A COURSE IN MIRACLES

CONCORDANCE

to
Volume One: Text

by
BARBARA FINDEISEN

First printing March, 1983
Printed in the United States of America by
Coleman Graphics
99 Milbar Blvd.
Farmingdale, N.Y. 11735

ISBN # 0-942-494-45-8

The material in this volume is from

"A COURSE IN MIRACLES"

and is used by permission
of the copyright owner,
The Foundation for Inner Peace.

FIRST LINE INDEX OF ITALICIZED MEDITATIONS

Text Pg.

alone — "I am not alone, and I would not intrude the past upon my Guest." 307

answer — "The answer that I give my brother is What I am asking for." 604

belongs — What is God's belongs to everyone, and is his due. 503

brother — "Let me know this brother as I know myself." 66

choose — "Choose once again if you would take your place among the saviors of the world, or would remain in hell, and hold your brothers there." 619

Christ — "Christ is in me, and where He is God must be, for Christ is part of Him." 152

created — "I am as God created me." 620

decided — I must have decided wrongly, because I am not at peace. 83

Decision — Rules For Decision. 581-3

Father — "Forgive us our illusions, Father, and help us to accept our true relationship with You..." 326

fruits — "By their fruits ye shall know them, And they shall know themselves." 161

give — "To have, give all to all." 98

guiltless — "What I experience I will make manifest." 255

holy instant — "I desire this holy instant for myself, That I may share it with my brother, whom I love." 358

Holy Spirit — "The Holy Spirit leads me unto Christ, And where else would I go?" 239

I — I am here only to be truly helpful. 24

incomplete — "God Himself is incomplete without me." 165

injustice — "By this do I deny the Presence of the Father and the Son." 524

know — "Because I will to know myself, I see you as God's Son and my brother." 155

1

know — "I do not know the thing I am, and therefore do not know what I am doing, where I am, or how to look upon the world or on myself." 614

leadeth — "He leadeth me and knows the way, which I know not." 259

love — Perfect love casts our fear... Only perfect love exists. 12

love — "Teach only love, for that is what you are." 87

peace — "To have peace, teach peace to learn it." 100

power — All power is of God. 188

release — "I give you to the Holy Spirit as part of myself." 306

responsible — "I am responsible for what I see." 418

same — What is the same can not be different, And what is one can not have separate parts. 484

Son of God — "Behold the Son of God, and look upon his purity and be still." 247

spirit — Spirit is in a state of grace forever. 7

thank — "I thank you, Father, for your perfect Son, And in his glory will I see my own." 595

thoughts — Thoughts increase by being given away. 67

truth — "The truth is true." 253

vigilant — "Be vigilant only for God and His Kingdom." 101

want — "Is this what I would see? Do I want this?" 432

world — "Do I desire a world I rule instead of one that rules me?" world — In this world you need not have tribulation because I have overcome the world. 431-2
  51

worthy — "I who am host to God am worthy of Him." 356

ABANDON

you — God did not *abandon* you. 276

ABILITY(IES)

developed — *Abilities* must be developed before you can use them. 94

ego — All harmfulness of your *abilities* lies in the ego's judgment.   **157**

ego — You cannot look on your *abilities* through the eyes of the ego, or you will judge them as it does.   **157**

Holy Spirit — All *abilities* should be given over to the Holy Spirit.   **110**

Holy Spirit — The Holy Spirit merely reminds you of the natural use of your *abilities*.   **157**

Holy Spirit's — All helpfulness of your *abilities* lies in the Holy Spirit's judgment.   **157**

meaningless — When they are perfect, *abilities* are meaningless.   **94**

potentials — *Abilities are potentials, not accomplishments.*   **94**

situation — In an impossible situation, you can develop your *abilities* to the point where they can get you out of it.   **94**

uncertainty — The introduction of *abilities* into being was the beginning of uncertainty, because *abilities* are potentials, not accomplishments.   **94**

unified — Different *abilities* become unified if applied long enough to one goal.   **110**

ABUNDANCE

teach — give, therefore, of your *abundance,* and teach your brothers theirs.   **119**

ACCOMPLISH(ED)

possible — What is possible has not yet been *accomplished.*   **169**

purpose — For your purpose was given you by God, and you must *accomplish* it because it is His Will.   **204**

yours — What has been *accomplished* for you must be yours.   **204**

ACCOMPLISHMENTS

God — *Accomplishments* of God are not gradual.   **105**

God's — God's *accomplishments* are not yours, but yours   104
       are like His.

Holy Spirit — The Holy Spirit would you accept His *ac-*   278
       complishments as yours, because He did
       them for you.

results — *Accomplishments* are results that have been   94
       achieved.

ACCUSE

understand — To *accuse* is not to understand.   262

ACCUSER

role — The role of the *accuser* will appear in many places   613
       and in many forms.

ACKNOWLEDGEMENT

God — God has never ceased to acknowledge you and   177
       in His *acknowledgement of you lies your being.*

healing — Do not look to the god of sickness for healing   177
       but only to the God of love, for healing
       is the *acknowledgement* of Him.

your — Your *acknowledgement* of your Father is the *acknow-* 177
       ledgement of yourself as you really are.

ADJUSTMENT(S)

belief — *Adjustment* is a change; a shift in perception, or   399
       a belief that was so before has been
       made different.

blind — The blind become accustomed to their world   416
       by their *adjustments* to it.

distortion — Every *adjustment* is a distortion, and calls   399
       upon defenses to uphold it against
       reality.

ego — *Adjustments* of any kind are of the ego.   400

knowledge — Knowledge reqires no *adjustment*, and is   399
       lost if any shift or change is under-
       taken.

sin — The belief in sin is an *adjustment*.   399

AFRAID

Holy Spirit — Whenever you are *afraid* you are deceived, and your mind cannot serve the Holy Spirit.   19

mind — Whenever you are *afraid* it is a sure sign that you have allowed your mind to mis-create and have not allowed me to guide it.   25

nothing — You may believe your are afraid of nothing-ness, but you really are *afraid* of no-thing.   172

peace — If you are *afraid*, you will inevitable value wrongly, and by endowing all thoughts with equal power will inevitably destroy peace.   16

you — You are *afraid* of your brothers and of your Father and of yourself.   198

ALONE

sick — To be *alone* must mean you are apart, and if you are, you cannot but be sick.   562

ALTAR(S)

Atonement — Christ has placed the Atonement on the *altar* for you.   207

beliefs — *Altars* are beliefs, but God and His creations are beyond beliefs because they are beyond question.   102

Christ — At God's *altar* Christ waits for the restoration of Himself in you.   187

Christ — Welcome me not into a manger, but into the *altar* to holiness, where holiness abides in perfect peace.   287

defiled — You have defiled the *altar* but not the world.   207

free — Be willing, for an instant, to leave your *altars* free of what you placed upon them, and what is really there you cannot fail to see.   419

gifts — You have not left open and unoccupied the *altar* where the gifts belong.   419

5

God — Every *altar* to God is part of you, because the   **186**
     light he created is one with Him.

God — No *altar* stands to God without His Son.   **269**

God — Only at the *altar* of God will you find peace.   **173**

holiest — The holiest of *altars* is set where once sin was   **510**
     believed to be.

home — No one but sees his chosen home as an *altar* to   **397**
     himself.

mind — You holy mind is *altar* unto God, and where He   **575**
     is no idols can abide.

perceptions — Bring your perceptions of the world to   **207**
     this *altar*, for it is the *altar* to truth.

sin — Where sin once was perceived will rise a world   **510**
     that will become an *altar* to the truth,
     and you will join the lights of Heaven
     there, and sing their song of gratitude
     and praise.

thought — The *altar* is perfectly clear in thought, be-   **108**
     cause it is a reflection of perfect
     Thought.

ALTERNATIVE(S)

mind — *Alternatives* are in your mind to use, and you can   **617**
     see yourself another way.

ANGER

Assault — Projection means *anger*, *anger* fosters assault,
     and assault promotes fear.   **85**

attacked — *Anger* cannot occur unless you believe you   **84**
     been attacked, that your attack is justi-
     fied in return, and that you are in no
     way responsible for it.

ego — Whenever you are angry you can be sure you   **297**
     have formed a special relationship
     which the ego has "blessed," for *anger*
     is its blessing.

ego — It is impossible for the ego to enter into any relationship without *anger*, for the ego believes that *anger* makes friends.   **295**

guilt — *Anger* takes many forms, but it cannot long deceive those who will learn love brings no guilt at all, and what brings guilt cannot be love and must be *anger*.   **297**

guilty — All *anger* is nothing more than an attempt to make someone feel guilty.   **297**

justified — *Anger* is never justified.   **593**

projection — *Anger* without projection is impossible.   **89**

responsibility — *Anger* always involves projection of separation, which must ultimately be accepted as one's own responsibility, rather than being blamed on others.   **84**

ANGRY

God — God is not *angry*.   **320**

ANSWER(S)

fear — Blessed are you who are willing to ask the truth of God without fear, for only thus can you learn that His *answer* is the release from fear.   **197**

God — What God gave *answer* to is answered and is gone.   **511**

God's — God's *answer* lies where the belief in sin must be, for only there can its effects be utterly undone and without cause.   **515**

Holy Spirit — The *answer* of the Holy Spirit is both many and one, as long as you believe the One is many.   **196**

Holy Spirit — Only the Holy Spirit can *answer* God for you, for only He knows what God is.   **262**

honest — An honest *answer* asks no sacrifice, because it answers questions truly asked.   **534**

loss — An *answer* which demands the slightest loss to anyone has not resolved the problem, but has added to it and made it greater and harder to resolve and more unfair.   **501**

love — *Answer* your brother's call for love, and yours is answered.   **203**

many — One with many *answers* can have no *answer*.   **533**

misunderstood — You have heard the *answer* but you have misunderstood the question.   **197**

receive — Seek not to *answer*, but merely to receive the *answer as it is given*.   **355**

received — There are many *answers* you have received but not yet heard.   **153**

Source — Where would the *answer* be but in the Source?   **427**

us — Not one of us but has the *answer* in him, to give to any one who asks it of him.   **197**

you — Where are you but there, where this same *answer* is?   **427**

your — Your *answer* is the proof of what you learned.   **602**

ANXIETY

ego — When you are anxious, realize that *anxiety* comes from capriciousness of ego, and know this need not be.   **57**

ego — Even if he is fully aware of *anxiety* he does not perceive its source as his own ego identification, and he always tries to handle it by making some sort of insane "arrangement" with the world.   **206**

mind — Without *anxiety* the mind is wholly kind, and because it extends beneficience it is beneficient.   **92**

APPEARANCE(S)

beyond — Reality does not deceive at all, and if you fail to see **beyond** *appearance* you are **deceived**.   **597**

brother — Forgive your brother all *appearances*, that are but ancient lessons you have taught yourself about the sinfulness in you.   **605**

changed — *Appearances* desceive but can be changed.   **597**

guilt — As your brother is healed are you made free   **599**
     of guilt, for his *appearance* is your own
     to you.

mind — *Appearances* can but deceive the mind that wants   **590**
     to be deceived.

miracle — There is no false *appearance* but will fade if you   **599**
     request a miracle instead.

unreal — *Appearances* are shown to be unreal because   **598**
     they change.

APPETITE(S)

body — Body *appetites* are not physical in origin.   **53**

mechanisms — *Appetites* are "getting" mechanisms,   **52**
     representing the ego's need to confirm
     itself.

APPRECIATION

full — Only one equal gift can be offered to Sons of God,   **97**
     and that is full *appreciation.*

God — God Himself created you in understanding, in   **113**
     appreciation, and in love.

God — God does not need your *appreciation,* but you do.   **88**

love — You cannot love what you do not appreciate, for   **88**
     fear makes *appreciation* impossible.

love — Understanding brings *appreciation* and *appreciation*   **115**
     brings love.

response — Only *appreciation* is an appropriate response   **201**
     to your brother.

understanding — Understanding is *appreciation* because   **113**
     what you understand you can identify
     with, and by making it part of you, you
     have accepted it with love.

ARROGANCE

Heaven — Only in *arrogance* could you conceive that you   **615**
     must make the way to Heaven plain.

love — *Arrogance* is the denial of love, because love   **178**
     shares and *arrogance* withholds.

ARROGANT

He — It is not *arrogant* to be as He created you, nor to make use of what He gave to answer all His Son's mistakes and set him free.   **518**

ASK

answer — *Ask* anything of God's Son and His Father will answer you, for Christ is not deceived in His Father and His Father is not deceived in Him.   **197**

taking — When you refuse to *ask* it is because you believe asking is taking rather than sharing.   **197**

ASKING

everything — *Asking* for everything you will receive it.   **366**

ASLEEP

crucified — While you perceive the Son of God as crucified you are *asleep*.   **194**

ASSAULT

body — *Assault* can ultimately be made only on the body.   **85**

fear — Projection means anger, anger fosters *assault*, and *assault promotes fear*.   **85**

Outrageous — I elected, for your sake and mine, to demonstrate that the most outrageous *assault*, as judged by the ego, does not matter.   **86**

ATONED

responsibility — If the sole responsibility of the miracle worker is to accept the Atonement for himself, then responsibility for what is *atoned* for cannot by yours.   **79**

ATONEMENT

acceptance — Acceptance of the *Atonement* is the end of separation.   **220**

acceptance — The acceptance of the *Atonement* by everyone is only a matter of time.   **18**

accepting - Accepting the *Atonement* for yourself means not to give support to someone's dream of sickness and of death.   **555**

accepting — By accepting the *Atonement* you are deciding against the belief that you can be alone, thus dispelling the idea of separation and affirming your true identification with the whole Kingdom as literally part of you.   **122**

afraid — When you are afraid you have placed yourself in a position where you need *Atonement*.   **26**

all — *Atonement* is for all, because it is the way to undo the belief that anything is for you alone.   **156**

ally — Be an ally of God and not the ego in seeking how the *Atonement* can come to you.   **325**

altar — The *Atonement* belongs at the center of the inner alter where it undoes the separation and restores the wholeness of mind.   **18**

atone — The *Atonement* cannot come to those who think they must first atone, but only to those who offer it simple willingness to make way for it.   **355**

awareness — The full awareness of the *Atonement* is the recognition that the separation never occurred.   **90**

blessing — The *Atonement* epitomizes harmlessness and sheds only blessing.   **33**

commitment — The *Atonement* is a total commitment.   **17**

condition — *Atonement* teaches you the true condition of the Son of God.   **261**

correction — The *Atonement* is the correction of the belief in nothingness.   **28**

crucifixion — The crucifixion did not establish the *Atonement;* the resurrection did.   **32**

curriculum — The curriculum of the *Atonement* is the opposite of the curriculum you have established for yourself, but so is its outcome.   **129**

defense — The *Atonement* is the only defense that cannot be used destructively, because it is not a device you made.   **16**

11

end — The circle of the *Atonement* has no end.   263

errors — My part in the *Atonement* is the cancelling out of   6
        all errors that you could not otherwise
        correct.

escape — *Atonement* teaches you how to escape forever   275
        from everything that you have taught
        yourself in the past, by showing you
        only what you are now.

fear — Joining the *Atonement* is the way out of fear.   74

fear — No one can look upon the fear of God unterrified   393
        unless he has accepted the *Atonement*
        and learned illusions are not real.

fear — The undoing of fear is an essential part of the   2
        Atonement value of miracles.

forgiven — The forgiven are the means of the *Atonement*.

gentle — The *Atonement* is so gentle you need but   271
        whisper to it and all its power will rush
        to your assistance and support.

gift — The *Atonement* is the only gift that is worthy of   19
        being offered at the Altar of God,
        because of the value of the altar itself.

guilt — The *Atonement* has always been interpreted as   224
        release from guilt, and this is correct if
        it is understood.

heal — The *Atonement* can only heal.   16

holiness — The *Atonement* does not make holy. You were   270
        created holy. It merely brings un-
        holiness to holiness, or what you made
        to what you are.

I — I am in charge of the process of the *Atonement*, which   6
        I undertook to begin.

invulnerable — Those who accept the *Atonement* are in-   257
        vulnerable.

Kingdom — The *Atonement* is the guarantee of the safety   74
        of the Kingdom, and the union of the
        Sonship in its protection.

learning — The *Atonement* was built into the space-time   16
        belief to set a limit on the need for
        belief itself, and ultimately to make
        learning complete.

lesson — The *Atonement* is the final lesson.   17

light — The *Atonement* can be accepted within you only   17
by the releasing of the inner light.

light —   The *Atonement* is perfectly clear because it   33
exists in light.

lost — The *Atonement* is the way back to what was never   219
lost.

love — *Atonement* cannot be separate because it comes   156
from love.

love — Perfect love is the *Atonement*.   26

mind — The *Atonement* gives you the power of a healed   76
mind, but the power to create is of God.

My — My part in the *Atonement* is not complete until   76
you join it and give it away.

need — The *Atonement* is the one need in this world   89
that is universal.

part — Everyone has a special part to play in the   262
Atonement, but the message given to
each one is always the same; God's Son
is guiltless.

past — The *Atonement* is a device by which you can free   17
yourself from the past as you go ahead.

peace — You cannot abide in peace unless you accept   163
the *Atonement*, because (it) is the way to
peace.

power — The power of God and all his love, without   325
limit, will support you as you seek only
your place in the plan of *Atonement*
arising from His Love.

prefer — *Atonement* is not welcomed by those who prefer   362
pain and destruction.

purpose —   The ability (to work miracles) in the   6
potential, the achievement is its
expression, and the *Atonement*, which is
the natural profession of the Children
of God, is the purpose.

purpose — The purpose of the *Atonement* is to save the   79
past in purified form only.

purpose — The purpose of the *Atonement* is to restore everything to you; or rather, to restore it to your awareness.   9

real — *Atonement* becomes real and visible to those who use it.   260

reevaluation — *Atonement* brings a reevaluation of everything you cherish, for it is the means by which the Holy Spirit can separate the false from the true, which you have accepted into your mind without distinction.   243

separation — It was only after the separation that the *Atonement* and the conditions necessary for its fulfillment were planned.   16

sharing — The *Atonement* is a lesson in sharing, which is given you because you have forgotten how to do it.   157

sharing — The *Atonement* must be understood as a pure act of sharing.   75

sin — It is extremely difficult to reach *Atonement* by fighting against sin.   363

sin — No one accepts *Atonement* for himself who still accepts sin as his goal.   362

spirit — The *Atonement* restores spirit to its proper place.   9

talents — When the *Atonement* is completed, all talents will be shared by all Sons of God.   10

time — *Atonement* works all the time and in all dimensions of time.   2

time — The *Atonement* is in time but not for time.   283

time — The *Atonement* saves time, but like the miracle it serves, does not abolish it.   17

truth — The *Atonement* radiates nothing but truth.   33

understood — If you already understood the difference between truth and illusion, the *Atonement* would have no meaning.   357

wholeness — The *Atonement* is not the price of your wholeness, but it is the price of your awareness of your wholeness.   209

you — You have a part to play in the *Atonement,* but the plan of the *Atonement* is beyond you.   **157**

ATONEMENT PRINCIPLE

Atonement — The *Atonement principle* was in effect long before the Atonement began.   **16**

love — The *Atonement principle* was love, and the Atonement was an act of love.   **16**

perception — (You are) under the *Atonement principle,* where perception is healed.   **3**

separation — The *Atonement principle* and the separation began at the same time.   **69**

separation — (The Holy Spirit) came into being with the separation, inspiring the *Atonement principle* at the same time.   **68**

ATONING

undoing — *"Atoning"* means "undoing."   **2**

ATTACK

blessed — Those who *attack* do not know they are blessed.   **119**

blind — You reinforce this every time you *attack* your brother, for the *attack* must blind you to yourself.   **340**

body — *Attack* can only be an assumed purpose of the body, because apart from the mind the body has no purpose at all.   **143**

Christ — *Attack* makes Christ your enemy, and God along with Him.   **491**

communication — There is no *attack* but there is unlimited communication and therefore unlimited power and wholeness.   **143**

creator — It seems safer to *attack* another or yourself than to *attack* the great Creator of the universe, Whose power you know.   **449**

denying — When you *attack* you are denying yourself.   **170**

depriving — *Attack* could never promote *attack* unless you perceived it as a means of depriving you of something you want.   **119**

destructive — *Attack* in any form is equally destructive.   **460**

different — Because you are not different, you cannot *attack*.   **450**

Different — Only the different can *attack*.   **450**

"evil" — You could not recognize your "evil" thoughts as long as you see value in *attack*.   **616**

fear — Fear and *attack* are inevitably associated.   **202**

fear — If only *attack* produces fear and if you see *attack* as the call for help that it is, the unreality of fear must dawn on you.   **202**

fear — It is as certain you will fear what you *attack* as it is sure that you will love what you perceive as sinless.   **451**

forgiveness — In your forgiveness will you understand His Love for you; through your *attack* believe He hates you, thinking Heaven must be hell.   **492**

form — *Attack* in any form has placed your foot upon the twisted stairway that leads from Heaven.   **459**

forms — The seeming gentler forms of *attack* are no less certain in their witnessing, or their results.   **459**

foundation — *Attack* has no foundation.   **593**

frailty — The show of strength *attack* would use to cover frailty conceals it not, for how can the unreal be hidden?   **451**

function — *Attack* is a response to function unfulfilled as you perceive the function.   **569**

grandeur — You believe that *attack* is grandeur.   **226**

guilt — *Attack* makes guilt real, and if it is real there is no way to overcome it.   **223**

guilt — Without guilt, *attack* is impossible.   **223**

guilty — By *attack* do you assert that you are guilty and must give as you deserve. — 606

healing — Every *attack* is a step away from (what you truly want), and every healing thought brings it closer. — 182

helplessness — Healing comes of power, and *attack* of helplessness. — 432

illusions — *Attack* has power to make illusions real. — 589

innocence — The wish to be unfairly treated is a compromise attempt that would combine *attack* and innocence. — 525

justification — You cannot be attacked, *attack* has no justification, and you are responsible for what you believe. — 84

justified — You have a differential view of when *attack* is justified, and when you think it is unfair and not to be allowed. — 522

justified — *Attack* is never justified. — 593

keeps — Everyone you *attack* keeps it and cherishes it by holding it against you. — 256

learned — Teach *attack* in any form and you have learned it, and it will hurt you. — 92

love — *Attack* will always yield to love if it is brought to love, and not hidden from it. — 265

love — Offer *attack* and love will remain hidden, for it can only live in peace. — 217

loving — What is not loving must be an *attack*. — 461

mind — If you will realize that all the *attack* you perceive is in your own mind and nowhere else, you will at last have placed its source, and where it begins it must end. — 207

murder — The sole intent of *attack* is murder. — 460

patience — Every *attack* is a call for His patience, since His patience can translate *attack* into blessing. — 119

peace — If you want peace, you must abandon the teacher of *attack*. — 278

physical — *Attack* is always physical. — 140

poor — Those who *attack* are poor. 205

projection — Projection and *attack* are inevitably related, because projection is always a means of justifying *attack*. 89

relationships — It is only by *attack* without forgiveness that the ego can ensure the guilt that holds relationships together. 295

relinquished — That is why *attack* is never discrete, and must be relinquished entirely. 114

safe — *Attack* is neither safe nor dangerous. It is impossible. 450

salvation — The ego believes in atonement through *attack*, being fully committed to the insane notion that *attack* is salvation. 223

satisfy — You will *attack* what does not satisfy, and thus you will not see you made it up. 588

separate — To *attack* is to separate. 142

separation — *Attack* promotes separation. 140

sin — *Attack* and sin are bound as one illusion, each the cause and aim and justifier of the other. 490

stranger — *Attack* is always made upon a stranger. 37

understanding — When you *attack* any part of God and His Kingdom, your understanding is not perfect, and what you really want is therefore lost to you. 182

unfairness — Unfairness and *attack* are one mistake so firmly joined that where one is perceived the other must be seen. 523

weakness — The power of the holiness and the weakness of *attack* are both being brought into your awareness. 310

work — *Attack* manifestly does not work and cannot protect you. 209

you — There is nothing you could *attack* that is not part of you. 454

you — For you are always the first point of your *attack*, and if this has never been, it has no consequences. 210

your — You will never realize the utter uselessness of   **210**
     attack except by recognizing that your
     attack on yourself has no effect.

yourself — If you recognize that you are part of God,   **170**
     you will understand why it is that you
     always *attack* yourself first.

ATTACKED

brother — Neither your brother nor yourself can be   **429**
     attacked alone.

light — What disappears in light is not *attacked*.   **270**

suffer — No one can suffer if he does not see himself   **560**
     attacked, and losing by attack.

you — You cannot be *attacked*, attack has no justification,   **84**
     and you are responsible for what you
     believe.

ATTACKING

others — By *attacking* others, you are literally *attacking*   **231**
     what is not there.

AUTHORITY

authorship — The issue of *authority* is really a question   **43**
     of authorship.

AUTHORITY PROBLEM

evil — (The *authority problem*) is the "root of all evil."   **43**

inconceivable — The *authority problem*, because it accepts   **43**
     the one inconceivable thought as its
     premise, can produce only ideas that
     are inconceivable.

meaningful — Only in this world is the idea of an   **46**
     authority problem meaningful.

mind — You cannot resolve the *authority problem* by   **44**
     depreciating the power of your mind.

power — The *authority problem* (is) based on the concept   **77**
     of usurping God's power.

you — You have the *authority problem* because you believe   **43**
     you are the author of yourself.

AUTHORSHIP

denial — All fear comes ultimately, and sometimes by way of very devious routes, from the denial of *Authorship*.   **44**

dispute — The dispute over *authorship* has left such uncertainty in your mind that it may even doubt whether you exist at all.   **43**

problem — The problem everyone must decide is the fundamental question of *authorship*.   **44**

AUTONOMY

ego — Belief in the *autonomy* of the ego costs you the knowledge of your dependence on God, in which your freedom lies.   **189**

ego's — If the ego's goal of *autonomy* could be accomplished, God's purpose could be defeated, and this is impossible.   **190**

goal — The ego always attacks on behalf of salvation. Believing it has the power to do this it does nothing else, because its goal of *autonomy* is nothing else.   **189**

His — (God) has included you in His *Autonomy*.   **189**

you — You can only establish your *autonomy* by identifying with Him, and fulfilling your function as it exists in truth.   **190**

AWAKE

I — If I live in you, you are *awake*.   **194**

learn — You are not yet *awake*, but you can learn how to awaken.   **162**

remember — You do not remember being *awake*.   **169**

sleeping — You cannot dream some dreams and wake from some, for you are either sleeping or *awake*.   **569**

AWAKEN

call — You will *awaken* to your own call, for the call to awake is within you.   **194**

I — I will *awaken* you as surely as I awakened my self.   **204**

AWAKENING

Kingdom — *Awakening* runs easily and gladly through the Kingdom, in answer to the call for God.   **131**

Son — The *awakening* of His Son begins with investment in the real world, and by this he will learn to re-invest in himself.   **212**

AWAKING

Christ — *Awaking* unto Christ is following the laws of love of your own free will, and out of quiet recognition of the truth in them.   **236**

His — His plan for your *awaking* is as perfect as yours is fallible.   **262**

learn — God's Son will learn the lesson of *awaking*.   **250**

AWARE

interpretation — You cannot be *aware* without interpretation, for what you perceive is your interpretation.   **192**

AWARENESS

join — Join your *awareness* to what has been already joined.   **422**

BARRIERS

God — God breaks no *barriers*, neither did he make them.   **260**

release — When you release *(barriers)* they are gone.   **260**

BEGINNINGS

created —- You who made delay can leave time behind simply by recognizing that neither *beginnings* nor endings were created by the eternal.   **180**

God — There are no *beginnings* and no endings in God, whose universe is Himself.   **180**

BEHAVIOR

beliefs — All *behavior* teaches beliefs that motivate it.   **88**

level — *Behavior* is not the level for teaching or learning, since you can act in accordance with what you do not believe.   **111**

BEING

assailed — It is only your awareness that needs protection since *being* cannot be assailed.   **102**

communication — Existence as well as *being* rest on communication.   **64**

doubtful — A real sense of *being* cannot be yours while you are doubtful of what you are.   **102**

doubts — Doubts about *being* must not enter your mind, or you cannot know what you are with certainty.   **102**

extended — *Being* must be extended.   **122**

God — God, who encompasses all *being,* created beings who have everything individually but who want to share it to increase their joy.   **64**

God — Because God shared His *Being* with you, you can know Him.   **127**

having — The equality of having and *being* is not yet perceived.   **99**

Kingdom — *Being* alone lives in the Kingdom, where everything lives in God without question.   **94**

knowledge — You can be perceived with meaning only by the Holy Spirit because your *being* is the knowledge of God.   **116**

mind — *Being* is completely without these distinctions. It is a state in which the mind is in communication with everything that is real.   **64**

mind — In the state of *being* the mind gives everything always.   **64**

sharing — *Being* is known by sharing.   **127**

threatened — *Being* is never threatened.   **91**

BELIEF(S)

attack — *Beliefs* will never openly attack each other because conflicting outcomes are impossible.   **464**

body — Your *beliefs* converge upon the body, the ego's chosen home, which you believe is yours.   **452**

compromise — Such is the power of *belief.* It cannot compromise.   **439**

conflicted — *Belief* does not require vigilance unless it is conflicted.   **115**

existence — *Belief* produces the acceptance of existence.   **11**

God — God and His creations are beyond *belief,* because they are beyond question.   **102**

impossible — The *belief* that you must have the impossible in order to be happy is at variance with the principle of creation.   **151**

loses — The whole *belief* that someone loses but reflects the underlying tenet God must be insane.   **496**

neutral — No *belief* is neutral.   **464**

perception — And since *belief* determines perception, you do not perceive what it means and therefore do not accept it.   **192**

perceptions — It is not until *beliefs* are fixed that perceptions stabilize.   **192**

premises — Whatever these *beliefs* may be, they are the premises that will determine what you accept into your mind.   **124**

real — All *beliefs* are real to the believer.   **45**

War — An unrecognized *belief* is a decision to war in secret, where the results of conflict are kept unknown and never brought to reason to be considered sensible or not.   **464**

weakness — *Belief* in enemies is *belief* in weakness, and what is weak is not the Will of God.   **451**

BELIEF SYSTEM

insane — You cannot evaluate an insane *belief system* from within it.   **164**

insane — You have built your whole insane *belief system* because you think you would be helpless in God's Presence and you would save yourself from His Love because you think it would crush you into nothingness.   **226**

BELIEVE(S)

accept — To *believe* is to accept and appreciate.   **154**

attack — You cannot be attacked, attack has no justification, and you are responsible for what you *believe*.   **84**

destroyed — Nothing the Son of God *believes* can be destroyed.   **508**

gifts — What you *believe* you are determines your gifts.   **105**

manifest — You will *believe* in what you manifest, and as you look out so will you see in.   **214**

see — It is impossible not to *believe* what you see, but it is equally impossible to see what you do not *believe*.   **192**

see — You see what you *believe* is there, and you *believe* it because you want it there.   **487**

teach — What you *believe* you will teach.   **86**

true — If you *believe* in truth and illusion, you cannot tell which is true.   **195**

BIBLE VERSES EXPLAINED

Alpha — "Alpha and Omega, the beginning and the end"   **37**

betrayest — "Betrayest thou the Son of Man with a kiss."   **87**

blessed — "Blessed are the pure in heart for they shall see God."   **33**

blessed — "Blessed are ye who have not seen and still believe."   **192**

children — "Except ye become as little children"   **10**

death — "There is no death."   **9**

Father — "Father forgive them for they know not what they do."   **24**

God — "Be still and know that I am God."   **47**

God — "Fear God and keep His commandments."   **37**

God — "For God so loved the world that He gave His only begotten Son that whosoever believeth in Him should not perish but have everlasting life."   **28**

God — "God created man in his own image and like-ness." 40

God — "God is not mocked." 10

Gods — "Thou shalt have no other Gods before you." 55

Golden — Golden Rule 7

He — "When He shall appear (or be perceived) we shall be like Him, for we shall see Him as He is." 35

I — "I am come as a light into the world." 81

I — "I am with you always." 107

I — "I come not to bring peace but a sword." 87

I — "I will visit the sins of the fathers unto the third and fourth generation." 80

I — "If I go I will send you another comforter and he will abide with you." 67

judge — "Judge not that ye be not judged." 41

Kingdom — "All power and glory are yours because the Kingdom is His." 130

Kingdom — "The Kingdom of Heaven is within you." 54

Kingdom — "Thine is the Kingdom" 81

know — "Know thyself" 36

lamb — "Lamb of God who taketh away the sins of the world" 33

lead — "Lead us not into temptation." 7

lies — "Lies of the serpent" 14

many — "Many are called but few are chosen." 39

meek — "The meek shall inherit the earth." 17

mind — "Be of one mind." 24

mind — "May the mind be in you that was also in Christ Jesus." 67

my — "My peace I give unto you." 172

peace — "The peace of God which passeth understand-ing" 16

praise — "Praise God." 64

Remembrance — "Do this in Remembrance of Me." 24

root — "The root of all evil"   43

seek — "Seek and ye shall find."   60

seek — "Seek ye first the Kingdom of Heaven."   44

sell — "Sell all you have and give to the poor and follow   205
me."

sow — "As ye sow so shall ye reap."   80

Story — story of the prodigal son   138

turning — "turning the other cheek"   75

vengeance — "Vengeance is mine, sayeth the Lord."   32

wages — "The wages of sin is death."   175

wicked — "The wicked shall perish."   80

word — "The word (or thought) was made flesh."   141

yoke — "My yoke is easy and my burden light."   71

BLAME(S)

ego — Self*blame* is therefore ego identification, and as   187
much an ego defense as blaming
others.

harbor — As *blame* is withdrawn from without, there is   187
a strong tendency to harbor it within.

undone — *Blame* must be undone, not seen elsewhere.   187

BLAMELESS

God — God knows His Son as wholly *blameless* as Him-   187
self, and He is approached through the
appreciation of His Son.

BLAMELESSNESS

Christ — The *blamelessness* of Christ is the proof that the   221
ego never was, and never can be.

BLASPHEMOUS

depressed — If God knows His children as wholly   178
joyous, it is *blasphemous* to feel de-
pressed.

guilty — If God knows His children as wholly sinless,   178
it is *blasphemous* to perceive of them as
guilty.

suffering — If God knows His children as wholly without pain, it is *blasphemous* to perceive
suffering anywhere.   178

BLASPHEMY

destructive — *Blasphemy* is self-destructive, not God-   176
destructive.

forms — All of these illusions, and the many other   178
forms that *blasphemy* may take, are
refusals to accept creation as it is.

sick — *(Blasphemy)* means you are not willing to know   176
yourself in order to be sick.

BLESS

one — To *bless* but one gives blessing to them all as one.   518

BLESSED

me — *Blessed* are you who teach with me.

world — Yes, you are *blessed* indeed. Yet in this world,   251
you do not know it.

BLESSING(S)

afraid — Be not afraid of *blessing,* for the One Who   535
blesses you loves all the world, and
leaves nothing within the world that
could be feared.

Atonement — Refuse to accept anyone as without the   264
blessing of the Atonement, and bring
him into it by blessing him.

brothers — Do not ask for *blessings* without *blessing*   154
(your brothers), for only in this way
can you learn how blessed you are.

charity — What can it be but universal *blessing* to look   449
on what your Father loves with
charity?

Father — The children of Heaven live in the light of the   261
blessing of their Father, because they
know that they are sinless.

fearful — If you shrink from *blessing*, the world indeed will seem fearful, for you have withheld its peace and comfort, leaving it to die. 536

gentleness — You cannot even give a *blessing* in perfect gentleness. 261

offer — If you offer *blessing* it must come first to yourself. 251

sacrifice — Creating is the opposite of loss as *blessing* is the opposite of sacrifice. 122

sin — If the Holy Spirit can commute each sentence that you laid upon yourself into a *blessing*, then it cannot be a sin. 494

you — You do not need God's *blessing* because that you have forever, but you do need yours. 118

BODY(IES)

abilities — The *body* is merely part of your experience in the physical world. Its abilities can be and frequently are overevaluated. 20

abilities — The *body* is nothing more than a framework for developing abilities, which is quite apart from what they are used for. 111

allegiance — The *body* is seen as capable of shifting allegiance from one voice to the other, making the concepts of both health and sickness meaningful. 144

anger — (The destruction of the) *body* does not justify anger. 85

another — In the *body* of another you will see the use to which you have put yours. 140

apart — The *body* is outside you, and but seems to surround you, shutting you off from others and keeping you apart from them. 360

Atonement — The many *body* fantasies in which minds engage arise from the distorted belief that the *body* can be used as a means of attaining Atonement. 17

attack — Do not let (the *body*) reflect your decision to attack.   146

attack — If you use the *body* for attack, it is harmful to you.   140

Believe — Behold the *body* and you will believe that you are there.   483

Brother — If you see a brother as a *body*, you have established a condition in which uniting with him becomes impossible.   371

Brother — The *body* does not separate you from your brother, and if you think it does you are insane.   428

Brother — While you see a brother as a *body* apart from you and separate in his cell, you are demanding sacrifice of him and you.   504

Brother's — Your brother's *body* is as little use to you as it is to him.   405

Change — The *body* does not change.   566

Christ — The Christ in you inhabits not a *body*. Yet He is in you. And thus it must be that you are not within a *body*.   482

Communication — The *body* is a limit imposed on the universal communication that is an eternal property of mind.   360

Communication — To be with a *body* is not communication.   297

Communication — To see the *body* as anything except a means of communication is to limit your mind and to hurt yourself.   143

Condition — The condition of the *body* lies in your interpretation of its function.   144

Create — The *body* cannot create, and the belief that it can, a fundamental error, produces all physical symptoms.   19

Depression — When you equate yourself with a *body*, you will always experience depression.   140

Dies — The *body* no more dies than it can feel.   389

Differences — Differences are only of the *body*.   435

29

Do — To do anything involves the *body*. 363

Dreaming — The *body* is the central figure in the dreaming of the world. 543

Ego — The *body* is the means by which the ego tries to make the unholy relationship seem real. 410

Ego — The *body* is the symbol of the ego, as the ego is the symbol of the separation. 300

Ego — The *body*, in service of ego, can hurt other *bodies*, but this cannot occur unless the *body* has already been confused with the mind. 111

Ego — The ego separates through the *body*. 140

Ego — The ego uses the *body* for attack, pleasure, and pride. 97

Ego — To the ego, the *body* is to attack with. 143

Ego's — The *body* is the ego's home by its own election. 60

End — (The *body* is) an end and not a means in your interpretation, and this always means you still find sin attractive. 362

Enemy — As "something" is the *body* asked to be God's enemy, replacing what He is with littleness, limit and despair. 567

Exist — At no single instant does the *body* exist at all. 362

Exist — The (*body*) is clearly a separation device and therefore does not exist. 97

externals — The eyes of the *body* rest on externals and cannot go beyond. 443

eyes — Everything the eyes of the *body* can see is a mistake, an error in perception, a distorted fragment of the whole without the meaning that the whole would give. 442

eyes — You look still with the eyes of the *body* and they can see but thorns. 398

faith — The *body* is the great seeming betrayer of faith. 386

faith — You still place too much faith in the *body* as a source of strength. 362

fear — Fear of the *body*, with which the ego identifies so   **60**
closely, makes no sense.

fear — It is only the messengers of fear that see the   **384**
body, for they look for what can suffer.

fear — It is not evident that what the eyes of the *body*   **484**
perceive fills you with fear.

fear — Whatever fear directs the *body* to do is painful.   **387**

feeling — Certainly (what the *body*) is made of is not   **387**
precious, and just as certainly it has no
feeling.

forgive — *Bodies* cannot forgive.   **297**

forgotten — There is one thing you have never done;   **362**
You have not utterly forgotten the
body.

form — The eyes of the *body* see only form.   **442**

friend — The *body* (is) the ego's friend.   **93**

function — The *body* has no function of itself, because   **145**
it is not an end.

goal — The *body* will seem to be whatever is the means   **386**
for reaching the goal you assign it.

goal — The *body*, innocent of any goal, is your excuse   **564**
for variable goals you hold, and force
the *body* to maintain.

God — The *body* that is asked to be a god will be attacked,   **567**
because its nothingness has not been
recognized.

God — God cannot come into a *body*, nor can you join   **364**
Him there.

God — In this sense the *body* does become a temple to   **142**
God; His Voice abides in it by directing
the use to which it is put.

guilt — The *body* will remain guilt's messenger, and will   **368**
act as it directs as long as you believe
guilt is real.

guilt — The glitter of guilt you laid upon the *body* would   **389**
kill it.

guilt — Under fear's orders, the *body* will pursue guilt,   **387**
serving its master whose attraction to
guilt maintains the whole illusion of its
existence.

guilty — A *body* cannot be guilty, for it can do nothing of itself.   359

hate — You hate (the *body*), yet you think it is yourself, and that, without it, would your self be lost.   560

hate — You who think you hate your *body* deceive yourself.   359

heal — The *body* cannot heal because it cannot make itself sick.   371

healed — A broken *body* shows the mind has not been healed.   529

healing — Let (the *body*) have healing as its purpose.   527

health — Health or sickness (of the *body*) depends entirely on how the mind perceives it, and the purpose that the mind would use it for. 371

health — The *body* is not the source of its own health.   143

holiness — True holiness of (the *body*) lies at the inner altar around which the structure is built.   18

Holy Spirit — The Holy Spirit reaches through (the *body*) to others.   140

Holy Spirit — The Holy Spirit sees the *body* only as a means of communication, and because communication is sharing, it becomes communion. 97

Holy Spirit's — The Holy Spirit's messengers are sent far beyond the *body*, calling the mind to join in holy communion and be at peace.   384

idea — The *body* is a tiny fence around a little part of a glorious and complete idea.   364

idol — The *body* is the ego's idol, the belief in Sin made flesh and then projected outward.   409

idolatry — Any relationship in which the *body* enters is based not on love, but on idolatry.   407

illness — Perceiving the *body* as a separate entity cannot but foster illness, because it is not there.   **142**

immovable - This *body* only seems to be immovable.   **446**

insane — It is insane to use the *body* as the scapegoat for guilt, directing its attack and blaming it for what you wished it to do.   **360**

instant — The unholy instant is the time of *bodies*.   **410**

joined — Minds are joined; *bodies* are not.   **359**

judgment — If you see the *body* you have chosen judgment and not vision.   **410**

judgment — Who sees a brother's *body* has laid a judgment on him and sees him not.   **410**

know — The *body* cannot know.   **364**

know — (The *body*) does not know what seeing is; what listening is for.   **558**

lead - (The *body*) can never lead where you would not be.   **607**

life — The *body* can become a sign of life, a promise of redemption, and a breath of immortality to those grown sick of breathing in the fetid scent of death.   **527**

limit — (The *body*) does not limit you, merely because you would not have it so.   **361**

limited — You are not limited by the *body*, and thought cannot be made flesh.   **143**

limits — To accept the limits of a *body* is to impose these limits on each brother whom you see.   **504**

little — The *body* is little and limited, and only those whom you would see without the limits the ego would impose on them can offer you the gift of freedom.   **301**

littleness — Do not let (the *body*) be an image of your own perception of littleness.   **146**

lives — The *body* neither lives or dies, because it cannot contain you who are life.   **96**

love — It is only the awareness of the *body* that makes love seem limited.   **364**

love — Love knows no *bodies,* and reaches to everything created like itself.   365

love — The *body* is a limit on love.   364

meaningless — *Bodies* may battle, but the clash of forms is meaningless.   462

meaningless — Sights and sounds the *body* can perceive are meaningless.

means — (The *body)* is a means, and not an end.   386

messages — From the world of *bodies,* made by insanity, insane messages seem to be returned to the mind that made it.   367

messages - Like any communication medium the *body* receives and sends the messages it is given.   387

mind — Do not allow the *body* to be a mirror of a split mind.   146

mind — Each *body* seems to house a separate mind, a disconnected thought, living alone and in no way joined to the thought by which it was created.   365

mind — *Bodies* cannot forgive. They can only do as the mind directs.   297

mind — If the mind can heal the *body,* but the *body* cannot heal the mind, then the mind must be stronger than the *body.*   97

mind — The *body* is easily brought into alignment with a mind that has learned to look beyond it toward the light.   22

mind — The *body* is released because the mind acknowledges "this is not done to me, but I am doing this."   553

mind — The *body* represents the gap between the little bit of mind you call your own and all rest of what is really yours.   560

minds — Minds need not the *body* to communicate.   405

minds — You do not perceive your brother as the Holy Spirit does, because you do not regard *bodies* solely as a means of joining minds, and uniting them with yours and mine.   140

miracle — The miracle is much like the *body* in that both are learning aids for facilitating a state in which they become unnecessary.   **9**

miracles — Miracles transcend the *body*.   **2**

misthought — The *body* can act wrongly only when it is responding to misthought.   **19**

misuse — If you misuse (the *body*) you will misunderstand it, because you have already done so by misusing it.   **141**

names — (The *body*) tells you but the names you gave to it to use when you call forth the witnesses to its reality.   **538**

nothing — Of itself the *body* can do nothing.   **472**

nothing — (The *body*) is nothing.   **389**

offer — *Bodies* can neither offer nor accept hold out nor take.   **397**

outside — The *body* is outside you, and but seems to surround you, shutting you off from others and keeping you apart from them.   **360**

past — Only its past and future make (the *body*) seem real.   **362**

perception — You can use your *body* best to help you enlarge your perception so you can achieve real vision, of which the physical eye is incapable.   **12**

pleasure — It is impossible to seek for pleasure through the *body* and not find pain.   **386**

pleasure — The Holy Spirit does not demand you sacrifice the hope of the *body's* pleasure; it has no hope of pleasure.   **384**

purpose — Perception of the *body* can be unified only by one purpose.   **142**

purpose — The *body* can but serve your purpose. As you look on it, so it will seem to be.   **389**

purpose — The *body* has no purpose and must be solitary.   **463**

purposeless — This *body*, purposeless within itself,   **538**
holds all your memories and all your
hopes.

reality — As long as you perceive your *body* as your   **305**
reality, so long will you perceive your-
self as lonely and deprived.

reason — If you would defend the *body* against your   **428**
reason, you will not understand the
body, or yourself.

relationships — The *body* is the ego's chosen weapon for   **407**
seeking power through relationships.

release — Release your *body* from imprisonment, and   **607**
you will see no one a prisoner to what
you have escaped.

sacrifice — The *body* is a loss, and can be made to sacri-   **504**
fice.

sacrifice — The little that the *body* fences off becomes   **504**
the self, preserved through sacrifice of
all the rest.

salvation — (The nothingness of the *body*) is your salva-   **567**
tion from which you would flee.

separate — Only *bodies* can be separate and therefore   **428**
unreal.

separate — The *body* is separate, and therefore cannot be   **97**
part of you.

separate — This separating off is symbolized, in your   **516**
perception, by a *body* which is clearly
separate and a thing apart.

separation — If you choose to see the *body* you behold a   **614**
world of separation, unrelated things,
and happenings that make no sense at
all.

separation — The *body* could not separate your minds   **564**
unless you wanted it to be a cause of
separation and of distance seen between you.

sick — A sick *body* does not make any sense.   **145**

sick — (The *body*) will be sick because you do not know   **564**
what loving means.

sick — Your perception of the *body* can clearly be sick, but project not this upon the *body*.   **359**

sin — The *body* was made to be a sacrifice to sin, and in the darkness so it still is seen.   **423**

sin — (The eyes of the *body*) adjust to sin, unable to over-look it in any form and seeing it every-where, in everything.   **413**

sinful — (The *body*) is not sinful, but neither is it sinless.   **410**

solve — The thought of bodies is the sign of faith-lessness, for *bodies* cannot solve any-thing.   **343**

spirit — The spirit (is) almost inaccessible to the mind and entirely inaccessible to the *body*.   **38**

symbol — The *body* is the symbol of what you think you are.   **97**

temple — You cannot make the *body* the Holy Spirit's temple, and it will never be the seat of love.   **407**

there — (The *body*) is not there.   **360**

truth — (Use the *body*) for truth, and you will see it truly.   **141**

union — The union of *bodies* thus becomes a way in which they would keep minds apart.   **297**

unite — While you believe that *bodies* can unite, you will find guilt attractive and believe that sin precious.   **377**

value — The only value your *body* has is to enable you to bring your brothers to the bridge with you, and to be released together there.   **322**

voices — The *body* exists in a world that seems to contain two voices fighting for its possession.   **144**

vulnerability — (The vulnerability of the *body*) is its own best argument that you cannot be of God.   **60**

wariness — There is a wariness that is aroused by learning that the *body* is not real.   **564**

weaknesses — (The "inherent" weaknesses of the *body*) set up limitations on what you would do, and keep your purpose limited and weak.   **564**

whole — In this world not even the *body* is perceived as   **142**
    whole.

you — You cannot conceive of you apart from (the *body*.)   **480**

BONDAGE

freedom — Since freedom and *bondage* are irreconcilable,   **174**
    their laws cannot be understood to-
    gether.

freedom — For the Love of God, no longer seek for   **321**
    union in separation, nor for freedom in
    bondage.

freedom — You must choose between total freedom and   **303**
    total *bondage,* for there are no alterna-
    tives but these.

BORN

past — To be *born* again is to let the past go, and look   **234**
    without condemnation on the present.

BRAIN

interpret — The *brain* cannot interpret what your vision   **436**
    sees.

interprets - The *brain* interprets to the body, of which it   **436**
    is a part.

BRIDGE

transition — The *bridge* is nothing more than a transi-   **322**
    tion in the perspective of reality.

BROTHER(S)

accept — In (union with me) you will accept all our   **302**
    brothers.

against — You think you hold against your *brother* what   **344**
    he has done to you. But what you really
    blame him for is what you did to him.

answer — (Your *brothers*) will answer you if you learn to   **154**
    ask only truth of them.

answered — When you joined your *brother* you answered   **354**
    me.

assurance — In (your *brother*) is your assurance that God is here, and with you now.   **475**

attack — In separation from your *brother* was the first attack upon yourself begun.   **540**

attacked — Again and again have you attacked your *brother* because you saw in him a shadow figure in your private world.   **231**

be — Where you would have your *brother* be, there will you think you are.   **287**

beauty — Ask them to learn of the reality of your *brother, because this is what you will perceive brother, because this is what you will perceive* in him and you will see your beauty reflected in his.   **198**

believe — Believe in your *brothers* because I believe in you, and you will learn that my belief in you is justified.   **154**

blessing — Whenever you deny a blessing to your *brother* you will feel deprived.   **117**

blessing — You need the blessing you can offer (your *brother*.)   **118**

body — When you look on your *brother* as a (body), his power and glory are "lost" to you, and so are yours.   **141**

call — Forget not that (the call of your *brother*) is yours, and answer him with me.   **287**

change — It is not up to you to change your *brother*, but merely to accept him as he is.   **156**

choice — It is your choice whether (your *brothers*) support the ego or the Holy Spirit in you.   **284**

Christ — Reach out to all your *brothers* and touch them with the touch of Christ.   **235**

Christ — The Christ in you can see your *brother* truly.   **477**

co-creator — (Your *brother*) is a co-creator with God with you.   **127**

condemn — Think who your *brother* is before you would condemn him.   **394**

condemn — When you condemn a *brother* you are saying: **243**
"I who was guilty choose to remain so."

continuity — In timeless union with (your *brothers*) is   **235**
your continuity, unbroken because it is
wholly shared.

create — Whenever you heal a *brother*, by recognizing his   **127**
worth, you are acknowledging his
power to create and yours.

created — Your *brother* is as He created him.   **476**

creation — What is within your *brother* still contains all   **479**
of creation, everything created and
creating, born and unborn as yet, still
in the future or apparently gone by.

creations — Accept your *brother* in this world and accept   **163**
nothing else, for in him you will find
your creations because he created
them with you.

darkness — Would you hold the past against (your   **235**
brothers) For if you do, you are choosing
to remain in the darkness that is not
there, and refusing to accept the light
that is offered you.

darkness — Behold your *brothers* in their freedom, and   **254**
learn of them how to be free of dark-
ness.

death — Your *brother* thinks he holds the hand of death.   **571**

debt — In learning to escape from illusions, your debt to   **61**
your *brother* is something you must
never forget.

deceived — Do not be deceived in your *brother*, and see   **197**
only his loving thoughts as his reality.

decision — (Your *brother*) will be imprisoned or released   **132**
according to your decision, and so will
you.

deny — Why would you insist on denying (your *brother*)   **206**
For to do so is to deny yourself, and
impoverish both.

dissociated — (Your *brother*) may have dissociated the   **72**
Call for God, just as you have.

dream — A dream is given you in which (your *brother*) is your savior, not your enemy in hate. 571

enemy — You had decided that your brother is your enemy. 563

errors — If you point out the errors of your *brother's* ego you must be seeing through yours, because the Holy Spirit does not perceive his errors. 155

errors — (The errors of your *brother*) do not come from the truth that is in him, and only this truth is yours. 156

errors — (The errors of your *brother*) cannot change this, and can have no effect at all on the truth in you. 156

errors — (Your *brother's*) errors are all past, and by perceiving him without them you are releasing him. 234

faith — You will raise your eyes in faith (with your *brother*), or not at all. 394

fear — Those who would free their *brothers* from the body can have no fear. 422

find — In (your *brother*) you will find yourself or lose yourself. 132

forgetful — Our *brothers* are forgetful. That is why they need your remembrance of me and of Him Who created me. 113

forgiveness — Withhold forgiveness from your *brother* and you attack him. 460

forsake — Forsake not now your *brother*. 440

forsake — You forsake yourself and God if you forsake any of your *brothers*. 76

freedom — You have denied (the freedom of your *brother*), and by doing so you have denied the witness unto yours. 243

friend — Your *brother* is your friend because His Father created him like you. 466

function — Futility of function not fulfilled will haunt you while your *brother* lies asleep, till what has been assigned to you is done and he is risen from the past. 477

41

gently — Look gently on your *brother*, and remember the
      ego's weakness is revealed in both your
      sight.   **425**

gift — Offer your *brother* the gift of lilies, not the crown
      of thorns, the gift of love and not the
      "gift" of fear.   **396**

gladness — Because you taught (your *brothers*) gladness
      and release, they will become your
      teachers in release and gladness.   **254**

God — God loves every *brother* as he loves you, neither
      less nor more.   **292**

God — Only God Himself is more than (your *brothers*),
      but they are not less than He is.   **162**

guilt — In any union with a *brother*, in which you seek to
      lay your guilt upon him, or share it
      with him or perceive his own, you will
      feel guilty.   **245**

guiltless — No one who condemns a *brother* can see
      himself as guiltless and in the peace of
      God.   **247**

guiltlessness — (The guiltlessness of your *brother*) is
      your Atonement.   **259**

healing — You share the real world as you share
      Heaven and (the healing of your *brother*)
      is yours.   **198**

hear — Hear of your *brother* what you would have me to
      hear of you, for you would not want
      me to be deceived.   **153**

holiness — The holiness in you belongs to (your *brother*.)   **479**

holiness — (The holiness of your *brother*) is your for-
      giveness.   **443**

Holy Spirit — By guiding your *brothers* home, you are
      but following (the Holy Spirit.)   **209**

Holy Spirit — If you point out the errors of your *brother's*
      ego you must be seeing through yours,
      because the Holy Spirit does not per-
      ceive his errors.   **155**

Holy Spirit — It is only the Holy Spirit in (your *brother*)
      that never changes His mind.   **113**

Holy Spirit — Remember that the Holy Spirit is in (your *brother*) and His voice speaks to you through him. **153**

Holy Spirit — Your *brother* does not have to be aware of the Holy Spirit in himself or in you for this miracle to occur. **72**

hurt — Show (your *brother*) that he cannot hurt you, and hold nothing against him, or you hold it against yourself. **75**

illusion — No illusion you have ever held against (a *brother*) has touched his innocence in any way. **247**

illusion — Your holy *brother*, sight of whom is your release, is no illusion. **411**

insanely — When a *brother* acts insanely, he is offering you an opportunity to bless him. **118**

joy — Do not attribute your denial of joy to (your *brothers*), or you cannot see the spark in them that would bring joy to you. **176**

judge — Judge not (your *brother*) for you will hear no song of liberation for yourself. **505**

judge — You may believe that you judge your *brothers* by the messages they give you, but you have judged them by the messages you give to them. **176**

justifying — My *brothers* and yours are constantly engaged in justifying the unjustifiable. **87**

know — I will bring (your gratitude to your *brother*) to God, for you, knowing that to know your *brother* is to know God. **62**

know — You do not know your creations because you do not know your *brothers*, who created them with you. **127**

know — Your *brother* may not know who he is, but there is a light in his mind that does know. **153**

knowledge — When you have seen your *brothers* as yourself you will be released to knowledge, having learned to free yourself through Him who knows freedom. **242**

laws — Look on your *brother* and behold in him the whole reversal of the laws that seem to rule this world.   **476**

light — You have found your *brother* and you will light each other's ways.   **354**

littleness — Do not allow (your *brother*) to belittle himself in your mind but give him freedom from his belief in littleness, and thus excape from yours.   **141**

lost — . . . What your *brother* loses you have lost, and what he gains is what is given you.   **609**

love — Within yourself you love your *brother* with a perfect love.   **349**

loving — As a loving *brother* I am deeply concerned with your mind, and urge you to follow my example as you look at yourself and at your *brother*, and see in both the glorious creations of a glorious Father.   **57**

merciful — Be merciful unto your *brother*.   **593**

message — The message your *brother* gives you is up to you.   **153**

mind — Do not accept your *brother's* variable perception of himself for his split mind is yours, and you will not accept your healing without his.   **198**

mind — Your mind is so powerful that you can look in (your *brothers'* minds) and enlighten them, as I can enlighten yours.   **113**

mirror — Your *brother* is the mirror in which you see the image of yourself as long as perception lasts.   **118**

misused — You do not realize how much you have misused your *brothers* by seeing them as sources of ego support.   **284**

need - What except your *brothers* can you need?   **240**

obscure — Let no dark cloud out of your past obscure (your *brother*) from you, for truth lies only in the present, and you will find it if you seek it there.   **234**

offer — What you offer to your *brother* you offer to Him, because He cannot go beyond your offering in His giving.   **162**

"outrageous" — Recognize what does not matter and if your *brothers* ask for something "outrageous," do it because it doesn't matter.   **206**

part — Do not try to hurt (your *brother*) when he fails to take the part that you assigned to him, in what you dreamed your life was meant to be.   **570**

part — Be certain, if you do your part (your *brother*) will do his, for he will join you where you stand.   **556**

patience — Your patience with your *brother* is your patience with yourself.   **81**

peace — Look with peace upon your *brothers*, and God will come rushing into your heart in gratitude for your gift to Him.   **117**

peace — When peace is not with you and when you suffer pain of any kind, you have beheld some sin within your *brother*, and have rejoiced at what you thought was there.   **473**

picture — The picture of your *brother* that you see means nothing.   **532**

picture — The picture of your *brother* that you see is wholly absent and has never been.   **532**

problems — Salvation is not found by those who use their *brothers* to resolve problems that are not there.   **245**

purpose — When *brothers* join in purpose in the world of fear they stand already at the edge of the real world.   **592**

reality — Ask to learn the reality of your *brother*, because this is what you will perceive in him, and you will see your beauty reflected in his.   **198**

receive — You will receive of your *brother* according to   **394**
    your choice.

recognize — You who are not at war must look for   **108**
    brothers and recognize all whom you see
    as *brothers,* because only equals are at
    peace.

relationship — Your relationship with your *brother* has   **369**
    been uprooted from the world of
    shadows, and its unholy purpose has
    been safely brought through the bar-
    riers of guilt, washed with forgiveness,
    and set shining and firmly rooted in the
    world of light.

release — Every *brother* has the power to release you, if   **192**
    you choose to be free.

request — It is only you, therefore, who have made the   **206**
    request outrageous and every request
    of a *brother* is for you.

responsibility — Never forget your responsibility to   **132**
    (your *brother*) because it is your re-
    sponsibility to yourself.

return — As you bring back (your *brother*), so will you   **186**
    return.

right — Your *brother* is as right as you are, and if you   **156**
    think he is wrong, you are condemning
    yourself.

road — This *brother* neither leads nor follows us, but   **604**
    walks beside us on the selfsame road.

role — Do not describe a role to (your *brother*) that you   **570**
    image would bring happiness to you.

salvation — In your *brother's* hands is your salvation.   **393**

savior — Either you are the savior (of your *brother*) or his   **440**
    judge, offering him sanctuary or
    condemnation.

savior — Let (your *brother*) be to you the savior from   **399**
    illusions, and look on him with the new
    vision that looks upon the lilies and
    brings you joy.

savior — (Your *brother*) is your savior from the dreams of fear. **475**

see — As you see (your *brother*), you will see yourself. **132**

see — And as (the light of truth) shines your *brothers* see it, and realizing that this light is not what you have made, they see in you more than you see. **253**

sick — Do not allow your *brother* to be sick, for if he is, have you abandoned him to his own dream by sharing it with him. **554**

sick — When a *brother* is sick, he is not asking for peace, and therefore does not know he has it. **172**

sin — Your *brother* has in him the power to forgive your sin, as you for him. **394**

sinless — It is impossible to see your *brother* as sinless and yet to look on him as a body. **410**

sinless — See (your *brother*) as sinless and there can be no fear in you. **402**

sins — Let your awareness of your *brother* not be blocked by your perception of his sins and of his body. **443**

specialness — All the tribute you have given special-ness belongs to (your *brother*), and thus returns to you. **479**

stranger — The *brother* who stands beside you still seems to be a stranger. **393**

symbol — You have decided that your *brother* is a symbol for "hateful-love," a "weakened power," and above all, "a living death." **531**

task — Your task (to your *brother*) is to tell him he is right. **155**

teach — Only (your *brothers*) can teach you what you are, for your learning is the result of what you taught them. **162**

together — In truth you and your *brother* stand together with nothing in between. **446**

together — You and your *brother* will yet come together in my name, and your sanity will be restored. **59**

treat — As you treat (your *brother*), you will treat yourself.   132

truth — You and your *brother* stand together in the holy presence of truth.   340

unlikely — That you are what your *brother* made of you seems most unlikely.   612

waken — The light in you will waken your *brothers*, and they will not leave you asleep.   254

wholeness — You cannot be hurt and do not want to show your *brother* anything except your wholeness.   75

willingness — Look on your *brother* with the willingness to see him as he is.   595

witness — Every *brother* you meet becomes witness for Christ or for the ego, depending on what you perceive in him.   191

world — With you, (your *brother*) thinks the world he made, made him.   420

yourself — You must see your *brother* as yourself.   483

CAUSE

effect — *cause* and effect are one, not separate.   517

effects — See the new effects of *cause* accepted now, with consequences here.   548

effects — The *cause* produces the effects, which then bear witness to the *cause*, and not themselves.   540

faith — There is *cause* for faith.   344

faithlessness — There is no *cause* for faithlessness.   344

fear — If you fear, there is a present *cause*.   519

future — A future *cause* as yet has no effects.   519

God — God is the only *Cause*, and guilt is not of Him.   256

healing — The *cause* of healing is the only *Cause* of everything.   551

reflections — Dwell not on suffering and sin, for they are but reflections of their *cause*.   540

remembering — Remembering a *cause* can but produce illusions of its presence, not effects.   547

CAUSELESS

be — The *causeless* cannot be.   **256**

communication — You will learn communication with oneness only when you learn to deny the *causeless*, and accept the cause of God as yours.   **256**

Son of God — What (the Son of God) has made is *causeless*, having no effects at all.   **550**

truth — What never was is *causeless*, and is not there to interfere with truth.   **344**

CERTAINTY

action — *Certainty* does not require action.   **36**

finding — There is a way of finding *certainty* right here and now.   **555**

God — *Certainty* is of God for you.   **102**

God — Inspiration is of the Holy Spirit, and *certainty* is of God, according to His laws.   **109**

CHANGE

blessing — *change* is the only thing that can be made a blessing here, where purpose is not fixed, however changeless it appears to be.   **572**

cause — *Change* must have a cause that will endure or else it will not last.   **548**

fearful — *Change* is always fearful to the separated, because they cannot conceive it as a move towards healing the separation.   **48**

function — You cannot *change* because your function has been fixed by God.   **572**

fundamental — The fundamental *change* will occur with the *change* of mind in the thinker.   **99**

God — *Change* is the greatest gift that God gave to all that you would make eternal. to ensure that only heaven would not pass away.   **572**

illusion — *Change* is an illusion, taught by those who cannot see themselves as guiltless.   **282**

immortality — There is no *change* in immortality, and Heaven knows it not.   **566**

peace — You believe that if you allow no *change* to enter into your ego you will find peace.   **48**

CHANGELESSNESS

brother — Your brother has a *changelessness* in him beyond appearance and deception, both.   **598**

CHAOS

consistency — *Chaos* and consistency cannot co-exist for long since they are mutually exclusive.   **101**

ego — The ego is *chaos*, and if it were all of you, no order at all would be possible.   **273**

gods — Your gods do not bring *chaos*; you are endowing them with *chaos*, and accepting it of them.   **174**

law — No law of *chaos* could compel belief but for the emphasis on form and disregard of content.   **458**

law — The first law of *chaos* is that the truth is different for everyone.   **455**

law — The second law of *chaos* is that each one must sin and therefore deserves attack and death.   **455**

law — The third law of *chaos* is, if God cannot be mistaken, He must accept His Son's belief in what he is and hate him for it.   **456**

law — The fourth law of *chaos* is the belief that you have what you have taken.   **456**

lawlessness — *Chaos* is lawlessness, and has no laws.   **458**

love — Lack of faith in love in any form attests to *chaos* as reality.   **459**

sin — From the belief in sin, the faith in *chaos* must follow.   **459**

CHAOTIC

meaning — Creation is perfectly lawful, and the *chaotic* is without meaing, because it is without God.   **174**

CHARITABLE

abundance — Only those who have a real and lasting   **52**
sense of abundance can be *charitable*.

CHARITY

another — *Charity* is a way of looking at another as if he   **23**
had already gone far beyond his actual
accomplishments in time.

ego — Equality is beyone (the grasp of the ego), and   **52**
charity becomes impossible.

help — The *charity* that is accorded (to another) is an   **23**
acknowledgement that he needs help,
and a recognition that he will accept it.

love — *Charity* is really a weaker reflection of a much   **23**
more powerful love-encompassment
that is far beyond any form of *charity*
you can conceive of as yet.

perfection — Healing rests on *charity*, and is a way of   **23**
perceiving the perfection of another,
even if you cannot perceive it in yourself.

right-mindedness — *Charity* is essential to right-   **23**
mindedness in the limited sense in
which it can now be attained.

world — *Charity* still lies within the limitations of this   **23**
world.

CHILD(REN) OF GOD, (SON(S) OF GOD, GOD'S SON(S), HIS SON(S))

asks — The *Son of God* asks only this: that you return to   **491**
him what is his due, that you may share
in it with him.

awe — Awe is inappropriate in connection with *Sons of*   **13**
God, because you should not experience
awe in the presence of your equals.

blessed — The *Son of God* is always blessed as one.   **430**

bound — The *Son of God* cannot be bound by time nor   **495**
place nor anything God did not will.

case — There can be no case against a *Child of God*, and   **81**
every witness to guilt in God's creation
is bearing false witness to God Himself.

certain — What can be more certain than a *Son of God*.   **404**

choice — The *Son of God* can make no choice the Holy Spirit cannot employ on his behalf, and not against himself.   **493**

Christ — Every *Child of God* is one in Christ, for his being is in Christ as Christ's is in God.   **213**

comfort — The *Children of God* are entitled to perfect comfort that comes from perfect trust.   **19**

confusion — There is no confusion in the mind of a *Son of God*, whose will must be the Will of the Father, because the Father's Will is His Son.   **125**

created — *Child of God*, you were created to create the good, the beautiful, and the holy.   **12**

created — The power of the *Sons of God* is present all the time, because they were created as creators.   **88**

crucified — In the calm light of truth, let us recognize that you believe you have crucified *God's Son*.   **224**

darkness — There is no darkness anywhere in (*God's Son*), for he is whole.   **235**

deceived — Be not deceived in *God's Son*, for he is one with himself and one with his Father.   **198**

equal — Because *God's* equal *sons* have everything, they cannot compete.   **108**

equal — *God's Sons* are equal in will, all being the Will of their Father.   **135**

faith — Your faith in a (*Son of God*) is your faith in yourself.   **153**

Father — The *Son of God* has both Father and Son, because he is both Father and Son.   **182**

Fatherhood — No *Son of God* remains outside His Fatherhood.   **366**

God — (*The Son of God's*) slavery is as complete as his freedom, for he will obey only the god he accepts.   **193**

God — (*God's plan for salvation*) must have been accepted   426
by the *Son of God*, for what God wills for
him he must receive.

god's — Hear only God's Answer in *His Sons*, and you   154
are answered.

guilt — The *Son of God* **believes he** is lost in guilt, **alone**   246
in a dark **world** where pain is **pressing**
everywhere upon him from without.

guiltless — The idea that the guiltless *Son of God* can   243
attack himself and make himself guilty
is insane.

guiltless — The redeemed son of man is the guiltless   225
Son of God, and to recognize him is your
redemption.

guiltless — You do not believe the *Son of God* is guiltless,   243
because you see the past, and see him
not.

guilty — You have no idea that you are failing the *Son*   223
of God by seeing him as guilty.

happy — A *Son of God* is happy only when we knows he is   126
with God.

ιeal — The power to heal the *Son of God* is given you   429
because he must be one with you.

holy — The *Children of God* are holy and the miracle   3
honors their holiness, which can be
hidden but never lost.

Holy Trinity — The *Son of God* is part of the Holy Trinity,   35
but the Trinity itself is one.

honor — Give only honor to the *Sons of* the living *God*,   119
and count yourself among them gladly.

hurt — No one can hurt the *Son of God*.   256

idols — *God's Son* knows no idols, but he does know His   172
Father.

illusions — Every *Son of God* has the power to deny illu-   172
sions anywhere in the Kingdom,
merely by denying them completely in
himself.

imprisoned — God is not mocked; no more *His Son* can   430
be imprisoned save by his own desire.

inheritance — You have not failed to increase the inheritance of the *Sons of God,* and thus have not failed to secure it for yourself.   **123**

know — Know the *Sons of God* and you will know all creation.   **127**

love — You are for the *(Son of God)* or against him; either you love him or attack him, protect his unity or see him shattered and slain by your attack.   **430**

loving — *(Children of God)* are the work of God, and His Work is wholly loving and wholly loveable.   **7**

loving — *God's Son* is still as loving as his Father.   **236**

meaning — The meaning of the *Son of God* lies solely in his relationship with his Creator.   **406**

mistake — The one mistake (of *God's Son*) is he thinks (his idols) real.   **590**

one — *God's Son* is one.   **332**

perfect — *God's Son* is perfect or he cannot be *God's Son.*   **595**

power — Nothing made by a *Child of God* is without power.   **44**

power — The power of the *Sons of God* is present all the time, because they were created as creators.   **88**

power — The power you have over the *Son of God* is not a threat to his reality.   **430**

power — There is no limit to the power of a *Son of God,* but he can limit the expression of his power as much as he chooses.   **58**

powerless — No one believes the *Son of God* is powerless.   **430**

prevail — Nothing can prevail against a *Son of God* who commends his Spirit into the Hands of his Father.   **35**

rejection — (The *Sons of God*) must learn to teach that all forms of rejection are meaningless.   **88**

relationship — The *Son of God* has invented an unholy relationship between him and his Father.   **406**

relationship — The real relationship (of the *Son of God*) is one of perfect union and unbroken continuity.   **406**

salvation — The influence (of the *Sons of God*) on each other is without limit, and must be used for their joint salvation.   **88**

salvation — Whenever two *Sons of God* meet, they are given another chance at salvation.   **132**

share — *God's Sons* have nothing they do not share.   **197**

sick — To believe a *Son of God* is sick is to worship the same idol that he does.   **171**

sick — To believe that a *Son of God* can be sick is to believe that part of God can suffer.   **171**

sinlessness — *God's Son* has found a witness unto his sinlessness and not his sins.   **500**

sinners — No one is punished for sins, and the *Sons of God* are not sinners.   **88**

"sins" — The betrayal of the *Son of God* lies only in illusions, and all his "sins" are but his own imagining.   **327**

specialness — The specialness of *God's Sons* stems from inclusion, not exclusion.   **10**

strangers — God is not a stranger to *His Sons*, and His Sons are not strangers to each other.   **36**

teacher — One *child of God* is the only teacher sufficiently worthy to teach another.   **119**

understands — And so is Heaven's Son prepared to be himself, and to remember that the *Son of God* knows everything His Father understands and understands it perfectly with Him.   **591**

waiting — All the *Sons of God* are waiting for your return, just as you are waiting for theirs.   **79**

worth — Seek not to appraise the worth of *God's Son* whom he created holy, for to do so is to evaluate his Father and judge against Him.   **258**

you — You are a *child of God*, a priceless part of His Kingdom, which He created as part of Him.   **94**

CHOICE

basis — There is no basis for a *choice* in this complex and over-complicated world.   **509**

death — The *choice* is yours to make between a sleeping death and dreams of evil or a happy wakening and joy of life.   **541**

end — There is no *choice* where every end is sure.   **608**

free — What you would choose between is not a *choice* and gives but the illusion it is free, for it will have one outcome either way.   **603**

freedom — (The freedom of *choice*) is the same power as the freedom to create, but its application is different.   **70**

function — There is no *choice* of function anywhere.   **533**

Heaven — A *choice* made with the power of Heaven to uphold it cannot be undone.   **444**

illusion — That there is *choice* is an illusion.   **509**

lose — The *choice* you fear to lose you never had.   **533**

oppose — To oppose (God) is to make a *choice* against yourself, and choose that you be bound.   **5ˆ5**

power — There is a *choice* that you have power to make when you have seen the real alternatives.   **609**

purpose — Recognize that in (your) *choice* the purpose of the world you see is chosen and will be justified.   **489**

rationale — There is a rationale for *choice*.   **129**

real — Real *choice* is no illusion.   **607**

real — The real world is the area of *choice* made real, not in the outcome, but in the perception of alternatives for *choice*.   **509**

true — It is true indeed there is no *choice* at all within the world.   **608**

vision — Vision or judgment is your *choice*, but never both of these.   **405**

witness — You will see the witness to the *choice* you made, and learn from this to recognize which one you chose.   **415**

CHOOSE

again — You will hear and you will *choose* again.   **621**

brother — You can teach (your brother) only that he is as you would have him, and what you *choose* he be is but your choice for you.   **429**

Christ — You always *choose* between your weakness and the strength of Christ in you.   **620**

God — You can never *choose* except between God and the ego.   **332**

Holy Spirit — By teaching what to *choose*, the Holy Spirit will ultimately teach you that you need not *choose* at all.   **101**

real — What you *choose* is what you think is real.

CHOOSING

control — You are in control of the outcomes of your *choosing*.   **607**

Holy Spirit — The Holy Spirit is one way of *choosing*.   **70**

Holy Spirit — *Choosing* through the Holy Spirit will lead you to the Kingdom.   **102**

mind — *Choosing* depends on a split mind.   **70**

CHRIST

abundance — The abundance of *Christ* is the natural result of choosing to follow Him.   **10**

acceptance — *Christ* waits for your acceptance of Him as yourself, and of His Wholeness as yours.   **187**

alone — Where *Christ* has entered no one is alone, for never could he find a home in separateness.   **438**

altar — *Christ* is at God's altar waiting to welcome His Son.   **187**

bodies — No one who carries *Christ* in him can fail to recognize Him everywhere, except in bodies.   **482**

body — The *Christ* in you inhabits not a body.   **482**

changelessness — The *Christ* as revealed to you now has no past, for He is changeless, and in his changelessness lies your release.   **234**

child — Every child of God is one in *Christ*, for his being is in *Christ* as *Christ's* is in God.   **213**

dwell — *Christ* has come to dwell in the abode you set for Him before time was, in calm eternity.   **622**

ego — *Christ* does rise above the ego and all its works, and ascends to the Father and His Kingdom.   **192**

face — If you see glimpses of the face of *Christ* behind the veil, looking between the snow white petals of the lilies you have received and given as your gift, you will behold your brother's face and recognize it.   **396**

forgiveness — *(Christ)* still holds forgiveness out to you, to share His holiness.   **394**

forgiveness — A risen *Christ* becomes the symbol of the Son of God's forgiveness on himself, the sign he looks upon himself as healed and whole.   **396**

God — *Christ* is the Son of God, Who lives in his Creator and shines with His glory.   **187**

hand — (The hand of *Christ*) holds all His brothers in Himself.   **474**

holiness — (The holiness of *Christ*) is yours because He is the only Power that is real in you.   **620**

holiness — (The holiness of *Christ*) directs the body through the mind at one with him.   **482**

Host — *(Christ)* is Host to God.   **304**

interpret — Let the *Christ* in you interpret for you, and do not try to limit what you see by narrow little beliefs that are unworthy of God's Son.   **192**

invisible — *Christ* is invisible to you because of what you have made visible to yourself.   **218**

knows — The *(Christ)* knows where you are going and leads you there in gentleness and blessing all the way.   **474**

like — *Christ* comes to what is like Himself, the same,   **438**
not different.

love — *Christ's* eyes are open and He will look on what-   **212**
ever you see with love if you accept His
vision as yours.

love — The *Christ's* eyes are open and He in you remem-   **602**
bers God with all the certainty with
which He knows His Love.

love — *Christ* is the extension of the Love and the Love-   **187**
liness of God, as perfect as His Creator
and at peace with Him.

majesty — What appears to hide the face of *Christ* is   **620**
powerless before His majesty, and
disappears before His holy sight.

miracle — The miracle is an expression of the inner   **4**
awareness of *Christ* and the acceptance
of His Atonement.

Own — Until *Christ* comes into His Own, the Son of God   **192**
will see himself as Fatherless.

perceive — Learning of *Christ* is easy, for to perceive   **192**
with Him involves no strain at all.

perceptions — The perceptions (of *Christ*) are your
natural awareness, and it is only the   **192**
distortions you introduce that tire you.

present — *(Christ)* lives within you in the quiet present,   **237**
and waits for you to leave the past be-
hind and enter into the world he holds
out to you in love.

purpose — From the purpose (of *Christ*) comes the   **478**
means for effortless accomplishment
and rest.

purpose — The purpose (of *Christ*) folds the body in His   **482**
light and fills it with the holiness that
shines from Him.

rejoice — And none who looks upon the *Christ* in you   **444**
but will rejoice.

relationship — Who is drawn to *Christ* is drawn to God   **438**
as surely as both are drawn to every
holy relationship, the home prepared
for them as earth is turned to Heaven.

sacrifice — In the Presence (of *Christ*) the whole idea of sacrifice loses all meaning.   **304**

savior — Each one finds his savior when he is ready to look upon the face of *Christ,* and see Him sinless.   **403**

separate — *Christ* is the Son of God Who is in no way separate from His Father, Whose every thought is as loving as the Thought of His Father by which He was created.   **197**

separate — You and your brother stand before (*Christ*) now to let Him draw aside the veil that seems to keep you separate and apart.   **483**

sight — The sight of *Christ* is all there is to see.   **475**

speaks — If you hear but your own voice, and *Christ* speaks through you, you will hear Him.   **192**

still — The *Christ* in you is very still.   **473**

task — It cannot be hard to do the task that *Christ* appointed you to do, since it is He Who does it.   **482**

tenderness — *Christ* calls to all with equal tenderness, seeing no leaders and no followers, and hearing but one answer to them all.   **604**

time — It is in your power to make this season holy, for it is in your power to make the time of *Christ* be now.   **302**

truth — The *Christ* in you looks only on the truth, and sees no condemnation that could need forgiveness.   **473**

vision — The vision of *Christ* is given the very instant that it is perceived.   **254**

vision — The vision (of *Christ*) is given quickly and gladly to anyone who is but willing to see his brother as sinless.   **441**

witness — (*Christ*) sees for you, as your witness to the real world.   **232**

world — *Christ* is the Holy Spirit's manifestation, looking always on the real world, and calling forth its witnesses and drawing them to you.   **232**

world — *(Christ)* looks quietly on the real world which   **213**
he would share with you because He
knows of the Father's love for Him.

world — Through the eyes of *Christ* only the real world   **216**
exists and only the real world can be
seen.

CHRIST, FIRST COMING OF

creation — The *First Coming of Christ* is merely another   **58**
name for the creation, for Christ is the
Son of God.

CHRIST, SECOND COMING OF

ego's — The *Second Coming of Christ* means nothing more   **58**
than the end of the ego's rule and
healing of the mind.

reality — The *Second Coming of Christ* is the awareness of   **159**
reality, not its return.

sense — The *Second Coming of Christ* is merely the return   **158**
of sense.

CHRISTMAS (THE TIME OF CHRIST)

Holy Spirit — This *Christmas* give the Holy Spirit every-   **304**
thing that would hurt you.

joy — Let no despair darken the joy of *Christmas*, for *the*   **306**
time of Christ is meaningless apart from
joy.

Message — The message of *the time of Christ* is the percep-   **306**
tion that we are deprived of nothing.

star — The sign of *Christmas* is a star, a light in darkness.   **304**

CHURCH

altar — A *church* is where an altar is, and the presence of   **86**
the altar is what makes the church
holy.

foundation — Only you can be the foundation of God's   **86**
church.

purpose — A *church* that does not inspire love has a   86
hidden altar that is not serving the
purpose for which God intended it.

CLARITY
confusion — *Clarity* undoes confusion by definition, and   188
to look upon darkness through limit
must dispel it.

COMFORT
need — God's Son is indeed in need of *comfort*, for he   184
knows not what he does, believing his
will not his own.

COMFORTER(S)
deceived — Do not be deceived by the dark *comforters*,   185
and never let them enter the mind of
God's Son, for they have no place in His
temple.

God — Know then Who abides with you merely by   184
recognizing what is there already, and
do not be satisfied with imaginary
comforters, for the *Comforter* of God is in
you.

God's — Only God's *Comforter* can comfort you.   185

rest — Your *Comforter* will rest you, but you cannot.   184

COMMUNICATE
His — Since only beings of a like order can truly *communi-*   64
cate, His creations naturally *communicate*
with Him and like Him.

Holy Spirit — God can *communicate* only to the Holy   261
Spirit in your mind.

Holy Spirit — Leave what you would *communicate* to the   266
Holy Spirit, because only He shares the
knowledge of what you are with God.

join — To *communicate* is to join and to attack is to   142
separate.

minds — Only minds *communicate*.   111

relationship — In each holy relationship is the ability to *communicate* instead of separate reborn. **437**

COMMUNICATING

abandoned — It is clearly insane to believe that by *communicating* you will be abandoned. **297**

COMMUNICATION

body — The body is a limit imposed on the universal *communication* that is an eternal property of mind. **360**

communicate — The willingness to communicate attracts *communication* to it, and overcomes loneliness completely. **298**

creation — Creation and *communication* are synonymous. **63**

Creator — You remain in close *communication* with (your Creator), and with everything that is within Him, as it is within yourself. **259**

direct — *Communication* is perfectly direct and perfectly united. **107**

divided — *Communication* between what cannot be divided cannot cease. **269**

free — *Communication* is totally free, because nothing discordant ever enters. **107**

God — *(Communication* belongs to God) and is therefore like Him. **107**

God — *Communication* with God is life. Nothing without it is at all. **262**

God — The *communication* that God placed within you, joining your mind with His, cannot be broken. **250**

happy — Unlearn isolation through His loving guidance, and learn of all the happy *communication* that you have thrown away but could not lose. **259**

healing — Healing is the Holy Spirit's form of *communication* in this world, and the only one He accepts. **111**

Holy Spirit — The Holy Spirit is the highest *communica-* 4
tion medium.

Holy Spirit — The Holy Spirit knows with Whom you 266
are in perfect *communication.*

Holy Spirit's — The Holy Spirit's function is entirely 266
communication.

interference — All interference in the *communication* 269
that God Himself wills with His Son is
quite impossible here.

language — (The language you made) has no meaning, 266
for its purpose is not *communication,* but
rather for the disruption of *communica-*
tion.

miracles — Miracles are temporary devices of *communica-* 4
tion.

perfect — You will not be able to accept perfect *communi-* 290
cation as long as you would hide it from
yourself.

relationships — *Communication* remains the only means 300
by which you can establish real rela-
tionships, which have no limits, having
been established by God.

restored — *Communication* must have been restored to
those who join, for this they could not
do through their bodies.

secret — God has no secret *communications,* for everything of Him is perfectly open and
freely accessible to all, being for all.

separation — *Communication* ends separation. 140

separation — You have regarded the separation as a 265
means for breaking your *communication*
with your Father.

true — The Holy Spirit will separate out all that has 266
meaning, dropping off the rest and
offering your true *communication* to
those who would communicate as truly
with you.

unlimited — *Communication* must be unlimited in order 300

to have meaning, and deprived of
meaning, it will not satisfy you
completely.

unlimited — There is no attack, but there is unlimited   **143**
communication and therefore unlimited
power and wholeness.

whole — Your whole *communication* is like a baby's.

COMMUNION

fear — You want *communion*, not the feast of fear.   **385**

natural — *Communion*, not prayer, is the natural state of   **41**
those who know.

unlimited — (The Son of God) is free, unlimited in his   **399**
communion with all that is within him.

COMPETITION

conflicts — Do not underestimate your need to be vigil-   **108**
ant against (the idea of *competition*),
because all your conflicts come from it.

COMPLETE

brother — His Will is brought together as you join in   **486**
Will, that you be made *complete* by offer-
ing completion to your brother.

creation — Creation gives no separate person and no   **587**
separate thing the power to *complete* the
Son of God.

creations — You seek but for your own completion, and   **315**
it is (your creations) who render you
complete.

God's — (The Son of God) was created that you might   **571**
be whole, for only the *complete* can be
part of God's completion which created
you.

special — To seek a special person or a thing to add to   **586**
yourself to make yourself *complete,* can
only mean that you believe some form
is missing.

will — Your will to be *complete* is but God's Will, and this   **587**
is given you by being His.

COMPLETION

awareness — Refuse not the awareness of your *completion,* and seek not to restore it to yourself.   **298**

bridge — Across the bridge is your *completion,* for you will be wholly in God, willing for nothing special, but only to be wholly like to Him, completing Him by your *completion.*   **315**

ego — To the ego, *completion* lies in triumph, and in the extension of the "victory" even to the final triumph over God.   **318**

function — *Completion* is the function of God's Son.   **587**

idol — Behind the search for every idol lies the yearning for *completion.*   **586**

ritual — The ritual of *completion* cannot complete, for life arises not from death, nor Heaven from hell.   **319**

union — The Holy Spirit knows that *completion* lies first in union, and then in the extension of union.   **318**

you — You seek but your own *completion,* and it is they who render you complete.   **315**

COMPLEXITY

God — *Complexity* is not of God.   **508**

COMPROMISE

accept — *Compromise* is to accept but part of what you want, to take a little and give up the rest.   **460**

conflict — Mistake not truce for peace, nor *compromise* for the escape from conflict.   **461**

salvation — (Salvation) is denied where *compromise* has been accepted, for *compromise* is the belief salvation is impossible.   **460**

salvation — (If *compromise*) is possible, salvation is attack.   **461**

CONCEPT(S)

changing — *Concepts* are needed while perception lasts, and changing *concepts* is salvation's task. **616**

cruel — Let the cruel *concept* of yourself be changed to one that brings the peace of God. **617**

forgiveness — Should one brother dawn upon your sight as wholly worthy of forgiveness, then your *concept* of yourself is wholly changed. **616**

given — *(Concepts)* are not given, so they must be made. **611**

God — God has given you His Son to save from every *concept* that he ever held. **618**

idols — *(Concepts)* are the ideas of idols, painted with the brushes of the world, which cannot make a single picture representing truth. **611**

learning — Apart from learning, *(concepts)* do not exist. **611**

maintain — *Concepts* maintain the world. **611**

salvation — Salvation can be seen as nothing more than the escape from *concepts*. **613**

self — A *concept* of the self is meaningless, for no one here can see what it is for, and therefore cannot picture what it is. **611**

self — The *concept* of the self has always been the great preoccupation of the world. **613**

self — You will make many *concepts* of the self as learning goes along. **613**

truth — You who believe that you can choose to see the Son of God as you would have him be, forget not that no *concept* of yourself will stand against the truth of what you are. **615**

truth — The *concept* of the self stands like a shield, a silent barricade before the truth, and hides it from your sight. **617**

world — Your *concept* of the world depends on this *concept* of the self. **612**

you — There can be no *concept* that can stand for what you are. **613**

yourself — The *concept* of yourself that you now hold 617
would guarantee your function here
remain forever unaccomplished and
undone.

CONDEMN

self-accused — Only the self-accused *condemn*. 606

yourself — You can only *condemn* yourself, and by so 222
doing you cannot know that you are
God's Son.

CONDEMNATION

attack — If you did not feel guilty you could not attack, 220
for *condemnation* is the root of attack.

God — You have condemned yourself, but *condemnation* 143
is not of God.

Holy Spirit — (The Holy Spirit) will teach you to see 156
yourself without *condemnation,* by learn-
ing how to look on everything without
it.

judgment — Judgment and *condemnation* are behind you, 234
and unless you bring them with you,
you will see that you are free of them.

results — If all *condemnation* is unreal, and it must be 143
unreal since it is a form of attack, then
it can have no results.

sin — Sin and *condemnation* are the same, and belief in 243
one is faith in the other, calling for
punishment instead of love.

Son — There is no *condemnation* in the Son, for there is 187
no *condemnation* in the Father.

world — The part you play in salvaging the world from 540
condemnation is your own escape.

world — The world's escape from *condemnation* is a need 540
which those within the world are
joined in sharing.

CONDEMNED

accuser — What is *condemned* can never be returned to its accuser, who had hated it, and hates it still as a symbol of his fear. — 530

brother — However much you wish (your brother) be *condemned,* God is in him. — 521

losing — When anyone is seen as losing he has been *condemned.* — 501

CONFLICT(S)

answer — In *conflict* there can be no answer and no resolution, for its purpose is to make no resolution possible, and to ensure no answer will be plain. — 533

choice — It is *conflict* that makes choice possible. — 508

choice — There is no *conflict* in the choice between truth and illusion. — 315

competition — Do not underestimate your need to be vigilant against (the idea of competition), because all your *conflicts* come from it. — 108

doubt — There must be doubt before there can be *conflict.* — 475

ego — The crucifixion was the result of clearly opposed thought systems; the perfect symbol of the *"conflict"* between the ego and the Son of God. — 88

ego — *Conflict* within you must imply that you believe the ego has the power to be victorious. — 452

ego's — The real *conflict* you experience is between the ego's idle wishes and the Will of God, which you share. — 189

evil — *Conflict* is the root of all evil, for being blind it does not see whom it attacks. — 184

fear — The first corrective step in undoing the error is to know first that the *conflict* is an expression of fear. — 26

fear — *Conflict* is fearful for it is the birth of fear. — 454

illusions — *Conflict* enters the instant the choice seems to be one between illusions, but this choice does not matter. — 315

illusions — *Conflict* is the choice between illusions, one   **454**
to be crowned as real, the other vanquished and despised.

knowledge — Only the oneness of knowledge is free of   **46**
conflict.

levels — Spirit has no levels, and all *conflict* arises from   **37**
the concept of levels.

peace — *Conflict* and peace are opposites.   **455**

released — To be released from *conflict* means that it is   **461**
over.

resolved — *Conflict* cannot be ultimately resolved until   **29**
all parts of the Sonship have returned.

sanity — There can be no *conflict* between sanity and   **99**
insanity.

you — You are in *conflict.*   **533**

CONFUSED

believe — Somehow you believe that what is totally   **600**
confused is easier to learn and understand.

CONFUSION

Kingdom — There is no *confusion* in the Kingdom, because there is only one meaning.   **107**

life — All *confusion* comes from not extending life,   **118**
because that it is not the Will of your Creator.

limited — *Confusion* is not limited.   **523**

meaning — It is apparent that *confusion* interferes with   **107**
meaning, and therefore prevents the learner from appreciating it.

share — You share *confusion* and you are confused, for in   **556**
the gap no stable self exists.

world — *Confusion* follows on *confusion* here, for on *confusion* has this world been based, and   **566**
there is nothing else it rests upon.

CONSCIOUSNESS

ego — *Consciousness* is correctly identified as the domain of the ego.　　37

level — *Consciousness,* the level of perception, was the first split introduced into the mind after the separation, making the mind a perceiver rather than a creator.　　37

mind — *Consciousness,* the level of perception, was the first split introduced into the mind after the separation, making the mind a perceiver rather than a creator.　　37

sickness — Unstated and unheart in *consciousness* is every pledge to sickness.　　560

state — *Consciousness* is the state that induces action, though it does not inspire it.　　5

CONSISTENCY

chaos — Chaos and *consistency* cannot coexist for long, since they are mutually exclusive.　　101

chaos — Your *consistency* is called on despite chaos.　　101

CONTENT

ego — The ego is incapable of understanding *content,* and is totally unconcerned with it.　　274

form — Take not form for *content,* for the form is but a means for *content.*　　485

form — What you consider *content* is not *content* at all. It is merely form, and nothing else.　　274

CONTROL

yourself — You who cannot even *control* yourself should hardly aspire to *control* the universe.　　218

CORRECT

yourself — You cannot *correct* yourself.　　156

CORRECTION

brother — *Correction* cannot be accepted or refused by you without your brother.　　428

God — *Correction* is of God, Who does not know of arrogance.　　156

left — *Correction* must be left to the One who knows   531
correction and forgiveness are the same.

see — *Correction* is for all who cannot see.   212

working — The working out of all *correction* takes no   520
time at all.

CORRUPTION

dedicated — You who are dedicated to the incorruptible   389
have been given through your accep-
tance the power to release from *corruption*.

CREATE

ability — Since creative ability rests in the mind, every-   29
thing you *create* is necessarily a matter
of will.

desire — To desire wholly is to *create*, and creating can-   100
not be difficult if God Himself created
you as a creator.

God — You can *create* as (God) did, and your dissociation   162
will not alter this.

love — To *create* is to love.   104

power — Apart from (the Source, the Son) has no power   420
to *create*, and what he makes is mean-
ingless.

power — The Atonement gives you the power of a   76
healed mind, but the power to *create* is
of God.

Sonship — Because the Sonship must *create* as one, you   162
remember creation whenever you
recognize part of creation.

will — Since creative ability rests in the mind, every-   29
thing you *create* is necessarily a matter
of will.

will — Your will to *create* was given you by your Creator.   29

world — In this world it is impossible to *create*.   333

you — You cannot *create* in this divided state, and you   117
must be vigilant against this divided
state because only peace can be extended.

CREATED

attack — You do not know your creations simply be-   169
cause you would decide against them
as long as your mind is split, and to
attack what you have *created* is impossible.

difference — You do not know the difference between   195
what you have made and what you
have *created*.

nothing — Nothing that ever was *created* but is yours.   299

safe — Everything that was *created* is perfectly safe,   169
because the laws of God protect it by
His love.

true — Anything that God *created* is as true as He is.   89

you — You were *created* only to create, neither to see or   252
do.

CREATION

circle — The circle of *creation* has no end.   550

communication — *Creation* and communication are   63
synonymous.

cornerstone — The cornerstone of God's *creation* is you,   179
for His thought system is light.

error — You can never make your misperceptions true,   38
and your *creation* is beyond your own
error.

eternity — The mission of redemption will be fulfilled   250
as surely as the *creation* will remain un-
changed throughout eternity.

expressed — The full power of *creation* cannot be ex-   76
pressed as long as any of God's ideas
are withheld from the Kingdom.

fatherhood — Fatherhood is *creation*.   550

given — This requires God's endowment of the Son   14
with free will, because all loving *creation*
is freely given in one continuous line,
in which all aspects are of the same
order.

God — *Creation* is the Will of God.   139

God — God cherishes *creation* as the perfect Father that   486
He is.

73

God — Your *creation* by God is the only foundation that cannot be shaken, because the light is in it.   45

interrupted — *Creation* cannot be interrupted.   241

joy — Unless you take part in the *creation* (God's) joy is not complete, because yours is incomplete.   64

limited — You have died to limit what He created, and so you believe that all *creation* is limited.   180

love — All fear is implicit in (miscreation) and all love in (*creation.*)   28

manner — You were created through His laws and by His Will, and the manner of your *creation* established you a creator.   174

means — *Creation* is the means for God's extension, and what is His must be His Son's as well.   462

miracle — The miracle of *creation* has never ceased, having the holy stamp of immortality upon it.   278

miracle — This is the miracle of *creation;* that it is one forever.   241

reality — *Creation* proves reality because it shares the function all *creation* shares.   559

sharing — If *creation* is sharing, it cannot create what is unlike itself.   176

Son of God — What the Son of God knew in *creation* he must know again.   592

source — *Creation* is your Source and your only real function.   40

will — *Creation* is your will because it is (God's.)   182

CREATIONS

acceptance — Acceptance of your *creations* is the oneness of creation, without which you could never be complete.   315

belong — Your *creations* belong in you, as you belong in God.   104

brother — Follow my example as you look at yourself   57
and at your brother, and see in both
the glorious *creations* of a glorious
Father.

establish — As miracles in this world join you to your   242
brothers, so do your *creations* establish
your fatherhood in Heaven.

extended — Extension cannot be blocked, and it has no   180
voids. It continues forever, however
much it is denied. Your denial of its
reality may arrest it in time, but not in
eternity. That is why your *creations* have
not ceased to be extended, and why so
much is waiting for your return.

God — God and His *creations* are completely dependent   19
on each other.

God — *Creations* of God do not merely reflect truth, they   272
are truth.

God — The Kingdom of Heaven is the spirit's right,   50
whose beauty and dignity are far
beyond doubt, beyond perception,
and stand forever as the mark of the
Love of God for His *creations*, who are
wholly worthy of Him and only of Him.

God — The *creations* of God do not create myths, al-   53
though creative effort can be turned
to mythology.

holy — Our *creations* are as holy as we are, and we are the   139
Sons of God Himself, as holy as He is.

know — You may not know your own *creations*, but you   123
can no more interfere with their reality
than your unawareness of your spirit
can interfere with its being.

love — Through our *creations* we extend our love, and   139
thus increase the joy of the Holy
Trinity.

love — The law of creation is that you love your *creations*   169
as yourself, because they are part of
you.

protected — Your *creations* are protected for you, because   **123**
the Holy Spirit, Who is in your mind,
knows of them and can bring them into
your awareness whenever you will let
Him.

safe — Be confident that your *creations* are as safe as you   **54**
are.

sleep — knowing your *creations* and your Creator, you   **169**
will have no wish to sleep, but only the
desire to waken and be glad.

Son's — The Son's *creations* are like his Father's.   **420**

yours — The *creations* of every Son of God are yours,   **123**
since your creation belongs to every-
one, being created for the Sonship as
a whole.

CREATIVE

likeness — Because of your likeness to your Creator,   **14**
you are *creative*.

power — The *creative* power of God and his creations is   **104**
limitless, but they are not in reciprocal
relationship.

Thought — As God's *creative* Thought proceeds from   **104**
Him to you, so must your creative
thought proceed from you to your
creations.

CREATOR

apart — You can do nothing apart from (your *Creator*)   **119**
and do nothing apart from him.

depart — You can temporize and you are capable of   **18**
enormous procrastination, but you
cannot depart entirely from your
Creator.

God — Everything God created knows its *Creator*.   **270**

influence — Nothing created not by your *Creator* has any   **420**
influence over you.

power — Nothing you made has any power over you   **441**
unless you still would be apart from
your *Creator*, and with a will opposed
to His.

Prime — (God) is the Prime *Creator*, because He created His co-creators.   **105**

separate — You cannot spearate yourself from your *Creator*, Who created you by sharing His Being with you.   **112**

Son — The Son gives Fatherhood to his *Creator* and receives the gift that he has given Him.   **550**

will — Your will to create was given you by your *Creator*, Who was expressing the same Will in His creation.   **29**

wills — You know what your *Creator* wills is possible, but what you made believes it is not so.   **440**

CROSS

deciding — Each day, each hour and minute you are deciding between the *cross* and the resurrection, between the ego and the Holy Spirit.   **255**

journey — The journey to the *cross* should be the last "useless journey."   **47**

rugged — Do not make the pathetic error of "clinging to the old rugged *cross*."   **47**

CRUCIFIED

asked — You are not asked to be *crucified*, which was part of my own teaching contribution.   **85**

God's — Until you realize that God's Son cannot be *crucified*, this is the world you will see.   **220**

reacted — You have probably reacted for years as if you were being *crucified*.   **85**

CRUCIFIXION

afraid — You are not really afraid of crucifixion.   **225**

Atonement — The *crucifixion* did not establish the Atonement; the resurrection did.   **32**

ego — I have said that the *crucifixion* is the symbol of the ego.   **224**

ego's — *Crucifixion* is always the ego's aim.   **264**

fear — I have also told you that the *crucifixion* was the last useless journey the Sonship need take, and that it represents release from fear to anyone who understands it. 85

meaning — The real meaning of the *crucifixion* lies in the apparent intensity of the assault of some of the Sons of God upon another. 85

message — The whole message of the *crucifixion* was simply that I did not (believe in betrayal.) 87

message — The message of the *crucifixion* is perfectly clear: Teach only love for that is what you are. 87

message — The message the *crucifixion* was intended to teach was that it is not necessary to perceive any form of assault in persecution, because you cannot be persecuted. 85

message — The only message of the *crucifixion* is, you can overcome the cross. 47

misunderstood — The Apostles often misunderstood (the *crucifixion*), and for the same reason that anyone misunderstands it. 87

peace — (The *crucifixion* was intended as) the call for peace. 87

seen — If the *crucifixion* is seen from an upside down point of view, it does appear as if God permitted and even encouraged one of His Sons to suffer because he was good. 33

sign — Let no dark sign of *crucifixion* intervene between the journey and its purpose. 396

thought — The *crucifixion* was the result of clearly opposed thought systems, the perfect symbol of the "conflict" between the ego and the Son of God. 88

CRUCIFY

guilty — Whom you perceive as guilty, you would crucify. 264

CURRICULUM

attack — This attempt at "learning" has so weakened your mind that you cannot love, for the *curriculum* you have chosen is against love, and amounts to a course in how to attack yourself. 211

conflicted — Their conflicted *curriculum* teaches that all directions exist, and gives them no rationale for choice. 129

content — It is not only the direction of the *curriculum* that must be unconflicted, but also the content. 130

depressing — You who have tried to learn what you do not want should take heart, for although the *curriculum* you set is depressing indeed, it is merely ridiculous if you look at it. 211

goal — The goal of the *curriculum*, regardless of the teacher you choose, is "know theyself." 132

goal — To achieve the goal of the *curriculum* you cannot listen to the ego, whose purpose is to defeat its own will. 132

goals — Do not attempt to teach yourself what you do not understand, and do not try to set up *curriculum* goals where yours have clearly failed. 210

Holy Spirit — The *curriculum* (of the Holy Spirit) is never depressing, because it is a *curriculum* of joy. 141

Holy Spirit — The *curriculum* (of the Holy Spirit) is totally unambiguous, because the goal is not divided and the means and the end are in complete accord. 211

meaningful — A meaningful *curriculum* cannot be inconsistent. 129

DARKNESS

attack — Only in *darkness* does your specialness appear to be attack. **493**

Christ — Beyond this *darkness* and yet still within you is the vision of Christ, Who looks on all in light. **232**

Christ — Not one illusion is accorded faith, and not one spot of *darkness* still remains to hide the face of Christ from anyone. **622**

commitment — A firm commitment to *darkness* or nothingness, however, is impossible. **34**

dispelled — Let the *darkness* be dispelled by Him who knows the light. **449**

entered — Everyone here has entered *darkness*, yet no one has entered it alone. **488**

escape — Escape from *darkness* involves two stages: The recognition that *darkness* cannot hide. This step usually entails fear. Second, the recognition that there is nothing you want to hide even if you could. **8**

forgive — On earth this means forgive your brother that the *darkness* may be lifted from your mind. **568**

happiness — Not one ray of *darkness* can be seen by those who will make their Father's happiness complete, and theirs along with His. **486**

holiness — Holiness can never really be hidden in *darkness*, but you can deceive yourself about it. **8**

Holy Spirit — The Holy Spirit is the radiance that you must let banish the idea of *darkness*. **69**

light — *Darkness* is abolished by light. **28**

light — *Darkness* is lack of light. **9**

light — Light cannot enter *darkness* when a mind believes in *darkness* and will not let it go. **267**

love — There is no *darkness* that the light of love will not dispel, unless it is cancealed from love's beneficence. **265**

savior — Within the *darkness* see the savior from the 486
dark, and understand your brother as his Father's Mind
shows him to you.

scarcity — (*Darkness*) is an example of the "scarcity" 9
belief, from which only error can
proceed.

see — It is in (*darkness*) that what you see you made. 232

see — Who can say that he prefers the *darkness* and 492
maintain he wants to see?

seeing — *Darkness* cannot be seen, for it is nothing more 276
than a condition in which seeing be-
comes impossible.

understanding — Put no confidence at all in *darkness* to 276
illuminate your understanding, for if
you do, you contradict the light, and
thereby think you see the *darkness*.

vision — Let *darkness* go and all you made you will no 232
longer see, for sight of it depends on
denying vision.

you — This *darkness* is in you. 233

DEAD

forgotten — Let the *dead* and gone be peacefully for- 512
gotten.

DEATH

accept — Perhaps you are willing to accept even *death* to 207
deny your Father.

appeal — The fear of *death* will go as its appeal is yielded 390
to love's real attraction.

atone — No one can die for ayone, and *death* does not 383
atone for sin.

attraction — What would you feel and think if *death* held 391
no attraction for you? Very simply,
you would remember your Father.

attraction — It is the attraction of *death* that makes life 392
seem to be ugly, cruel and tyrannical.

attraction — What seems to be the fear of *death* is really 388
its attraction.

belief — There is no *death*, but there is a belief in *death*.　　**46**

betrayed — For in the dark and secret place is the realization that you have betrayed God's Son by condemning him to *death*.　　**224**

brother — To you and your brother, in whose special relationship the Holy Spirit entered, it is given to release and be released from the dedication to *death*.　　**388**

conflict — *Death* is an attempt to resolve conflict by not deciding at all.　　**97**

conflict — The retreat to *death* is not the end of conflict.　　**390**

dedication — Your dedication is not to *death* nor to its master.　　**388**

desire — When you are tempted to yield to the desire for *death*, remember that I did not die.　　**217**

die — No one can die unless he chooses *death*.　　**388**

ego — *Death* is the result of the thought we call the ego, as surely as life is the result of the Thought of God.　　**388**

ego — To the ego the goal is *death*, which is its end.　　**280**

ego — Wanting to kill you as the final expression of its feeling for you, (the ego) lets you live but to await *death*.　　**216**

ego — You are no more afraid of *death* than of the ego.　　**392**

ego — You will think that *death* comes from God and not the ego because, by confusing yourself with the ego, you believe that you want *death*.　　**217**

ego's — The *death* penalty is the ego's ultimate goal, for it fully believes that you are a criminal, as deserving of *death* as God knows you are deserving of life.　　**216**

exist — I could demonstrate that *death* does not exist.　　**9**

fear — Those who fear *death* see not how often and how loudly they call to it, and bid it come to save them from communication.　　**389**

God — The *death* of God, if it were possible, would be your *death*.　　**452**

investment — The Holy Spirit guides you into life eternal, but you must relinquish your investment in *death*, or you will not see life though it is all around you. 209

kill — A murderer is frightened, and those who kill fear *death*. 400

law — Not one law of *death* you bind (your brother) to will you escape. 476

life — *Death* is the opposite to peace, because it is the opposite of life. 541

life — It cannot be the "sinner's" wish for *death* is as strong as is God's Will for life. 494

life — While it could perhaps be argued that *death* suggests there was life, no one would claim that it proves there is life. 228

living — There is no *death* because the living share the function their Creator gave to them. 573

me — When you learn to make me manifest, you will never see *death*. 217

nothing — Nothing is accomplished through *death*, because *death* is nothing. 96

peace — Awaken and forget all thoughts of *death* and you will find you have the peace of God. 541

price — You pay no price for life for that was given you, but you do pay a price for *death*, and a very heavy one. 209

purpose — When you accepted the Holy Spirit's purpose in place of the ego's, you renounced *death*, replacing it with life. 388

resurrection — Now you are part of resurrection, not of *death*. 512

safety — *Death* is seen as safety, the great savior from the light of truth, the answer to the Answer, the silencer of the Voice That speaks for God. 389

sin — The arrogance of sin, the pride of guilt, the sepulchre of separation, all are part of your unrecognized dedication to *death*. 389

Will — For *death* is not your Father's Will nor yours, and
whatever is true is the Will of the
Father.   **209**

will — God's Son cannot will *death* for himself, because
His Father is Life and His Son is like
Him.   **182**

world — Leave the world of *death* behind, and return
quietly to Heaven.   **262**

world — God does love the real world, and those who
perceive its reality cannot see the
world of *death*.   **207**

world — Those who serve the lord of *death* have come to
worship in a separated world, each
with his tiny spear and rusted sword,
to keep his ancient promises to die.   **571**

you — Nothing you made but has the mark of *death*
upon it.   **237**

DECEIT

impossible — Yet you can learn the truth about yourself
from the Holy Spirit, Who will teach
you that, as part of God, *deceit* in you
is impossible.   **199**

perceive — When you perceive yourself without *deceit*
you will accept the real world in place
of the false one you have made.   **199**

DECEIVED

choose — Those who choose to be *deceived* will merely
attack direct approaches, because they
seem to encroach upon deception and
strike at it.   **252**

God — For it God is not *deceived* in you, you can be *deceived*
only in yourself.   **199**

DECIDE

Christ — *Decide* with (Christ), who has decided to abide
with you.   **287**

God — *Decide* for God through Him.   **286**

DECIDING

value — The value of *deciding* in advance what you want   341
to happen is simply that you will
perceive the situation as a means to
make it happen.

volition — Only your own volition seems to make   261
deciding hard.

DECISION(S)

cannot — And yet, you cannot make *decisions* by yourself.   584

conclusion — For a *decision* is a conclusion based on   464
everything that you believe.

depend — And no one walks upon the earth but must   586
depend on your *decision*, that he learn
death has no power over him, because
he shares your freedom as he shares
your will.

destructively — Whenever you choose to make *decisions*   256
for yourself, you are thinking destruc-
tively, and the *decision* will be wrong.

difficult - *Decision* cannot be difficult.   83

every — Every *decision* you make is for Heaven or for   286
hell, and brings you the awareness of
what you decided for.

every — Every *decision* you make stems from what you   285
think you are, and represents the value
that you put upon yourself.

function — Before you make any *decisions* for yourself,   260
remember that you have decided
against your function in Heaven, and
then consider carefully whether you
want to make *decisions* here.

God — When you have learned how to decide with God,   260
all *decisions* become as easy and as right
as breathing.

Holy Spirit — Make no *decisions* about what it is or where   260
it lies, but ask the Holy Spirit every-
thing, and leave all *decisions* to His
gentle counsel.

Holy Spirit — The power of *decision*, which you made in   265 place of the power of creation, (the Holy Spirit) would teach you how to use on your behalf.

I — I can offer my strength to make yours invincible, but I cannot oppose your *decision* without competing with it and thereby violating God's Will for you.   **135**

idols — You will not make *decisions* by yourself whatever you decide. For they are made with idols or with God.   **584**

impossible — Forget not that it has been your *decision* to make everything that is natural and easy to you impossible.   **356**

joint — All things are possible through our joint *decision*, but mine alone cannot help you.   **134**

power — The power of *decision* is your one remaining freedom as a prisoner of this world.   **215**

powerful — My *decision* cannot overcome yours, because yours is as powerful as mine.   **134**

results — *Decisions* cause results because they are not made in isolation.   **584**

rules for decision:
1. "Today I will make no decisions by myself."   **581**
2. "If I make no *decisions* by myself, This is the day that will be given me."   **582**
3. "I have no question. I forgot what to decide."   **582**
4. "At least I can decide I do not like what I feel now."   **583**
5. "And so I hope I have been wrong."   **583**
6. "I want another way to look at this. Perhaps there is another way to look at this. What can I lose by asking?"   **583**

salvation — Every *decision* you undertake alone but signifies that you would define what salvation is, and what you would be saved from.   **257-258**

Son of God's — (The Son of God's) power of *decision* is the determiner of every situation in which he seems to find himself by chance or accident.   **418**

Sonship — Every *decision* is made for the Whole Sonship, directed in and out, and influencing a constellation larger than anything you ever dreamed of. **257**

truth — Would you deny the truth of God's *decision*, and place your pitiful appraisal of yourself in place of His calm and unswerving value of His Son? **257**

wrong — Through His power and glory all your wrong *decisions* are undone completely, releasing you and your brother from every imprisoning thought any part of the Sonship holds. **133**

wrong — Wrong *decisions* have no power, because they are not true. **133**

yourself — It will never happen that you must make *decisions* for yourself. **257**

DEFENSE(S)

acceptance — The truth itself needs no *defense*, but you do need *defense* against your acceptance of the gift of death. **335**

Atonement — Since the separation, *defenses* have been used almost entirely against the Atonement, and thus maintain the separation. **17**

Atonement — The Atonement is the only *defense* that cannot be used destructively because it is not a device you made. **16**

attack — It is hard to believe a *defense* that cannot attack is the best *defense*. **17**

do — It is essential to realize that all *defenses* do what they would defend. **334**

ego — Consider what the ego wants *defenses* for. Always to justify what goes against the truth, flies in the face of reason and makes no sense. **446**

gifts — Every *defense* operates by giving gifts, and the gift is always a miniature of the thought system the *defense* protects, set in a golden frame. **334**

made — *Defenses*, like everything you made, must be   **268**
gently turned to your own good,
translated by the Holy Spirit from
means of self-destruction to means of
preservation and release.

making — *Defense* is of your making.   **268**

need — And you need no *defense*.   **445**

sin — Belief in sin needs great *defense*, and at enormous   **446**
cost.

truth — The best *defense*, as always, is not to attack   **32**
another's position, but rather to
protect the truth.

truth — The truth itself needs no *defense*, but you do   **335**
need *defense* against your acceptance of
the gift of death.

weaken — Everything that needs *defense* you do not   **445**
want, for anything that needs *defense*
will weaken you.

DEFENSIVE

illusion — Forget not, when you feel the need arise to be   **446**
defensive about anything, you have
identified yourself with an illusion.

DELUSIONAL

condemnation — (The *delusional*) do not wish to die, yet   **231**
they will not let condemnation go.

destructive — The *delusional* can be very destructive, for   **231**
they do not recognize they have
condemned themselves.

past — You consider it "natural" to use your past ex-   **233**
perience as the reference point from
which to judge the present. Yet this is
unnatural because it is *delusional*.

reality — For to believe reality is what you would have   **234**
it be according to your use for it is
delusional.

recognize — Yet what is within (the *delusional*) do not   **231**
see, for the reality of their brothers
they cannot recognize.

system — You can surely regard a *delusional* system without fear, for it cannot have any effects if its source is not real. 188

truth — The *delusional* believe that truth will assail them, and they do not recognize it because they prefer the delusion. 136

DENIAL

accept — And if you accept *denial*, you can accept its undoing. 177

defense — Yet *denial* is a defense, and so it is as capable of being used positively as well as negatively. 118

error — In the service of the right mind the *denial* of error frees the mind, and re-establishes the freedom of the will. 16

error — *Denial* of error is a strong defense of truth, but *denial* of truth results in miscreation, the projections of the ego. 16

error — This is the proper use of *denial*. It is not used to hide anything, but to correct error. 16

God — Your *denial* of (God) therefore means that you love Him, and that you know He loves you. 176

insanity — But this is what *denial* does, for by it you accept insanity, believing you can make a private world and rule your own perception. 232

love — And *denial* is as total as love. 183

miscreation — *Denial* of error is a strong defense of truth, but *denial* of truth results in miscreation, the projections of the ego. 16

power — *Denial* has no power in itself, but you can give it the power of your mind, whose power is without limit. 118

protective — True *denial* is a powerful protective device. 16

DENIED

cannot — But what is really asked for cannot be *denied*. 587

DENY

denied — Seek to *deny* and you will feel denied.   **503**

Holy Spirit — Anything you *deny* that (the Holy Spirit)   **252**
knows to be true you have denied
yourself, and He must therefore teach
you not to *deny* it.

Holy Spirit — You can *deny* (the Holy Spirit), but you   **278**
cannot call on Him in vain.

yourself — You cannot *deny* part of yourself, because the   **183**
rest will seem to be separate and
therefore without meaning.

DEPRESSION

death — *Depression* speaks of death, and vanity of real   **526**
concern with anything at all.

deprived — *Depression* comes from the sense of being   **57**
deprived of something you want and
do not have.

God — *Depression* means that you have forsworn God.   **175**

isolation — *Depression* is isolation, and so it could not   **176**
have been created.

DEPRIVATION

attack — *Deprivation* breeds attack, being the belief that   **305**
attack is justified.

attack — And as long as you would retain the *deprivation*,   **305**
attack becomes salvation and sacrifice
becomes love.

blame — If your brothers are part of you and you blame   **187**
them for your *deprivation*, you are
blaming yourself.

DEPRIVE

seek — Seek to *deprive*, and you have been deprived.   **503**

DEPRIVED

decisions — Remember that you are *deprived* of nothing   **57**
except by your own decisions, and then
decide otherwise.

DESIRE

receive — For it what you *desire* you receive, and happiness is constant, then you need ask for it but once to have it always.　　**434**

request — Yet he will ask because *desire* is a request, an asking for, and made by one whom God Himself will never fail to answer.　　**434**

want — *Desire* what you want, and you will look on it and think it real.　　**433**

DESTROY

himself — No one can will to *destroy* himself.　　**171**

DESTRUCTION

ego — Yet without your alliance in your own *destruction*, the ego could not hold you to the past.　　**324**

function — But if you interpret your function as *destruction*, you will lose sight of the present and hold on to the past to ensure a destructive future.　　**230**

image — Yet the *destruction* is no more real then the image, although those who make idols do worship them.　　**171**

DESTRUCTIVE

love — For you see love as *destructive*, and your only question is who is to be destroyed, you or another?　　**303**

nothing — Nothing *destructive* was or ever will be.　　**248**

wish — For your wish to make *destructive* what cannot destroy can have no real effect at all.　　**359**

"DEVIL"

God — The *"devil"* deceives by lies, and builds Kingdoms in which everything is in direction opposition to God.　　**45**

God — (The *"devil"*) is perceived as a force in combat with God, battling Him for possession of His creations.　　**45**

separation — The mind can make the belief in separation very real and very fearful, and this belief is the *"devil."*　　**45**

souls — Yet (the *"devil"*) attracts men rather then repels them, and they are willing to "sell" him their souls in return for gifts of no real worth.   45

DEVOTION

brother — *Devotion* to a brother cannot set you back either. It can lead only to mutual progress.   47

divided — Your divided *devotion* has given you the two voices, and you must choose at which altar you want to serve.   70

power — Do not underestimate the power of the *devotion* of God's Son, nor the power the god he worships has over him.   193

result — The result of genuine *devotion* is inspiration, a word which properly understood is the opposite of fatigue.   47

DIE

born — You were not born to *die*.   572

can — Yet, no one can *die* for anyone, and death does not atone for sin.   383

cannot — You are not sick and you cannot *die*.   177

hatred — It will torment you while you live, but the hatred (of the ego) is not satisfied until you *die*.   216-217

separate — For if you could really separate yourself from the Mind of God you would *die*.   207

DIFFERENCE

Sons of God — There is no *difference* among the Sons of God.   518

DIRECTION

Holy Spirit — Any *direction* that would lead you where the Holy Spirit leads you not, goes nowhere.   252

DISBELIEVE

attack — To *disbelieve* is to side against, or to attack.   154

DISCOMFORT

correction — *Discomfort* is aroused only to bring the need   **22-23**
    for correction into awareness.

DISINHERITED

Sonship — There can be no *disinherited* parts of the   **209**
    Sonship, for God is whole and all His
    extensions are like Him.

DISSOCIATION

afraid — And you have replaced your knowledge by an   **170**
    awareness of dreams because you are
    afraid of your *dissociation* not of what
    you have dissociated.

decision — Knowledge must precede *dissociation,* so that **169-170**
    dissociation is nothing more than a
    decision to forget.

delusion — *Dissociation* is not a solution; it is a delusion.   **136**

knowledge — Yet any part of knowledge threatens   **427**
    dissociation as much as all of it.

reality — Yet to give up the *dissociation* of reality brings   **170**
    more than merely lack of fear.

thinking — *Dissociation* is a distorted process of thinking   **267**
    whereby two belief systems which
    cannot coexist are both maintained.

truth — What has been forgotten then appears to be   **170**
    fearful, but only because the *dissociation*
    is an attack on truth.

DISTORTION(S)

correct — The way to correct *distortions* is to withdraw   **35**
    your faith in them.

DOUBT(S)

Christ — Christ has no *doubt*, and from His certainty His   **475**
    quiet comes.

Christ — (Christ) will exchange His certainty for all   **475**
    your *doubts*, if you agree that He is one
    with you, and that this oneness is
    endless, timeless, and within your
    grasp because your hands are His.

conflict — There must be *doubt* before there can be   475
    conflict.

every — And every *doubt* must be about yourself.   475

DREAM(S)

accept — Accept the *dream* He gave instead of yours.   542

alien — Nothing at all has happened but that you have   551
    put yourself to sleep, and dreamed a
    dream in which you were an alien to
    yourself, and but a part of someone
    else's *dream*.

arrange - In *dreams* you arrange everything.   350

body — The body is the central figure in the dreaming of   543
    the world. There is no *dream* without it,
    nor does it exist without the *dream* in
    which it acts as if it were a person to be
    seen and be believed.

brother — *Dream* softly of your sinless brother, who   543
    unites with you in holy innocence.

brother — It is no *dream* to love your brother as yourself.   357

brother — Like you, your brother thinks he is a *dream*.   556

brother's — Join not your brother's *dream*, but join with   557
    him, and where you join His Son the
    Father is.

cause — You may cause a *dream*, but never will you give   551
    it real effects.

caused — Yet what you fail to recognize is that what   351
    caused the *dream* has not gone with it.

caused — Yet if you are the dreamer, you perceive this   551
    much at least: That you have caused
    the *dream*, and can accept another *dream*
    as well.

change — It is not difficult to change a *dream* when once   542
    the dreamer has been recognized.

chaotic — *Dreams* are chaotic because they are governed   350
    by your conflicting wishes, and
    therefore they have no concern with
    what is true.

choice — The choice is not between which *dreams* to keep, but only if you want to live in *dreams* or to waken from them. **569**

Christ — Beyond your darkest *dreams* (Christ) sees God's guiltless Son within you, shining in perfect radiance that is undimmed by your *dreams*. **233**

crucifixion — The *dream* of crucifixion still lies heavy on your eyes, but what you see in *dreams* is not reality. **194**

dark — Your dark *dreams* are but the senseless, isolated scripts you write in sleep. **597**

defense — God's Son needs no defense against his *dreams*. **590**

disappear — *Dreams* disappear when light has come and you can see. **232**

done — Yet what is done in *dreams* has not been really done. **327**

ego's — Your *dreams* contain many of the ego's symbols and they have confused you. **94**

escape — And yet the *dream* cannot escape its origin. **351**

evil — Remember if you share an evil *dream*, you will believe you are the *dream* you share. **558**

evil — It is the sharing of evil *dreams* of hate and malice, bitterness and death, of sin and suffering and pain and loss, that makes them real. **558**

eyes — Let not the *dream* take hold to close your eyes. **352**

fear — The *dreams* you think you like would hold you back as much as those in which the fear is seen. For every *dream* is but a *dream* of fear, no matter what the form it seems to take. **569**

fearful — Nothing more fearful than an idle *dream* has terrified God's Son, and made him think he has lost his innocense, denied his Father, and made war upon himself. **542**

fearful — Refuse to be a part of fearful *dreams* whatever   **555**
      form they take, for you will lose
      identity in them.

figures — For you could not react at all to figures in a   **545**
      dream you knew that you were
      dreaming.

forgiving — Forgiving *dreams* are kind to everyone who   **579**
      figures in the *dream*. And so they bring
      the dreamer full release from *dreams* of
      fear.

forgiving — Forgiving *dreams* have little need to last.   **579**

forgiving — Forgiving *dreams* remind you that you live in   **579**
      safety and have not attacked yourself.

forgiving — Forgiving *dreams* are means to step aside **571-572**
      from dreaming of a world outside
      yourself.

forgiving — But in forgiving *dreams* is no one asked to be   **551**
      the victim and the sufferer.

free — You are asked to let yourself be free of all the   **590**
      dreams of what you never were, and
      seek no more to substitute the
      strength of idle wishes for the Will of
      God.

God — God is the Alternate to *dreams* of fear.   **558**

God — That is why God placed the Holy Spirit in you,   **252**
      where you placed the *dream*.

happy — Happy *dreams* come true, not because they are   **357**
      dreams, but only because they are
      happy.

hatred — Let us not delay this, for your *dreams* of hatred   **204**
      will not leave you without help, and
      Help is here.

Heaven — Yet heaven is sure. This is no *dream*.   **352**

Holy Spirit — In these lie your true perceptions, for   **238**
      the Holy Spirit corrects the world of
      dreams, where all perception is.

Holy Spirit — Yet the Holy Spirit, too, has use for sleep,   **147**
      and can use *dreams* on behalf of waking,
      if you will let Him.

Holy Spirit — (The Holy Spirit) brings forgiving *dreams*,   **542**
in which the choice is not who is the
murderer and who shall be the victim.

Holy Spirit — The Holy Spirit, ever practical in His   **351**
wisdom, accepts your *dreams* and uses
them as means for waking.

Holy Spirit — Because unless the Holy Spirit gives the   **571**
dream its function, it was made for hate,
and will continue in death's services.

hope — Yet nothing in the world of *dreams* remains   **571**
without the hope of change and
betterment, for here is not where
changelessness is found.

identity — Identity in *dreams* is meaningless because the   **556**
dreamer and the *dream* are one.

illusion — It is impossible to convince the dreamer that   **327**
this is so, for *dreams* are what they are
because of their illusion of reality.

illusion — The *dream* is but illusion in the mind.   **556**

illusions — *Dreams* are illusions of joining, because they   **146**
reflect the ego's distorted notions
about what joining is.

judgment — The *dream* of judgment is a children's game,   **579**
in which the child becomes the father,
powerful, but with the little wisdom of
a child.

judgment — And what was once a *dream* of judgment   **579**
now has changed into a *dream* where all
is joy, because that is the purpose that
it has.

lasting — Nothing lasting lies in *dreams,* and the Holy   **96**
Spirit, shining with the Light from God
Himself, speaks only for what lasts
forever.

like — The *dreams* you think you like would hold you   **569**
back as much as those in which fear is
seen.

love — Yet the *dreams* of love lead unto knowledge.   **238**

love — The end of dreaming is the end of fear, and love **554**
was never in the world of *dreams.*

mind — It is the *dream* you fear, and not the mind. **556**

miracle — The miracle establishes you *dream* a *dream*, and **552**
that its content is not true.

nightmares — Nightmares are childish *dreams.* **578**

oblivion — If you decide to have and give and be nothing **251**
except a *dream,* you must direct your
thoughts unto oblivion.

pardon — Only dreams of pardon can be shared. **597**

perception — (*Dreams*) are the best example you could **350**
have of how perception can be used to
substitute illusions for truth.

power — *Dreams* show you that you have the power to **351**
make a world as you would have it be,
and that because you want it you see it.

real — You recognize from your own experience that **169**
what you see in *dreams* you think is real
while you are asleep.

reality — The *dream* of crucifixion still lies heavy on your **194**
eyes, but what you see in *dreams* is not
reality.

reason — *Dreams* have no reason in them. **431**

relationship — Nor is your holy relationship a *dream.* **357**

sacred — There is no area of your perception that it has **251-252**
not touched, and your *dream* is sacred to
you.

salvation — There can be no salvation in the *dream* as **578**
you are dreaming it.

savior — So perfectly can you forgive (your brother) his **568**
illusions he becomes your savior from
your *dreams.*

see — The instant that he sees (*dreams*) as they are they **544**
have no more effects on him, because
he understands he gave them their
effects by causing them and making
them seem real.

separate — Look not to separate *dreams* for meaning. **597**

shared — When *dreams* are shared, they lose the function of attack and separation, even though it was for this that every dream was made.   **571**

tantrums — *Dreams* are perceptual temper tantrums, in which you literally scream, "I want it thus!"   **350**

travel — You travel but in *dreams,* while safe at home.   **240**

true — They are *dreams* because they are not true.   **568**

wake — When you wake you will see the truth around you and you will no longer believe in *dreams*, because they will have no reality for you.   **94**

waken — No one can waken from a *dream* the world is dreaming for him.   **541**

waken — What you seem to waken to is but another form of the world you see in *dreams*.   **351**

waking — The *dream* of waking is easily transferred to its reality.   **352**

wanted — *Dreams* are not wanted more or less.   **569**

witnesses — Your dreams are witnesses to his, and his attest the truth of yours.   **556**

world — Yet (*dreams*) are a way of looking at the world, and changing it to suit the ego better.   **350**

world — The dreaming of the world is but a part of your own *dream* you gave away, and saw as if it were its start and ending, both.   **542**

DREAMER

awake — The *dreamer* of a dream is not awake, but does not know he sleeps.   **551**

evil — You share no evil dreams if you forgive the *dreamer*, and perceive that he is not the dream he made.   **558**

miracle — The miracle does not awaken you, but merely shows you who the *dreamer* is.   **551**

world — You are the *dreamer* of the world of dreams.   **542**

DREAMING

fear — The end of *dreaming* is the end of fear, and love was never in the world of dreams. 554

minds — Yet in the *dreaming* has this been reversed, and separate minds are seen as bodies, which are separated and cannot join. 554

time — All your time is spent in *dreaming*. 351

world — No one asleep and *dreaming* in the world remembers his attack upon himself. 544

world — The *dreaming* of the world takes many forms, because the body seeks in many ways to prove it is autonomous and real. 543

you — But for this change in content of the dream, it must be realized that it is you who dreamed the *dreaming* that you do not like. 551

EASTER

brother — This *Easter*, look with different eyes upon your brother. 398

forgiveness — This *Easter* I would have the gift of your forgiveness offered by you to me, and returned by me to you. 396

joy — The time of *Easter* is a time of joy, and not of mourning. 397

peace — For *Easter* is the sign of peace, not pain. 396

salvation — *Easter* is the time of your salvation, along with mine. 397

song — The song of *Easter* is the glad refrain the Son of God was never crucified. 398

EFFECT(S)

cause — *Effects* do not create their cause, but they establish its causation. 550

cause — Cause and *effect* are one, not separate. 517

God — What God has given cannot be a loss, and what is not of Him has no *effects*. 557

healing — The healing of *effect* without the cause can merely shift *effects* to other forms. 517

EGO(S)

abundance — The *ego* never gives out of abundance, because it was made as a substitute for it.   52

afraid — And now the *ego* is afraid.   425

afraid — Do not be afraid of the *ego*.   121

afraid — Listen to what the *ego* says, and see what it directs you to see, and it is sure that you will see yourself as tiny, vulnerable and afraid.   425

afraid — The most inventive activities of the *ego* have never done more than obscure the question, because you have the answer and the *ego* is afraid of you.   93

afraid — You must recognize that the last thing the *ego* wishes you to realize is that you are afraid of it.   189

aim — The sole aim of the *(ego)* is to lose the function of everything.   145

allegiance — Aware of its weakness the *ego* wants your allegiance, but not as you really are.   116

allies — Unless you do believe it you will not side with it, and the *ego* feels badly in need of allies, though not brothers.   93

analyzes — The *ego* analyzes; the Holy Spirit accepts.   190

answer — The *ego* has never given you a sensible answer to anything.   129

Atonement — Excluding yourself from the Atonement is the *ego's* last-ditch defense of its own existence.   82

attack — Believing in the power of attack, the *ego* wants attack.   147

attack — The *ego* believes in atonement through attack, being fully committed to the insane notion that attack is salvation.   223

attack — I have repeatedly emphasized that the *ego* does believe it can attack God, and tries to persuade you that you have done this.   116 attack — (The *ego's*) profound sense of vulnerability renders it incapable of judgment except in terms of attack.   **166**

attack — The *ego* depends solely on your willingness to attack it.   **166**

attack — The *ego* is, therefore, particularly likely to attack you when you react lovingly, because it has evaluated you as unloving and you are going against its judgment.   **164**

attack — The *ego* teaches you to attack yourself because you are guilty, and this must increase the guilt, for guilt is the result of attack.   **223**

attack — This is such a fearful state that it can only turn to other *egos* and try to unite with them in a feeble attempt at identification, or attack them in an equally feeble show of strength.   **53**

attack — The *ego* will attack your motives as soon as they become clearly out of accord with its perception of you.   **164**

attacks — The *ego* always attacks on behalf of separation.   **189**

attacks — This means that the *ego* attacks what is preserving it, which must result in extreme anxiety.   **114**

attacks — Unaware that the belief cannot be established and obsessed with the conviction that separation is salvation, the *ego* attacks everything it perceives by breaking it into small disconnected parts, without meaningful relationships and therefore without meaning.   **191**

bargain — (The *ego*) is always willing to strike a bargain, but it cannot understand that to be like another means that no bargains are possible.   **104**

being — But there is a corollary; if only knowledge has being and *ego* has no knowledge, then the *ego* has no being.   **145**

belief — Belief is an *ego* function, and as long as your origin is open to belief you are regarding it from an *ego* viewpoint. **52**

belief — The *ego* is a device for maintaining this belief, but it is still only your decision to use the device that enables it to endure. **62**

belief — The *ego* is nothing more than a part of your belief about yourself. **61**

believes — (The *ego*) literally believes that every time it deprives someone of something, it has increased. **113**

believes — The *ego* believes that this is what you did because it believes that it is you. **77**

believes — The *ego* believes it is completely on its own, which is merely another way of describing how it thinks it originated. **53**

believes — They are problems of understanding, since their presence implies a belief that what you are is up to you to decide. The *ego* believes this totally, being fully committed to it. **116**

Bible — The Bible is a fearful thing in the *ego's* judgment. **80**

body — Regarding the body as an end, the *ego* has no real use for it because it is not an end. **144**

body — Since the *ego* cannot obliterate the impulse to communicate because it is also the impulse to create, it can only teach you that the body can both communicate and create, and therefore does not need the mind. **111**

body — The *ego* regards the body as its home, and tries to satisfy itself through the body. **53**

body — The *ego* uses the body to conspire against your mind, and because the *ego* realizes that its "enemy" can end them both merely by recognizing they are not part of you, they join in the attack together. **93**

body — The *ego* uses the body for attack, for pleasure and for pride. **97**

body — For the *ego* would limit everyone to a body for its   **300**
own purposes, and while you think it
has a purpose, you will choose to utilize
the means by which it tries to turn its
purpose into accomplishment.

brother — In effect, if you follow the *ego's* dictates you   **229**
will react to your brother as though he
were someone else, and this will surely
prevent you from recognizing him as
he is.

brothers — Instead, (the *ego*) bids you look upon your   **244**
brothers, and see the guilt in them.

brothers — Projecting its insane belief that you have   **119**
been treacherous to your Creator, (the
ego) believes your brothers, who are as
incapable of this as you are, are out to
take God from you.

capriciousness — When you are anxious, realize that   **57**
anxiety comes from the capriciousness
of the *ego*, and this need not be.

chaos — The *ego* will always substitute chaos for mean-   **191**
ing, for if separation is salvation,
harmony is threat.

charity — Equality is beyond (the *ego's*) grasp, and   **52**
charity becomes impossible.

clash — *Egos* can clash in any situation, but spirit cannot   **49**
clash at all.

communication — (The *ego's*) communication is con-   **63**
trolled by its need to protect itself, and
it will disrupt communication when it
experiences threat.

communication — The *ego* is thus against communica-   **63**
tion, except insofar as it is utilized to
establish separateness rather than to
abolish it.

comparisons — The *ego* literally lives by comparisons.   **52**

competitive — The *ego,* on the other hand, always de-   **104**
mands reciprocal rights, because it is
competitive rather than loving.

complexity — Complexity is of the *ego*, and is nothing more than the *ego's* attempt to obscure the obvious.   **289**

condemnation — Make no one fearful, for his guilt is yours, and by obeying the *ego's* harsh commandments you bring its condemnation on yourself, and you will not escape the punishment it offers those who obey it.   **243**

conflict — Yet this is so only from the viewpoint of the *ego*, for the *ego* believes in solving conflict through fragmentation, and does not perceive the situation as a whole.   **342**

confusion — The *ego* is expert only in confusion.   **129**

confusion — You may have carried the *ego's* reasoning to its logical conclusion, which is total confusion about everything.   **124**

continuance — The *ego's* whole continuance depends on its belief you cannot learn this course.   **442**

continuity — The continuity of (the *ego*) would keep you in time, while the Holy Spirit would release you from it.   **230**

contradictory — The introduction of reason into the *ego's* thought system is the beginning of its undoing, for reason and the *ego* are contradictory.   **442**

control — The *ego* is thrown further off balance because it keeps its primary motivation from your awareness, and raises control rather than sanity to predominance.   **59**

crucifixion — You do not even suspect this murderous but insane idea lies hidden there, for the *ego's* destructive urge is so intense that nothing short of the crucifixion of God's Son can ultimately satisfy it.   **223-224**

damn — Thus does the *ego* damn, and reason save.   **442**

dead — The *ego* wants you dead but not itself.   **280**

death — No one who follows the *ego's* teaching is without the fear of death.   **280**

death — The death penalty is the *ego's* ultimate goal, for it fully believes you are a criminal, as deserving of death as God knows you are deserving of life. **216**

death — So does the *ego* find the death it seeks, returning it to you. **388**

death — Wanting to kill you as the final expression of its feeling for you, (the *ego*) lets you live but to await death. **216**

deceived — The *ego* is deceived by everything you do, especially when you respond to the Holy Spirit, because at such times its confusion increases. **164**

decision — The Holy Spirit, like the *ego*, is a decision. **78**

decisions — The *ego's* decisions are always wrong, because they are based on the error they were made to uphold. **80**

defeat — The *ego* always marches to defeat, because it thinks that triumph over you is possible. **452**

defend — A more honest statement would be that those who want the *ego* are predisposed to defend it. **144**

defense — (The *ego*) believes the best defense is attack, and wants you to believe it. **93**

delay — Delay is of the *ego*, because time is its concept. **72**

delusional — The *ego*, then, is nothing more than a delusional system in which you made your own father. **179**

demand — For although the *ego* urges you again and again to get it, it leaves you nothing, for what you get it will demand of you. **239**

denial — That is why the *ego* is the denial of free will. **130**

dependency — The *ego* sees all dependency as threatening, and has twisted even your longing for God into a means of establishing itself. **189**

deprived — That is why everyone who identifies with the *ego* feels deprived. **206**

desirable — This is because the *ego* perceives nothing as wholly desirable.   **126**

desperate — The *ego* is desperate because it opposes literally invincible odds, whether you are asleep or awake.   **56**

dictates — (The *ego*) dictates endless prescriptions for avoiding catastrophic outcomes.   **145**

disheartened — The disheartened are useless to themselves and to me, but only the *ego* can be disheartened.   **58**

dissolves — When the *ego* was made, God placed in the mind the call to joy. This call is so strong that the *ego* dissolves at its sound.   **69**

divide — The *ego* always seeks to divide and separate.   **110**

doctrine — For it is the *ego's* fundamental doctrine that what you do to others you have escaped.   **295**

doubt — The *ego* speaks against His creation, and therefore engenders doubt.   **102**

error — Holding error clearly in mind, and protecting what it has made real, the *ego* proceeds to the next step in its thought system: Error is real and truth is error.   **191**

error — Only the form of error attracts the *ego*.   **442**

errors — To the *ego* it is kind and right and good to point out errors and "correct" them.   **155**

escape — Think not the *ego* will enable you to find escape from what it wants.   **456**

eternal — God is as incapable of creating the perishable as the *ego* is of making the eternal.   **50**

exist — Without your own allegiance, protection, and love, the *ego* cannot exist.   **58**

exploit — The *ego* tries to exploit all situations into forms of praise for itself in order to overcome its doubts.   **49**

failure — Failure is of the *ego*, not of God.   **250**

faith — Therefore, (the *ego*) seeks to split off segments 342
of the situation and deal with them
separately, for it has faith in separation
and not in wholeness.

false — No one can doubt the *ego's* skill in building up 145
false cases.

father — And either the *ego*, which you made, is your 179
father, or its whole thought system
will not stand.

Father — The *ego* looks straight at the Father and does 191
not see Him, for it has denied His Son.

fear — Yet we have repeatedly emphasized the need to 202
recognize fear and face it without dis-
guiise as a crucial step in the undoing of
the *ego*.

fear — Fear in association with sin the *ego* deems quite 423
appropriate, and smiles approvingly.

fear — Yet (the *ego*) must engender fear in order to 281
maintain itself.

fear — For the *ego* must seem to keep fear from you to 281
hold your allegiance.

fear — Recognize only that the *ego's* goal, which you 190
have pursued so diligently, has merely
brought fear, and it becomes difficult
to maintain that fear is happiness. Upheld by fear, this is what the *ego* would
have you believe.

fear — Produced by fear, the *ego* reproduces fear. This is 115
its allegiance, and this allegiance makes
it treacherous to love because you are
love.

fear — (The basic threat to the *ego*) is the recognition 190
that whatever seems to separate you
from God is only fear.

fear — Minimizing fear, but not its undoing, is the *ego's* 189
constant effort, and is indeed a skill at
which it is very ingenious.

feel — The *ego* is incapable of knowing how you feel. 145

forgive — Forgiveness becomes impossible, for the *ego* 296
believes that to forgive another is to lose him.

forgiveness — The *ego*, too, has a plan of forgiveness be- 157
cause you are asking for one, though not of the right teacher. The *ego's* plan, of course, makes no sense and will not work.

forgotten — The *ego* can be completely forgotten at any 122
time, because it is a totally incredible belief, and no one can keep a belief he has judged to be unbelievable.

form — To the *ego*, if the form is acceptable the content 274
must be.

freedom — The *ego* cannot accept this freedom, and will 79
oppose it at every possible moment and in every possible way.

function — God gave you a very lofty function that you 50
are not meeting. Your *ego* has chosen to be afraid instead of meeting it.

functions — The *ego* believes that all functions belong to 158
it, even though it has no idea what they are.

gifts — Suffering and sacrifice are the gifts with which 296
the *ego* would "bless" all unions.

giving — If you can accept the concept that the world is 67
one of ideas, the whole belief in the false association the *ego* makes between giving and losing is gone.

goal — The *ego's* goal is quite explicitly *ego* autonomy. 188

goal — The *ego's* goal is as unified as the Holy Spirit's, 110
and it is because of this that their goals can never be reconciled in any way or to any extent.

God — And so the *ego* seems to demand less of you than 303
God, and of the two is judged as the lesser of two evils, one to be feared a little, perhaps, but the other to be destroyed.

God — Bringing the *ego* to God is but to bring error to truth, where it stands corrected because it is the opposite of what it meets.   **270**

God — Thoughts of God are unacceptable to the *ego*, because they clearly point to the nonexistence of the *ego* itself. The *ego* therefore either distorts them or refuses to accept them.   **59**

God — To the *ego* the *ego* is God, and guiltlessness must be interpreted as the final guilt that fully justifies murder.   **224**

God — You react to your *ego* much as God does to His creations — with love, protection and charity.   **52**

God — Your *ego* is never at stake because God did not create it.   **49**

grandeur — The *ego* does not understand the difference between grandeur and grandiosity, because it sees no difrerence between miracle impulses and ego-alien beliefs of its own.   **166**

grandeur — The *ego* is immobilized in the presence of God's grandeur, because His grandeur establishes your freedom.   **166**

guide — Let me repeat that the *ego's* qualifications as a guide are singularly unfortunate, and that it is a remarkably poor choice as a teacher of salvation.   **158**

guilt — In the *ego's* teaching, then, there is no escape from guilt.   **223**

guilt — For the *ego* really believes that it can get and keep by making guilty.   **295**

guilt — If the *ego* is a symbol of separation, it is also the symbol of guilt.   **77**

guilt — The *ego* is the choice for guilt; the Holy Spirit the choice for guiltlessness.   **255**

guilt — The *ego* tells you all is black with guilt within you, and bids you not to look.   **244**

guilt — The *ego* will assure you now that it is impossible for you to see no guilt in anyone. 439

guilt — Forgetfulness, sleep and even death become the *ego's* best advice for dealing with the perceived and harsh intrusion of guillt on peace. 248

guilt — To the *ego,* the guiltless are guilty. 224

guilt — Whenever you respond to your *ego* you will experience guilt, and you will fear punishment. 77

guilty — If you identify yourself with the *ego*, you must perceive yourself as guilty. 77

guilty — For the *ego* really believes it can get and keep by making guilty. 295

hatred — It will torment you while you live but (the hatred of the *ego*) is not satisfied until you die. 217

Heaven — (The *ego*) speaks to you of Heaven, but assures you that Heaven is not for you. 280

Heaven — The *ego* teaches that Heaven is here and now because the future is hell. 281

hell — When (the *ego*) becomes overtly savage, it offers you hell. 228

home — The *ego* has built a shabby and unsheltering home for you, because it cannot build otherwise. 50

Holy Spirit — The *ego* cannot ask the Holy Spirit for anything, because there is complete communication failure between them. 151

Holy Spirit — I have said before that the Holy Spirit is God's Answer to the *ego*. 72

Holy Spirit's — And now you recognize that it was not the *ego* that joined the Holy Spirit's purpose, and so there must be something else. 424

honesty — It sounds insane when it is stated with perfect honesty, but the *ego* never looks on what it does with perfect honesty. 179

host — You are unwilling to recognize that the *ego*,   **303**
     which you invited, is treacherous only
     to those who think they are its host.

host — The idea is simply this: you believe it is possible   **302**
     to be host to the *ego* or hostage to God.

humility — Humility is a lesson for the *ego*, not for the   **50**
     spirit.

hurt — Everything the *ego* tells you that you need will   **238**
     hurt you.

idea — All that the *ego* is, is an idea that it is possible   **419**
     that things can happen to the Son of
     God without his will; and thus without
     the Will of his Creator, Whose will
     cannot be separate from his own.

idea — For though the *ego* takes many forms, it is always   **302**
     the same idea.

identification — The *ego* is a confusion in identification.   **121**

identify — You who identify with your *ego* cannot   **55**
     believe God loves you.

identity — Those who have joined their brothers have   **424**
     detached themselves from their belief
     that their identity lies in the *ego*.

idol — The body is the *ego's* idol; the belief in sin made   **409**
     flesh and then projected outward.

idols — Homeless, the *ego* seeks as many bodies as it can   **407**
     collect to place its idols in, and so
     establish them as temples to itself.

-illusions — *Ego-illusions* are quite specific, although the   **63**
     mind is naturally abstract.

images — In every case you have thought wrongly   **57**
     about some brother God created, and
     are perceiving images your *ego* makes in
     a darkened glass.

immortality — And out of its unwillingness for you to   **280**
     find peace even in death, (the *ego*) offers
     you immortality in hell.

impossible — The *ego's* wishes do not mean anything,   **125**
     because the *ego* wishes for the
     impossible.

insane — Either God or the *ego* is insane.   179

interprets — Nothing the *ego* perceives is interpreted correctly.   80

inward — Loudly the *ego* tells you not to look inward, for if you do your eyes will light on sin, and God will strike you blind.   424

journey — Do you realize that the *ego* must set you on a journey that cannot but lead to a sense of futility and depression?   208

joy — The *ego* is afraid of the spirit's joy, because once you have experienced it you will withdraw all protection from the *ego*, and become totally without investment in fear.   50

judge — The *ego* as a judge gives anything but an impartial judgment.   144

judgment — The *ego* cannot survive without judgment, and is laid aside accordingly.   54

judgment — The *ego* should be brought to judgment and found wanting there.   58

judgment — The *ego* speaks in judgment, and the Holy Spirit reverses its decision, much as a higher court has the power to reverse a lower court's decisions in this world.   80

kill — For the *ego* does want to kill you, and if you identify with it you must believe its goal is yours.   224

kingdom — The calm being of God's kingdom, which in your sane mind is perfectly conscious, is ruthlessly banished from the part of the mind the *ego* rules.   56

Kingdom — The *ego* can keep you in exile from the Kingdom, but in the Kingdom itself it has no power.   75

Kingdom — The *ego* cannot prevail against the Kingdom because the Sonship is united.   74

know — The *ego* cannot afford to know anything.   115

know — (Spirit and *ego*) are fundamentally irreconcil-   **48**
able, because spirit cannot perceive and
the *ego* cannot know.

know — You cannot understand the conflict until you   **93**
fully understand the basic fact that the
ego cannot know anything.

knowledge — If you speak from the *ego* you are dis-   **47**
claiming knowledge instead of
affirming it, and are thus disspiriting
yourself.

knows — Even if you could disregard the Holy Spirit   **129**
entirely, which is impossible, you could
still learn nothing from the *ego*, because
the *ego* knows nothing.

law — "Giving to get" is an inescapable law of the *ego*,   **52**
which always evaluates itself in
relation to other *egos*.

laws — The *ego* cannot oppose the laws of God any more   **78**
than you can, but it can interpret them
according to what it wants, just as you
can.

laws — (The *ego*) is the product of the misapplication of   **121**
the laws of God by distorted minds that
are misusing their power.

laws — The *ego's* laws are strict, and breaches are severe-   **243**
ly punished.

laws — And those who follow (the laws of the *ego*)   **243**
believe that they are guilty, and so they
must condemn.

learn — Nevertheless, the *ego* can learn, even though its   **48**
maker can be misguided.

learn — Therefore (the *ego*) does not really learn at all.   **109**

learning — The distractions of the *ego* may seem to   **128**
interfere with your learning, but the
ego has no power to distract you from
learning unless you give it the power to
do so.

learning — Preoccupations with problems set up to be incapable of solution are favorite *ego* devices for impeding learning progress.   **61**

life — (The *ego*) tells you this life is your existence, because it is its own.   **55**

logical — (The *ego*) is perfectly logical but clearly insane.   **114**

loneliness — For the *ego* will always teach that loneliness is solved by guilt, and that communication is the cause of loneliness.   **297**

love — Being unable to love, the *ego* would be totally inadequate in love's presence, for it could not respond at all.   **208**

love — Follow (the teaching of the *ego*), then, and you will search for love, but will not recognize it.   **208**

love — For the *ego* cannot love, and in its frantic search for love it is seeking what it is afraid to find.   **208**

love — Its evaluation of you, however, is the exact opposite of the Holy Spirit's, because the *ego* does not love you.   **164**

love — No love in this world is without this ambivalence the concept is beyond its understanding.   **55**

love — (The *ego*) does not find love, for that is not what it is seeking.   **215**

love — The *ego* is certain that love is dangerous, and this is always its central teaching.   **207-208**

love — The *ego* will therefore distort love, and teach you that love really calls forth the responses the *ego* can teach.   **208**

love — Yet the *ego*, though encouraging the search for love very actively, makes one provision; do not find it.   **208**

loves - For what the *ego* loves, it kills for its obedience.   **389**

meaning — Analyzing to attack meaning the *ego* succeeds in overlooking it, and is left with a series of fragmented perceptions which it unifies on behalf of itself.   191

meaningless — This is where the *ego* is forced to appeal to "mysteries," insisting that you must accept the meaningless to save yourself.   157

meet — Be certain that it is impossible God and the *ego*, or yourself and it, will ever meet.   452

messages — The *ego's* messages are always sent away from you, in the belief that for your message of attack and guilt will someone other than yourself suffer.   387

mind — The *ego* is the part of the mind that believes in division.   77

mind — The *ego* is the part of the mind that believes your existence is defined by separation.   63

mind — (The *ego*) projects conflict from your mind to other minds, in an attempt to persuade you that you have gotten rid of the problem.   121

mind — The *ego* therefore wants to engage your mind in its own delusional system, because otherwise the light of your understanding would dispel it.   116

mind — The *ego*, which is not real, attempts to persuade the mind, which is real, that the mind is the *ego's* learning device; and further, that the body is more real than the mind is.   93

mind — This is because *ego* believes that mind is dangerous, and that to make mindless is to heal.   147

mind — To the *ego* the mind is private, and only the body can be shared.   296

mind — Using its own warped version of the laws of God, the *ego* utilizes the power of mind only to defeat the mind's real purpose.   121

mind — Your mind and mine can unite in shining your *ego* away, releasing the strength of God into everything you think and do. **58**

nothing — And the *ego* is nothing, whether you invite it in or not. **184**

nothing — You will not succeed in being partial hostage to the *ego*, for it keeps no bargains and would leave you nothing. **303**

"Now" — "Now" has no meaning to the *ego*. **229**

oblivion — As long as (the *ego*) is reasonably satisfied with you, as its reasoning goes, it offers you oblivion. **228**

oppose — To think you can oppose the Will of God is a real delusion. The *ego* believes it can, and that it can offer you its own "will" as a gift. **110**

opposes — The *ego* therefore opposes all appreciation, all recognition, all sane perception and all knowledge. **115**

pain — The *ego* rewards fidelity to it with pain, for faith in it is pain. **243**

past — The *ego* invests heavily in the past, and in the end believes that the past is the only aspect of time that is meaningful. **229**

past — By the notion of paying for the past in the future, (the *ego*) believes the past becomes the determiner of the future, making them continuous without an intervening present. **229**

past - The *ego* cannot tolerate release from the past, and although the past is over, the *ego* tries to preserve its image by responding as if it were present. **229**

payment — While it is obvious that what the *ego* does demands payment it never seems to be demanding it of you. **303**

peace — No obstacle to peace can be surmounted through (the help of the *ego*.) **393**

peace — Peace is the *ego's* greatest enemy, because, according to its interpretation of reality, war is the guarantee of its survival.   73

perceive — The *ego* is a wrong-minded attempt to perceive yourself as you wish to be, rather than as you are.   37

perceives — He also makes an *ego* for everyone else he perceives, which is equally variable.   51

perception — The *ego's* perception has no counterpart in God, but the Holy Spirit remains the bridge between perception and knowledge.   90

picture — The *ego's* picture of you is deprived, unloving and vulnerable.   118

possession — The *ego* wants to have things for salvation, for possession is its law.   238

possession — Possession for its own sake is the *ego's* fundamental creed, a basic cornerstone in the churches it builds to itself.   238

power — Yet the one claim (of the *ego*) to your allegiance is that it can give power to you.   189

present — (The *ego*) dictates your reactions to those you meet in the present from a past reference point, obscuring their present reality.   229

present — For the *ego* regards the present only as a brief transition to the future, in which it brings the past to the future by interpreting the present in past terms.   229

prevail — The *ego* cannot prevail against a totality that includes God, and any totality must include God.   122

problems — And thus (the *ego*) seeks to guarantee there will be no solution.   332

projection — The projection of the *ego* makes it appear as if God's Will is outside yourself, and therefore not yours.   182

projection — The *ego* uses projection only to destroy your perception of both yourself and your brothers.   89

projects — The *ego* projects to exclude, and therefore to deceive. 91

punishment — The *ego* believes that by punishing itself it will mitigate the punishment of God. 78

punishment — Whenever you respond to your *ego* you will experience guilt, and you will fear punishment. 77

purpose — (The *ego*) is much more vigilant than you are, because it is perfectly certain of its purpose. 189

purpose — From the beginning, then, (the purpose of the *ego*) is to be separate, sufficient unto itself and independent of any power except its own. 188-189

purpose — The *ego's* purpose is fear, because only the fearful can be egotistic. 77

question — The *ego* does not know what a real question is, although it asks an endless number. 146

question — Faith and belief have shifted, and you have asked the question the *ego* will never ask. 427

questioning — The *ego* is the questioning aspect of the post-separation self, which was made rather than created. 37

questions — (The *ego*) is capable of asking questions but not of receiving meaningful answers, because these would involve knowledge and cannot be perceived. 37

real — (The *ego's*) whole perception of other *egos* as real is only an attempt to convince itself that it is real. 52

"reality" — For the *ego* is itself an illusion, and only illusions can be the witnesses to its "reality." 319

reason — And what your reason tells you now the *ego* would not hear. 424

reinterpreted — The *ego* will not be destroyed because it is part of your thought, but because it 80-81 is uncreative and therefore unsharing, it will be reinterpreted to release you from fear.

rejected — While the *ego* is equally unaware of spirit, it does perceive itself as being rejected by something greater than itself.   53

relationship — It is this studied interference (of the *ego*) that makes it difficult for you to recognize your holy relationship for what it is.   400

relationships — The *ego* is the self-appointed mediator of all relationships, making whatever adjustments it deems necessary and interposing them between those who would meet, to keep them separate and prevent their union.   400

relationships — And thus (the *ego*) embarks on an endless, unrewarding chain of special relationships, forged out of anger and dedicated to but one insane belief; that you more anger you invest outside yourself, the safer you become.   295

relationships — For it is the *ego's* fixed belief that all relationships depend on adjustments, to make of them what it would have them be.   400

release — The *ego* will make every effort to recover and mobilize its energy against your release.   166

remembers — For the *ego* remembers everything you have done that has offended it, and seeks retribution of you.   324

return — The *ego* can accept the idea that return is necessary because it can so easily make the idea seem difficult.   90

rights — The *ego*, on the other hand, always demands reciprocal rights, because it is competitive rather than loving.   104

sacrifice — No partial sacrifice will appease (the *ego*), for 303
    it is an invader who but seems to offer
    kindness, but always to make the
    sacrifice complete.

sane — The *ego* is not sane. It represents a delusional 77
    system, and speaks for it.

satisfied — You must have noticed an outstanding 144
    characteristic of every end the *ego* has
    accepted as its own. When you have
    achieved it, it has not satisfied you.

save — Of your *ego* you can do nothing to save yourself 50
    or others, but of your spirit you can do
    everything for the salvaton of both.

scarcity — (The *ego*) is therefore continually preoccupied 52
    with the belief in scarcity that gave rise
    to it.

search — The search the *ego* undertakes is bound to be 208
    defeated.

secrets — (The *ego*) does not open up its secrets and bid 393
    you look on them and go beyond them.

self — The *ego* tries to find (power and glory) in yourself 132
    alone, because it does not know where
    to look.

self-inflation — Self-inflation of the *ego* is its alternative 165
    to the grandeur of God.

separate — The *ego* regards itself as separate and outside 93
    its maker, thus speaking for the part of
    your mind that believes you are
    separate and outside the Mind of God.

separate — What teaches you that you cannot separate 450
    denies the *ego*.

separation — The *ego* arose from separation, and its 55
    continued existence depends on your
    continuing belief in the separation.

separation — The *ego* believes that power, under- 190
    standing and truth lie in separation,
    and to establish this belief it must
    attack.

separation — The *ego* is the symbol of separation, just as 73
the Holy Spirit is the symbol of peace.

separation — The body is the symbol of the *ego*, as the *ego* 300
is the symbol of the separation.

separation — Separation remains the *ego's* chosen 274
condition.

separation — Where the *ego* sees salvation it sees separa- 239
tion, and so you lose whatever you
have gotten in its name.

sickness — The *ego* has a profound investment in sick- 144
ness.

sin — The *ego* brings sin to fear demanding punishment. 376

sin — The *ego* does not perceive sin as lack of love, but as 78
a positive act of assault.

sin — The *ego* does not think it possible that love, not 376
fear, is really called upon by sin and
always answers.

sin — (The *ego*) doubts not your belief and faith in sin. 423

sin — Forget not that the *ego* has dedicated the body to 387
the goal of sin, and places in it all its
faith that this can be accomplished.

sin — It can indeed be said that the *ego* made its world on 375
sin.

sin — The idea of sin is wholly sacrosanct to the thought 375
system (of the *ego*), and quite
unapproachable except with reverence
and awe.

sin — There is no stone in all the *ego's* embattled citadel 376
more heavily defended than the idea
that sin is real.

sin — To the *ego* sin means death and so atonement is 383
achieved through murder.

situation — The *ego* believes the situation brings the 341
experience.

soul — The *ego* is trying to teach you how to gain the 211
whole world and lose you own soul.

speaks — (The voices of the Holy Spirit and the *ego*) 80
speak for different interpretations of

the same thing simultaneously; or almost simultaneously, for the *ego* always speaks first.

spirit — While the *ego* is equally unaware of spirit, it does perceive itself as being rejected by something greater than itself.   **53**

strength — The *ego* teaches that your strength is in you alone.   **133**

stress — "Self-esteem" is always vulnerable to stress, a term which refers to any perceived threat to the *ego's* existence.

strong — The *ego* becomes strong in strife.   **73**

study — The study of the *ego* is not the study of the mind.   **274**

study — (Those who study the *ego*) but study form with meaningless content.   **274**

survival — (Survival of the *ego*) depends on your belief you are exempt from its evil intentions.   **295**

suspiciousness — The *ego* is capable of suspiciousness at best and viciousness at worst.   **164**

taught — Spirit need not be taught but the *ego* must be.   **48**

teach — The *ego* does not know what it is trying to teach.   **129**

teach — The *ego* tries to teach you that you want to oppose God's Will.   **130**

teaches — That is why the *ego* is insane; it teaches you are not what you are.   **108**

teaches — The *ego* teaches thus: Death is the end as far as hope of Heaven goes.   **281**

teaches — The *ego* teaches you always encounter your past, and because your dreams were not holy, the future cannot be, and the present is without meaning.   **229**

thought — The *ego* is quite literally a fearful thought.   **77**

time — The *ego* is an ally of time but not a friend.   **280**

time — The *ego* literally lives on borrowed time, and its days are numbered.   **158**

time — The *ego* regards the function of time as one of extending itself in place of eternity.   **230**

time — All the waste that time seems to bring with it is due but to your identification with the *ego* which uses time to support its belief in destruction. **280**

time - Do not fear the Last Judgment, but welcome it and do not wait, for the *ego's* time is borrowed from your eternity. **158**

time — Delay is of the *ego*, because time is its concept. **72**

tolerate — The *ego* depends solely on your willingness to tolerate it. **166**

traitor — (The *ego*) is a traitor to you who believe that you have been treacherous to your Father. **217**

transcending — Our success in transcending the *ego* is guaranteed by God. **137**

true — The *ego* never was and never will be part of (your Godlike mind) but through the *ego* you can hear and teach and learn what is not true. **91**

trust — Being the part of your mind that does not believe it is responsible for itself, and being without allegiance to God, the *ego* is incapable of trust. **119**

truth — The *ego* cannot protect you against truth, and in its presence the *ego* is dispelled. **224**

truth — (The *ego*) wants no part of truth, because the *ego* itself is not true. **116**

undermining — Undermining the *ego's* thought system must be perceived as painful, even though this is anything but true. **52**

understand — The *ego* does not understand, appreciate or love what it makes. **113**

undone - The *ego* is always being undone, and does suspect your motives. **108**

unpredictable — (The *ego* is) unpredictable in its responses, because it has no idea of what it perceives. **158**

unshared — The existence (of the *ego*) is unshared. **75**

variation — Everyone makes an *ego* or a self for himself, which is subject to enormous variation because of its instability.   **51**

viciousness — (The *ego*) shifts to viciousness when you decide not to tolerate self-abasement and seek relief.   **166**

vigilant — The *ego* exerts maximal vigilance about what it permits into awareness, and this is not the way a balanced mind holds together.   **59**

vigilant — You must be vigilant against the *ego*.   **101**

wants — For what the *ego* really wants you do not realize.   **297**

war — Every response to the *ego* is a call to war, and war does deprive you of peace.   **128**

war — Surely you realize the *ego* is at war with God.   **452**

war — The *ego's* friend is not part of you, because the *ego* perceives itself at war, and therefore in need of allies.   **108**

weakness — The *ego* despises weakness, even though it makes every effort to induce it.   **147**

weakness — The *ego* would not have you see its weakness, and learn it has no power to keep you from the truth.   **393**

without — To the *ego*, to give up anything implies that you will have to do without it.   **52**

witnesses — The *ego* does not call upon witnesses who would disagree with its case, nor does the Holy Spirit.   **144**

world — The *ego* made the world as it perceives it, but the Holy Spirit, the reinterpreter of what the *ego* made, sees the world as a teching device for bringing you home.   **74**

world — (The world of the *ego*) does not exist.   **117**

wrong — (The) *ego* is always wrong no matter what it says or does.   **155**

you — The *ego* does not regard itself as part of you.   **93**

EMOTION(S)

manifestations — Your manifestations of *emotions* are the opposite of what the *emotions* are.   **231**

two — You have but two *emotions*, and one you made and one was given to you.   **232**

two — You have but two *emotions*, love and fear.   **230**

EMPATHIZE(S)

strength — Yet of this you may be sure; if you will merely sit quietly by and let the Holy Spirit relate through you, you will *empathize* with strength, and will gain in strength and not in weakness.   **307**

weaken — The ego always *empathizes* to weaken, and to weaken is always to attack.   **307**

EMPATHY

past — All you have learned of *empathy* is from the past.   **307**

past — Do not use *empathy* to make the past real, and so perpetuate it.   **307**

suffering — (*Empathy*) does not mean to join in suffering, for that is what you must refuse to understand.   **307**

ENCOUNTER

holy — The Holy Spirit teaches that you always meet yourself, and the *encounter* is holy because you are.   **229**

holy — Every holy *encounter* in which you enter fully will teach you (someone else is not someone else.)   **132**

holy — When you meet anyone, remember it is a holy encounter.   **132**

ENDS

means — Perception is a part of what it is your purpose to behold, for means and *ends* are never separate.   **483**

ENDINGS

eternal — You who made delay can leave time behind simply by recognizing that neither beginnings nor *endings* were created by the eternal.　　　**180**

ENEMY

yourself — You have no *enemy* except yourself, and you are *enemy* indeed to him because you do not know him as yourself.　　　**523**

EQUAL

Sons of God — Only one *equal* gift can be offered to the *equal* Sons of God, and that is full appreciation.　　　**97**

EQUALITY

ego — *Equality* is beyond (the ego's) grasp, and charity becomes impossible.　　　**52**

oneness — There is no order of difficulty in miracles because all of God's Sons are of equal value, and their *equality* is their oneness.　　　**194**

ERROR(S)

Atonement — Atonement undoes all *errors* in this re spect, and thus uproots the source of fear.　　　**7**

attack — If you attack *error* in another you will hurt yourself.　　　**37**

attractive — An *error* is not attractive.　　　**376**

brother's — Let all your brother's *errors* be to you nothing except a chance to see the workings of the Helper given you to see the world He made instead of yours.　　　**488**

concentrate — To concentrate on *error* is only a further *error.*　　　**28**

conflict — The first corrective step in undoing the *error* is to know first and conflict is the expression of fear.　　　**26**

corrected — *Error* can be corrected, and the wrong made right.　　　**374**

corrected — *Errors* of any kind can be corrected because   455
    they are untrue.

correction — *Errors* are quickly recognized and quickly   378
    given to correction, to be healed, not
    hidden.

correction — *Errors* are of the ego and correction of *errors*   155
    lies in the relinquishment of the ego.

decide — The only way out of *error* is to decide you do   125
    not have to decide anything.

faithlessness — Use not your *error* as the justification   386
    for your faithlessness.

fear — Any attempt to resolve the *error* through at-   28
    tempting the mastery of fear is useless.

Holy Spirit — Unless (giving them to the Holy Spirit)   156
    becomes the one way in which you
    handle all *errors*, you cannot understand
    how all *errors* are undone.

Holy Spirit — What has no effect does not exist, and to   158
    the Holy Spirit the effects of *error* are
    non existent.

Holy Spirit — When you react to *error* you are not   155
    listening to the Holy Spirit.

limitation — This sense of limitation is where all *errors*   157
    arise.

magnitude — You may be very surprised to hear how   348
    different is reality from what you see.
    You do not realize the magnitude of
    that one *error*.

mind — Only the mind is capable of *error*.   19

nothing — Any way you handle *error* results in nothing.   145

occurred — The escape (from fear) is brought about by   15
    your acceptance of the Atonement,
    which enables you to realize that your
    errors never really occurred.

original — When you seem to see some twisted form of   348
    the original *error* rising to frighten you,
    say only, "God is not fear, but love,"
    and it will dissappear.

perceive — To perceive *errors* in anyone and to react to them as if they were real, is to make them real to you.   **156**

power — To interpret *error* is to give it power, and having done this you will overlook truth.   **200**

punishment — It is sin that calls for punishment, not *error*.   **377**

purpose — There is another purpose in the world that *error* made, because it has another Maker who can reconcile its goal with His Creator's purpose.   **487**

reality — No illusions can rise to meet your sight, for reality leaves no room for any *error*.   **233**

sin — It is essential that *error* be not confused with sin, and it is this distinction that makes salvation possible.   **374**

true — If you want to believe in *error*, you would have to make it real because it is not true.   **200**

truth — *Error* cannot threaten truth, which can always withstand it.   **7**

truth — That one *error* which brought truth to illusion, infinity to time, and life to death, was all you ever made.   **347**

truth — Truth overcomes all error, and those who live in *error* and emptiness can never find lasting solace.   **35**

uncorrected — Uncorrected *error* of any kind deceives you about the power that is in you to make correction.   **428**

understand — You do not understand how to overlook *errors*, or you would not make them.   **157**

ETERNAL

dedication — Let you dedication be to the *eternal*, and learn how not to interfere with it and make it slave to time.   **374**

end — What seems *eternal* all will have an end.   **572**

faith — Faith in the *eternal* is always justified, for the   386
         eternal is forever kind, infinite in its
         patience and wholly loving.

loved — Only the *eternal* can be loved, for love does not   177
         die.

peace — The *eternal* are in peace and joy forever.   105

re-created — The Bible speaks of a new Heaven and a   194
         new earth, yet this cannot be literally
         true, for the *eternal* are not re-created.

remember — If you would remember eternity you must   178
         look only on the *eternal*.

unite — (The *eternal*) can unite only with what is already   386
         at peace in you, immortal as itself.

world — When you learn to make me manifest, you will   217
         never see death. For you will have
         looked upon the deathless in your self,
         and you will see only the *eternal* in
         yourself as you look out upon a world
         that cannot die.

you — What you think you do to the *eternal* you do to   374
         you.

ETERNITY

accept — If you will accept only what is timeless as real,   177
         you will begin to understand *eternity*
         and make it yours.

creation — *eternity* is the indelible stamp of creation.   105

dwell — You dwell not here but in *eternity*.   240

God — *Eternity* is an idea of God, so the Holy Spirit   73
         understands it perfectly.

joy — Only joy increases forever, since joy and *eternity*   105
         are inseparable.

mind — Time and *eternity* are both in your mind, and will   168
         conflict until you perceive time solely
         as a means to regain eternity.

miracle — Each miracle of joining is a mighty herald of   405
         eternity.

peace — *Eternity* and peace are as closely related as time   73
         and war.

place — Your place is only in *eternity*, where God Himself   79
placed you forever.

time — *Eternity* is one time, its only dimension being   163
"always."

time — *Eternity* itself is beyond all time.   272

time — Neither time nor season means anything in   301
eternity.

time — The little breath of *eternity* that runs through   405
time like a golden light is all the same,
nothing before it, nothing afterwards.

time — Time and *eternity* cannot both be real, because   178
they contradict each other.

yours — *Eternity* is yours, because He created you   104
eternal.

EVALUATION(S)

conflicting — You have two conflicting *evaluations* of   164
yourself in your mind, and they cannot
both be true.

God's — If truth is indivisible, your *evaluation* of yourself   167
must be God's.

EVIL

exist — Innocence is wisdom because it is unaware of   33
evil, and *evil* does not exist.

EVOLUTION

incomprehensible — (*Evolution*) is incomprehensible in   17
temporal terms, because you return as
you go forward.

process — *Evolution* is a process in which you seem to   17
proceed from one degree to the next.

EXCEPTIONS

perceive — Make no *exceptions* yourself or you will not   193
perceive what has been accomplished
for you.

resurrection — The resurrection is the Will of God,   198
which knows no time and no *exceptions*.

EXIST

size — What does not *exist* has no size and no measure.　194

EXISTENCE

communication — *Existence* as well as being rest on communication.　64

EXPECT

invite — You see what you *expect*, and you *expect* what you invite.　214

EXPERIENCE(S)

beliefs — Perceptions are built up on the basis of *experience*, and *experience* leads to beliefs.　192

I — I am leading you to a new kind of *experience* that you will become less and less willing to deny.　192

teach — Yet different *experiences* lead to different beliefs, and experience does teach.　192

EXTEND

aspect — To *extend* is a fundamental aspect of God which He gave to His Son.　14

project — What you project or *extend* is up to you, but you must do one or the other, for that is a law of mind, and you must look in before you look out.　215

real — What you project or *extend* is real for you.　106

EXTENSION

blocked — *Extension* cannot be blocked, and it has no voids.　180

forever — (*Extension*) continues forever, however much it is denied.　180

God — You make by projection, but God creates by *extension*.　179

love — Without projection there can be no anger, but it is also true that without *extension* there can be no love.　120

oneness — *Extension* (of the Father and Son) is the result   132
of their oneness, holding their unity
together by extending Their joint Will.

projection — The inappropriate use of *extension*, or   14
projection, occurs when you believe
that some emptiness or lack exists in
you, and that you can fill it with your
own ideas instead of truth.

radiance — *Extension*, as undertaken by God, is similar to   14
the inner radiance that the children of
the Father inherit from Him.

FACTS

change — It is indeed possible for you to deny *facts*,   151
although it is impossible for you to
change them.

FAIL

anything — No one will *fail* in anything.   342

God — God will not *fail* nor ever has in anything.   260

loving — *Fail* not in your function of loving in a loveless   260
place made out of darkness and deceit,
for thus are darkness and deceit
undone.

FAILURE

ego — *Failure* is of the ego, not of God.   250

sense — Accept your sense of *failure* as nothing more   298
than a mistake in who you are.

FAIR

God — (God) is wholly *fair* to everyone.   498

World — The world is *fair* because the Holy Spirit has   524
brought injustice to the light within,
and there has all unfairness been
resolved and been replaced with justice
and with love.

FAIRNESS

vengeance — *Fairness* and vengeance are impossible, for   498
each one contradicts and other and
denies that it is real.

FAITH

belief — *Faith* can be rewarded only in terms of the belief in which the *faith* was placed. — 243

brother — Be tempted not to snatch away from gift of *faith* you offered to your brother. — 353

chains — *Faith* can keep the Son of God in chains as long as he believes he is in chains. — 421

desire — *Faith* and desire go hand in hand, for everyone believes in what he wants. — 419

ego — The ego rewards fidelity to it with pain, for *faith* in it is pain. — 243

equal — It is impossible to place equal *faith* in opposite directions. — 421

faithful — What you had *faith* in still is faithful, and watches over you with *faith* so gentle yet so strong that it would lift you far beyond the veil, and place the Son of God safely within the sure protection of this Father. — 395

fear — *Faith* is the opposite of fear, as much a part of love as fear is of attack. — 373

fearful — Have *faith* in Him who walks with you, so that your fearful concept of yourself may change. — 616

forgive — There is nothing *faith* cannot forgive. — 374

forgiven — Through the eyes of *faith* the Son of God is seen already forgiven, free of all the guilt he laid upon himself. — 373

freedom — By *faith* you offer the gift of freedom from the past, which you perceived. — 373

give — Give *faith* to one another, for *faith* and hope and mercy are yours to give. — 394

goal — *Faith* is still a learning goal, no longer needed when the lesson has been learned. — 374

goal — Your *faith* must grow to meet the goal that has been set. — 343

God — *Faith* is the gift of God, through Him Whom God has given you. — 373

heal — To have *faith* is to heal. — 373

Him — You call for *faith* because of Him Who walks with you in every situation. 344

holiness — As holiness and *faith* go hand in hand, so must its *faith* go everywhere with it. 343

holiness — *Faith* unites you in the holiness you see, not through the body's eyes, but in the sight of Him Who joined you and in Whom you are united. 373

Holy Spirit — Offer your *faith* to (the Holy Spirit) and (He) will place it gently in the holy place where it belongs. 253

Holy Spirit's — *Faith* arises from the Holy Spirit's perception, and is the sign you share it with him. 373

Holy Spirit's — *Faith* is implicit in the acceptance of the Holy Spirit's purpose, and this *faith* is all-inclusive. 342

illusions — *Faith* given to illusions does not lack power, for by it does the Son of God believe that he is powerless. 421

innocence — *Faith* in innocence is *faith* in sin if the belief excludes one living thing and holds it out, apart from its forgiveness. 439

justified — There is no justification for faithlessness, but *faith* is always justified. 373

knowledge — *Faith* is as easily exchanged for knowledge as is the real world. 373

lack — If you lack *faith* ask that it be restored to you where it was lost, and seek not to have it made up to you elsewhere, as if you had been unjustly deprived of it. 343

lack — It is impossible that the Son of God lack *faith*, but he can choose where he would have it be. 421

lack — Your lack of *faith* in the power that heals all pain arises from your wish to retain some aspects of reality for fantasy. 327

limitations — Faithlessness would always limit and attack; *faith* would remove all limitations and make whole. 372

135

messenger — (*Faith*) is the messenger of the new per- 373
ception, sent forth to gather witnesses
unto its coming, and to return their
messages to you.

nothing — Your *faith* in nothing is deceiving you. 253

obstacles — Faithlessness would interpose illusions 372
between the Son of God and his
Creator; *faith* would remove all
obstacles that seem to rise between
them.

past — You will accept your treasure, and if you place 243
your *faith* in the past, the future will be
like it.

peace — *Faith* brings peace, and so it calls on truth to 374
enter and make lovely what has already
been prepared for loveliness.

power — The power of *faith* is never recognized if it is 421
placed in sin.

problem — There is no problem in any situation that 342
faith will not solve.

purpose — Your *faith* will call the others to serve your 344
purpose, as the same purpose calls
forth the *faith* in you.

quiet — Be quiet in your *faith* in Him who loves you, and 258
would lead you out of insanity.

reason — Your *faith* is moving inward, past insanity and 424
on to reason.

relationship — Your holy relationship with its new 373
purpose offers you *faith* to give your
brother.

reward — *Faith* makes the power of belief, and where it 243
is invested determines its reward.

rewards — Do not abandon *faith* now that the rewards 338
of *faith* are being introduced.

sin — What *faith* you give to sin you take away from 421
holiness.

thankful — Be you thankful that only little *faith* is asked 497
of you.

truth — Faithlessness is wholly dedicated to illusions; *faith* wholly to truth.   372

truth — Peace without *faith* will never be attained, for what is dedicated to truth as its only goal is brought to truth by *faith*.   371

truth — The goal of truth requires *faith*.   342

truth — The strain of refusing *faith* to truth is enormous, and far greater than you realize.   345

union — *Faith* is the acknowledgement of union.   373

unreal — *Faith* in the unreal leads to adjustments in reality to make it fit the goal of madness.   419

FAITHFUL

conflicting — You cannot be *faithful* to two masters who ask conflicting things of you.   327

FAITHLESSNESS

apart — Your *faithlessness* has driven you apart, and so you do not recognize salvation in each other.   373

attack — You do not see how great the devastation wrought by your *faithlessness*, for *faithlessness* is an attack that seems to be justified by its results.   373

bodies — The thought of bodies is the sign of *faithlessness*, for bodies cannot solve anything.   343

forgiveness — *Faithlessness* looks upon the Son of God and judges him unworthy of forgiveness.   373

illusion — *Faithlessness* is the servant of illusion, and wholly faithful to its master.   343

illusion — The goal of illusion is as closely tied to *faithlessness* as faith to truth.   343

illusions — Do not overlook our earlier statement that *faithlessness* leads straight to illusions.   371

illusions — *Faithlessness* is wholly dedicated to illusions, faith wholly to truth.   372

illusions — *Faithlessness* would interpose illusions bet-   372
ween the Son of God and his Creator,
faith would remove all obstacles that
seem to rise between them.

justification — There is no justification for *faithlessness,*   373
but faith is always justified.

kingdoms — As *faithlessness* will keep your little king-   374
doms barren and separate, so will faith
help the Holy Spirit prepare the
ground for the most holy garden that
he would make of it.

lack — *Faithlessness* is not lack of faith but faith in no-   421
thing.

limit — *Faithlessness* would always limit and attack; faith   372
would remove all limitations and make
whole.

perception — *Faithlessness* is the perception of a brother   371
as a body, and the body cannot be used
for purposes of union.

sickness — *Faithlessness* is sickness.   562

Son of God — Think carefully before you let yourself   345
use *faithlessness* against (the Son of God.)

truth — *Faithlessness* used against truth will always   343
destory faith.

use — Use not your *faithlessness.*   343

FANTASY(IES)

body — *Fantasies* have made your body your "enemy;"   360
weak, vulnerable and treacherous,
worthy of the hate that you invest in it.

confusion — Only *fantasies* make confusion in choosing   320
possible, and they are totally unreal.

distortions — *Fantasies* of any kind are distortions,   12
because they always involve twisting
perception into unreality.

ego — The symbols of *fantasy* are of the ego, and of these   159
you will find many.

fearful — What can be fearful but *fantasy*, and who turns to *fantasy* unless he despairs of finding satisfaction in reality?   **158**

illusion — *Fantasy* solutions bring out the illusion of experience, and the illusion of peace is not the condition in which truth can enter.   **342**

impossible — It is impossible to act out *fantasies*.   **360**

impossible — The impossible can happen only in *fantasy*.   **159**

knowledge — Every *fantasy*, be it of love or hate, deprives you of knowledge, for *fantasies* are the veil behind which truth is hidden.   **316**

means — *Fantasies* are a means of making false associations and attempting to obtain pleasure from them.   **13**

no — Hear not the call of hate, and see no *fantasies*.   **316**

past — There is no *fantasy* that does not contain the goal of retribution for the past.   **324**

past — How can you change the past except in *fantasy*.   **324**

reality — *Fantasy* is an attempt to control reality according to false needs.   **12**

reality — *Fantasies* change reality.   **327**

satisfaction — It is certain that you will never find satisfaction in *fantasy*, so that your only hope is to change your mind about reality.   **158**

truth — What you use in *fantasy* you deny to truth.   **327**

vision — *Fantasy* is a distorted form of vision.   **12**

FEAR(S)

afraid — In your disordered state of mind, you are not afraid of *fear*.   **225**

alive — No one who lives in *fear* is really alive.   **30**

appeal — Having taught you to accept only loving thoughts in others and to regard everything else as an appeal for help, (the Holy Spirit) has taught you *fear* itself is an appeal for help.   **202**

Atonement — Joining the Atonement is the way out of *fear*.   **74**

attack — It is as certain you will *fear* what you attack as it is sure that you will love what you perceive as sinless.   **451**

author — God is not the author of *fear*. You are.   **49**

banish — You who have tried to banish love have not succeeded, but you who choose to banish *fear* must succeed.   **204**

body — The circle of *fear* lies just below the level the body sees, and seems to be the whole foundation on which the world is based.   **367**

cause — *Fear* cannot be real without a cause and God is the only Cause.   **151**

conflict — *Fear* is always a sign of strain arising whenever what you want conflicts with what you do.   **25**

correction — The correction of *fear* is your responsibility.   **25**

create — As long as you believe *fear* is possible, you will not create.   **152**

created — You cannot make the unreal because the absence of reality is fearful, and *fear* cannot be created.   **152**

dissociation — *Fear* produces dissociation, because it induces separation.   **112**

effects — (The effects of *fear*) can be dispelled merely by denying their reality.   **188**

emotion — *Fear* is both a fragmented and a fragmenting emotion.   **347**

escape — The escape (from *fear*) is brought about by your acceptance of the Atonement, which enables you to realize that your errors never really occurred.   **15**

exceptions — Exceptions are fearful because they are made by *fear*.   **112**

faith — Faith is the opposite of *fear*, as much a part of love as *fear* is of attack.   **373**

forgive — Those you do not forgive you *fear*.   393

forgiveness — The emptiness engendered by *fear* must   9
be replaced by forgiveness.

forms — (*Fear*) has many forms, for the content of   230
individual illusions differs greatly.

gladden — *Fear* does not gladden.   112

God — All *fear* is ultimately reducible to the basic mis-   15
perception that you have the ability to
usurp the power of God.

God — The *fear* of God is *fear* of life, and not of death.   461

guilt — Love contains the end of guilt, as surely as *fear*   382
depends on it.

guilt — The messengers of *fear* are harshly ordered to   382
seek out guilt, and cherish every scrap
of evil and of sin that they can find,
losing none of them on pain of death,
and laying them respectfully before
their lord and master.

hate — Hate must father *fear*, and look upon its father   602
as itself.

hell — What you see is hell, for *fear* is hell.   617

Holy One — You retain thousands of little scraps of *fear*   56
that prevent the Holy One from
entering.

Holy Spirit — If you do not protect (*fear*), the Holy Spirit   202
will reinterpret it.

Holy Spirit — The Holy Spirit cannot teach through   297
fear.

idol — Whenever you feel *fear* in any form, be sure you   579
made an idol, and believe it will betray
you.

judgment — *Fear* is a judgment never justified.   596

look — Do not be afraid to look upon *fear*, for it cannot   188
be seen.

loss — *Fear* is a symptom of your own deep sense of loss.   202

love — As love must look past *fear*, so must *fear* see   382
love not.

love — *Fear* and love are the only emotions of which   202
     you are capable.

love — *Fear* and love cannot co-exist, and if it is impos-   66
     sible to be wholly fearful and remain
     alive, the only possible whole state is
     that of love.

love — *Fear* arises from lack of love.   26

love — *Fear* demands the sacrifice of love, for in love's   564
     presence *fear* cannot abide.

love — *Fear* is a call for love, in unconscious recognition   202
     of what has been denied.

love — *Fear* is attracted to what love sees not, and each   382
     believes that what the other looks
     upon does not exist.

love — No one reaches love with *fear* beside him.   393

love — Perfect love casts out *fear*.   12

love — There is no *fear* in perfect love.   204

love — Where *fear* has gone there love must come,   558
     because there are but these
     alternatives.

love — You have denied *(fear's)* power to conceal love,   202
     which was its only purpose.

love — You react with *fear* to love, and draw away from   231
     it.

madness — *Fear* will reign in madness, and will seem to   452
     have replaced love there.

make — *Fear* and love make or create depending upon   114
     whether the ego or the Holy Spirit
     begets or inspires them, but they will
     return to the mind of the thinker and
     they will affect his total perception.

meaning — *(Fear's)* presence has no meaning but to show   596
     you wrote a fearful script, and are
     afraid accordingly.

meaningless — In the security of reality, *fear* is totally   151
     meaningless.

mind — Whenever there is *fear*, it is because you have   26
     not made up your mind.

miracles — By choosing the miracle you have rejected *fear,* if only temporarily.　　**28**

miracles — There is nothing (miracles) cannot do, but they cannot be performed in the spirit of *fear* or doubt.　　**15**

miscreation — All *fear* is implicit in (miscreation.)　　**28**

miscreations — Both the separation and the *fear* are miscreations that must be undone for the restoration of the temple, and for the opening of the altar to receive the Atonement.　　**18**

nothing — *Fear* is really nothing and love is everything.　　**28**

peace — *Fear* not to cross to the abode of peace and perfect happiness.　　**315**

present — *Fear* is not of the present, but only of the past and future, which do not exist.　　**281**

produces — *(Fear)* produces a state that does not exist.　　**12**

real — Be not afraid, therefore, for what you will be looking at is the source of *fear,* and you are beginning to learn that *fear* is not real.　　**188**

reality — *Fear* lies not in reality, but in the minds of children who do not understand reality.　　**198**

recognize — To recognize *fear* is not enough to escape from it, although the recognition is necessary to demonstrate the need for escape.　　**201**

recoils — Everyone draws nigh unto what he loves, and recoils from what he *fears.*　　**231**

removing — The means for removing *fear* is in yourself, and you have demonstrated this by giving it.　　**202**

responsibility — The correction of *fear* is your responsibility.　　**25**

see — The more you look at *fear* the less you see it, and the clearer what it conceals becomes.　　**267**

self-controlled — *Fear* cannot be controlled by me, but it can be self-controlled.　　**25**

separate — (The conditions that have brought *fear*   25
about) always entail a willingness to be
separate.

separation — Before the separation the mind was invul-   18
nerable to *fear*, because *fear* did not
exist.

separation — Your investment (in *fear*) is great now   50
because *fear* is a witness to the separa-
tion, and your ego rejoices when you
witness to it.

thing — The thing you *fear* is gone.   243

thoughts — The presence of *fear* shows you have raised   25
body thoughts to the level of mind.

unknown — You do not *fear* the unknown but the   204
known.

untrue — All aspects of *fear* are untrue because they do   12
not exist at the creative level, and
therefore do not exist at all.

weak — How weak is *fear*, how little and how meaning-   446
less.

world — The world contains no *fear* that you laid not   383
upon it.

world — Your private world is filled with figures of *fear*   231
you have invited to it, and all the love
your brothers offer you, you do not
see.

FEARFUL

brother — You must be *fearful* if you believe that your   119
brother is attacking you to tear the
Kingdom of Heaven from you.

chosen — When you are *fearful*, you have chosen wrong-   25
ly.

exclude — What you exclude from yourself seems *fear-*   305
ful, for you endow it with fear and try
to cast it out, though it is part of you.

forgotten — You are *fearful* because you have forgotten.   170

Holy Spirit — Errors (the Holy Spirit) will correct, but   423
this makes no one *fearful*.

144

FINDING

seeking — Seeking and *finding* are the same, and if you seek for two goals you will find them, but you will recognize neither.　215

FLESH

body — If you choose the *flesh* you will never escape the body as your own reality, for you have chosen that you want it so.　614

spirit — You see the *flesh* or recognize the spirit.　614

FORGETTING

remembering — *Forgetting* is merely a way of remembering better.　109

FORGIVE(S)

brother — *Forgive* your brother and you cannot separate yourself from him nor from his Father.　486

faith — (In your relationship) you will recognize that there is nothing faith cannot *forgive*.　374

fear — Those you do not *forgive* you fear.　393

God's — You must *forgive* God's Son entirely.　595

healed — Who *forgives* is healed.　528

illusions — Whom you *forgive* is given power to *forgive* you your illusions.　568

learn — Ask to learn how to *forgive*, and to restore what always was to your unforgiving mind.　260

nothing — There is nothing to *forgive*.　256

overlook — To *forgive* is to overlook.　156

remember — To *forgive* is merely to remember only the loving thoughts you gave in the past and those that were given you.　330

sin — No one *forgives* unless he has believed in sin, and still believes that he has much to be forgiven.　509

willing — Be willing to *forgive* the Son of God for what he did not do.　330

FORGIVEN

accomplished — Ask not to be *forgiven* for this has al-   260
ready been accomplished.

illusions — All that must be *forgiven* are the illusions you   325
have held against your brothers.

illusions — (The reality of illusions you held against   325
your brothers) has no past, and only
illusions can be *forgiven*.

join — What has been *forgiven* must join, for nothing   510
stands between to keep them separate
and apart.

understood — All things must be first *forgiven*, and then   591
understood.

FORGIVENESS

accepted — For your *forgiveness*, offered unto him, has   616
been accepted now for both of you.

all — *Forgiveness* is for all.   493

attack — Unjustified *forgiveness* is attack. And this is all   594
the world can ever give.

brother — *Forgiveness* takes away what stands between   516
your brother and yourself.

brother — Think not that your *forgiveness* of your broth-   404
er serves but you two alone.

brother — Withhold *forgiveness* from your brother and   460
you attack him.

brother — (Your brother) waits for your *forgiveness* only   468
that he may return it unto you.

communication — *Forgiveness* lies in communication as   297
surely as damnation lies in guilt.

complete — Before complete *forgiveness* you still stand   393
unforgiving.

complete — *Forgiveness*, once complete, brings timeless-   579
ness so close the song of Heaven can
be heard, not with the ears, but with
the holiness that never left the altar
that abides forever deep within the
Son of God.

complete — In complete *forgiveness*, in which you recog-   298
nize that there is nothing to forgive,
you are absolved completely.

146

dreamer — *Forgiveness* separates the dreamer from the evil dream, and thus releases him.   **558**

end — Yet even *forgiveness* is not the end. (It) does make lovely, but it does not create.   **369**

fear — *Forgiveness* that is learned of me does not use fear to undo fear.   **157**

function — *Forgiveness* is the only function meaningful in time.   **493**

guilt — If what you offer is complete *forgiveness* you must have let guilt go, accepting the Atonement for yourself and learning you are guiltless.   **251**

guilty — I ask for your *forgiveness*, for if you are guilty, so must I be.   **385**

heal — *Forgiveness* recognized as merited will heal.   **594**

healing — *Forgiveness* is not real unless it brings a healing to your brother and yourself.   **528**

healing — *Forgiveness* is the healing of the perception of separation.   **41**

healing — *(Forgiveness)* is the source of healing, but it is the messenger of love and not its source.   **369**

Holy Spirit — *(Forgiveness)* is the means the Holy Spirit uses to translate specialness from sin into salvation.   **493**

Holy Spirit — *Forgiveness* through the Holy Spirit lies simply in looking beyond error from the beginning, and thus keeping it unreal for you.   **157**

Holy Spirit's — Follow the Holy Spirit's teaching in *forgiveness*, then, because *forgiveness* is His function and He knows how to fulfill it perfectly.   **158**

illusion — *Forgiveness* is release from all illusion, and that is why it is impossible but partly to forgive.   **470**

kind — In kind *forgiveness* will the world sparkle and shine, and everything you once thought sinful now will be reinterpreted as part of Heaven.   **452**

Love — In your *forgiveness* will you understand His Love 492
for you; through your attack believe
He hates you, thinking Heaven must
be hell.

love — Nothing in boundless love could need *forgiveness.* 509

miracle — *(Forgiveness)* gives the miracle its strength to 594
overlook illusions.

miracles — Only *forgiveness* offers miracles. 503

one — *Forgiveness* cannot be for one and not the other. 528

peace — *Forgiveness* is your peace, for herein lies the end 572
of separation and the dream of danger
and destruction, sin and death; of madness and of murder, grief and loss.

receive — It is sure he would receive *(forgiveness)* wholly 470
the instant that he gave it so.

remembering — *Forgiveness* is a selective remembering, 330
based not on your selection.

responsibility — Your sole responsibility must be to 503
take *forgiveness* for yourself.

sane — *Forgiveness* is the only sane response. 593

see — You will see *forgiveness* where you have given it. 328

sinned — You need no *forgiveness,* for the wholly pure 486
have never sinned.

suffer — No one in whom true *forgiveness* rests can 528
suffer.

transforms — *Forgiveness* literally transforms vision, and 329
lets you see the real world reaching
quietly and gently across chaos, removing all illusions that had twisted
your perception and fixed it on the
past.

truth — What is *forgiveness* but a willingness that truth be 516
true?

truth — *Forgiveness* is the means by which the truth is 532
represented temporarily.

untrue — *Forgiveness* removes only the untrue, lifting 370
shadows from the world and carrying
it, safe and sure within its gentleness,

to the bright world of new and clean perception.

withheld — *Forgiveness* cannot be withheld a little.   **461**

world — *Forgiveness* turns the world of sin into a world of   **510** glory, wonderful to see.

world — The world has much to offer to your peace, and   **488** many chances to extend your own *forgiveness*.

world's — *Forgiveness* is the world's equivalent of Heaven's justice.   **509**

FORM(S)

means — Take not the *form* for content, for the *form* is   **485** but a means for content.

mistakes — Let not the *form* of his mistakes keep you   **443** from him whose holiness is yours.

mistakes — Only mistakes have different *form* and so   **443** they can deceive.

reason — Reason will tell you that if *form* is not reality it   **443** must be an illusion, and is not there to see.

true — You can change *form* because it is not true.

FREE

brother — *Free* your brother here, as I freed you.   **395**

forgive — Whom you forgive is *free*, and what you give   **394** you share.

God — (God) joins with you in willing you be *free*.   **585**

offering — By offering freedom you will be *free*.   **135**

Son — The Son whom God created is as *free* as God   **513** created him.

taught — You may have taught freedom, but you have   **311** not learned how to be *free*.

will — Unless you do your will you are not *free*.   **585**

FREE WILL

freedom — *Free will* must lead to freedom.   **44**

God's — This requires God's endowment of the Son   14
with *free will,* because all loving creation
is freely given in one continuous line,
in which all aspects are of the same
order.

joy — Your *free will* was given you for your joy in creat-   15
ing the perfect.

miscreate — A *free will* cannot miscreate, because it   16
recognizes only truth.

FREEDOM

body — Do you want *freedom* of the body or of the mind?   447
For both you cannot have.

body — *Freedom* of the body has no meaning, and so the   447
mind is dedicated to serve illusions.

bondage — Since *freedom* and bondage are irreconcilable,   174
their laws cannot be understood to-
gether.

bondage — For the Love of God, no longer seek for   321
union in separation, nor for *freedom* in
bondage.

brother — (Your brother) has no need but this; that you   491
allow him *freedom* to complete the task
God gave to him.

cause — You have cause for *freedom* now.   520

Christ — The time of Christ is the time appointed for   302
the gift of *freedom,* offered to everyone.

creation — *Freedom* is creation, because it is love.   135

gift — *Freedom* is the only gift you can offer to God's   135
Sons, being an acknowledgement of
what they are and what He is.

gift — Behold the gift of *freedom* that I gave the Holy   395
Spirit for (you and your brother.)

give — You are not free to give up *freedom,* but only to   174
deny it.

learned — It is of them who learned of *freedom* that you   403
should ask what *freedom* is.

offering — By offering *freedom* you will be free.   135

150

real — Real *freedom* depends on welcoming reality, and   **184**
of your guests only the Holy Spirit is
real.

results — Those who choose *freedom* will experience only   **403**
its results.

step — The first step toward *freedom* involves a sorting   **30**
out of the false from the true.

taught — You could never have taught *freedom* unless   **312**
you did believe in it.

total — You must choose between total *freedom* and total   **303**
bondage, for there are no alternatives
but these.

tyranny — *Freedom* cannot be learned by tyranny of any   **135**
kind, and the perfect equality of all
God's Sons cannot be recognized
through the opinion of one mind over
another.

vision — There is another vision and another Voice in   **426**
which your *freedom* lies, awaiting your
choice.

yearns — No one but yearns for *freedom* and tries to find   **447**
it.

FUNCTION(S)

accept — Accept the *function* that has been assigned to   **496**
you in God's Own plan to show His
Son that hell and Heaven are different,
not the same.

accept — No one who does not accept his *function* can   **139**
understand what it is, and no one can
accept his *function* unless he knows
what he is.

being — *Functions* are part of being since they arise from   **143**
it, but the relationship is not reciprocal.

brother's — To let (your brother's) *function* be fulfilled   **491**
is but the means to let yours be.

called — You have been called, together with your   **350**
brother, to the most holy *function* this
world contains.

confusion — The confusion of *function* is so typical of the   158
ego that you should be quite familiar
with it by now.

create — God gave you the *function* to create in eternity.   156

creative — Your whole creative *function* lies in your com-   189
plete dependence on God, Whose
function He shares with you.

ego — The ego teaches that your *function* on earth is   228
destruction, and you have no *function* at
all in Heaven.

fulfill — You will never rest until you know your *function*   183
and fulfill it, for only in this can your
will and your Father's be wholly joined.

God — The *function* God Himself gave your mind   124
through His you may deny, but you
cannot prevent.

God — God gave you a very lofty *function* that you are   50
not meeting.

God — You who have God must be as God, for His *func-*   184
tion became yours with His gift.

healing — Accept only the *function* of healing in time, be   156
cause that is what time is for.

knowable — (The *function* of God's Son), because it is not   139
unknown to His Creator, is forever
knowable to him.

lonely — The lonely ones are those who see no *function* in   493
the world for them to fill, no place
where they are needed, and no aim
which only they can perfectly fulfill.

made — You made neither yourself nor your *function*.   138

only — However much he overlooks the masterpiece in   486
him and sees only a frame of darkness,
it is still your only *function* to behold in
(your brother) what he sees not.

see — As you see (your brother) so do you define the   492
function he will have for you, until you
see him differently and let him be what
God appointed that he be to you.

shares — God shares His *function* with you in Heaven, and the Holy Spirit shares His with you on earth.   **214**

sin — Your *function* is to show your brother sin can have no cause.   **527**

special — To each his special *function* is designed to be perceived as possible, and more and more desired, as it proves to him that it is an alternative he really wants.   **496**

special — Without your special *function* has the world no meaning for you.   **505**

special — Your special *function* shows you nothing else but perfect justice can prevail for you.   **500**

special — Your special *function* is the special form in which the fact that God is not insane appears most sensible and meaningful to you.   **495**

your — Your *function* here is only to decide against deciding what you want, in recognition that you do not know.   **260**

FUTURE

continuous — Past, present and *future* are not continuous, unless you force continuity on them.   **234**

expiation — The *future*, in time, is always associated with expiation, and only guilt could induce a sense of a need for expiation.   **222**

GAP

body — The body represents the *gap* between the little bit of mind you call your own and all the rest of what is really yours.   **560**

brother — Either there is a *gap* between you and your brother, or you are as one.   **561**

brother — The *gap* between your brother and yourself was never there.   **592**

love — Look at the little *gap* and you behold the innocence and emptiness of sin that you will see within yourself, when you have lost the fear of recognizing love.   **559**

nothing — In the *gap* is nothing.

promise — Whoever says "There is no *gap* between my mind and yours" has kept God's promise, not his tiny oath to be forever faithful unto death.   560

toys — The *gap* that is not there is filled with toys in countless forms.   589

truth — There is no *gap* that separates the truth from dreams and from illusions.   559

GARDEN OF EDEN

mind — The *Garden of Eden,* or the pre-separation condition, was a state of mind in which nothing was needed.   14

GET

taking — You believe in a world that takes, because you believe that you can *get* by taking.   197

GIFT(S)

bodies — *Gifts* are not made through bodies, if they be truly given and received.   397

brother — Each little *gift* you offer to your brother lights up the world.   449

brother's — Let all your brother's *gifts* be seen in light of charity and kindness offered you.   543

creations — Your *gifts* to yourself are meaningless, but your *gifts* to your creations are like His, because they are given in His Name.   178

ego — The *gifts* you offer to the ego are always experienced as sacrifices, but the *gifts* you offer to the Kingdom are *gifts* to you.   120

escape — Do not try to escape the *gift* of God He so freely and so gladly offers you.   257

evaluation — Each *gift* is an evaluation of the receiver and the giver.   397

extend — Save no dark secrets that He cannot use, but offer Him the tiny *gifts* He can extend forever.   449

Father — There is no *gift* the Father asks of you but that you see in all creation the shining glory of His *gift* to you.   **571**

God — God gave Himself to you in your creation, and His *gifts* are eternal.   **177**

God — God is your heritage, because His one *gift* is Himself.   **181**

God — Each *gift* but adds to the supply. For God is fair.   **501**

God's — God's *gifts* have no reality apart from your receiving them.   **325**

Holy Spirit — (The Holy Spirit) always gives His *gifts* in place of yours.   **278**

Holy Spirit — What the Holy Spirit does with *gifts* you give each other, to whom He offers them, and where and when, is up to Him.   **449**

I — The *gift* of union is the only *gift* that I was born to give.   **302**

I — The only *gift* I can accept of you is the *gift* I gave to you.   **301**

Kingdom — Out of your *gifts* to Him the Kingdom will be restored to His Son.   **178**

life — The *gift* of life is yours to give, because it was given you.   **118**

limitless — The *gift* of God to you is limitless.   **518**

obscure — Behind the dark doors you have closed lies nothing, because nothing can obscure the *gift* of God.   **269**

offered — Can you offer guilt to God? You cannot, then, offer it to His Son. For they are not apart and *gifts* to one are offered to the other.   **269**

reluctantly — To give reluctantly is not to gain the *gift*, because you are reluctant to accept it.   **501**

savior — Forget not that it is your savior to whom the *gift* is offered.   **397**

Sons of God — Only one equal *gift* can be offered to equal Sons of God, and that is full appreciation.   **97**

two — Two *gifts* are offered you. Each is complete, and cannot be partially accepted. **335**

GIVE(S)

everyone — You *give* to one another for everyone, and in your gift is everyone made glad. **405**

forget — Forget not Who has given you the gifts you *give*, and through your not forgetting this, will you remember Who gave the gifts to Him to *give* to you. **405**

God — Everything you *give* to God is yours. **264**

God — What God *gives* has always been. **221**

hands — Into the hands that *give*, the gift is given. **394**

His — What you *give* is His, and giving it, you learn to understand His gift to you. **486**

Holy Spirit's — The Holy Spirit's first lesson was: "To have, *give* all to all." **99**

limit — *Give*, then, without limit and without end, to learn how much He has given you. **181**

lost — Nothing you *give* is lost to you or anyone, but cherished and preserved in Heaven, where all of the treasures given to God's Son are kept for him, and offered anyone who but holds out his hand in willingness they be received. **501**

much — You do not see how much you now can *give*, because of everything you have received. **566**

receive — To *give* is no more blessed than to receive. But neither is it less. **430**

received — *Give* as you have received. **346**

share — Whom you forgive is free, and what you *give* you share. **394**

value — What you *give* is the exact measure of the value you put upon it. **154**

GIVEN

God — To whom God gives Himself, He is *given*. **270**

missing — Only what you have not *given* can be lacking in any situation. **343**

GIVING

Father — *Giving* Himself is all (the Father) knows, and so it is all knowledge. **260**

first — In time and *giving* comes first, though (*giving* and receiving) are simultaneous in eternity, where they cannot be separated. **163**

function — *Giving* of yourself is the function (God) gave you. **133**

having — Having appears to be the opposite of *giving*. **99**

having — Unless he gives he will not know he has, for *giving* is the proof of having. **567**

keep — *Giving* (something) is how you keep it. **121**

receive — By *giving* you receive. **154**

receiving — The cost of *giving* is receiving. **256**

willingness — The recognition of having is the willingness for *giving*, and only by this willingness can you recognize what you have. **154**

GLORIOUS

God — Yet the Son of God cannot hide his glory, for God wills him to be *glorius*, and gave him the light that shines in him. **185**

God — You cannot, then, be less *glorious* than (God) is. **162**

GLORY

gift — *Glory* is God's gift to you, because that is what He is. **133**

God's — God's *glory* and His Son's belong to you in truth. **269**

Holy Spirit — Banish not power from your mind, but let all that would hide your *glory* be brought to the judgment of the Holy Spirit, and there undone. **269**

inheritance — *Glory* is your inheritance, given you by your Creator that you might extend it. **186**

obscured — In darkness you have obscured the *glory* God gave you, and the power He bestowed upon His guiltless Son. **269**

power — Power and *glory* belong to God alone. **133**

restored — Look not for what has been removed, but for the *glory* that has been restored for you to see. — 378

saved — You are not saved from anything, but you are saved for *glory*. — 186

united — All *glory* lies in (God and His Sons) because they are united. — 136

GOAL(S)

accepted — You may be attempting to follow a very long road to the *goal* you have accepted. — 363

accomplishment — The *goal* establishes the fact that everyone involved in it will play his part in its accomplishment. — 342

bodies — Bodies have no *goal*. — 472

body's — Whenever you attempt to reach a *goal* in which the body's betterment is cast as major beneficiary, you try to bring about your death. — 574

chosen — You have chosen but the *goal* of God, from which your true intent was never absent. — 339

clarification — The clarification of the *goal* belongs at the beginning, for it is this which will determine the outcome. — 341

dedicate — To dedicate yourself to both (truth and illusion) is to set up a *goal* forever impossible to attain, for part of it is sought through the body, thought of as a means for seeking out reality through attack. — 372

eternal — Look straight at every image that rises to delay you, for the *goal* is inevitable because it is eternal. — 204

forgiveness — If you but knew the glorious *goal* that lies beyond forgiveness, you would not keep hold on any thought, however light the touch of evil on it may appear to be. — 571

happen — Without a clearcut positive *goal*, set at the   **341**
      outset, the situation just seems to
      happen, and makes no sense until it has
      already happened.

Holy Spirits's — The Holy Spirit's *goal* gives one inter-   **597**
      pretation, meaningful to you and to
      your brother.

learning — Your learning *goal* has been not to learn, and   **210**
      this cannot lead to successful learning.

light — Let us then join quickly in an instant of light,   **353**
      and it will be enough to remind you
      that your *goal* is light.

love — The *goal* of love is but your right, and it still   **204**
      belongs to you despite your dreams.

meaningful — The situation now has meaning, but only   **341**
      because the *goal* has made it
      meaningful.

means — If a *goal* is possible to reach, the means to do so   **410**
      must be possible as well.

means — Think you not the *goal* itself will gladly arrange   **340**
      the means for its accomplishment?

means — Yet the *goal* is fixed, firm, and unalterable, and   **340**
      the means will surely fall in place
      because the *goal* is sure.

reality — The *goal's* reality will call forth and accomplish   **344**
      every miracle needed for its
      fulfillment.

seek — Yet seeking and finding are the same, and if you   **215**
      seek for two *goals* you will find them,
      but you will recognize neither.

sin — The *goal* of sin induces the perception of a fearful   **419**
      world to justify its purpose.

true — The true becomes what can be used to meet the   **341**
      goal.

truth — But you will advance, because your *goal* is the   **353**
      advance from fear to truth.

GOD

absent — If you believe you are absent from *God* you will   **181**
      believe He is absent from you.

absent — There is no time, no place, no state where *God* is absent. 563

accomplishments — *God* does not take steps, because His accomplishments are not gradual. 105

accord — *God* cannot be out of accord with Himself, and you cannot be out of accord with Him. 112

accord — If your mind could be out of accord with *God's*, you would be willing without meaning. 117

afraid — You are afraid of *God* because you ear your brother. 393

afraid — You are afraid of *God* because you fear your love cannot enter where it is not welcome. 226

against — *God* holds nothing against anyone, for He is incapable of illusions of any kind. 325

alone — *God* would not have us be alone because He does not will to be alone. 139

asks — *God* asks for nothing and His Son, like Him, need ask for nothing. 561

bargain — To believe it is possible to get much for little is to believe that you can bargain with *God*. 154

beginnings — There are no beginnings or endings in *God*, whose universe is Himself. 180

being — All being is in (*God*) Who is all Being. 110

blessed — (*God*) blessed His children with a way of thinking that could raise their perceptions so high they could reach almost back to Him. 68

blessed — *God* blessed His Son forever. 186

body — *God* did not make the body. 97

brother — You could no more know *God* alone than He knows you without your brother. 366

brothers — *God* will come to you only as you will give Him to your brothers. 63

Call — Our task is the joyous one of waking to the Call for *God*. 71

160

Call — What we can accomplish together has no limit, because the Call for *God* is the call to the unlimited.   **71**

call — Your Father has not denied you, He does not retaliate, but He does call you to return.   **177**

care — You cannot choose to escape the care of *God*.   **82**

"Cause" — "Cause" is a term properly belonging to *God*, and his "Effect" is His Son.   **28**

children — *God* knows His children with perfect certainty.   **37**

children — *God* watches over His children and denies them nothing.   **126**

co-creator — Think not He wills to bind you, Who has made you co-creator of the universe along with Him.   **585**

co-creator — *God* extends outward beyond limits and beyond time, and you who are co-creator with Him extend His Kingdom forever and beyond limit.   **105**

comfortless — (The relinquishment of your false decision-making prerogative) was accomplished for you by the Will of *God*, Who has not left you comfortless.   **125**

commended — *God* commended His Spirit to you, and asks that you commend yours to Him.   **82**

communicate — You communicate fully with *God*, as He does with you.   **104**

condemned — *God* has never condemned His Son, and being guiltless he is eternal.   **223**

confidence — It is impossible the confidence of *God* should be misplaced.   **406**

conflicted — *God* is not conflicted.   **95**

contradict — *God* does not contradict Himself, and His Sons, who are like Him, cannot contradict themselves of Him.   **139**

corruption — What *God* creates is safe from all corruption, unchanged and perfect in eternity.   **485**

create' — (Communication with *God*) is an ongoing   **104**
process in which you share, and
because you share it, you are inspired
to create like *God*.

create — The final step is *God's*, because it is but *God* who   **591**
could create a perfect Son and share
His Fatherhood with him.

create — To think like *God* is to share His certainty of   **105**
what you are, and to create like Him is
to share the perfect Love He shares
with you.

created — (*God*) created you for Himself, but He gave   **168**
you the power to create for yourself so
you would be like Him.

created — *God* created you to create.   **90**

created — *God* Himself created the law by creating by it.   **106**

created — *God* in His devotion to you created you de-   **151**
voted to everything, and gave you
what you are devoted to.

created — *God*, who encompasses all being, created   **64**
beings who have everything
individually, but who want to share it
to increase their joy.

created — In creation you are not in a reciprocal relation   **104**
to *God*, since He created you, but you
did not create Him.

created — Teaching aims at change, but *God* created   **95**
only the changeless.

created — *God* created His Sons by extending His   **90**
Thought, and retaining the extensions
of His Thought in His Mind.

created — *God* created nothing beside you, and nothing   **168**
beside you exists.

create — (*God*) created you for Himself, but He gave you   **168**
the power to create for yourself so you
would be like Him.

created — What *God* created cannot be attacked, for   **465**
there is nothing in the universe unlike
itself.

created — What *God* has created needs no frame, for what He has created He supports and frames within Himself.   **485**

created — You cannot be anywhere *God* did not put you, and *God* created you as part of Him.   **89**

creates — Only what *God* creates is irreversible and unchangeable.   **78**

creates — The Mind that was in me is in you, for *God* creates with perfect fairness.   **80**

creates — What *God* creates is eternal.   **68**

creating — *God* is as incapable of creating the perishable as the ego is of making the eternal.   **50**

creation — *God* gave Himself to you in your creation, and His gifts are eternal.   **177**

creation — What can upset you except the ephemeral and how can the ephemeral be real if you are *God's* only creation and He created you eternal?   **168**

creations — (*God*) does not teach, because His creations are changeless.   **105**

creations — *God* knew His creations were good.   **30**

creative — As *God's* creative Thought proceeds from Him to you, so must your creative thought proceed from you to your creations.   **104**

Creator — (*God*) is the Prime Creator, because He created His co-creators.   **105**

death — The death of *God*, if it were possible, would be your death.   **452**

deceive — Listen and do not question what you hear, for *God* does not deceive.   **167**

deception — Listen only to *God*, who is as incapable of deception as the Spirit He created.   **50**

decide — *God* will never decide against you, or He would be deciding against Himself.   **168**

denial — Allegiance to the denial of *God* is the ego's religion.   **176**

denied — (*God*) has not denied you.   **177**

deny — Do not forget, however, that to deny *God* will   176
    inevitably result in projection, and you
    will believe that others and not
    yourself have done this to you.

deny — When you deny (*God*) you are insane.   177

dependent — By (*God's* willingness to share His func-   189
    tion), He became as dependent on you
    as you are on Him.

dependent — *God* and His creations are completely de-   19
    pendent on each other.

ego — Whom *God* has joined as one, the ego cannot put   332
    asunder.

enter — You cannot enter the Presence of *God* if you   187
    attack His Son.

equally — *God* gives only equally.   127

eternal — No one created by *God* can find joy in anything   138
    except the eternal, not because He is
    deprived of anything else, but because
    nothing else is worthy of him.

eternity — *God* offers you the continuity of eternity in   79
    exchange.

everyone — To everyone has *God* entrusted all, because   618
    a partial savior would be one who is but
    partly saved.

everything — (*God*) will give you everything but for the   170
    asking.

extend — *God* Himself has established what you can   101
    extend with perfect safety.

extended — *God* extended Himself to His creations and   14
    imbued them with the same loving will
    to create.

extends — Far beyond your little world but still in you,   286
    (*God*) extends forever.

fact — In (the Innocense of *God*) your mind knows *God*,   34
    for *God* is not symbolic; He is fact.

fear — *God* is not the author of fear. You are.   49

fear — *God* were fear indeed if he whom He created   602
    innocent could be a slave to guilt.

fear — The fear of *God* is but the fear of loss of idols.   575

fear — The fear of *God* is nothing to you now.   398

fear — The fear of *God* is the fear of life, and not of death.   393

fear — To look upon the fear of *God* does need some preparation.   393

fear — What seems to be fear of *God* is really fear of your own reality.   149

First — *God* is First in the sense that He is first in the Holy Trinity Itself.   105

forget — *God* willed not His son forget Him.   601

forgiven — And now in *God* forgiven, for you chose to look upon your brother as a friend.   586

forgiveness — *God* asks for your forgiveness.   471

forgiveness — No one would dare to look upon the (fear of *God*) without complete forgiveness of his brother in his heart.   393

function — *God* does not share His function with a body.   462

gave — *God* gave you all there is.   577

gift — *God* has given you a gift that you both have and are.   110

gifts — The gifts you offer to the Kingdom will always be treasured by *God* because they belong to His beloved Sons, who belong to Him.   120

give — *God* would give Himself through you.   286

give — Your ability to accept (*God*) depends on your willingness to give as He gives.   181

given — *God* has given you everything.   56

gives — *God* gives; He does not take.   197

guarantee — The guarantee of *God* will hold against all obstacles.   404

happiness — *God* wills you perfect happiness now.   163

healing — Your minds are not separate, and *God* has only one channel for healing because He has but one Son.   171

heritage — *God* is your heritage, because His one gift is Himself.   181

hides — *God* hides nothing from His Son, even though   185
His Son would hide himself.

hold — (*God*) does not hold your "evil" deeds against   32
you.

home — You are at home in *God*, dreaming of exile but   169
perfectly capable of awakening to
reality.

honors — *God* honored even the miscreations of His   68
children because they had made them.

host — You believe it is possible to be host to the ego or   302
hostage to *God*.

humble — Be humble before (*God*) yet great in Him.   288

idea — In one sense the ego's fear of *God* is at least   60
logical, since the idea of Him does
dispel the ego.

idols — When you have experienced the protection of   175
God, the making of idols becomes
inconceivable.

in — You are in *God*.   109

inevitable — *God* is inevitable, and you cannot avoid   50
Him any more than He can avoid you.

insane — Either *God* or the ego is insane.   179

jealous — *God* is not jealous of the gods you make but   172
you are.

joined — Nothing can come between what *God* has   347
joined and what the Holy Spirit sees as
one.

joy — When the ego was made, *God* placed in mind the   69
call to joy.

Kingdom — *God* has kept the Kingdom for you, but He   64
cannot share His joy with you until you
know it with your whole mind.

knows — what (*God*) knows exists forever changelessly.   587

lack — Without you there would be a lack in *God*, a   475
Heaven incomplete, a son without a
Father.

laws — If you (disobey the laws of *God*), and only if you   133
do, you will feel lonely and helpless,

because you are denying yourself everything.

laws — You cannot exempt yourself from (the laws of God), although you can disobey them. **133**

learn — As part of His Thought, you cannot think apart from *God*. **78**

leave — *God* did not leave His children comfortless, even though they chose to leave Him. **70**

life — The death penalty is the ego's ultimate goal, for it fully believes that you are a criminal, as deserving of death as *God* knows you are deserving of life. **216**

light — (The light of *God*) was never obscured, because it is His Will to share it. **105**

limit — *God* does not limit His gifts in any way. **104**

lonely — The constant going out of His Love is blocked when His channels are closed, and (*God*) is lonely when the minds He created do not communicate fully with Him. **64**

lonely — *God* is lonely without His Sons, and they are lonely without Him. **19**

love — *God* will never cease to love His Son, and His Son will never cease to love Him. **117**

love — You have not attacked *God* and you do love Him. **171**

Love — But see the Love of *God* in you, and you will see it everywhere because it is everywhere. **120**

Love — The Love of *God* is in everything He created, for His Son is everywhere. **177**

Love — You who could give the Love of *God* to everything you see and touch and remember, are literally denying Heaven to yourself. **126**

loves — You are (*God's*) care, because He loves you. **82**

loving — Very gently does *God* shine upon Himself, *God* loving the extension of Himself that is His Son. **213**

Majesty — Recognizing the Majesty of *God* as your brother is to accept your own inheritance.   127

meaning — *God's* meaning waits in the Kingdom, because that is where He placed it.   108

meaning — How can you who are *God's* meaning perceive yourself as absent from it?   108

means — (*God*) does not will anyone to suffer for a wrong decision, including you. That is why He has given you the means for undoing it.   133

Means — *God* is a Means as well as End.   479

meets — Everything meets in *God*, because everything was created by Him and in Him.   90

memory — How instantly the memory of *God* arises in the mind that has no fear to keep the memory away!   549

memory — The memory of *God* cannot shine in a mind that has obliterated it and wants to keep it so.   218

memory — The memory of *God* comes to the quiet mind.   452

memory — The memory of *God* is obscured in minds that have become illusions' battleground.   455

memory — The memory (of *God*) shines in your mind and cannot be obliterated.   218

memory — The memory of *God* shines not alone.   479

memory — Under the ego's dark foundation is the memory of *God*, and it is of this that you are really afraid.   225

mercy — *God* asks your mercy on His Son and on Himself. Deny Them not.   471

mercy — *God* offers only mercy.   43

mind — *God* has lit your mind Himself, and keeps your mind lit by His Light because His Light is what your mind is.   109

Mind — *God* changes not His Mind about His Son with passing circumstance, which has no   476 meaning in eternity where He abides, and you with Him.

Mind — *God* does not change His Mind about you, for He is not uncertain of Himself.   168

Mind — *God* has given you a place in His Mind that is yours forever.   181

Mind — (The Mind of *God*) cannot be lessened.   181

Mind — What is unlike *God* cannot enter His Mind, because it was not His Thought and therefore does not belong to Him.   185

Mind — You are altogether irreplaceable in the Mind of *God*.   167

Mind — Your value is in *God's* Mind, and therefore not in yours alone.   167

miracles — All miracles mean life, and *God* is the Giver of Life.   1

need — *God* would respond to every need, whatever form it takes.   299

one — If you were one with *God* and recognized this oneness, you would know His power is yours.   449

Oneness — *God's* Oneness and ours are not separate, because His Oneness encompasses ours.   136

part — You are part of *God*, as your sons are part of His Sons.   104

peace — *God* knows you only in peace, and this is your reality.   39

peace — The peace of *God* lies in that message, and so the peace of *God* lies in you.   91

peace — (The peace of *God*) is complete, and you must be included in it.   133

plan — *God's* plan is simple; never circular and self-defeating.   426

possible — To *God* all things are possible.   194

praised — *God* is praised whenever any mind learns to be wholly helpful.   65

protected — (*God*) protected both your creations and 312
    you together, keeping one with you
    what you would exclude.

quiet — *God* is very quiet for there is no conflict in Him. 184

real — When you are afraid, be still and know that *God* is 49
    real, and you are His beloved Son in
    whom He is well pleased.

real — Nothing beyond *God* can happen, because no- 168
    thing except Him is real.

receive — Those who receive the Father are one with 306
    Him, being host to Him Who created
    them.

recognition — The recognition of *God* is the recognition 136
    of yourself.

remember — If you would remember your Father, let 274
    the Holy Spirit order your thoughts
    and give only the answer with which
    He answers you.

remember — It is impossible to remember *God* in secret 274
    and alone.

remembers — (*God*) remembers nothing, having always 292
    known you exactly as He knows you
    now.

rests — *God* rests with you in quiet, undefended and 446
    wholly undefending, for in this quiet
    state alone is strength and power.

retaliate — *God* does not retaliate, but He does call you 177
    to return.

retribution — *God* does not believe in retribution. 32

revelation — *God* does not need revelation returned to 65
    Him, which would clearly be
    impossible, but He does want it
    brought to others.

secrets — *God* has no secrets. 435

separate — Your recognition that whatever seems to 190
    separate you from *God* is only fear,
    regardless of the form it takes and
    quite apart from how the ego wants
    you to experience it, is therefore the
    basic ego threat.

separation — There is no separation of *God* and His creation.   **136**

sickness — Sickness and separation are not of *God*, but the Kingdom is.   **106**

sin — *God*, Who created neither sin nor death, wills not that you be bound by them.   **389**

Son — *God* and His beloved Son do not think differently.   **495**

Son — It should especially be noted that *God* has only one Son.   **29**

stranger — *God* is not a stranger to His Sons, and His Sons are not strangers to each other.   **36**

strangers — You are not strangers in the house of *God*.   **454**

strength — Those with the strength of *God* in their awareness could never think of battle.   **463**

suffer — *God* wills no one suffer.   **133**

teach — *God* does not teach.   **95**

thanks — *God* offers thanks to the Holy host who would receive Him, and lets Him enter and abide where He would be.   **306**

think — To think like *God* is to share His certainty of what you are, and to create like Him is to share the perfect Love He shares with you.   **105**

Thoughts — (*God*) has no Thoughts except the Self-extending, and in this your will must be included.   **426**

Thoughts — (The Thoughts of *God*) are perfectly united within themselves and with each other.   **90**

time — Time applies neither to (*God*) nor to what He created.   **105**

trusts — *God* Himself trusts you, and therefore your trustworthiness is beyond question.   **125**

undoing — *God* has given you the means for undoing what you have made.   **178**

unfulfillment — Unless you create you are unfulfilled, but *God* does not know unfulfillment and therefore you must create.   **123**

171

universe — Can you exclude yourself from the universe, or from *God* Who is the universe?   180

unworthy — Be certain *God* did not entrust His Son to the unworthy.   438

Voice — The Voice for *God* comes from your own altars to Him.   70

Voice — The Voice for *God* is always quiet, because it speaks of peace.   70

Voice — (The Voice for *God*) reminds you always that all hope is yours because of His care.   82

Voice — The Voice for *God* speaks only for belief beyond question, which is the preparation for being without question.   102

Voice — (The Voice of *God*) will be heard.   250

Voice — (The Voice of *God*) will teach you how to distinguish between pain and joy, and will lead you out of the confusion you have made.   125

Voice — Why should you listen to the endless insane calls you think are made upon you, when you can know the Voice for *God* is in you?   82

Voice — You cannot hear the Voice for *God* in yourself alone, because you are not alone.   153

weeps — *God* weeps at the "sacrifice" of His children who believe they are lost to Him.   82

welcome — *God's* welcome waits for us all, and He will welcome us as I am welcoming you.   137

will — The seeds of sickness and the shame of guilt (*God*) cannot bridge, for He cannot destroy the alien will that He created not.   554

will — *God* Himself keeps your will alive by transmitting it from His Mind to yours as long as there is time.   69

will — (*God*) would only have you learn your will and follow it, not in the spirit of sacrifice and submission, but in the gladness of freedom.   193

Will — If you were not part of *God* His Will would not be unified.   **180**

Will — You are the same as *God* Himself is One, and not divided in His Will.   **486**

Will — You exist because *God* shared His Will with you, that His creation might create.   **558**

wills — Everything *God* wills is not only possible, but has already happened.   **356**

wills — (*God*) wills His Son have everything.   **516**

wills — What *God* wills is whole, and part of him because His Will is one.   **475**

GOD'S WILL, WILL OF GOD

afraid — It is not, then, *The Will of God* of which you are afraid, but yours.   **149**

afraid — You are afraid to know *God's Will,* because you believe it is not yours.   **182**

ask — You must ask what *God's Will* is in everything, because it is yours.   **181**

boundaries — (*God's Will*) has no boundaries because it created all things.   **131**

boundless — (*God's Will*) is boundless in strength, love and peace.   **130**

changeless — (*God's Will*) does not vacillate, being changeless forever.   **133**

Christ — Christ will always offer you *The Will of God,* in recognition that you share it with Him.   **237**

content — You will be content with nothing but (*God's*) Will.   **287**

created — Creation is the *Will of God.* His Will created you to create.   **139**

die — You cannot crucify God's son, for *God's Will* cannot die.   **194**

disobeying — Disobeying *God's Will* is meaningful only to the insane.   **123**

done — Whatever your reactions to the Holy Spirit's Voice may be, whatever voice you choose to listen to, whatever strange thoughts may occur to you, *God's Will* is done.   **249**

fear — Fear of (*God's Will*) is one of the strangest beliefs the human mind has ever made.   **149**

forced — Yet the wish for other experience will block its accomplishment, because *God's Will* cannot be forced on you.   **131**

forever — (Your healing) is still (*God's*) *Will* for you, and His Will must stand forever and in all things.   **148**

fulfill — To fulfill the *The Will of God* perfectly is the only joy and peace that can be fully known, because it is the only function that can be fully experienced.   **131**

Holy Spirit — (The Holy Spirit) cannot conceive of God without you, because it is not *God's Will* to be without you.   **130**

Holy Spirit — The Holy Spirit is the way in which *God's Will* is done on earth as it is in Heaven.   **70**

illusion — (*God's*) *Will* has saved you, not from yourself but from your illusion of yourself.   **138**

join — (*God's*) *Will* is brought together as you join in will.   **486**

joined — *The Will of God* forever lies in those whose hands are joined.   **593**

know — Would you know the *Will of God* for you? Ask it of me who knows it for you and you will find it.   **137**

know — You do not know what (*God's Will*) is, but the Holy Spirit remembers it for you.   **181**

Love — It is (*God's*) *Will* that you share His Love for you, and look upon yourself as lovingly as He conceived of you before the world began, and as He knows you still.   **476**

one — *God's Will* is one, not many.   **380**

one — *God's Will* is that His Son be one, and united with Him in His oneness.   **182**

oppose — If you are opposing (*God's*) *Will* how can you have knowledge?   **128**

oppose — To think you can oppose *The Will of God* is a real delusion.   **110**

oppose — You still oppose *The Will of God* just by a little.   **380**

opposite — You also believe it is possible to do the opposite of *God's Will.*   **124**

opposition — (*God's Will*) has no opposition, for there is none beside it.   **380**

own — To hear *The Will of your Father* is to know your own.   **182**

possible — Remember, then, that *God's Will* is already possible, and nothing else will ever be.   **152**

power — The *Will of God* is without limit, and all power and glory lie within it.   **130**

prevail — Nothing can prevail against our united wills because nothing can prevail against *God's (Will.)*   **137**

remember — Ultimately everyone must remember *The Will of God,* because ultimately everyone must remember himself.   **151**

resurrection — The resurrection is the *Will of God* which knows no time and no exceptions.   **193**

salvation — *God's Will* is your salvation.   **163**

shares — It is never God who coerces you, because He shares *His Will* with you.   **130**

strain — There is no strain in doing *God's Will* as soon as you recognize that it is also your own.   **26**

thought — *God's Will* is thought. It cannot be contradicted by thought.   **139**

unchangeable — Because *God's Will* is unchangeable, no conflict of will is possible.   **117**

you — You are *God's Will.*   **119, 131**

GOOD

evil — *Good* can withstand any form of evil, as light abolishes forms of darkness.   **33**

work — Only the *good* can work.   **161**

GRACE

body — *Grace* is not given to a body, but to a mind.   **373**

brother — Do you, then, offer *grace* and blessing to your   374
     brother, for you stand at the same altar
     where *grace* was laid for both of you.

God — The *grace* of God rests gently on forgiving eyes,   492
     and everything they look on speaks of
     Him to the beholder.

healed — Be you healed by *grace* together, that you may   374
     heal through faith.

Heaven — There is no *grace* of Heaven that you cannot   394
     offer to one another, and receive from
     your most holy Friend.

Love — To all who share the Love of God the *grace* is   445
     given to the givers of what they have
     received.

state — *Grace* is the natural state of every Son of God.   126

GRANDEUR

awakening — My birth in you is your awakening to   287
     grandeur.

bless — From your *grandeur* you can only bless, because   166
     your *grandeur* is your abundance.

brothers — You will find the place of truth as you see   227
     it in your brothers, for though they
     may deceive themselves, like you they
     long for the *grandeur* that is in them.

deceive — Your *grandeur* will never deceive you, but your   167
     illusions will.

delusional — Your *grandeur* is not delusional because   166
     you did not make it.

despair — If you are willing to look upon your *grandeur*   166
     you cannot despair, and therefore you
     cannot want the ego.

ego — Whenever you become aware of (*grandeur*), how-   165
     ever dimly, you abandon the ego
     automatically, because in the presence
     of the *grandeur* of God the
     meaninglessness of the ego becomes
     perfectly apparent.

ego — Your *grandeur* is God's answer to the ego, because it is true.   **166**

God — *Grandeur* is of God, and only of Him.   **165**

God's — *Grandeur* is the right of God's Son, and no illusions can satisfy him or save him from what he is.   **227**

illusions — *Grandeur* is totally without illusions, and because it is real is compellingly convincing.   **166**

littleness — Littleness and *grandeur* cannot coexist, nor is it possible for them to alternate.   **166**

GRANDIOSITY

attack — You made *grandiosity* and are afraid of it because it is a form of attack, but your grandeur is of God, Who created it out of His Love.   **166**

competitiveness — The essence of *grandiosity* is competitiveness, because it always involves attack.   **165**

delusional — Grandiosity is delusional, because it is used to replace your grandeur.   **167**

despair — *Grandiosity* is always a cover for despair.   **165**

help — Beneath all the *grandiosity* you hold so dear is your real call for help.   **227**

littleness — (*Grandiosity*) is an attempt to counteract your littleness, based on the belief that the littleness is real.   **165**

GRATEFUL

ability — I do not need gratitude, but you need to develop your weakened ability to be *grateful*, or you cannot appreciate God.   **88**

GRATITUDE

brother — *Gratitude* is due (your brother) for both his loving thoughts and his appeals for help, for both are capable of bringing love into your awareness if you perceive them truly.   **201**

brother — Through your *gratitude* you come to know   62
your brother, and one moment of real
recognition makes everyone your
brother because each of them is of your
Father.

God — The *gratitude* of God is freely offered to everyone   486
who shares His purpose.

I — I do not need *gratitude*, but you need to develop your   88
weakened ability to be grateful.

GREAT RAYS

extend — And from this light will the *Great Rays* extend   354
back into darkness and forward unto
God, to shine away the past and so
make room for His eternal Presence, in
which everything is radiant in the
light.

Holy Spirit — As the ego would limit your perception   299
of your brothers to the body, so would
the Holy Spirit release your vision and
let you see the *Great Rays* shining from
them, so unlimited that they reach to
God.

obscured — In many only the spark remains, for the   175
Great Rays are obscured. Yet God has
kept the spark alive so that the *Rays* can
never be completely forgotten.

relationship — The *Great Rays* would establish the total   321
lack of value of the special relationship
if they were seen.

unseen — If you but see the little spark you will learn of   175
the greater light, for the *Rays* are there
unseen.

GRIEVANCE(S)

love — Whatever reminds you of your past *grievances*   330
attracts you and seems to go by the
name of love, no matter how distorted
the associations by which you arrive at
the connection may be.

GUEST(S)

come — Your *Guest* has come.   565

determine — You are free to determine who shall be your *guest*, and how long he shall remain with you.   184

gifts — You cannot see your *Guest*, but you can see the gifts He brought.   566

Holy Spirit — Real freedom depends on welcoming reality, and of your *guests* only the Holy Spirit is real.   184

welcome — They will be healed when you accept your gifts, because your *guest* will welcome everyone whose feet have touched the holy ground whereon you stand, and where His gifts for them are laid.   566

GUIDANCE

accept — You must accept *guidance* from within.   134

evaluative — *Guidance* is evaluative, because it implies there is a right way and also a wrong way, one to be chosen and the other to be avoided.   69

fear — Unable to follow (false) guidance without fear, he associates fear with *guidance,* and refuses to follow any *guidance* at all.   125

Holy Spirit — You believe that to ask for *guidance* of the Holy Spirit is to ask for deprivation.   197

meaningless — The *guidance* must be what you want or it will be meaningless to you.   134

miracles — (And by so) limiting the *guidance* that you would accept, you are unable to depend on miracles to answer all your problems for you.   277

my — The reason you need my help is because you have denied your own guide and therefore need *guidance.*   54

separation — Before the separation you did not need *guidance.*   69

GUIDE

errors — If you do not follow this *Guide*, your errors will not be corrected. **157**

God — By this refusal to attempt to teach yourself what you do not know, the *Guide* Whom God has given you will speak to you. **277**

miracles — You cannot be your *guide* to miracles, for it is you who made them necessary. **277**

purpose — The purpose of this *Guide* is merely to remind you of what you want. **149**

purpose — (This *Guide*) is merely making every possible effort, within the limits you impose on Him, to re-establish your own will in your awareness. **149**

GUILT

Atonement — The moment that you realize *guilt* is insane, wholly unjustified and wholly without reason, you will not fear to look on the Atonement and accept it wholly. **246**

Atonement — When you have accepted the Atonement for yourself, you will realize there is no *guilt* in God's Son. **222**

Atonement — If *guilt* were real, Atonement would not be. **246**

attack — *Guilt* is the symbol of attack on God. **77**

attack — *Guilt* remains the only thing that hides the Father, for *guilt* is the attack upon His Son. **242**

attack — To the extent to which you value *guilt*, to that extent will you perceive a world in which attack is justified. **487**

attraction — In this world the attraction of *guilt* stands between (the Father and the Son.) **301**

attraction — The attraction of *guilt* produces fear of love, for love would never look on *guilt* at all. **382**

attraction — The attraction of *guilt* is found in sin, not error. **376**

attraction — The attraction of *guilt* has value to you only   295
because you have not looked at what it
is, and have judged it completely in the
dark.

attraction — But this is what you must remember; the   301
attraction of *guilt* opposes the
attraction of God.

blessed — What is truly blessed is incapable of giving   77
rise to *guilt*, and must give rise to joy.

blind — *Guilt* makes you blind, for while you see one   243
spot of *guilt* within you, you will not see
the light.

brothers — A sick and suffering you but represents   525
your brother's *guilt*; the witness that
you send lest he forget the injuries he
gave, from which you swear he never
will escape.

burden — The burden of *guilt* is heavy but God would   262
not have you bound by it.

Christ — *Guilt* hides Christ from your sight, for it is the   221
denial of the blamelessness of God's
Son.

Christ — Would you see in me the symbol of *guilt* or the   385
end of *guilt*, remembering that what I
signify to you you see within yourself?

communication — In the holy instant *guilt* holds no   297
attraction, since communication has
been restored.

compromise — There is no compromise that you can   255
make with *guilt*, and escape the pain
that only guiltlessness allays.

continuity — *Guilt* is a way of holding past and future in   222
your mind to ensure the ego's
continuity.

damnation — Forgiveness lies in communication as   297
surely as damnation lies in *guilt*.

dangerous — What *guilt* has wrought is ugly, fearful and   323
very dangerous.

denial — *Guilt* hides Christ from your sight, for it is the denial of the blamelessness of God's Son. 221

dispell — You cannot dispell *guilt* by making it real and then atoning for it. 223

displaced — You have displaced your *guilt* to your body from your mind. 359

disruptive — *Guilt* is always disruptive. 77

ego — *Guilt* is the only need the ego has, and as long as you identify with it, guilt will remain attractive to you. 297

ego — We said before that the ego attempts to maintain and increase *guilt*, but in such a way that you do not recognize what it would do to you. 295

ego — Without *guilt* the ego has no life, and God's Son is without *guilt*. 221

ego's — In the ego's teaching, then, there is no escape from *guilt*. 223

ego's — (The ego's belief in *guilt*) is the belief from which all guilt really stems. 77

end — The end of *guilt* is in your hands to give. 385

exclude — Through *guilt* you exclude your Father and your brothers from yourself. 305

Father — It is *guilt* that has obscured the Father from you, and it is *guilt* that has driven you insane. 220

Father — *Guilt* remains the only thing that hides the Father, for *guilt* is the attack upon His Son. 242

fearful — Make no one fearful, for his *guilt* is yours, and by obeying the ego's harsh commandments you bring its condemnation on yourself, and you will not escape the punishment it offers those who obey it. 243

feelings — *Guilt* feelings are preservers of time. 79

feelings — (Feelings of *guilt*) induce fears of retaliation   **79**
        or abandonment, and thus ensure that
        the future will be like the past.

function — This entails the recognition that *guilt* is   **255**
        interference, not salvation, and serves
        no useful function at all.

function — For in the end, whatever form it takes, your   **260**
        guilt arises from your failure to fulfill
        your function in God's Mind with all of
        yours.

God — Can you offer *guilt* to God? You cannot, then,   **269**
        offer it to His Son.

God's — Let the holiness of God's Son shine away the   **222**
        cloud of *guilt* that darkens your mind,
        and by accepting his purity as yours,
        learn of him that it is yours.

guiltlessness — Keep not *guilt* and guiltlessness apart,   **265**
        for your belief that you can have them
        both in meaningless.

guiltlessness — You believe that *guilt* and guiltlessness   **255**
        are both of value, each representing an
        escape from what the other does not
        offer you.

happiness — Whenever the pain of *guilt* seems to attract   **255**
        you, remember that if you yield to it,
        you are deciding against your
        happiness, and will not learn how to be
        happy.

Holy Spirit — The Holy Spirit knows that all salvation is   **258**
        escape from *guilt*.

Holy Spirit's — The undoing of *guilt* is an essential part   **217**
        of the Holy Spirit's teaching.

idea — The idea of *guilt* brings a belief in condemnation   **222**
        of one by another, projecting
        separation in place of unity.

illusion — Now no one need suffer, for you have come   **323**
        too far to yield to the illusion of the
        beauty and holiness of *guilt*.

illusions — Here is the joyful statement that there are no forms of evil that can overcome the Will of God; the glad acknowledgement that *guilt* has not succeeded by your wish to make illusions real. 595

innocense — Cannot you see *guilt* where God knows there is perfect innocence? 244

innocence — There can be no attraction of *guilt* in innocence. 451

invest — What you invest in *guilt* you withdraw from God. 301

kindnesses — (Your kindnesses and every loving thought you ever had) are beyond destruction and beyond *guilt*. 76

Kingdom — In Heaven there is no *guilt*, because the Kingdom is attained through the Atonement, which releases you to create. 77

loss — Whatever way the game of *guilt* is played, there must be loss. 523

love — Love and *guilt* cannot coexist, and to accept one is to deny the other. 221

made — Remember you made *guilt*, and that your plan for the escape from *guilt* has been to bring Atonement to it, and make salvation fearful. 356

mind — *Guilt* is always in your mind, which has condemned itself. 243

minds — Minds that are joined and recognize they are, can feel no *guilt*. 489

over — For *guilt* is over. 547

past — You can hold onto the past only through *guilt*. 222

peace — Peace and *guilt* are antithetical, and the Father can be remembered only in peace. 221

project — Project (*guilt*) not, for while you do, it cannot be undone. 243

projected — You have projected *guilt* blindly and indiscriminately, but you have not uncovered its source. 224

punished — *Guilt* establishes that you will be punished   222
for what you have done, and thus
depends on one-dimensional time,
proceeding from past to future.

punishment — *Guilt* asks for punishment, and its   515
request is granted.

reason — Give no reality to *guilt*, and see no reason for it.   246

reason — The end of *guilt* will never come as long as you   246
believe there is a reason for it.

reason — Your *guilt* is without reason because it is not   247
in the Mind of God, where you are.

release - Release from *guilt* as you would be released.   247

release - Release from *guilt* is the ego's whole undoing.   243

remembering — Yet, characteristically, the ego at-   223
tempts to get rid of *guilt* from its
viewpoint only, for much as the ego
wants to retain *guilt* you find it
intolerable, since *guilt* stands in the way
of your remembering God, whose pull
is so strong that you cannot resist it.

retain — If you are to retain *guilt*, as the ego insists, you   223
cannot be you.

sense — Nor could (the Apostles) speak of the cruci-   87
fixion entirely without anger, because
their sense of *guilt* made them angry.

separation — The acceptance of *guilt* into the mind of   220
God's Son was the beginning of the
separation, as the acceptance of the
Atonement is its end.

sin — Where can *guilt* be when the belief in sin is gone?   385

symbol — Wish not to make yourself a living symbol of   525
his *guilt*, for you will not escape the
death you made for him.

thinking — Guilt is a sure sign that your thinking is   78
unnatural.

thought — *Guilt* feelings are always a sign that you do   78
not know (your thought was created
by God.)

thoughts — *Guilt* is inescapable by those who believe they order their own thoughts, and must therefore obey their dictates.   **78**

world — Send forth to all the world the joyous message of the end of *guilt*, and all the world will answer.   **385**

world — The world you see is a delusional system of those made mad by *guilt*.   **220**

GUILTLESS

attack — What can attack the *guiltless*   **390**

brother — See your brother as *guiltless* as I look on you, and overlook the sins he thinks he sees within himself.   **395**

Christ — You will see (Christ) as you learn the Son of God is *guiltless*.   **221**

eternity — You are not *guiltless* in time, but in eternity.   **221**

God — Unless you are *guiltless* you cannot know God.   **261**

invulnerable — You are invulnerable because you are guiltless.   **222**

love — There is no fear in love, for love is *guiltless*.   **247**

Son of God - Only as you look on (the Son of God) as *guiltless can you understand his oneness.*   **222**

Son of God — For God has never condemned His Son, and being *guiltless* he is eternal.   **223**

Son of God - The Son of God is *guiltless* now, and the brightness of his purity shines untouched forever in God's mind.   **222**

understandng — The *guiltless* and the guilty are totally incapable of understanding one another.   **261**

you — Unless you are *guiltless* you cannot know God, Whose will is that you know Him. Therefore, you must be *guiltless*.   **261**

GUILTLESSNESS

Atonement — The Atonement was established as a means of restoring *guiltlessness* to minds that have denied it, and thus denied Heaven to itself.   **261**

brother's — When you accept a brother's *guiltlessness* you will see the Atonement in him. **259**

establish — How can you, so firmly bound to guilt and committed so to remain, establish for yourself your *guiltlessness.* **277**

guilty — See no one, then, as guilty and you will affirm the truth of *guiltlessness* unto yourself. **245**

happy — Yet you are whole only in your *guiltlessness,* and only in your *guiltlessness* can you be happy. **255**

invulnerability — *Guiltlessness* is invulnerability. **256**

pain — Perhaps you are accustomed to using *guiltlessness* merely to offset the pain of guilt, and do not look upon it as having value in itself. **255**

protect — And you do not realize that it is only your *guiltlessness* that can protect you. **224**

restore — Yet you restore *guiltlessness* to whomever you see as guiltless. **264**

Son of God — Deny your world and judge him not, for his eternal *guiltlessness* is in the Mind of his Father, and protects him forever. **222**

state — The state of *guiltlessness* is only the condition in which what is not there has been removed from the disordered mind that thought it was. **259**

value — You believe that guilt and *guiltlessness* are both of value, each representing an escape from what the other does not offer you. **255**

GUILTY

alone - To be alone is to be *guilty.* **290**

attack — If you did not feel *guilty* you could not attack, for condemnation is the root of attack. **220**

attack — The ego teaches you to attack yourself because you are *guilty,* and this must increase the guilt, for guilt is the result of attack. **223**

attack — Yet to make *guilty* is direct attack, although it   296
     does not seem to be.

believe — But those who believe they are *guilty* will   257
     respond to guilt, because they think it
     is salvation, and will not refuse to see it
     and side with it.

condemn — The *guilty* always condemn, and having   242
     done so they will still condemn, linking
     the future to the past as is the ego's
     law.

ego — For as long as you feel *guilty* you are listening to   217
     the voice of the ego, which tells you
     that you have been treacherous to God
     and therefore deserve death.

ego — If you identify with the ego, you must perceive   77
     yourself as *guilty*.

error — If you allow yourself to feel *guilty*, you will   83
     reinforce the error rather than allow it
     to be undone for you.

God - Very simply, the attempt to make *guilty* is always   317
     directed against God.

God's — Yet you will not realize this until you accept the   220
     eternal fact that God's Son is not *guilty*.

HALLUCINATIONS

disappear — *Hallucinations* disappear when they are   413
     recognized for what they are.

dispel — Yet you are not asked to dispel your *hallucina-*   128
     tions alone.

means — (*Hallucinations*) are the means by which the   413
     outside world, projected from within,
     adjusts to sin and seems to witness to
     its reality.

purpose — One thing is sure; *hallucinations* serve a   413
     purpose, and when that purpose is no
     longer held they disappear.

removed — If you do not want (*hallucinations*) on the basis   128
     of loss of peace, they will be removed
     from your mind for you.

HAPPINESS

ask — And if you do not have (*happiness*) always, being   **434**
what it is, you did not ask for it.

constancy — The constancy of *happiness* has no excep-   **434**
tions; no change of any kind.

constant — *Happiness* must be constant, because it is   **433**
attained by giving up the wish for the
inconstant.

content - Be not content with future *happiness.*   **520**

decide — If he sees his *happiness* as ever changing, now   **433**
this, now that, and now an elusive
shadow attached to nothing, he does
decide against it.

decides — No one decides against his *happiness,* but he   **433**
may do so if he does not see he does it.

fear — You can be sure indeed that any seeming *happiness*   **439**
that does not last is really fear.

fear — Recognize only that the ego's goal, which you   **190**
have pursued so diligently, has merely
brought fear, and it becomes difficult
to maintain that fear is *happiness.*
Upheld by fear, this is what the ego
would have you believe.

following — Think not that *happiness* is ever found by   **609**
following a road away from it.

glad — Be you glad that you are told where *happiness*   **573**
abides, and seek no longer elsewhere.

God — For nothing God created is apart from *happiness,*   **333**
and nothing god created but would
extend *happiness* as its Creator did.

God's — Learn of (God's) *happiness* which is yours.   **276**

misery — The Holy Spirit cannot teach without this   **252**
contrast, for you believe that misery is
happiness.

reason — Reason will tell you that you cannot ask for   **434**
happiness inconstantly.

will — But it is given you to know that God's function is   **190**
yours, and *happiness* cannot be found
apart from your joint will.

world — It needs but two who would have *happiness* this day to promise it to all the world.   **584**

HAPPY

decision — Be *happy;* and you gave the power of decision to Him Who must decide for God for you.   **418**

immutable — You cannot be *happy* unless you do what you will truly, and you cannot change this because it is immutable.   **182**

world — In this world, it is impossible to create. Yet it is possible to make *happy.*   **333**

HATE

ancient — An ancient *hate* is passing from the world.   **592**

call — Hear not the call of *hate,* and see no fantasies.   **316**

call — See in the call of *hate,* and in every fantasy that rises to delay you, but the call for help that rises ceaselessly from you to your Creator.   **316**

cause — When ancient memories of *hate* appear, remember that their cause is gone.   **548**

fear — For *hate* must father fear, and look upon its father as itself.   **602**

hide — It is essential to bring (*hate*) into sight, and to make no attempt to hide it.   **314**

illusion — For *hate* is an illusion, and what can change was never love.   **314**

limit — You cannot limit *hate.*   **314**

love — For *hate* to be maintained, love must be feared; and only sometimes present, sometimes gone.   **564**

love — For it is the attempt to balance *hate* with love that makes love meaningless to you.   **314**

symbols — The symbols of *hate* against the symbols of love play out a conflict that does not exist.   **314**

target — Yet *hate* must have a target.   **431**

understand — You do not understand Who calls to you   **602**
beyond each form of *hate;* each call to
war.

HATRED

look — You may wonder why it is so crucial that you   **225**
look upon your *hatred* and realize its full
extent.

love — As long as the illusion of *hatred* lasts, so long will   **315**
love be an illusion to you.

love — Do not let your *hatred* stand in the way of love,   **204**
for nothing can withstand the Love of
Christ for His Father, or His Father's
Love for Him.

love — The holiest of all spots on earth is where an   **522**
ancient *hatred* has become a present
love.

mind — That is why you must realize that your *hatred* is   **207**
in your mind and not outside it before
you can get rid of it; and why you must
get rid of it before you can perceive the
world as it really is.

strength — You associate love with weakness and *hatred*   **226**
with strength, and your own real
power seems to you as your real
weakness.

HAVING

being — This is how *having* and being are ultimately   **108**
reconciled, not in the Kingdom, but in
your mind.

giving — At this point, the equality of *having* and giving   **99**
is not perceived. Until it is, *having*
appears to be the opposite of giving.

giving — You learn first that *having* rests on giving, and   **102**
not on getting.

recognition — The recognition of *having* is the willing-   **154**
ness for giving, and only by this
willingness can you recognize what
you have.

HEAL

brothers — *Heal* your brothers simply by accepting God   **171**
for them.

decision — If sickness is separation, the decision to *heal*   **182**
and to be healed is the first step toward
recognizing what you truly want.

faith — To have faith is to *heal*.   **373**

God — To *heal* is the only kind of thinking in this world   **105**
that resembles the Thought of God,
and because of he elements they share,
can transfer easily to it.

hate — And it will be impossible for you to hate what   **447**
serves whom you would *heal*.

healed — And being healed, the power to *heal* must also   **565**
now be yours.

perception — To *heal*, then, is to correct perception in   **106**
your brother and yourself by sharing
the Holy Spirit with him.

remembering — When you *heal*, you are remembering   **109**
the laws of God and forgetting the laws
of the ego.

Son of God — Every situation, properly perceived, be-   **371**
comes an opportunity to *heal* the Son of
God.

unite — Therefore, to *heal* is to unite with those who are   **136**
like you, because perceiving this
likeness is to recognize the Father.

whole — To *heal* is to make whole.   **595**

yourself — You can *heal* only yourself, for only God's   **183**
Son needs healing.

HEALED

body — The body is *healed* because you came without   **371**
it, and joined the Mind in which all
healing rests.

brother — Your healing saves him pain as well as you,   **529**
and you are *healed* because you wished
him well.

cause — You have accepted healing's cause, and so it   **565**
must be you are *healed*.

fearful — The fearful are not *healed*, and cannot heal.   **535**

forgives — Who forgives is *healed*.   **528**

forgiving — Let yourself be *healed* that you may be forgiving, offering salvation to your brother and yourself.   **529**

goal — For to be *healed* is to perceive one goal, because you have accepted only one and want but one.   **215**

heal — Be *healed* that you may heal, and suffer not the laws of sin to be applied to you.   **539**

heal — The only way to heal is to be *healed*.   **535**

offer — But he can let himself be *healed* and thus offer the other what he has received.   **535**

Son of God — (The Son of God) is *healed* because you offered faith to him, giving him to the Holy Spirit and releasing him from every demand your ego would make of him.   **371**

wish — If you wish only to be *healed*, you heal.   **535**

HEALER(S)

contribution — The only meaningful contribution the *healer* can make is to present an example of one whose direction has been changed for him, and who no longer believes in nightmares of any kind.   **160**

"fearful" — The "fearful" *healer* is a contradiction in terms, and is therefore a concept that only a conflicted mind could possibly perceive as meaningful.   **112**

heal — There have been many *healers* who did not heal themselves.   **82**

Holy Spirit — Unless the *healer* always heals by (the Holy Spirit) the results will vary.   **112**

readiness — The *healers* who relies on his own readiness is endangering his understanding.   **22**

unhealed — All unhealed *healers* follow the ego's plan for forgiveness in one form or another.   **159**

unhealed — By definition, (the unhealed *healer*) is trying to give what he has not received.   **159**

unhealed — Every *healer* who searches fantasies for   **159**
            truth must be unhealed, because he
            does not know where to look for truth,
            and therefore does not have the
            answer to the problem of healing.

unhealed — If an unhealed *healer* is a theologian, for   **159**
            example, he may begin with the
            premise, "I am a miserable sinner, and
            so are you."

unhealed — It my help someone to point out where he is   **160**
            heading, but the point is lost unless he
            is also helped to change his direction.
            The unhealed *healer* cannot do this for
            him, since he cannot do it for himself.

unhealed — Nothing real has happened to the unhealed   **160**
            healer, and he must learn from his own
            teaching.

unhealed — The lesson (of the unhealed *healer*) is limited   **112**
            by his own ingratitude, which is a
            lesson in sickness.

unhealed — (The unhealed *healer*) cannot correct, be-   **160**
            cause he is not working correctively.

unhealed — The unhealed *healer* obviously does not   **111**
            understand his own vocation.

unhealed — The unhealed *healer* therefore does not   **160**
            know how to give, and consequently
            cannot share.

unhealed — The unhealed *healer* wants gratitude from   **112**
            his brothers, but he is not grateful to
            them.

HEALING

ability — *Healing* is the one ability everyone can develop,   **111**
            and must develope if he is to be healed.

afraid — But if you are afraid of *healing,* then it cannot   **535**
            come through you.

apparent — But *healing* is apparent in specific instances,   **536**
            and generalizes to include them all.

Atonement — The Atonement, or the final miracle, is a   **19**
            remedy and any type of *healing* is a
            result.

Atonement — The miracle is the means, the Atonement   **19**
  is the principle, and *healing* is the result.

body — (The body) needs no *healing*.   **371**

charity — This is because *healing* rests on charity, and   **23**
  charity is a way of perceiving the
  perfection of another even if you
  cannot perceive it in yourself.

Christ — *Healing* is the love of Christ for His Father and   **203**
  for Himself.

Christ — *Healing* reflects (the joint will of Christ and   **134**
  you.)

communication — *Healing* is the result of using the body   **142**
  solely for communication.

content — Be you content with *healing*, for Christ's gift   **242**
  you can bestow, and your Father's gift
  you cannot lose.

counted — *Healing* can be counted on because it is in-   **112**
  spired by His voice, and is in accord
  with His laws.

creating — *Healing* is not creating; it is reparation.   **69**

danger — *Healing* is a way of forgetting the sense of   **110**
  danger the ego has induced in you, by
  not recognizing its existence in your
  brother.

decision — *Healing* is release from the fear of waking   **147**
  and the substitution of the decision to
  wake.

differences — *Healing* is the way to undo the belief in   **110**
  differences, being the only way to
  perceiving the Sonship as one.

effort — Nothing employed for *healing* represents an   **547**
  effort to do anything at all.

everyone — *Healing* must be for everyone, because he   **502**
  does not merit an attack of any kind.

exceptions — Fear always makes exceptions. *Healing*   **112**
  never does.

extend — Your *healing* will extend, and will be brought to   **537**
  problems you thought were not your
  own.

fear — All *healing* is essentially the release from fear.   **19**

fear — The only thing that is required for a *healing* is a lack of fear.   **535**

frightening — Is *healing* frightening? To many, yes.   **528**

gladden — Fear does not gladden. *Healing* does.   **112**

God — *Healing* does not come directly from God Who knows His creations as perfectly whole. Yet *healing* is still of God, because it proceeds from His voice and from His laws.   **109**

God — Do not look to the god of sickness for *healing* but only to the God of love, for *healing* is the acknowledgement of Him.   **177**

God — He has not learned that every mind God created is equally worthy of (*healing*) because God created it whole.   **85**

God — For God gave *healing* not apart from sickness, nor established remedy where sickness cannot be.   **372**

God's Son — Forget not that the *healing* of God's Son is all the world is for.   **476**

harmony — *Healing* always produces harmony, because it proceeds from integration.   **112**

health — Your *healing*, then, is part of His health, since it is part of His wholeness.   **148**

Holy Spirit — The Holy Spirit does not work by chance, and *healing* that is of Him always works.   **112**

Holy Spirit's — *Healing* is the Holy Spirit's form of communication in this world, and the only one He accepts.   **111**

idea — The Holy Spirit is the idea of *healing*. Being the Call for God, it is also the idea of God.   **72**

knowledge — *Healing*, then, is a way of approaching knowledge by thinking in accordance with the laws of God, and recognizing their universality.   **110**

knowledge — What is *healing* but the removal of all that stands in the way of knowledge?   **188**

lawful — All *healing* must proceed in lawful manner, in accord with laws that have been properly perceived but never violated.   **537**

love — The decision to wake is the reflection of the will to love, since all *healing* involves replacing fear with love.   **147**

mind — Help and *healing* are the normal expressions of a mind that is working through the body, but not in it.   **142**

mind — Yet must all *healing* come about because the mind is recognized as not within the body, and its innocence is quite apart from it, and where all *healing* is.   **551**

minds — *Healing* is the effect of minds that join, as sickness comes from minds that separate.   **553**

miracle — *Healing* is not a miracle.   **19**

miracle — A miracle of *healing* proves that separation is without effect.   **529**

mysterious — *Healing* is not mysterious.   **160**

need — Would you bring anything else to the Sonship, recognizing your need of *healing* for yourself? For in this lies the beginning of the return to knowledge; the foundation on which God will help build again the thought system you share with Him.   **180**

need — You have learned your need of *healing*.   **180**

need — You need (*healing*) because you do not understand yourself, and therefore know not what you do.   **183**

offer — Everyone you offer *healing* to returns it.   **256**

one — For *healing* will be one or not at all, its oneness being where the *healing* is.   **561**

pain — He does not join in pain, understanding that *healing* pain is not accomplished by delusional attempts to enter into it, and lighten it by sharing the delusion.   **307**

past — All *healing* is release from the past.   **240**

power — For *healing* comes of power, and attack of helplessness.   **432**

present — (*Healing*) must be accomplished in the present to release the future.   **230**

protection — However, as long as time persists, *healing* is needed as a means of protection.   **23**

sacrifice — Who, then, fears *healing*. Only those to whom their brother's sacrifice and pain are seen to represent their own serenity.   **530**

separation — Before (the separation) there was no need for *healing,* for no one was comfortless.   **68**

separation — *Healing* is an ability that developed after the separation, before which it was unnecessary.   **23**

separation — *Healing* is the way in which separation is overcome.   **134**

sin — If you choose sin instead of *healing,* you would condemn the Son of God to what can never be corrected.   **429**

Sonship — That is why it makes no difference to what part or by what part of the Sonship the *healing* is offered. Every part benefits, and benefits equally.   **66**

Sonship — And in your *healing* is the Sonship healed because your wills are joined.   **448**

specialness — This is the law the miracle obeys; that *healing* sees no specialness at all.   **529**

step — Step gently aside, and let *healing* be done for you.   **307**

strengthens — *Healing* only strengthens.   **111**

suffering — *Healing* replaces suffering.   **536**

thought — *Healing* is a thought by which two minds perceive their oneness and become glad.   **66**

time — *Healing* in time is needed, for joy cannot establish its eternal reign where sorrow dwells.   **240**

truth — Because you see them as they are, you offer them your acceptance of their truth, so   **35**

they can accept it for themselves. This
is the *healing* that the miracle induces.

understanding — *Healing* thus becomes a lesson in 183
understanding, and the more you
practice it the better teacher and
learner you become.

understood — Yet if *healing* is consistent it cannot be 112
inconsistently understood.

venture — That is why *healing* is a collaborative venture. 134

whole — *Healing* is a sign that you want to make whole. 183

wholeness — By your *healing* you learn of wholeness, 110
and by learning of wholeness you learn
to remember God.

will — That is why *healing* is the beginning of the recog- 182
nition that your will is His.

world — Thus is your *healing* everything the world re- 536
quires, that it may be healed.

HEALTH

Holy Spirit — *Health* is seen as the natural state of 146
everything when interpretation is left
to the Holy Spirit, who perceives no
attack on anything.

home — Your home is built upon your brother's *health,* 562
upon his happiness, his sinlessness,
and everything his Father promised
him.

life — *Health* is the beginning of the proper perspective 146
on life under the guidance of the one
Teacher Who knows what life is, being
the Voice for Life itself.

lovelessly — *Health* is the result of relinquishing all 146
attempts to use the body lovelessly.

peace — *Health* is inner peace. 15

purpose — *Health* is therefore nothing more than united 143
purpose.

see — Your *health* is a result of your desire to see your 529
brother with no blood upon his hands,
nor guilt upon his heart made heavy
with the proof of sin.

world — *Health* in this world is the counterpart of value   **172**
    in Heaven.

HEAR
will — For you will *hear*, and you will choose again.   **621**

HEAVEN
advance — *Heaven* is joined with you in your advance to   **354**
    Heaven.

anywhere — Life not in Heaven is impossible, and what   **459**
    is not in *Heaven* is not anywhere.

choose — Until you choose *Heaven*, you are in hell and   **440**
    misery.

choose — You but choose whether to go toward *Heaven*,   **511**
    or away to nowhere.

completion — To everyone *Heaven* is completion. There   **318**
    can be no disagreement on this, be-
    cause both the ego and the Holy Spirit
    accept it.

contrast — *Heaven* is perfectly unambiguous. Everything   **248-249**
    is clear and bright, and calls forth one
    response. There is no darkness and
    there is no contrast.

death — And even though you know not *Heaven*, might   **228**
    it not be more desirable than death?

difficult — Think not the way to *Heaven's* gate is difficult   **511**
    at all.

gift — *Heaven* is the gift you owe your brother, the debt   **395**
    of gratitude you offer to the Son of
    God in thanks for what he is, and what
    his Father created him to be.

given — Each part of *Heaven* that you bring is given you.   **448**

God — Have faith in only this one thing, and it will be   **249**
    sufficient: God wills you be in *Heaven*,
    and nothing can keep you from it, or it
    from you.

God — And *Heaven* remains the Will of God for you.   **270**

God's Son — *Heaven* waits for his return, for it was   **178**
    created as the dwelling place of God's
    Son.

guilt — In *Heaven* there is no guilt, because the Kingdom is attained through the Atonement, which releases you to create.   77

hand — You can stretch out your hand and reach to *Heaven*.   360

hell — Yet neither oblivion nor hell is as unacceptable to you as *Heaven*.   228

hell — And so you walk toward *Heaven* or toward hell, but not alone.   491

home — *Heaven* is your home, and being in God it must also be in you.   213

home — *Heaven* waits for his return, for it was created as the dwelling place of God's Son. You are not at home anywhere else, or in any other condition.   178

homecoming — There will be great joy in *Heaven* on your homecoming, and the joy will be yours.   225

illusions — There is no part of *Heaven* you can take and weave into illusions.   440

joy — And how great will be the joy in *Heaven* when you join the mighty chorus to the Love of God!   511

joy — The joy of *Heaven*, which has no limit, is increased with each light that returns to take its rightful place within it.   323

knows — For *Heaven* knows you well, as you know *Heaven*.   381

oneness — *Heaven* is not a place nor a condition. It is merely an awareness of perfect oneness, and the knowledge that there is nothing else; nothing outside this oneness, and nothing else within.   359

purity — *Heaven* is the home of perfect purity, and God created it for you.   441

reflect — You can reflect *Heaven* here.   271

sure — Yet *Heaven* is sure.   352

threat — Your definition of *Heaven* is hell and oblivion, and the real *Heaven* is the greatest threat you think you could experience.   228

true — *Heaven* is wholly true.   **461**

unambiguous — *Heaven* is perfectly unambiguous.   **248**

union — *Heaven* itself is union with all creation, and with its one Creator.   **270**

union — For what is *Heaven* but union, direct and perfect, and without the veil of fear upon it?   **402**

value — When we are all united in *Heaven,* you will value nothing that you value here.   **248**

yours — There is no chance that *Heaven* will not be yours, for God is sure, and what He wills is as sure as He is.   **250**

yours — You do not have to know that *Heaven* is yours to make it so.   **250**

HELL

belief — The belief in *hell* is inescapable to those who identify with the ego.   **280**

belief — The belief in *hell* is what prevents you from understanding the present, because you are afraid of it.   **281**

ego — *Hell* is only what the ego has made of the present.   **281**

ego — The ego teaches that *hell* is in the future, for this is what all its teaching is directed to.   **280**

ego's — *Hell* is (the ego's) goal.   **280**

guilt — But the belief in guilt must lead to the belief in *hell,* and always does.   **281**

guilt — The appeal of *hell* lies only in the terrible attraction of guilt, which the ego holds out to those who place their faith in littleness.   **319**

Heaven — And so you walk toward Heaven or toward *hell,* but not alone.   **491**

Holy Spirit — The Holy Spirit teaches thus: There is no *hell.*   **281**

purpose — For we are one in purpose, and the end of *hell* is near.   **622**

salvation — To every part of true creation has the Lord of Love and Life entrusted all salvation from the misery of *hell.*   **617**

world — There is no place for *hell* within a world whose loveliness can yet be so intense and so inclusive it is but a step from there to Heaven. **621**

HELP

anger — Can anyone be justified in responding with anger to a brother's plea for *help*. **200**

appeal — If you believe that an appeal for *help* is something else you will react to something else. **200**

brother — Deny (a brother) your *help* and you will not recognize God's Answer to you. **201**

call — For the sake of your need, then, hear every call for *help* as what it is, so God can answer you. **201**

call — To fail to recognize a call for *help* is to refuse *help*. **201**

giving — By giving *help* you are asking for it, and if you perceive but one need in yourself you will be healed. **201**

loving — Every loving thought is true. Everything else is an appeal for healing and *help*, regardless of the form it takes. **200**

recognizing — There is nothing to prevent you from recognizing all calls for *help* as exactly what they are except your own imagined need to attack. **200**

HELPFUL

God's — The truly *helpful* are God's miracle workers, whom I direct until we are all united in the joy of the Kingdom. **65**

I — I will direct you to wherever you can be truly *helpful*, and to whoever can follow my guidance through you. **65**

invulnerable — The truly *helpful* are invulnerable, because they are not protecting their egos and so nothing can hurt them. **65**

HELPFULNESS

praise — Their *helpfulness* is their praise of God, and He will return their praise of Him because they are like Him, and they can rejoice together.   **65**

HELPLESS

deceive — Deceive yourself no longer that you are *helpless* in the face of what is done to you.   **418**

sin — Being *helpless* is the cost of sin.   **430**

Son of God — And those who see themselves as *helpless* must believe that they are not the Son of God.   **430**

HELPLESSNESS

attack — For healing comes of power, and attack of *helplessness*.   **432**

HIDDEN

apart — The *hidden* is kept apart, but value always lies in joint appreciation.   **265**

hide — For what you would hide is *hidden* from you.   **290**

shared — Nothing has *hidden* value, for what is *hidden* cannot be shared, and so its value is unknown.   **265**

terrify — And yet it is only the *hidden* that can terrify, not for what it is, but for its hiddenness.   **265**

HINDRANCE

God — There is no *hindrance* to the will of God, nor any need that you repeat again a journey that was over long ago.   **513**

little — A little *hindrance* can seem large indeed to those who do not understand that miracles are all the same.   **511**

HOLINESS

brother — But *holiness* would set your brother free, removing hatred by removing fear, not as a symptom, but at its source.   **422**

brother's — Before your brother's *holiness* the world is still, and peace descends on it in gentleness and blessing so complete that not one trace of conflict still remains to haunt you in the darkness of the night.   **475**

brother's — Be thankful, rather, it is given you to see (your brother's) *holiness* because it is the truth.   **479**

brother's — Make not (your brother's) holiness a sacrifice to your belief in sin.   **505**

brother's — Your brother's *holiness* is sacrament and benediction unto you.   **477**

brother's — Your brother's *holiness* shows you that God is one with him and you; that what he has is yours because you are not separate from him nor from his Father.   **475**

change — Time is inconceivable without change, yet *holiness* does not change.   **282**

content — Holy Child of God, when will you learn that only *holiness* can content you and give you peace?   **287**

contradiction — There is no contradiction in what *holiness* calls forth.   **272**

extension — Concern yourself not with the extension of *holiness,* for the nature of miracles you do not understand.   **309**

faith — As *holiness* and faith go hand in hand, so must its faith go everywhere with it.   **343**

faith — You did not set (the goal of *holiness*) because *holiness* cannot be seen except through faith, and your relationship was not holy because your faith in your brother was so limited and little.   **343**

faith — Faith and belief and vision are the means by which the goal of *holiness* is reached.   **421**

goal — But remember this; the goal of *holiness* was set for your relationship, and not by you.   **343**

God — Think but an instant just on this; you can behold the *holiness* God gave His Son.   **414**

guilt — And you will turn from time to *holiness,* as surely   272
  as the reflection of *holiness* calls every-
  one to lay all guilt aside.

healing — There is no contradiction in what *holiness*   272
  calls forth. Its one response is healing,
  without regard for what is brought to
  it.

holy — You must be holy if you offer *holiness.*   282

impartial — Yet will his perfect sinlessness release you   476
  both, for *holiness* is quite impartial, with
  one judgment made for all it looks
  upon.

innocence — For *holiness* is seen through holy eyes that   618
  look upon the innocence within, and
  thus expect to see it everywhere.

leads — The *holiness* that leads us is within us, as is our   399
  home.

life — The presence of *holiness* lives in everything that   271
  lives, for *holiness* created life, and leaves
  not what it created holy as itself.

power — For *holiness* is power, and by sharing it, it gains   293
  strength.

power — The power of *holiness* and the weakness of   310
  attack are both being brought into
  your awareness.

separation — All separation vanishes as *holiness* is   293
  shared.

shared — *Holiness* must be shared, for therein lies every-   264
  thing that makes it holy.

sin — For *holiness* is merely the result of letting the   410
  effects of sin be lifted, so what was
  always true is recognized.

temple — In the temple, *holiness* waits quietly for the   271
  return of them that love it.

time — *Holiness* lies not in time, but in eternity.   283

vision — For all who choose to look away from sin are   422
  given vision, and are led to *holiness.*

HOLY INSTANT

accept — It is impossible to accept the *holy instant* without reservation unless, just for an instant, you are willing to see no past or future.   **362**

answer — In the *holy instant,* you can bring the question to the answer, and receive the answer that was made for you.   **535**

answer — (The *holy instant*) is the answer.   **354**

answer — The *holy instant* is the interval in which the mind is still enough to hear an answer that is not entailed within the question asked.   **534**

attack — To attack your brother is not to lose the *(holy) instant,* but to make it powerless in its effects.   **340**

bodies — In the *holy instant* there are no bodies, and you experience only the attraction of God.   **301**

brothers — In this *holy instant* you will unchain all your brothers, and refuse to support either their weakness or your own.   **284**

calls — (The *holy instant*) calls you to be yourself, within its safe embrace.   **362**

case — The *holy instant* is nothing more than a special case, or an extreme example, of what every situation is meant to be.   **345**

Christ — And the extent to which you learn to accept (Christ) is the measure of the time in which the *holy instant* will be yours.   **289**

Christ — The *holy instant* is truly the time of Christ.   **302**

claim — You can claim the *holy instant* any time and anywhere you want it.   **288**

communication — The *holy instant* is a time in which you receive and give perfect communication.   **289**

communication — (the *holy instant*) is the recognition that all minds are in communication.   **289**

conflict — In the *holy instant* there is no conflict of needs, for there is only one.   **292**

determination — The *holy instant* is the result of your determination to be holy.   **354**

difficult — If you believe the *holy instant* is difficult for   356
you, it is because you have become the
arbiter of what is possible, and remain
unwilling to give place to One Who
Knows.

difficulty — Your difficulty with the *holy instant* arises   355
from your fixed conviction that you
are not worthy of it.

ego's — Against the ego's insane notion of salvation the   324
Holy Spirit gently lays the *holy instant.*

eternal — The *holy instant* is eternal, and your illusions   325
of time will not prevent the timeless
from being what it is, nor you from
experiencing it as it is.

eternity — The *holy instant* is a miniature of eternity.   335

eternity — For the *holy instant* reaches to eternity, and to   292
the Mind of God.

fails — The *holy instant* never fails.   337

fear — Do not be concerned with time, and fear not the   283
(holy instant) that will remove all fear.

fear — Fear not the *holy instant* will be denied you, for I   294
denied it not.

forever — You could live forever in the *holy instant,*   289
beginning now and reaching to eter-
nity, but for a very simple reason.

function — Never approach the *holy instant* after you   357
have tried to remove all fear and hatred
from your mind. That is its function.

God — Yet in the *holy instant* you unite directly with God,   292
and all your brothers join in Christ.

God — In the *holy instant,* in which you see yourself as   282
bright with freedom, you will remem-
ber God.

God's — What is the *holy instant* but God's appeal to you   434
to recognize what He has given you?

guilt — In the *holy instant* guilt holds no attraction, since   297
communication has been restored.

guilt — The *holy instant* is His most helpful aid in protecting you from the attraction of guilt, the real lure in the special relationship. 321

happened — The *holy instant* has not yet happened to you. 284

happens — In the *holy instant* nothing happens that has not always been. 293

healed — Come to the *holy instant* and be healed, for nothing that is there received is left behind on your returning to the world. 536

Heaven — The *holy instant* is a miniature of Heaven, sent you from Heaven. 335

holiness — From this *holy instant* wherein holiness was born again you will go forth in time without fear, and with no sense of change with time. 282

Holy Spirit — In the *holy instant* the power of the Holy Spirit will prevail, because you joined Him. 325

Holy Spirit — Offer the miracle of the *holy instant* through the Holy Spirit, and leave His giving it to you to Him. 283

Holy Spirit — (The Holy Spirit) joins with you to make the *holy instant* far greater than you can understand. 355

Holy Spirit's — The *holy instant* is the Holy Spirit's most useful learning device for teaching you love's meaning. 290

impossible — It is impossible that the *holy instant* will come to either of you without the other. And it will come to both at the request of either. 358

impossible — It is through the *holy instant* that what seems impossible is accomplished, making it evident that it is not impossible. 297

instant — The *holy instant* is this instant and every instant. 288

joined — You have joined with many in the *holy instant*, and they have joined with you. 339

laws — In the *holy instant* the laws of God prevail, and   293
    only they have meaning.

learning — The *holy instant* does not replace the need for   298
    learning, for the Holy Spirit must not
    leave you as your Teacher until the
    holy instant has extended far beyond
    time.

lesson — The *holy instant* thus becomes a lesson in how to   293
    hold all your brothers in your mind,
    experiencing not loss but completion.

love — For in the *holy instant*, free of the past, you see   292
    that love is in you, and you have no
    need to look without and snatch love
    guiltily from where you thought it
    was.

love — In the *holy instant* the condition of love is met, for   305
    minds are joined without the body's
    interference, and where there is com-
    munication there is peace.

love — In the *holy instant* you ask of love only what it   366
    offers everyone, neither less nor more.

love — In the *holy instant* you recognize the idea of love in   293
    you, and unite this idea with the Mind
    that thought it, and could not relin-
    quish it.

love — The *holy instant* in which you were united is but   369
    the messenger of love, sent from be-
    yong forgiveness to remind you of all
    that lies beyond it.

love — The *holy instant* is your invitation to love to enter   366
    into your bleak and joyless kingdom,
    and to transform it into a garden of
    peace and welcome.

message — Seek and find His message in the *holy instant*,   326
    where all illusions are forgiven.

miracle — The miracle of the *holy instant* lies in your   355
    willingness to let it be what it is.

miracle's — The *holy instant* is the miracle's abiding place.   535

need — In the *holy instant* you will recognize the only need the Sons of God share equally, and by this recognition you will join with me in offering what is needed.   294

one — There is but one *(holy instant.)*   405

past — In the *holy instant* it is understood that the past is gone, and with its passing the drive for vengeance has been uprooted and has disappeared.   325

peace — Peace will join you (in the *holy instant*), simply because you have been willing to let go the limits you have placed upon love, and joined it where it is and where it led you, in answer to its gentle call to be at peace.   362

preparation — The preparation for the *holy instant* belongs to Him Who gives it.   356

preparing — In preparing for the *holy instant,* do not attempt to make yourself holy to be ready to receive it.   355

problems — It is in (the *holy instant*) that all your problems should be brought and left.   533

received — You have received the *holy instant,* but you may have established a condition in which you cannot use it.   340

recognition — The *holy instant* is not an instant of creation, but of recognition.   419

relationship — In the *holy instant* you see in each relationship what it will be when you perceive only the present.   291

relationship — The *holy instant* is the shining example, the clear and unequivocal demonstration, of the meaning of every relationship and every situation, seen as a whole.   344

relationships — All your relationships are blessed in the *holy instant,* because the blessing is not limited.   292

relationships — In the *holy instant,* where the Great Rays replace the body of awareness, the recognition of relationships without limits is given you.   **300**

release — In these instants of release from physical restrictions, you experience much of what happens in the *holy instant;* the lifting of barriers of time and space, the sudden experience of peace and joy, and, above all, the lack of awareness of the body, and of the questioning whether or not all this is possible.   **361**

reminder — In the *holy instant* is His reminder that His Son will always be exactly as he was created.   **325**

request — (The *holy instant*) will come to both at the request of either.   **358**

separating — Start now to practice your little part in separating out the *holy instant.*   **284**

shared — The *(holy instant)* is shared and cannot be yours alone.   **282**

sin — The *holy instant* will replace all sin if you but carry its effects with you.   **539**

special — In the *holy instant* no one is special, for your personal needs intrude on no one to make your brothers seem different.   **291**

thanks — To give thanks to one another is to appreciate the *holy instant,* and thus enable its results to be accepted and shared.   **340**

timelessness — (the *holy instant*) is a picture of timelessness, set in a frame of time.   **335**

willingness — The *holy instant* does not come from your little willingness alone.   **355**

HOLY SPIRIT

abide — You must have set aside a place in which the *Holy Spirit* can abide, and where He is.   **426**

abilities — All abilities should therefore be given over to the *Holy Spirit,* who understands how to use them properly.   **110**

accepts — The ego analyzes; the *Holy Spirit* accepts. **190**

answer — Be certain any answer to a problem the *Holy* **501** Spirit solves will always be one in which no one loses.

Answer — Remember that the *Holy Spirit* is the Answer, **92** not the question.

Answer — (The *Holy Spirit*) is the Answer to everything, **146** because He knows what the answer to everything is.

answer — It is possible that (the answer of the *Holy* **153** *Spirit)* will not be heard.

answering — The *Holy Spirit* will not delay in answering **261** your every question what to do.

answers — The *Holy Spirit* does not speak first, but He **93** always answers.

ask — You can ask for everything of the *Holy Spirit*, be- **151** cause your requests to Him are real, being of your right mind.

Atonement — (The *Holy Spirit*) came into being with the **68** separation, as a protection, inspiring the Atonement principle at the same time.

Atonement — The *Holy Spirit* is God's Answer to the **69** separation; the means by which the Atonement heals until the whole mind returns to creating.

Atonement — The *Holy Spirit* is the Mind of the Atone- **68** ment.

Atonement — The *(Holy Spirit)* shares my trust and **62** accepts my Atonement decisions be- cause My Will is never out of accord with His.

atones — The *Holy Spirit* atones in all of us by undoing. **76**

attack — The *Holy Spirit's* perception leaves no ground **502** for an attack.

belief — The *Holy Spirit* will teach you to perceive **121** beyond your belief, because truth is beyond belief and His perception is true.

213

believe — Coming from God (the *Holy Spirit*) uses every-   **90**
thing for good, but He does not believe
in what is not true.

blessing — (The *Holy Spirit*) is the only blessing you can   **81**
truly give, because He is truly blessed.

blocks — The *Holy Spirit* merely teaches you how to re-   **261**
move the blocks that stand between
you and what you know.

body — The *Holy Spirit* sees the body only as a means of   **97**
communication, and because com-
munication is sharing, it becomes
communion.

body — The *Holy Spirit* teaches you to use your body only   **145**
to reach your brothers, so He can teach
His message through you.

bridge — The *Holy Spirit* is the bridge for the transfer of   **72**
perception to knowledge, so we can use
the terms as if they were related, because in His Mind they are.

bridge — The ego's perception has no counterpart in   **90**
God, but the *Holy Spirit* remains the
bridge between perception and knowledge.

brother — It is only the *Holy Spirit* in (your brother) that   **113**
never changes His mind.

brother — When you look with gentle graciousness   **379**
upon your brother, you are beholding
(the *Holy Spirit*).

call — The *Holy Spirit* is the call to awaken and be glad.   **71**

choice — The *Holy Spirit* is the part of your mind that   **70**
always speaks for the right choice,
because He speaks for God.

choice — The choice for the *Holy Spirit* is the choice for   **70**
God.

Christ — The *Holy Spirit* keeps the vision of Christ for   **212**
every Son of God who sleeps.

Christ's — The *Holy Spirit* serves Christ's purpose in   **483**
your mind, so that the aim of special-
ness can be corrected where the error
lies.

comforted — Be comforted, and feel the *Holy Spirit* watching over you in love and perfect confidence in what he sees. — **406**

commands — The *Holy Spirit* never commands. To command is to assume inequality which the *Holy Spirit* demonstrates does not exist. — **95**

communication — Remember that the *Holy Spirit* is the communication link between God the Father and His separated Sons. — **88**

communication — The *Holy Spirit* is the highest communication medium. — **4**

communication — The *Holy Spirit* mediates higher to lower communication, keeping the direct channel from God to you open for revelation. — **6**

communication — The *Holy Spirit,* Who leads to God, translates communication into being, just as He ultimately translates perception into knowledge. — **97**

communication — There is complete communication failure between (the ego and the *Holy Spirit*). — **151**

communion — (The *Holy Spirit*) is in communion with God always, and He is part of you. — **74**

concern — The concern and care (of the *Holy Spirit*) for you are limitless. — **298**

condemnation — Let the *Holy Spirit* remove all offenses of God's Son against Himself and perceive no one but through His guidance, for He would save you from all condemnation. — **198**

conflict — (The *Holy Spirit*) resolves the apparent conflict (illusions) engender by perceiving conflict as meaningless. — **115**

communication — By attacking nothing, (the *Holy Spirit*) presents no barrier to communication with God. — **91**

danger — The *Holy Spirit* is as vigilant as the ego to the   73
        call of danger, opposing it with His
        strength just as the ego welcomes it.

darkness — The *Holy Spirit* is the radiance that you must   69
        let banish the idea of darkness.

deceived — The *Holy Spirit* is not deceived by anything   164
        you do, because he never forgets what
        you are.

decision — The *Holy Spirit*, like the ego, is a decision.   78

decisions — Make no decisions about what (salvation) is   257
        or where it lies, but ask the *Holy Spirit*
        everything, and leave all decisions to
        His gentle counsel.

decisions — The decisions (of the *Holy Spirit*) are re-   258
        flections of what God knows about
        you, and in this light, error of any kind
        becomes impossible.

doubt — You whose mind is darkened by doubt and   249
        guilt, remember this: God gave the
        Holy Spirit to you, and gave Him the
        mission to remove all doubt and every
        trace of guilt His dear Son has laid upon
        himself.

dreams — The core of dreams the *Holy Spirit* gives is   569
        never one of fear.

dreams — The *Holy Spirit* makes no distinction among   96
        dreams. He merely shines them away.

dreams — (Your brother) asks for help in every dream   570
        he has, and you have help to give him if
        you perceive the function of the dream
        as (the *Holy Spirit*) perceives its
        function, Who can utilize all dreams as
        a means to fulfill the function given
        Him.

effects — You judge effects, but (the *Holy Spirit*) has   545
        judged their cause.

efforts — Being conflict free, (the *Holy Spirit*) maximizes   107
        all efforts and results.

ego — Remember, however, what the *Holy Spirit* rejects, the ego accepts. **100**

ego — The ego's goal is as unified as the *Holy Spirit's*, and it is because of this that their goals can never be reconciled in any way or to any extent. **110**

ego — (The *Holy Spirit*) can therefore perform the function of reinterpreting what the ego makes, not by destruction but by understanding. **73**

ego — The *Holy Spirit* has the task of undoing what the ego has made. **73**

ego's — Everything of which the *Holy Spirit* reminds you is in direct opposition to the ego's notions, because true and false perceptions are themselves opposed. **72**

ego's — (The ability of the *Holy Spirit*) to deal with symbols enables Him to work with the ego's beliefs in its own language. **73**

ego's — The *Holy Spirit* judges against the reality of the ego's thought system merely because He knows its foundation is not true. **165**

error — The *Holy Spirit* cannot distinguish between degrees of error, for if He taught that one form of sickness is more serious than another, He would be teaching that one error can be more real than another. **147**

error — The miracle dissolves error because the *Holy Spirit* identifies error as false or unreal. **3**

errors — The *Holy Spirit* never itemizes errors because He does not frighten children, and those who lack wisdom are children. **96**

evaluative — The *Holy Spirit* is evaluative and must be. He sorts out the true from the false in your mind, and teaches you to judge every thoght you allow to enter it in the light of what God put there. **100**

extends — The *Holy Spirit* extends and the ego projects. **89**

extends — The *Holy Spirit* extends by recognizing Him- 91
    self in every mind, and thus perceives
    them as one.

faith — The *Holy Spirit* can give you faith in holiness 419
    and vision to see it easily through.

faith — (The task of the *Holy Spirit* is) to atone for your 323
    unwillingness by His perfect faith, and
    it is His faith you share with Him (in
    the holy instant).

fear — No response given by (the *Holy Spirit*) will be one 153
    that would increase fear.

fear — Thus does the *Holy Spirit* replace fear with love 202
    and translate error into truth.

following — Following the *Holy Spirit* is therefore the 126
    easiest thing in the world, and the only
    thing that is easy, because it is not of
    the world.

forever — Nothing lasting lies in dreams, and the *Holy* 96
    Spirit, shining with the light from God
    Himself, speaks only for what lasts
    forever.

forgiveness — The *Holy Spirit* will teach you to re- 298
    member that forgiveness is not loss,
    but your salvation.

forgives — The *Holy Spirit* in you forgives all things in 156
    you and in your brother.

form — (The *Holy Spirit*) opposes the idea that dif- 107
    ferences in form are meaningful,
    emphasizing always that these
    differences do not matter.

freedom — (The *Holy Spirit's*) direction is freedom and 130
    His goal is God.

freedom — The *Holy Spirit* leads you steadily along the 130
    path of freedom, teaching you how to
    disregard or look beyond everything
    that would hold you back.

freedom — (The *Holy Spirit*) teaches you the difference 130
    between imprisonment and freedom.

function — Bringing illusion to truth, or the ego to God, is the *Holy Spirit's* only function.　　270

function — Extension of forgiveness is the *Holy Spirit's* function.　　449

function — It is the *Holy Spirit's* function to teach you how this oneness is experienced, what you must do that it can be experienced, and where you should go to do it.　　484

function — The function (of the *Holy Spirit*) is to distinguish only between the false and the true, replacing the false with the true.　　147

function — The *Holy Spirit* needs your special function, that His may be fulfilled.　　493

function — The *Holy Spirit's* main function is to teach you to tell (joy from pain.)　　124

function — The sole function (of the *Holy Spirit*) is to undo the questionable and thus lead to certainty.　　109

function — What is the *Holy Spirit's* special function but to release the holy Son of God from the imprisonment he made to keep himself from justice?　　506

function — You can rest assured that (the *Holy Spirit*) will not fulfill a function He does not see and recognize as His.　　531

gifts — The *Holy Spirit* understands how to increase your little gifts and make them mighty.　　462

give — (The *Holy Spirit*) cannot give you something you do not want.　　150

give — The *Holy Spirit* will give you only what is yours, and will take nothing in return.　　197

given — Because (the *Holy Spirit*) has been given you freely by God, you must give Him as you received Him.　　81

given — Whatever is given (the *Holy Spirit*) that is not of God is gone.　　205

glory — The *Holy Spirit* has promised the Father that through Him you would be released from littleness to glory.　　269

goal — All you need do is make the effort to learn, for the *Holy Spirit* has a unified goal for the effort. **110**

goal — The *Holy Spirit* knows the situation is as the goal determines it, and is experienced according to the goal. **342**

goal — Now (the *Holy Spirit*) will work with you to make (the goal) specific. **340**

goal — The means to meet the *Holy Spirit's* goal will come from the same source as does His purpose. **409**

God — I suggested before that you remind yourself to allow the *Holy Spirit* to decide for God for you. **99**

God — The *Holy Spirit* asks you to respond as God does, for He would teach you what you do not understand. **299**

God — The *Holy Spirit* can speak only for (what is true) because He speaks for God. **90**

God — (The *Holy Spirit*) is both God and you, as you are God and Him together. **312**

God — When I said that the *Holy Spirit's* function is to sort out the true from the false in your mind, I meant that He has the power to look into what you have hidden and recognize the Will of God there. **149**

God's — The *Holy Spirit* is God's Answer to the ego. **72**

God's — The *Holy Spirit* is God's attempt to free you of what He does not understand. **299**

God's — The *Holy Spirit* is the way in which God's Will is done on earth as it is in Heaven. **70**

guidance — As long as you avoid the guidance (of the *Holy Spirit*) in any way, you want to be weak. **125**

guidance — (The *Holy Spirit's*) promise is always: "Seek and you will find," and under His guidance you cannot be defeated. **208**

guidance — Under the guidance (of the *Holy Spirit*) you will travel light and journey lightly, for His sight is ever on the journey's end, which is His goal. — **239**

guidance — You will not trust the guidance of the *Holy Spirit*, or believe that it is for you, unless you hear it in others. — **153**

guide — The *Holy Spirit* is your guide in choosing. — **70**

guide — (The *Holy Spirit*) is your guide to salvation, because He holds the remembrance of things past and to come, and brings them to the present. — **74**

guide — The *Holy Spirit* will always guide you truly, because your joy is His. — **126**

guides — The *Holy Spirit* guides you into life eternal, but you must relinquish your investment in death, or you will not see life though it is all around you. — **209**

guiltlessness — The ego is the choice for guilt; the *Holy Spirit* the choice for guiltlessness. — **255**

guiltlessness — The *Holy Spirit* sees only guiltlessness, and in His gentleness He would release from fear and reestablish the reign of love. — **264**

heal — Accept the healing power (of the *Holy Spirit*) and use it for all He sends you, for He wills to heal the Son of God, in whom He is not deceived. — **198**

healing — As you heal you are healed, because the *Holy Spirit* sees no order of difficulty in healing. — **110**

healing — The *Holy Spirit* is the idea of healing. — **72**

healing — The *Holy Spirit* promotes healing by looking beyond it to what the children of God were before healing was needed, and will be when they have been healed. — **69**

Heaven — Call upon (the *Holy Spirit*), for Heaven is at His call. — **323**

221

help — Surely (the *Holy Spirit*) will not fail to help you, since help is His only purpose.   **205**

helping — (The *Holy Spirit*) is helping you to remember what you are.   **150**

hidden — (The *Holy Spirit*) cannot shine away what you keep hidden, for you have not offered it to Him and He cannot take it from you.   **204**

hide — What you hide the *Holy Spirit* cannot look upon.   **268**

home — The *Holy Spirit* remembers (your home) for you, and He will guide you to your home because that is His mission.   **209**

host — The *Holy Spirit* cannot speak to an unwelcoming host, because He will not be heard.   **183**

illusions — The *Holy Spirit* undoes illusions without attacking them, because He cannot perceive them at all.   **115**

impartiality — The *Holy Spirit* was given you with perfect impartiality, and only by recognizing Him impartially can you recognize him at all.   **91**

inequality — To command is to assume inequality, which the *Holy Spirit* demonstrates does not exist.   **95**

investment — (The *Holy Spirit*) has no investment in the things that he supplies, except to make certain that you will not use them on behalf of lingering in time.   **239**

invitation — I have already said that I can reach up and bring the *Holy Spirit* down to you, but I can bring Him to you only at your own invitation.   **67**

joy — The *Holy Spirit* never varies (about what you are), and so the one mood He engenders is joy.   **101**

joy — The *Holy Spirit* is the spirit of joy.   **69**

judge — The *Holy Spirit* does not teach you to judge others, because He does not want you to teach error and learn it yourself.   **101**

judgment — The ego speaks in judgment, and the *Holy Spirit* reverses its decision, much as a higher court has the power to reverse a lower court's decision in this world. 80

judgment — (The *Holy Spirit*) has perfect faith in your final judgment, because He knows that He will make it for you. 249

judgment — The judgment (of the *Holy Spirit*) must prevail, and He will give to you as you join your perception to His. 268

Kingdom — Wherever (the *Holy Spirit*) looks He sees Himself, and because He is united He offers the whole kingdom always. 91

knowledge — The word "know" is proper in this context, because the *Holy Spirit* is so close to knowledge that He calls it forth; or better, allows it to come. 68

knowledge — The word "knows" is correct here, because the *Holy Spirit* still holds knowledge safe in your mind through His impartial connection. 91

knowledge — The *Holy Spirit* is the Christ Mind which is aware of the knowledge that lies beyond perception. 68

knows — Like any good teacher, the *Holy Spirit* knows more than you do now, but He teaches only to make you equal with Him. 95

knows — The *Holy Spirit* knows that you both have and are everything. 56

knows — (The *Holy Spirit*) knows what to do with (what you do not want.) 205

laws — The *Holy Spirit's* ability to look beyond symbols into eternity enables Him to understand the laws of God, for which He speaks. 73

learner — The *Holy Spirit* needs a happy learner, in whom His mission can be happily accomplished. 252

learning — The *Holy Spirit*, as always, takes what you have made and translates it into a learning device.   **97**

led — In everything be led by (the *Holy Spirit*), and do not reconsider.   **258**

lesson — The *Holy Spirit*, seeing where you are but knowing you are elsewhere, begins his lesson in simplicity with the fundamental teaching that truth is true.   **253**

lesson — The *Holy Spirit's* first lesson was: "To have, give all to all."   **99**

lesson — The second lesson of the *Holy Spirit* is "To have peace, teach peace to learn it."   **100**

lesson — The third lesson of the *Holy Spirit* is: "Be vigilant only for God and His Kingdom.   **101**

light — (The *Holy Spirit*) holds the light, and you the darkness.   **268**

light — Whatever is in accord with this light (the *Holy Spirit*) retains, to strengthen the Kingdom in you.   **100**

light — (The *Holy Spirit*) will give you all things that do not block the way to light.   **239**

light — The light (of the *Holy Spirit*) is always the call to awaken, whatever you have been dreaming.   **96**

Light — The *Holy Spirit* is the Light in which Christ stands revealed.   **233**

love — It is perfectly obvious that if the *Holy Spirit* looks with love on all He perceives, He looks with love on you.   **163**

loving — The *Holy Spirit* will help you reinterpret everything that you perceive as fearful, and teach you that only what is loving is true.   **74**

meaning — The *Holy Spirit* is not concerned with form, being aware only of meaning.   **151**

meaningless — However, the *Holy Spirit* has the task of translating the useless into the useful, the meaningless into the meaningful, and the temporary into the timeless.　　105

mediator — The *Holy Spirit* is mediator between the interpretations of the ego and the knowledge of the spirit.　　73

memory — God is in your memory because of (the *Holy Spirit*).　　212

message — The meaning of the message (of the *Holy Spirit*) is always the same; only the meaning matters.　　107

message — The message (of the *Holy Spirit*) speaks of timelessness in time, and that is why Christ's vision looks on everything with love.　　241

messengers — If you send forth only the messengers the *Holy Spirit* gives you, wanting no messages but theirs, you will see fear no more.　　383

messengers — The *Holy Spirit* has given you love's messengers to send instead of those you trained through fear.　　383

mind — Since the *Holy Spirit* is in your mind, your mind can also believe only what is true.　　90

mind — (The *Holy Spirit*) always tells you that only the mind is real, because only the mind can be shared.　　97

mind — The *Holy Spirit* is in your right mind, as He was in mine.　　67

mind — The *Holy Spirit* recognizes (the part of the mind that is still for God) perfectly because it is His Own dwelling place, the place in the mind where He is at home.　　74

mind — The *Holy Spirit* will, of Himself, fill every mind that so makes room for Him.　　278

Mind — The *Holy Spirit* is not separate from (the Father and the Son), being in the Mind of both.　　241

Mind — The Mind (of the *Holy Spirit*) shone on you in your creation and brought your mind into being.   **58**

minds — The *Holy Spirit* has one direction for all minds, and the one He taught me is yours.   **137**

miracles — Miracles are the witnesses of (the *Holy Spirit*), and speak for His Presence.   **214**

miracles — The *Holy Spirit* is the mechanism of miracles.   **3**

mission — It is impossible the mission (of the *Holy Spirit*) fail.   **249**

motivation — The *Holy Spirit* is the motivation for miracle-mindedness; the decision to heal the separation by letting it go.   **69**

need — Only the *Holy Spirit* knows what you need.   **239**

need — (The *Holy Spirit*) will take nothing from you as long as you have any need of it.   **239**

needs — Leave, then, your needs to (the *Holy Spirit*).   **239**

open — The *Holy Spirit* asks of you but this: bring to Him every secret you have locked away from Him. Open every door to Him, and bid Him enter the darkness and lighten it away.   **268**

opposites — (The *Holy Spirit*) must work through opposites, because He must work with and for a mind that is in opposition.   **74**

pain — Do not leave any spot of pain hidden from the light (of the *Holy Spirit*), and search your mind carefully for any thoughts you may fear to uncover.   **227**

pain — The *Holy Spirit* will direct you only so as to avoid pain.   **124**

past — (The *Holy Spirit*) teaches that the past does not exist, a fact which belongs to the sphere of knowledge, and which therefore no one in the world can know.   **240**

peace — The ego is the symbol of separation, just as the *Holy Spirit* is the symbol of peace.   **73**

peace — The *Holy Spirit* counters this welcome (of the   73
    call of danger by the ego) by welcoming
    peace.

peace — When the peace in you has been extended to   379
    everyone, the *Holy Spirit's* function here
    will be accomplished.

perceive — (The *Holy Spirit*) separates the true from the   3
    false by His ability to perceive totally
    than selectively.

perceives — Perceiving equality, the *Holy Spirit* perceives   89
    equal needs.

perception — Although perception of any kind is unreal,   90
    you made it and the *Holy Spirit* can
    therefore use it well.

perception — The ego would prefer to believe that this   90
    memory (of knowledge) is impossible,
    yet it is your perception the *Holy Spirit*
    guides.

perception — The *Holy Spirit*, Who leads to God, trans-   97
    lates communication into being, just as
    He ultimately translates perception
    into knowledge.

perfect — The *Holy Spirit* begins by perceiving you as   89
    perfect.

power — (The *Holy Spirit*) teaches you that all power is   107
    yours.

power — This power (of the *Holy Spirit's* purpose) in-   345
    stantly transforms all situations into
    one sure and continuous means for
    establishing His purpose, and
    demonstrating its reality.

problem — Every problem is the same (to the *Holy Spirit*),   506
    because each one is solved in just the
    same respect and through the same
    approach.

problem — The *Holy Spirit* offers you release from every   506
    problem that you think you have.

problems — The *Holy Spirit* wants only to make His resolutions complete and perfect, and so He seeks and finds the source of problems where it is, and there undoes it. 332

promise — The promise (of the *Holy Spirit*) is always, "Seek and you will find," and under His guidance you cannot be defeated. 208

purpose — The *Holy Spirit* looks on the world as with one purpose, changelessly established. 595

purpose — The *Holy Spirit's* purpose now is yours. 521

purpose — The *Holy Spirit's* purpose is to let the presence of your holy Guests be known to you. 523

purpose — The practical application of the *Holy Spirit's* purpose is extremely simple, but it is unequivocal. 340

question — I asked you earlier, "Would you be hostage to the ego or host to God?" Let this question be asked you by the *Holy Spirit* every time you make a decision. 286

questions — The Answer merely undoes the question by establishing the fact that to question reality is to question meaninglessly. That is why the *Holy Spirit* never questions. 109

reawakened — The *Holy Spirit* is glad when you can learn from (my experiences), and be reawakened by them. 86

redemption — The *Holy Spirit* knows your part in the redemption, and who are seeking you and where to find them. 242

referred — (The *Holy Spirit*) is referred to as the Healer, the Comforter, and the Guide. 67

relationship — If you believed the *Holy Spirit* was there to accept the relationship, why would you now not still believe that He is there to purify what He has taken under His guidance? 338

relationship — (The *Holy Spirit*) offered your relation-   379
ship the gift of holiness, without which
it would have been forever impossible
to appreciate your brother.

relationship — The *Holy Spirit's* temple is not a body, but   407
a relationship.

release — For a teaching assignment such as His, (the   298
Holy Spirit) must use everything in this
world for your release.

remedy — Here is both (God's Son's) pain and his   227
healing, for the *Holy Spirit's* vision is
merciful and His remedy is quick.

remember — The *Holy Spirit* calls you both to remember   70
and to forget.

rest — The *Holy Spirit* asks that you offer Him a resting   379
place where you will rest in Him.

restore — Yet the *Holy Spirit* has saved (the meaning of   196
what you perceive) for you, and if you
will let him interpret it, He will restore
to you what you have thrown away.

return — The *Holy Spirit* tells you that even return is   90
unnecessary, because what never
happened cannot be difficult.

sacrifice — I have emphasized many times that the *Holy*   150
Spirit will never call upon you to
sacrifice anything.

sacrifice — The *Holy Spirit* never asks for sacrifice, but   125
the ego always does.

salvation — To each, (the *Holy Spirit*) gives each a special   493
function in salvation he alone can fill, a
part for only him.

sanity — Lay before the eternal sanity (of the *Holy Spirit*)   227
all your hurt, and let Him heal you.

see — You cannot see the *Holy Spirit*, but you can see His   214
manifestations.

see — You cannot see the *Holy Spirit*, but you can see   379
your brothers truly.

separate — The *Holy Spirit* is the frame God set around the part of Him that you would see as separate. — 485

separation — (The *Holy Spirit* came into being with the separation) as a protection, inspiring the Atonement principle at the same time. — 68

separation — All the *Holy Spirit* perceives in separation is that it must be undone. — 332

separation — (The *Holy Spirit*) reinterprets what the ego uses as an argument for separation into a demonstration against it. — 97

service — The gentle service that you give the *Holy Spirit* is service to yourself. — 448

Sons — The *Holy Spirit* will remain with the Sons of God, to bless their creations and keep them in the light of joy. — 68

Sonship — Every one will answer the Call of the *Holy Spirit*, or the Sonship cannot be as one. — 71

soul — The *Holy Spirit* teaches that you cannot lose your soul and there is no gain in the world, for of itself it profits nothing. — 212

speak — The *Holy Spirit* does not speak first, but He always answers. — 93

speaks — The *Holy Spirit* is the part of your mind that always speaks for the right choice, because He speaks for God. — 70

strength — The *Holy Spirit* always sides with you and your strength. — 125

takes — (The *Holy Spirit*) never takes anything back, because He wants you to keep it. — 97

teacher — The *Holy Spirit* is the perfect teacher. — 73

teaches — The *Holy Spirit* teaches that all strength is in God and therefore in you. — 133

teaches — The *Holy Spirit* teaches that you always meet yourself, and the encounter is holy because you are. — 229

teaches — The *Holy Spirit* teaches you that if you only   **132**
look at yourself you cannot find your-
self, because that is not what you are.

teaches — There is no inconsistency in what the *Holy*   **424**
Spirit teaches.

teaching — Only (the teaching of the *Holy Spirit*) will   **131**
release your will to God's, uniting it
with His power and glory and establishing them as yours.

teaching — The *Holy Spirit's* teaching is a lesson in re-   **107**
membering.

teaching — The *Holy Spirit,* therefore, must begin His   **252**
teaching by showing you what you can
never learn.

Thought — (The *Holy Spirit*) is a Thought of God, and   **241**
God has given Him to you because He
has no thoughts He does not share.

time — The *Holy Spirit* interprets time's purpose as ren-   **230**
dering the need for time unnecessary.

time — The *Holy Spirit* uses time, but does not believe in   **90**
it.

time — The *Holy Spirit* uses time in His Own way, and is   **280**
not bound by it.

time — The *Holy Spirit,* Who speaks for God in time, also   **81**
knows that time is meaningless.

Trinity — The *Holy Spirit* is the only part of the Holy   **67**
Trinity that has a symbolic function.

truly — (The *Holy Spirit's*) evaluation of you is based on   **164**
His knowledge of what you are, and so
He evaluates you truly.

trust — Trust (the *Holy Spirit*) to answer quickly, surely,   **258**
and with Love, for everyone who will
be touched in any way by the decision.

trust — You are asked to trust the *Holy Spirit* only be-   **182**
cause he speaks for you.

trustworthy — The *Holy Spirit* is perfectly trustworthy,   **125**
as you are.

truth — The ego tries to persuade you that it is up to you   99
   to decide which voice is true, but the
   Holy Spirit teaches you that truth was
   created by God, and your decision
   cannot change it.

understanding — (The understanding of the *Holy Spirit*)   74
   looks back to God in remembrance of
   me.

undertaken — This will you do, for nothing undertaken   379
   with the *Holy Spirit* remains unfinished.

undone — (The *Holy Spirit*) has already undone every-   221
   thing unworthy of the Son of God, for
   such was His mission, given Him by
   God.

unify — The *Holy Spirit* always seeks to unify and heal.   110

useless — However, the *Holy Spirit* has the task of trans-   105
   lating the useless into the useful, the
   meaningless into the meaningful, and
   the temporary into the timeless.

Voice — It is possible even in this world to hear only (the   69
   Voice of the *Holy Spirit*) and no other.

Voice — The *Holy Spirit's* Voice is as loud as your willing-   145
   ness to listen.

Voice — (The Voice of the *Holy Spirit*) brings to your   70
   mind the other way, remaining quiet
   even in the midst of the turmoil you
   may make.

Voice — The Voice of the *Holy Spirit* does not command,   70
   because it is incapable of arrogance.

Voice — (The Voice of the *Holy Spirit*) does not demand,   70
   because it does not seek control.

Voice — (The Voice of the *Holy Spirit*) does not over-   70
   come, because it does not attack.

Voice — (The Voice of the *Holy Spirit*) is compelling only   70
   because of what it reminds you of.

Voice — (The Voice of the *Holy Spirit*) is not weak in It-   72
   self, but It is limited by your unwilling-
   ness to hear it.

Voice — The Voice of the *Holy Spirit* is the call to Atonement, or the restoration of the integrity of the mind. 68

Voice — The Voice of the *Holy Spirit* is weak in you. That is why you must share it. 72

Voice — Yet by your listening (the Voice of the *Holy Spirit*) extends, because you have accepted what He says. 535

will — The *Holy Spirit* opposes any imprisoning of the will of a Son of God, knowing that the will of the Son is the Father's. 130

Will — This mind is the *Holy Spirit*, Whose Will is for God always. 71

work — The *Holy Spirit* must work through you to teach you He is in you. 109

world — The ego made the world as it perceives it, but the *Holy Spirit*, the reinterpreter of what the ego made, sees the world as a teaching device for bringing you home. 74

world — (The *Holy Spirit*) will show you the real world because God gave you heaven. 212

worth — Remembering you always, the *Holy Spirit* cannot let you forget your worth. 212

you — The *Holy Spirit* is in communication with God always, and He is part of you. 74

HOLY TRINITY

confusion — There is no confusion within the levels (of the *Holy trinity*), because They are of one Mind and one Will. 35

creations — Your creations are your gift to the *Holy trinity*, created in gratitude for your creation. 138

function — Unless you take your place in (the *Holy trinity*) and fulfill your function as part of It, the *Holy trinity* is as bereft as you are. 136

holy — The *Holy trinity* is holy because It is One. 135

Son of God — The Son of God is part of the *Holy trinity,* 35
but the Trinity itself is One.

HONOR(S)

brother — See not in (your brother) the sinfulness he 486
sees, but give him *honor* that you may
esteem yourself and him.

gift — Only *Honor* is a fitting gift for those whom God 119
created worthy of *honor,* and whom He
honors.

illusions — *Honor* is not due to illusions, for to *honor* 173
them is to *honor* nothing.

peace — Place *honor* where it is due, and peace will be 173
yours.

HOPE

hopeless — To place your *hope* where no *hope* lies must 484
make you hopeless.

HOPELESSNESS

choice — Yet is this *hopelessness* your choice while you 484
seek for hope where none is ever
found.

HOST

freedom — God would have His *host* abide in perfect 288
freedom.

God — The *host* of God needs not seek to find anything. 287

God — You who are *host* to God are also *host* to (your 312
creations.)

mind — It is your mind that is the *host* to Him. 288

power — God's power is forever on the side of His *host,* 287
for it protects only the peace in which
He dwells.

HUMILITY

littleness — *Humility* will never ask that you remain con- 355
tent with littleness.

HURT

death — In every wish (to *hurt* the Son of God) chooses death instead of what his Father wills for him. — **518**

power — Nothing can *hurt* unless you give it the power to do so. — **402**

IDEA(S)

delusional — Delusional *ideas* are not real thoughts, although you can believe in them. — **78**

ego — *Ideas* of the ego can conflict because they occur at different levels and also include opposite thoughts at the same level. — **75**

everything — Everything is an *idea*. — **67**

fail — No one can fail but your *idea* of him, and there is no betrayal but of this. — **569**

forces — *Ideas* are mighty forces, to be used and not held idly by. — **311**

free — You can enslave a body, but an *idea* is free, incapable of being kept in prison or limited in any way except by the mind that thought it. — **374**

hell — Hell and oblivion are *ideas* that you made up, and you are bent on demonstrating their reality to establish yours. — **228**

illusions — To believe *ideas* can leave their source is to invite illusions to be true, without success. — **517**

mind — Every *idea* begins in the mind of the thinker. — **91**

mind — *Ideas* are of the mind. — **515**

purpose — Every *idea* has a purpose, and its purpose is always the natural outcome of what it is. — **189**

result — The result of an *idea* is never separate from its source. — **372**

self — From an *idea* of self as two, there comes a necessary view of function split between the two. — **530**

share — An *idea* that you share you must have. — **92**

small — (An idol) could never be your will, because what shares in all creation cannot be content with small *ideas* and little things.   586

source — *Ideas* leave not their source, and their effects but seem to be apart from them.   515

spirit — *Ideas* of the spirit do not leave the mind that thinks them, nor can they conflict with each other.   75

IDENTIFICATION

brothers — (Miracles) are reflections of both your proper *identification* with your brothers, and of your awareness that your *identification* is maintained by extension.   123

your — Your *identification* is with the Father and with the Son.   135

IDENTITY

abides — Your *Identity* abides in (God the Father and the Son), and where they are, forever must you be.   570

changeless — Being yours (God) cannot change Himself, for your *Identity* is changeless.   277

choice — Choose once again what you would have (God's Son) be, remembering that every choice you make establishes your own *identity* as you will see it and believe it is.   621

God — It is impossible that God lose His *Identity*, for if He did, you would lose yours.   277

lost — Be confident that you have never lost your *Identity*, and the expressions which maintain it in wholeness and peace.   123

shared — Remember always that your *Identity* is shared, and that Its sharing is Its reality.   157

treasure — (The Son of God) would sacrifice his own *identity* with everything to find a little treasure of his own.   517

IDOL(S)

accept — *Idols* accept, but never make return.　　　**407**

before — Every *idol* that you raise to place before Him　　**320**
stands before you, in place of what you
are.

believed — (An *idol*) must be believed before it seems to　**576**
come to life, and given power that it
may be feared.

believes — No one believes in *idols* who has not enslaved　**575**
himself to littleness and loss.

brother — An *idol* is an image of your brother that you　**575**
would value more than what he is.

Christ — The world of *idols* is a veil across the face of　**576**
Christ, because its purpose is to sepa-
rate your brother from yourself.

cost — Do not choose an *idol* thoughtlessly, remember-　**593**
ing that he will pay the cost as well as
you.

death — And each will fail him, all excepting one; for he　**573**
will die, and does not understand the
idol that he seeks is but his death.

disappear — *Idols* must disappear, and leave no trace be-　**408**
hind their going.

dreams — All figures in dreams are *idols*, made to save　**578**
you from the dream.

fall — *Idols* must fall because they have no life, and what　**574**
is lifeless is a sign of death.

false — An *idol* is a false impression or a false belief,　**575**
some form of antiChrist, that consti-
tutes a gap between the Christ and
what you see.

fear — One way (that you can see) shows you an image,　**113**
or an *idol* that you may worship out of
fear, but will never love.

getting — An *idol* is a means of getting more. And it is　**577**
this that is against God's Will.

god — A sick god must be an *idol*, made in the image of　**171**
what its maker thinks he is.

God — An *idol* is beyond where God has set all things   576
    forever, and has left no room for anything to be except His Will.

God — No *idol* can establish you as more than God. But   577
    you will never be content with being less.

God — Your holy mind is an altar unto God, and where   575
    He is, no *idols* can abide.

hidden — Forget not, then, that *idols* must keep hidden   588
    what you are, not from the Mind of God, but from your own.

judge — Judge not, for he who judges will have need of   577
    idols, which will hold the judgment off from resting on himself.

limits — *Idols* are limits.   586

loss — Decide for *idols* and you ask for loss.   586

nothing — The *idols* are nothing, but their worshippers   171
    are the Sons of God in sickness.

pardon — What you see as having power to make an *idol*   595
    of the Son of God you will not pardon.

peace — It is vain to worship *idols* in the hope of peace.   574

power — Your *idols* do what you would have them do,   574
    and have the power you ascribe to them.

reality — *Idols* are but substitutes for your reality.   575

relationship — *(Idols)* do not understand what they are   407
    offered, and any relationship in which they enter has lost its meaning.

relationships — *(Idols)* have no relationships, for no one   407
    else is welcome there.

share — *Idols* do not share.   407

slave — The slave of *idols* is a willing slave.   577

thought — *(An idol)* is still a thought and cannot leave   576
    the mind that is its source.

toys — You do but dream, and *idols* are the toys you   578
    dream you play with.

truth — *(Idols)* were made that you might forget (the   589
    truth could never be attacked.)

truth — All *idols* of this world were made to keep the   **574**
truth within from being known to you,
and to maintain allegiance to the dream
that you must find what is outside
yourself to be complete and happy.

unrecognized — *Idols* are unrecognized as such, and   **575**
never seen for what they really are.

want — It is never the *idol* you want.   **587**

want — But you will understand that mighty changes   **590**
have been quickly brought about,
when you decide one very simple thing;
you do not want whatever you believe
an *idol* gives.

will — Beyond all *idols* stands his holy will to be but what   **587**
he is.

will — It is not your will to have (an *idol*).   **586**

worship — The destruction is no more real than the   **171**
image, although those who make *idols*
do worship them.

worship — Each *idol* that you worship when God calls   **573**
will never answer in His place.

worshipper — Each worshipper of *idols* hopes his special   **577**
deities will give him more than other
men possess.

IDOLATOR(S)

love — *Idolators* will always be afraid of love, for nothing   **408**
so severely threatens them as love's
approach.

you — You are an *idolator* no longer.   **408**

IDOLATRY

caricatures — All forms of *idolatry* are caricatures of   **171**
creation, taught by sick minds too
divided to know that creation shares
power and never usurps it.

past — *Idolatry* is past and meaningless.   **409**

sickness — Sickness is *idolatry*, because it is the belief   **171**
that power can be taken from you.

I (ME, MY MINE)

answer — *I* have called and you will answer.   59

Atonement — *I* am in charge of the process of Atone-   6
         ment, which I undertook to begin.

awe — I have stressed that awe is not an appropriate   13
         reaction to *me* because of our inherent
         equality.

brother — *I* bridge the distance as an elder brother to   5
         you on the one hand, and as a Son of
         God on the other.

brother — As a loving brother *I* am deeply concerned   57
         with your mind, and urge you to follow
         my example as you look at yourself and
         at your brother, and see in both the
         glorious creations of a glorious Father.

brother — As you come closer to a brother, you   63
         approach *me*, and as you withdraw
         from Him *I* become distant to you.

brother — If what you do to your brother, you do to *me*,   162
         and if you do everything for yourself
         because we are part of you, everything
         we do belongs to you as well.

call — *I* will come in response to a single unequivocal   56
         call.

choice — *I* cannot choose for you, but can help you make   39
         your own right choice.

decision — *I* am your model for decision.   71

devotion — *My* devotion to you is of (God), being born   139
         of *my* knowledge of myself and Him.

ego — *I* could not understand (the importance of the   51
         body and the ego) to you if *I* had not
         once been tempted to believe in them
         myself.

ego — *I* will never attack your ego, but *I* am trying to   48
         teach you how its thought system
         arose.

ego — *I* will substitute for your ego if you wish, but   50
         never for your spirit.

ego — When you unite with *me* you are uniting without   **136**
the ego, because *I* have renounced the
ego in myself and therefore cannot
unite with yours.

entrusted — *I* can be entrusted with your body and your   **51**
ego only because this enables you not
to be concerned with them, and lets me
teach you their unimportance.

error — As a man *I* did not attempt to counteract error   **39**
with knowledge, but to correct error
from the bottom up.

example — To use *my* experiences constructively, how-   **87**
ever, you must still follow *my* example
in how to perceive them.

faith — *My* faith in you is as strong as all the love *I* give   **247**
my Father.

Father — *I* am nothing without the Father, and you are   **135**
nothing without *me*, because by deny-
ing the Father you deny yourself.

Father — You cannot forget the Father because *I* am   **113**
with you, and *I* cannot forget Him.

fear — *I* have already indicated that you cannot ask *me* to   **27**
release you from fear. *I* know it does
not exist, but you do not.

forgiven — *I* have great need for lilies, for the Son of   **397**
God has not forgiven *me*.

goal — *I* will teach with you and live with you if you will   **49**
think with *me*, but *my* goal will always
be to absolve you finally from the need
for a teacher.

God — *I* come to you from our Father to offer you   **179**
everything again.

grace — *I* am made welcome in the state of grace, which   **383**
means you have at last forgiven *me*.

gratitude — Your gratitude to your brother is the only   **62**
gift *I* want.

heal — *I* can heal you, because *I* know you.   **172**

Holy Spirit — *I* am the manifestation of the Holy Spirit, and when you see *me* it will be because you have invited Him. — 215

Holy Spirit — *I* have already said that *I* can reach up and bring the Holy Spirit down to you, but *I* can bring Him to you only at your invitation. — 67

Holy Spirit — *I* hear only the Holy Spirit in you, Who speaks to *me* through you. — 153

Kingdom — *I* have chosen you to teach the Kingdom to the Kingdom. — 127

leave — *I* will never leave you or forsake you, because to forsake you would be to forsake *myself* and God Who created *me*. — 76

lesson — The lesson *I* was born to teach and still would teach to all my brothers, is that sacrifice is nowhere and love is everywhere. — 306

light — *I* am come as a light into a world that does deny itself everything. — 133

limits — *I* give you no limits because God lays none on you. — 147

love — *I* will love you and honor you and maintain complete respect for what you have made, but *I* will not uphold it unless it is true. — 56

loves — *I* love only what God loves with *me*, and because of this *I* treasure you beyond the value that you set on yourself, even unto the worth that God has placed upon you. — 247

loves — *I* love you for the truth in you, as God does. — 153

mind — *I* want to share *my* mind with you because we are of one Mind, and that Mind is ours. — 113

mind — *I* do work with your higher mind, the home of the Holy Spirit, whether you are asleep or awake, just as your ego does with your lower mind, which is its home. — 59

miracles — Ask *me* which miracles you should perform. — 7

miracles — *I* have asked you to perform miracles, and have made it clear that miracles are natural, corrective, healing and universal.   **15**

miracles — *I* inspire all miracles, which are really intercessions.   **3**

miracles — *I* will provide opportunities to do (miracles), but you must be ready and willing.   **6**

miracles — The interpersonal nature of the miracle is an essential ingredient, because it enables *me* to direct its application, and under *my* guidance miracles lead to the highly personal experience of revelation.   **7**

misperceptions — *I* cannot unite your will with God's for you, but *I* can erase all misperceptions from your mind if you will bring it under *my* guidance.   **39**

model — *I* am the model for rebirth, but rebirth itself is merely the dawning on your mind of what is already in it.   **86**

model — You have been asked to take *me* as your model for learning, since an extreme example is a particularly helpful learning device.   **84**

patience — *I* have shown you infinite patience because my will is that of our Father, from Whom *I* learned of infinite patience.   **81**

peace — *I* bring God's peace back to all His children because *I* received it of Him for us all.   **137**

perception — *My* one lesson, which *I* must teach as *I* learned it, is that no perception that is out of accord with the judgment of the Holy Spirit can be justified.   **87**

plan — *I* am making (God's) plan perfectly explicit to you, and will also tell you of your part in it, and how urgent it is to fulfill it.   **82**

power — To join with *me* is to restore His power to you because we are sharing it.   **136**

powerlessness — *I* demonstrated both the powerlessness of the body and the power of the mind.   **39**

"punished" — *I* was not "punished" because you were bad.   32

purpose — *My* purpose, then, is still to overcome the world.   133

relationship — For in your new relationship am *I* made welcome.   383

remember — *I* will always remember you, and in *my* remembrance of you lies your remembrance of yourself.   135

resurrection — *I* am your resurrection and your life.   193

revelations — Revelations are directly inspired by *me* because *I* am close to the Holy Spirit, and alert to the revelation-readiness of my brothers.   5

role — *My* role is only to unchain your will and set it free.   79

role — *My* role is to separate the true from the false, so truth can break through the barriers the ego has set up and can shine into your mind.   55

separate — "No man cometh unto the Father but by *me*" does not mean that *I* am in any way separate or different from you except in time, and time does not really exist.   5

share — Nor can you use what *I* have given you unless you share it.   398

strength — *My* strength will never be wanting, and if you choose to share it you will do so.   137

symbol — *I* became the symbol of your sin, and so *I* had to die instead of you.   383

teach — *I* can teach you, but only you can choose to listen to *my* teaching.   135

teacher — *I* am constantly being perceived as a teacher to be exalted or rejected, but *I* do not accept either perception of *myself.*   49

teaching — *I* am teaching you to associate misery with the ego and joy with the spirit.   62

time — You may think this implies that an enormous amount of time is necessary between readiness and mastery, but let *me* remind you that time and space are under *my* control.   29

trust — *My* trust in you is without limit, and without the fear that you will hear *me* not.   247

trust — You have very little trust in *me* as yet, but it will increase as you turn more and more often to *me* instead of to your ego for guidance.   61

truth — Believe that the truth is in *me*, for *I* know that it is in you.   197

truth — When you look within and see *me*, it will be because you have decided to manifest truth.   216

value — *I* know your value for you, and it is this value that makes you whole.   172

vigilance — Vigilance was required of *me* as much as of you, and those who choose to teach the same thing must be in agreement about what they believe.   103

will — *I* will with God that none of His Sons should suffer.   87

will — The Holy One shares *my* trust and accepts *my* Atonement decisions because *my* will is never out of accord with His.   62

will — Your will is as free as *mine*, and God Himself would not go against it.   135

witness — *I* will witness for anyone who lets *me*.   9

world — The world must therefore despise and reject *me*, because the world is the belief that love is impossible.   134

ILLUSION(S)

abandon — In the Name of God, be wholly willing to abandon all *illusions*.   316

attract — No *illusions* can attract a mind that has transcended them, and left them far behind.   408

battle — *Illusions* battle only with themselves.   **453**

beliefs — *Illusions* are but beliefs in what is not there.   **312**

change — To change *illusions* is to make no change.   **439**

chaos — The laws of chaos govern all *illusions*.   **459**

completion — Every *illusion* you accept into your mind by judging it to be attainable removes your own sense of completion, and thus denies the Wholeness of your Father.   **316**

connected — *Illusions* are always connected, as is truth.   **372**

dangerous — There is no reason to shrink from *illusions*, for they cannot be dangerous.   **188**

deceptions — *Illusions* are deceptions.   **167**

defense — Forget not when you feel the need to be defensive about anything, you have identified yourself with an *illusion*.   **447**

defense — Only *illusions* need defense because of weakness.   **445**

dispel — The only way to dispel *illusions* is to withdraw all investment from them, and they will have no life for you because you will have put them out of your mind.   **118**

escape — No one can escape from *illusions* unless he looks at them, for not looking is the way they are protected.   **188**

escape — The attempt to escape from one *illusion* into another must fail.   **315**

faith — Not one *illusion* is accorded faith, and not one spot of darkness still remains to hide the face of Christ from anyone.   **622**

fear — Certain it is *illusions* will bring fear because of the beliefs that they imply, not for their form.   **459**

fear — Every *illusion* is one of fear, whatever form it takes.   **315**

fear — It is the denial of *illusions* that calls on truth, for to deny *illusions* is to recognize that fear is meaningless.   **438**

Force — Within you is a Force that no *illusion* can resist. 446

forms — *Illusions* are but forms. 459

freedom — Freedom from *illusions* lies only in not believing them. 143

God — God does not wait upon *illusions* to let Him be Himself. 464

guilt — *Illusions* carry only guilt and suffering, sickness and death, to their believers. 439

hidden — You must look upon your *illusions* and not keep them hidden, because they do not rest on their own foundation. 226

hierarchy — All that a hierarchy of *illusions* can show is preference, not reality. 515

insane — *(Illusions)* have one thing in common; they are all insane. 230

investments — *Illusions* are investments. 118

join — And yet *illusions* cannot join. They are the same, and they are nothing. 453

Kingdom — Everything outside of the Kingdom is *illusion*. 103

laws — All *illusions* that you believe about yourself obey no laws. 589

love — *Illusions* have no place where love abides, protecting you from everything that is not true. 454

makes — The one who makes *(illusions)* does not see himself as making them, and their reality does not depend on him. 541

me — Forgive me your *illusions,* and release me from punishment for what I have not done. 385

meaning — *(Illusions)* are meaningful only to their maker, and so they have no meaning at all. 230

meaning — *Illusions* serve the purpose they were made to serve, and from their purpose they derive whatever meaning they seem to have. 517

mind — Your mind can be possessed by *illusions*, but spirit is eternally free. 9

miracle — The miracle, or the right answer, corrects *(illusions.)* 36

paid — You have paid very dearly for your *illusions*, and nothing you have paid for bought you peace. 385

pain — Every *illusion* carries pain and suffering in the dark folds of the heavy garments in which it hides its nothingness. 439

peace — For you have chosen to remain where he would have you, and no *illusion* can attack the peace of God together with His Son. 463

perpetuate — You cannot perpetuate an *illusion* about another without perpetuating it about yourself. 121

questioning — In your questioning of *illusions*, ask yourself if it is really sane to perceive what was as now. 233

questioning — Questioning *illusions* is the first step in undoing them. 36

real — No one can make one *illusion* real, and still escape the rest. 514

satisfy — For grandeur is the right of God's Son, and no *illusions* can satisfy him or save him from what he is. 227

savior — The savior from *illusions* has come to greet you, and lead you home with him. 399

Self — Only an *illusion* stands between you and the holy Self you share. 445

Self — You are your Self or an *illusion*. 558

separate — Not one *(illusion)* but rests on the belief that you are separate. 447

separation — The core of the separation *illusion* lies simply in the fantasy of destruction of love's meaning. 320

sights — *(Illusions)* are made up of sights that are not seen and sounds that are not heard. 230

sinless — No one who clings to one *illusion* can see him- 470
self as sinless, for he holds one error to
himself as lovely still.

solitude — Lead not your life in solitude, with one *illu-* 514
sion as your only friend.

"something" — Think what that instant brought; the 438
recognition that the "something else"
you thought was you is an *illusion*.

time — Time and space are one *illusion*, which takes 519
different forms.

triumph — *Illusions* cannot triumph over truth, nor can 453
they threaten it in any way.

true — If one belief so deeply valued here were true, 494
then every Thought God ever had is an
illusion.

truth — Every *illusion* is an assault on truth, and every 461
one does violence to the idea of love
because it seems to be of equal truth.

truth — Is it not welcome news to hear not one of the 441
illusions that you made replaced the
truth?

truth — It is impossible that one *illusion* be less amenable 515
to truth than are the rest.

truth — The opposite of *illusion* is not disillusionment 438
but truth.

truth — The seeming conflict between truth and *illusion* 312
can only be resolved by separating
yourself from the *illusion*, and not the
truth.

truth — To choose *(illusion)* is to let *(truth)* go. 332

truth — Truth and *illusion* have no connection. 372

truth — What you can decide between is fixed, because 255
there are no alternatives except truth
and *illusion*.

truth — When you try to bring truth to *illusions*, you are 328
trying to make *illusions* real, and keep
them by justifying your belief in them.

unanswered — Not one *illusion* still remains unanswered 512
in your mind.

war — The meeting of *illusions* leads to war.　　　**454**

willingness — Your willingness to let *illusions* go is all　　**557**
　　　the Healer of God's Son requires.

witnesses — *Illusions* have no witnesses and no effects.　**516**

world — (*Illusions*) make up a private world that cannot　**230**
　　　be shared.

IMAGE(S)

believe — You still believe you are an *image* of your own　**45**
　　　making.

destruction — The destruction is no more real than the　**171**
　　　image, although those who make idols
　　　do worship them.

God — God is no *image*, and His creations, as part of Him,　**272**
　　　hold Him in them in truth.

God — The *images* you make cannot prevail against what　**620**
　　　God Himself would have you be.

holiness — The *image* of holiness that shines in your　**271**
　　　mind is not obscure, and will not
　　　change.

minds — Let every *image* held of everyone be loosened　**602**
　　　from our minds and swept away.

perceived — *Images* are perceived, not know.　　**45**

perception — The word *"image"* is always perception-　**40**
　　　related, and not a part of knowledge.

see — All things you see are *images,* because you look on　**617**
　　　them as through a barrier that dims
　　　your sight and warps your vision so
　　　that you behold nothing with clarity.

sick — You believe that the sick things you have made　**178**
　　　are your real creations, because you
　　　believe that the sick *images* you perceive
　　　are the Sons of God.

strange — There are no strange *images* in the Mind of　**175**
　　　God, and what is not in His Mind
　　　cannot be in yours, because you are of
　　　one mind and that Mind belongs to
　　　Him.

symbolic — *Images* are symbolic and they stand for something else. **40**

time — There will come a time when *images* have all gone by and you will see you know not what they are. **613**

unworthy — They make up *images*, perceive them as unworthy, and attack them for their unworthiness. **117**

world — The world can teach no *images* of you unless you want to learn them. **613**

IMMORTAL

attacked — What is *immortal* cannot be attacked; what is but temporal has no effect. **479**

Father — (The Son of Life) is *immortal* as his Father. **572**

IMMORTALITY

Atonement — Accepting the Atonement teaches you what *immortality* is, for by accepting your guiltlessness you learn that the past has never been, and so the future is needless and will not be. **222**

brother — In your brother is the light of God's eternal promise of your *immortality*. **402**

constant — Spirit is immortal, and *immortality* is a constant state. **54**

God's — *Immortality* is (God's) Will for His Son, and His Son's will for himself. **182**

time — *Immortality* is the opposite of time, for time passes away while *immortality* is constant. **222**

IMPRISON

identification — When you *imprison* yourself, you are losing sight of your true identification with me and with the Father. **135**

love — Whom you seek to *imprison* you do not love. **135**

Son of God — You have taught yourself how to *imprison* the Son of God, a lesson so unthinkable that only the insane, in deepest sleep, could even dream of it. **275**

INCOMPLETE

idol — This is the purpose of an idol; that you will not look beyond it, to the source of the belief that you are *incomplete*. 586

sinned — Only if you had sinned could (you be *incomplete*). 586

INFINITY

alone — To be alone is to be separated from *infinity*, but how can this be if *infinity* has no end? 180

meaningless — *Infinity* is meaningless without you, and you are meaningless without God. 181

understood — *Infinity* cannot be understood by merely counting up its separate parts. 537

INHERITANCE

bought — Your *inheritance* can neither be bought nor sold. 209

joint — Together is your joint *inheritance* remembered and accepted by you both. 605

Kingdom — The *inheritance* of the Kingdom is the right of God's Son, given him in his creation. 262

recognition — Your *inheritance* awaits only the recognition that you have been redeemed. 209

INJUSTICE(S)

God — God knows of no *injustice*. 499

Holy Spirit — The Holy Spirit does not evaluate *injustices* as great or small, or more or less. 506

INNOCENCE

Atonement — Bring *innocence* to light, in answer to the call of the Atonement. 263

brother's — Attest (your brother's) *innocence* and not his guilt. 526

compromise — The wish to be unfairly treated is a compromise attempt that would combine attack and *innocence*. 525

evil — *Innocence* is wisdom because it is unaware of evil, and evil does not exist. 33

God — God offers you the means to see the *innocence* (of the Son of God.)   507

God — The *innocence* of God is the true state of mind of His Son.   34

guilt — There can be no attraction of guilt in *innocence*.   451

Holy Spirit — (The Holy Spirit) is the strong protector of the *innocence* that sets you free.   258

real — (*Innocence*) is not real until it is total.   34

release — From everyone whom you accord release from guilt, you will inevitably learn your *innocence*.   263

sacrifice — *Innocence* is incapable of sacrificing anything, because the innocent mind has everything and strives only to protect its wholeness.   33

savior's — This is the savior's vision; that he see his *innocence* in all he looks upon, and sees his own salvation everywhere.   618

shining — There is nothing in the Mind of God that does not share His shining *innocence*.   262

sight — The sight of *innocence* makes punishment impossible, and justice sure.   502

wisdom — It is not until their *innocence* becomes a viewpoint with universal application that it becomes wisdom.   33

yourself — You cannot give yourself your *innocence*, for you are too confused about yourself.   616

INNOCENT

brother — You think your brother is unfair to you because you think that one must be unfair to make the other *innocent*.   523

creation — I have said that only what God creates or what you create with the same will has any real existence. This, then, is all the *innocent* can see.   34

danger — What danger can assail the wholly *innocent*   390

exist — (*Innocent* or true perception) means you never see what does not exist, and always see what does.   34

perception — Because their hearts are pure, the *innocent* defend true perception, instead of defending themselves against it.   35

release — The *innocent* release in gratitude for their release.   607

safe — The *innocent* are safe because they share their innocence.   451

safety — The *innocent* see safety, and the pure in heart see God within His Son, and look unto the Son to lead them to the Father.   402

truly — *Innocent* or true perception means that you never misperceive and always see truly.   34

truly — Understanding the lesson of the Atonement, (the *innocent*) are without the wish to attack, and therefore they see truly.   35

uncontained — It is the nature of the *innocent* to be forever uncontained.   550

understanding — The understanding of the *innocent* is truth.   34

INSANE

creations — It must, however, be *insane* to believe that it is up to you to decide what God's creations are.   100

fear — Only the *insane* would choose fear in place of love, and only the *insane* could believe that love can be gained by attack.   190

protect — The *insane* protect their thought systems, but they do so insanely.   334

salvation — It would be madness to entrust salvation to the *insane*.   496

separation — The separation has nothing in it, no part, no "reason," and no attribute that is not *insane*.   334

wholly — You are not now wholly *insane*.   338

INSANELY

brother — When a brother behaves *insanely* you can heal him only by perceiving the sanity in him.   155

INSANITY

accept — You can accept *insanity* because you made it, but you cannot accept love because you did not.
226

adjust — Seek not to make the Son of God adjust to his *insanity*.
401

brother — Only if they share (*insanity*) does it seem fearful, and you do share in it until you look upon your brother with perfect faith and love and tenderness.
393

case — The case for *insanity* is strong to the insane.
191

deny — It is given you to learn how to deny *insanity*, and come forth from your private world in peace.
232

God — The Holy Spirit will restore your sanity because *insanity* is not the Will of God.
249

Holy Spirit — (The Holy Spirit) reverses the course of *insanity* and restores you to reason.
349

learn — You who know not what you do can learn what *insanity* is, and look beyond it.
232

madness — Not wholly mad, you have been willing to look on much of your *insanity* and recognize its madness.
424

outside — Inward is sanity; *insanity* is outside you.
348

reason — Hide not behind *insanity* in order to escape from reason.
429

reason — The part of mind where reason lies was dedicated, by your will in union with your Father's, to the undoing of *insanity*.
427

reason's — There is no reason in *insanity*, for it depends entirely on reason's absence.
427

sanity — Allowing *insanity* to enter your mind means that you have not judged sanity as wholly desirable.
117

sense — What makes no sense and has no meaning is *insanity*.
494

Son of God — No even what the Son of God made in *insanity* could be without a hidden spark of beauty that gentleness could release.
329

INSPIRATION

all — As a man and also one of God's creations, my right thinking, which came from the Holy Spirit or the Universal *Inspiration*, taught me first and foremost that this *Inspiration* is for all.   67

Holy Spirit — *Inspiration* is of the Holy Spirit, and certainty is of God according to His laws.   109

INSTANT

birth — Each *instant* is a clean, untarnished birth, in which the Son of God emerges from the past into the present.   281

blessed — In the blessed *instant* you will let go all your past learning, and the Holy Spirit will quickly offer you the whole lesson of peace.   283

ego's — (An *instant* is) long enough to transcend all of the ego's making, and ascend unto your Father.   283

eternal — Give the eternal *instant* that eternity may be remembered for you, in that shining *instant* of perfect release.   283

experience — The experience of an *instant*, however compelling it may be, is easily forgotten if you allow time to close over it.   340

Heaven — The tiny *instant* you would keep and make eternal, passed away in Heaven to soon for anything to notice it had come.   512

immortality — (An *instant* is) as long as it takes to remember immortality, and your immortal creations who share it with you.   283

love — What occurred within the *instant* that love entered in without attack will stay forever.   537

mind —'If you are tempted to be dispirited by thinking   **282**
how long it would take a change your
mind so completely, ask yourself,
"How long is an *instant*"

peace — The *instant* of peace is eternal because it is   **283**
without fear.

reborn — Every *instant* can you be reborn, and given life   **505**
again.

redeeming — In this redeeming *instant* lies Heaven.   **282**

INTERPRET

error — To *interpret* error is to give it power, and having   **200**
done this you will overlook truth.

solitude — Do not *interpret* out of solitude, for what you   **597**
see means nothing.

INTERPRETATION(S)

alien — What needs *interpretation* must be alien.   **437**

brother — Every *interpretation* you would lay upon a   **275**
brother is senseless.

brother's — Your *interpretation* of your brother's needs   **201**
are your *interpretation* of yours.

Holy Spirit — The Holy Spirit's goal gives one *interpreta-*   **597**
tion, meaningful to you and to your
brother.

justification — Your *interpretation* thus becomes the   **200**
justification for the response.

motivation — There is but one *interpretation* of motiva-   **200**
tion that makes any sense.

respond — Understand that you do not respond to any-   **200**
thing directly, but to your *interpretation*
of it.

INTERPRETER

one — We have one *Interpreter.*   **597**

INVEST

salvation — Insistence means investment, and what   **205**
you *invest* in is always related to your
notion of salvation.

INVESTMENT

relinquish — Yet to find the place (where you will see your vision changed) you must relinquish your *investment* in the world as you project it, allowing the Holy Spirit to extend the real world to you from the altar of God.   **207**

INVISIBLE

effects — Yet if you see the effects (of the *invisible*) you know it must be there. By perceiving what it does, you recognize its being.   **214**

Holy Spirit — The Holy Spirit is *invisible*, but you can see the results of His Presence, and through them you will learn that He is there.   **214**

see — You cannot see the *invisible*.   **214**

INVITATION

Holy Spirit — The Holy Spirit is there, although He cannot help you without your *invitation*.   **184**

perception — Your perception is the result of your *invitation*, coming to you as you sent for it.   **214**

INVITE

accept — You will accept only whom you *invite*.   **184**

INVULNERABILITY

attack — If you accept your *invulnerability*, you are recognizing that attack has no effect.   **209**

guiltlessness — The way to teach this simple lesson is merely this: guiltlessness is *invulnerability*.   **256**

make — Therefore, make your *invulnerability* manifest to everyone.   **256**

INVULNERABLE

guiltless — You are *invulnerable* because you are guiltless.   **222**

pure — Being wholly pure, you are *invulnerable*.   **223**

JOINED

unseparated — What is unseparated must be *joined*.   **561**

JOINING

present — Future loss is not your fear. But present *joining* is your dread.   **519**

JOURNEY

awakening — As you perceive the holy companions who travel with you, you will realize that there is no *journey*, but only an awakening.   **222**

choice — You came this far because the *journey* was your choice.   **395**

Christ — There is no *journey* but to walk with (Christ).   **475**

closes — The *journey* closes, ending at the place where it began.   **622**

darkness — You do not know (Who walks beside you on the way) because the *journey* into darkness has been long and cruel, and you have gone deep into it.   **353**

ego — Whenever fear intrudes anywhere along the road to peace, it is because the ego has attempted to join the *journey* with us and cannot do so.   **137**

end — The *journey's* end is at the place of peace.   **453**

end — You have reached the end of an ancient *journey*, not realizing yet that it is over.   **366**

endless — The *journey* that seemed endless is almost complete, for what is endless is very near.   **316**

exist — A *journey* from yourself does not exist.   **609**

Father — The *journey* the Son of God has set himself is useless indeed, but the *journey* on which his Father sets him is one of release and joy.   **221**

God — Ours is simply the *journey* back to God Who is our home.   **137**

God — The *journey* to God is merely the reawakening of the knowledge of where you are always, and what you are forever.   **139**

Holy Spirit — Whatever *journey* you choose to take, (the Holy Spirit) will go with you, waiting.   **183**

hopeless — There is no part of the *journey* that seems more hopeless and futile than standing where the road branches, and not deciding on which way to go.   **444**

lonely — The lonely *journey* fails because it has excluded what it would find.   **274**

me — On this *journey* you have chosen me as your companion instead of the ego.   **137**

peace — Content yourself with what you will as surely keep, and be not restless, for you undertake a quiet *journey* to the peace of God, where He would have you be in quietness.   **240**

purpose — A *journey* without a purpose is still meaningless, and even when it is over it seems to make no sense.   **393**

repeat — There is no hindrance to the Will of God, nor any need that you repeat again a *journey* that was over long ago.   **513**

together — The *journey* that we take together is the exchange of dark for light, of ignorance for understanding.   **264**

together — We begin the *journey* back by setting out together, and gather in our brothers as we continue together.   **137**

useless — Whenever you are tempted to undertake a useless *journey* that would lead away from light, remember what you really want, and say, "The Holy Spirit leads me unto Christ, And where else would I go? What need have I but to awake in Him?"   **239**

world — You will undertake a *journey* because you are not at home in this world.   **208**

JOY

beauty — Out of your *joy* you will create beauty in His   185
Name, for your *joy* could no more be
contained than His.

constancy — The constancy of *joy* is a condition quite   433
alien to your understanding.

cost — *Joy* has no cost.   592

created — Blessed Son of a wholly blessing Father, *joy*   262
was created for you.

depression — The opposite of *joy* is depression.   142

eternal — *Joy* is eternal.   439

eternity — Only *joy* increases forever, since *joy* and   105
eternity are inseparable.

find — You cannot find *joy* except as God does.   138

God's — (God's) *joy* lay in creating you, and He extends   138
His Fatherhood to you so that you can
extend yourself as He did.

heal — Those who attempt to heal without being wholly   66
joyous themselves call forth different
kinds of responses at the same time,
and thus deprive others of the *joy* of
responding whole-heartedly.

Holy Spirit — The Holy Spirit never varies on this point   101
(about what you are) and so the one
mood He engenders is *joy*.

inspire — If you inspire *joy* and others react to you with   161
joy, even though you are not
experiencing *joy* yourself there must be
something in you that is capable of
producing it.

know — You do not know your *joy* because you do not   123
know your own self-fullness.

love — There is no difference between love and *joy*.   66

misery — The search for *joy* in misery is senseless, for   439
how could *joy* be found in misery?

one — *Joy* calls forth an integrated willingness to share   66
it, and promotes the mind's natural
impulse to respond as one.

purpose — *Joy* is unified purpose.   143

seeks — Everyone seeks for what will bring him *joy* as he defines it.   **489**

sorrow — *Joy* cannot establish its eternal reign where sorrow dwells.   **240**

sorrow — *Joy* does not turn to sorrow, for the eternal cannot change.   **439**

sorrow — Sorrow can be turned to *joy*, for time gives way to the eternal.   **439**

source — What you seek for is a source of *joy* as you conceive it.   **473**

suffering — While you think that suffering and sin will bring you *joy*, so long they will be there for you to see.   **489**

unlimited — *Joy* is unlimited, because each shining thought of love extends its being and creates more of itself.   **450**

vision — *Joy* cannot be perceived except through constant vision.   **433**

want — What else but *joy* would you want?   **138**

JOYFUL

ego — What is *joyful* to you is painful to the ego, and as long as you are in doubt about what you are you will be confused about joy and pain.   **124**

JOYOUS

decided — Decision cannot be difficult. This is obvious, if you realize that you must have already decided not to be wholly *joyous* if that is how you feel.   **83**

love — Whenever you are not wholly *joyous*, it is because you have reacted with a lack of love to one of God's creations.   **82**

JUDGE

invisible — *Judge* not what is invisible to you or you will never see it, but wait in patience for its coming.   **405**

loves — No one who loves can *judge*, and what he sees is free of condemnation.   **411**

order — To order is to *judge*, and to arrange by judgment.   **273**

quietness — *Judge* not except in the quietness which is not of you.   **264**

sinner — *Judge* not because you cannot, not because you are a miserable sinner too.   **500**

understand — It is surely good advice to tell you not to *judge* what you do not understand.   **201**

JUDGING

everyone — Each one you see you place within the holy circle of Atonement or leave outside, *judging* him fit for crucifixion or redemption.   **264**

JUDGMENT

attack — *Judgment*, like any other defense, can be used to attack or protect; to hurt or to heal.   **58**

behold — Everything you behold without is a *judgment* of what you beheld within.   **216**

belief — In the end it does not matter whether your *judgment* is right or wrong. Either way you are placing your belief in the unreal.   **42**

brother — But forget not this; the role you give to (your brother) is given you, and you will walk the way you pointed out to him because it is your *judgment* on yourself.   **492**

condemnation — *Judgment* and condemnation are behind you, and unless you bring them with you, you will see that you are free of them.   **234**

damnation — Damnation is your *judgment* on yourself, and this you will project upon the world.   **415**

different — What is different calls for *judgment*, and this must come from someone "better," someone incapable of being like what he condemns, "above" it, sinless by comparison with it.   **465**

directions — *Judgment* will always give you false direc-   415
tions, but vision shows you where to
go.

escape — Escape from *judgment* simply lies in this: all   596
things have but one purpose, which
you share with all the world.

evaluation — The Last *Judgment* might be called a process   30
of right evaluation.

extend - Just as the separation occurred over millions of   30
years, the Last *Judgment* will extend
over a similarly long period, and
perhaps an even longer one.

fear — You will also regard *judgment* with fear, believing   43
that it will someday be used against
you.

fear — Your self-betrayal must result in fear, for fear is   579
judgment, leading surely to the frantic
search for idols and for death.

God — *Judgment* is not an attribute of God.   29

Holy Spirit — (The Holy Spirit) makes but one *judgment*;   507
that to hurt God's Son must be unfair
and therefore is not so.

illusion — The sword of *judgment* is the weapon that you   618
give to the illusion of yourself, that it
may fight to keep the space that holds
your brother off unoccupied by love.

imprisons — *Judgment* always imprisons because it   44
separates segments of reality by the
unstable scales of desire.

injustice — *Judgment* is an injustice to God's Son, and it is   578
justice that who judges him will not
escape the penalty he laid upon himself
within the dream he made.

knowledge — In the presence of knowledge all *judgment*   42
is automatically suspended and this is
the process that enables recognition to
replace perception.

life — You do not need *judgment* to organize your life,   42
and you certainly do not need it to
organize yourself.

miracles — The length of (the Last *Judgment*), however, can be shortened greatly by miracles, the device for shortening but not abolishing time.   **30**

past — *Judgment* always rests on the past, for past experience is the basis on which you judge.   **290**

perception — *Judgment* is symbolic because beyond perception there is no *judgment*.   **41**

price — There is a price you will pay for *judgment*, because *judgment* is the setting of a price. And as you set it you will pay it.   **154**

reality — You who would judge reality cannot see it, for whenever *judgment* enters reality has slipped away.   **237**

rejection — *Judgment* always involves rejection.   **42**

release — You have no idea of the tremendous release and deep peace that comes from meeting yourself and your brothers totally without *judgment*.   **42**

rightmindedness — Punishment is a concept totally opposed to rightmindedness, and the aim of the Last *Judgment* is to restore rightmindedness to you.   **30**

sane — Sane *judgment* would inevitably judge against the ego, and must be obliterated by the ego in the interest of its self-preservation.   **59**

separation — *Judgment* is not an attribute of God. It was brought into being only after the separation, when it became one of the many learning devices to be built into an overall plan.   **30**

Source — Remember the holy presence of the One given you to be the Source of *judgment*.   **391**

strain — The strain of constant *judgment* is virtually intolerable.   **43**

symbolic — *Judgment* is symbolic because beyond perception there is no *judgment*.   **41**

taught — *Judgment* you taught yourself; vision is learned   **411**
    from Him Who would undo your
    teaching.

value — *Judgment* has no value unless the goal is sin.   **411**

JUSTICE

awareness — (*Justice*) is awareness that giving and   **503**
    receiving are the same.

blind — *Justice*, being blind, is satisfied by being paid,   **498**
    it matters not by whom.

expedient — *Justice* is a temporary expedient, or an   **43**
    attempt to teach you the meaning of
    mercy.

God — God cannot be remembered until *justice* is loved   **507**
    instead of feared.

God — God ensured that *justice* would be done unto the   **499**
    Son He loves, and would protect from
    all unfairness you might seek to offer,
    believing vengeance is his proper due.

God — *Justice* does (God) know, and knows it well.   **498**

God's — God's *justice* rests in gentleness upon His Son,   **505**
    and keeps him safe from all injustice
    the world would lay upon him.

God's — God's *justice* warrants gratitude, not fear.   **501**

God's — In God's Own *justice* does He recognize all you   **499**
    deserve, but understands as well that
    you cannot accept it for your self.

Holy Spirit's — It is extremely hard for those who still   **498**
    believe sin meaningful to understand
    the Holy Spirit's *justice*.

Holy Spirit's — It is impossible for you to share the Holy   **498**
    Spirit's *justice* with a mind that can
    conceive of specialness at all.

insanity — Yet how could *justice* be defined without   **498**
    insanity where love means hate, and
    death is seen as victory and triumph
    over eternity and timelessness and
    life?

loser — Yet does the problem still remain unsolved, for only *justice* can set up a state in which there is no loser; no one left unfairly treated and deprived, and thus with grounds for vengeance.   **502**

love — Love and *justice* are not different.   **499**

love — Love without *justice* is impossible.   **500**

love — Without love is *justice* prejudiced and weak.   **500**

loving — And God rejoices as His Son receives what loving *justice* knows to be his due.   **499**

miracle — The miracle of *justice* can correct all errors.   **506**

punish — *Justice* cannot punish those who ask for punishment, but have a Judge Who knows that they are wholly innocent in truth.   **499**

sacrifice — *Justice* demands no sacrifice, for any sacrifice is made that sin may be preserved and kept.   **498**

same — *Justice* looks on all in the same way.   **498**

total — You would believe it safe to give but some mistakes to be corrected while you keep others to yourself, remember this: *justice* is total.   **507**

vengeance — Vengeance is alien to God's Mind because He knows of *justice*.   **498**

KINGDOM (OF HEAVEN)

alone — The *Kingdom of Heaven* cannot be found alone, and you who are the *Kingdom* cannot find yourself alone.   **132**

Atonement — In Heaven there is no guilt, because the *Kingdom* is attained through the Atonement, which releases you to create.   **77**

attack — When God created you He made you part of Him. That is why attack within the *Kingdom of Heaven* is impossible.   **93**

attention — To be in the *Kingdom of Heaven* is to merely focus your full attention on it.   **108**

awareness — The wholeness of the *Kingdom* does not   102
depend on your perception, but your
awareness of its wholeness does.

being — Being alone lives in the *Kingdom*, where every-   94
thing lives in God without question.

believed — You have believed you are without the   102
Kingdom, and have therefore excluded
yourself from it in your belief.

bereft — God in His knowledge is not waiting, but His   79
Kingdom is bereft while you wait.

certainty — There is only certainty (in the *Kingdom of*   106
Heaven.)

confusion — There is no confusion in the *Kingdom*, be-   107
cause there is only one meaning.

Creator — If you do not extend the *Kingdom* you are not   117
thinking with your Creator and
creating as He created.

darkness — No darkness abides anywhere in the *King-*   91
dom, but your part is only to allow no
darkness to abide in your own mind.

extending — The *Kingdom* is forever extending itself   123
because it is in the Mind of God.

fear — You can delay the completion of the *Kingdom*, but   81
you cannot introduce the concept of
fear into it.

guilt — Before the glorious radiance of the *Kingdom* guilt   248
melts away, and transformed into
kindness will never more be what it
was.

having — Remember that in the *Kingdom* there is no   64
difference between having and being,
as there is in existence.

identification — Your identification with the *Kingdom* is   116
totally beyond question except by you,
when you are thinking insanely.

idolators — There are no idolators in the *Kingdom*, but   172
there is great appreciation for
everything that God created, because
of the calm knowledge that each one is
part of Him.

illusion — Everything outside of the *Kingdom* is illusion. 103

illusions — (The *Kingdom of Heaven*) has not ceased to create because of the ego's illusions. 54

included — It is therefore essential to teach you that you must be included (in the *Kingdom of Heaven*), and that the belief that you are not is the only thing that you must exclude. 102

joy — The whole glory and perfect joy that is the *Kingdom* lies in you to give. 113

laws — See ye first the *Kingdom of Heaven*, because that is where the laws of God operate truly, and they can operate only truly because they are the laws of truth. 110

lost — Remember the *Kingdom* always, and remember that you who are part of the *Kingdom* cannot be lost. 80

love — You cannot remain within the *Kingdom* without love, and since the *Kingdom* is love, you believe that you are without it. 93

nothing — There is nothing else (besides the *Kingdom of Heaven*). 110

part — You are a child of God, a priceless part of His *Kingdom*, which He created as part of Him. 94

peace — The great peace of the *Kingdom of Heaven* shines in your mind forever, but it must shine outward to make you aware of it. 91

replace — You cannot replace the *Kingdom*, and you cannot replace yourself. 167

seeming — You who are the *Kingdom* are not concerned with seeming. 108

sell — You cannot sell the *Kingdom of Heaven*. 209

Son of God — The *Kingdom of Heaven* is the dwelling place of the Son of God, who left not his Father and dwells not apart from Him. 358

Sons — The *Kingdom of Heaven* includes all His Sons and their children, who are as like the Sons as they are like the Father. 127

teaching — In the *Kingdom* there is no teaching or learn-   **106**
ing, because there is no belief.

whole — To (God's perfect love) the Holy Spirit leads   **105**
you, that your joy may be complete
because the *Kingdom of God* is whole.

within — The *Kingdom of Heaven* is within you.   **197**

you — The *Kingdom of Heaven* is you.   **54**

you — You are the *Kingdom of Heaven,* but you have let the   **69**
belief in darkness enter your mind and
so you need a new light.

KNOW

acknowledge — It is true, just as you fear, that to   **310**
acknowledge Him is to deny all you
think you *know.*

certainty — To *know* is to be certain, and certainty is   **35**
strength.

learning — The essential thing is learning that you do   **275**
not *know.*

peace — Whenever you think you *know,* peace will depart   **278**
from you, because you have abandoned
the Teacher of peace.

true — What you think you *know* was never true.   **310**

unknowing — It is not possible to convince the un-   **267**
knowing that they *know.*

KNOWING

doing — *Knowing,* as we have already observed, does not   **39**
lead to doing.

interpretation — *Knowing* is not open to interpretation.   **40**

sharing — You who share His life must share it to know   **182**
it, for sharing is *knowing.*

truth — True perception is the basis for knowledge, but   **35**
knowing is the affirmation of truth and
beyond all perceptions.

KNOWLEDGE

adjustments — *Knowledge* requires no adjustments and,   **399**
in fact, is lost if any shift or change
is undertaken.

all — All *knowledge* must be yours, for in you is all *knowledge.*   **241**

altar — *Knowledge* comes from the altar within and is timeless because it is certain.   **36**

aspect — You are an aspect of *knowledge,* being in the Mind of God, Who knows you.   **240**

attainment — *Knowledge* is far beyond attainment of any kind.   **427**

changes — *Knowledge* never changes, so its constellation is permanent.   **144**

comparisons — *Knowledge* never involves comparisons. That is its main difference from everything the mind can grasp.   **54**

concern — *Knowledge* is far beyond your individual concern.   **242**

condition — (A condition in which opposites do not exist) is the condition of *knowledge.*   **195**

conditions — *Knowledge* can be restored only when you meet its conditions.   **128**

correction — *Knowledge* needs no correction.   **238**

Creator — *Knowledge* has but one law because it has but one Creator.   **487**

darkness — As darkness disappears in light, so ignorance fades away when *knowledge* dawns.   **267**

deceive — *Knowledge* cannot deceive, but perception can.   **45**

dissociation — Any part of *knowledge* threatens dissociation as much as all of it.   **427**

dissociation — *Knowledge* must precede dissociation, so that dissociation is nothing more than a decision to forget.   **169**

do — This cannot be an active process of correction, because, as I have already emphasized, *knowledge* does not do anything.   **38**

Father — You who are part of *(knowledge)* and all of it need only realize that it is of the Father, not of you.   **242**

flow — *Knowledge* is always ready to flow everywhere, but it cannot oppose.   **68**

free — The *knowledge* that illuminates not only sets you free, but also shows you clearly that you are free.   **15**

God — I have said that the last step in the reawakening of *knowledge* is taken by God.   **105**

God — Nothing can change the *knowledge,* given you by God, unto unknowingness.   **270**

God — You can deny God's *knowledge,* but you cannot change it.   **243**

God — You can know yourself only as God knows His Son, for *knowledge* is shared with God.   **162**

Holy Spirit — The word "know" is proper in this context, because the Holy Spirit is so close to *knowledge* that He calls it forth; or better, allows it to come.   **68**

Holy Spirit — Why would you struggle so frantically to anticipate all you cannot know, when all *knowledge* lies behind every decision the Holy Spirit makes for you?   **258**

illusions — *Knowledge* cannot dawn on a mind full of illusions, because truth and illusions are irreconcilable.   **174**

impersonal — Abstract thought applies to *knowledge* because *knowledge* is completely impersonal, and examples are irrelevant to its understanding.   **51**

ingenuity — Ingenuity is totally divorced from *knowledge,* because *knowledge* does not require ingenuity.   **40**

lack — Lack of *knowledge* of any kind is always associated with unwillingness to know, and this produces a total lack of *knowledge* simply because *knowledge* is total.   **165**

littleness — Not to question your littleness therefore is to deny all *knowledge.*   **165**

lovelessly — You are also incapable of *knowledge* because you can still perceive lovelessly.   **37**

one — *(Knowledge)* is all one and has no separate parts.   **41**

partial — The very real difference between perception and *knowledge* becomes quite apparent if you consider this: There is nothing partial about *knowledge*.   **240**

peace — *Knowledge* is not the motivation for learning this course. Peace is.   **128**

perception — *Knowledge* preceded both perception and time, and will ultimately replace them.   **36**

perception — *Knowledge* transcends the laws governing perception, because partial *knowledge* is impossible.   **41**

perception — This is because *knowledge* makes no attack upon perception. They are brought together, and only one continues past the gate where Oneness is.   **508**

power — *Knowledge* is power, and all power is of God.   **275**

reality — Being corrected (perception) gives place to *knowledge,* which is forever the only reality.   **219**

remembered — What you perceive as *(knowledge's)* attack is your own vague recognition that *knowledge* can always be remembered, never having been destroyed.   **39**

restored — *Knowledge* can be restored only when you meet its conditions.   **128**

revelation — *Knowledge* is the result of revelation and induces only thought.   **36**

stable — *Knowledge* is always stable, and it is quite evident that you are not.   **40**

strength — *Knowledge* provides the strength for creative thinking, but not for right doing.   **36**

timeless — *Knowledge* comes from the altar within and is timeless because it is certain.   **36**

total — *Knowledge* is total, and the ego does not believe in totality.   **115**

true — Perception's laws are opposite to truth, and what is true of *knowledge* is not true of anything that is apart from it.   **515**

union — The bridge that leads to union in yourself must lead to *knowledge,* for it was built with God beside you, and will lead you straight to Him where your completion rests, wholly comparable with His.   316

Will — *Knowledge* is His Will.   128

LACK

death — For you believe you can suffer *lack,* and *lack* is death.   574

deny — What you deny you *lack,* not because it is lacking, but because you have denied it in another and are therefore not aware of it in yourself.   118

God — While *lack* does not exist in the creation of God, it is very apparent in what you have made.   11

no — There is no *lack* (in God's Son).   561

separation — A sense of separation from God is the only *lack* you really need correct.   11

separation — Until the "separation," which is the meaning of the "fall," (there was no *lack*).   11

sin — (Perceiving sin as an act of assault) is necessary to the ego's survival because, as soon as you regard sin as a *lack,* you will automatically attempt to remedy the situation.   78

LANGUAGE(S)

interpreter — Your interpreter perceives the meaning in your alien *language.*   266

two — You speak two *languages* at once, and this must lead to unintelligibility.   266

LAST JUDGMENT

apply — You can, however, apply (your own *last judgment*) meaningfully, and at any time to everything you have made, and retain in your memory only what is creative and good.   30

death — The term *"Last Judgment"* is frightening not only   30
because it has been projected onto God,
but also because of the association of
"last" with death.

fear — Do not fear the *Last Judgment,* but welcome it and   158
do not wait, for the ego's time is bor-
rowed from your eternity.

healing — The *Last Judgment* is the final healing, not a   30
meting out of punishment, however
much you may think that punishment
is deserved.

ideas — The *Last Judgment* is one of the most threatening   29
ideas in your thinking.

life — If the meaning of the *Last Judgment* is objectively   30
examined, it is quite apparent that it is
really the doorway to life.

LAW(S)

adapted — *Laws* must be adapted to circumstances if   106
they are to maintain order.

apply — (The *law*) therefore produces abundance or   120
scarcity, depending on how you choose
to apply it.

brother — You place yourself under the *laws* you see as   477
ruling (your brother).

change — You cannot change *laws* you did not make, and   151
the *laws* of happiness were created for
you, not by you.

chaos — No *law* of chaos could compel belief but for the   458
emphasis on form and disregard of
content.

chaos — The *laws* of chaos can be brought to light,   455
though never understood.

chaos — The first *law* of chaos is that truth is different   455
for everyone.

chaos — The second *law* of chaos, dear indeed to every   455
worshipper of sin, is that each one
must sin, and therefore deserves
attack and death.

chaos — The third *law* of chaos is, if God cannot be mistaken, He must accept His Son's belief in what he is, and hate him for it. — 456

chaos — The fourth *law* of chaos is the belief you have what you have taken. — 456

chaos — The final *law* of chaos holds there is a substitute for love. — 457

chaotic — Chaotic *laws* are hardly meaningful, and therefore out of reason's sphere. — 455

communicated — *Laws* must be communicated if they are to be helpful. — 106

continuity — But remember that *laws* are set up to protect the continuity of the system in which the lawmaker believes. — 48

ego — "Giving to get" is an inescapable *law* of the ego, which always evaluates itself in relation to other egos. — 52

ego — To the ego, the *law* is perceived as a means of getting rid of something it does not want. — 120

ego — When you feel guilty, remember that the ego has indeed violated the *laws* of God, but you have not. — 57

God — Between the future and the past the *laws* of God must intervene, if you would free yourself. — 243

God — God Himself created the *law* by creating by it. — 106

God — God Himself has protected everything He created by His *laws*. — 174

God — (The *laws* of God) are of freedom, but yours are the *laws* of bondage. — 174

God — (The *laws* of God) govern you because they govern everything. — 133

God — (The *laws* of God) were established for your protection and are as inviolate as your safety. — 168

God — The *laws* of God work only for your good, and there are no other *laws* beside His. — 174

God — What God has given follows His *law,* and His   **403**
         alone.

God — Yet are (God's) *laws* reflected everywhere.   **487**

God — You were created through (the *laws* of God) and   **174**
         by His Will, and the manner of your
         creation established you a creator.

God's — God's *laws* hold only for your protection, and   **186**
         they never hold in vain.

God's — God's *laws* will keep your mind at peace because   **174**
         peace is His Will, and His *laws* are
         established to uphold it.

God's — (God's) definitions are his *laws,* for by them He   **175**
         established the universe as what it is.

God's — God's *laws* do not obtain directly to a world per-   **487**
         ception rules, for such a world could
         not have been created by the Mind to
         which perception has no meaning.

God's — You can violate God's *laws* in your imagination,   **168**
         but you cannot escape from them.

happiness — You cannot change *laws* you did not make,   **151**
         and the *laws* of happiness were created
         for you, not by you.

Holy Spirit — The Holy Spirit is the translator of the   **106**
         laws of God to those who do not under-
         stand them.

insane — Your insane *laws* were made to guarantee you   **403**
         would make mistakes, and give them
         power over you by accepting their
         results as your just due.

knowledge — Knowledge has but one *law* because it has   **487**
         but one Creator.

meaningless — *Laws* are not meaningless, since all   **110**
         meaning is contained by them and in
         them.

mind — I have said before that whether you project or   **215**
         extend is up to you, but you must do
         one or the other, for that is a *law* of the
         mind, and you must look in before you
         look out.

mind — The outstanding characteristic of the *laws* of the   **106**
mind as they operate in the world is
that by obeying them, and I assure you
that you must obey them, you can
arrive at diametrically opposed results.

perception's — Perception's basic *law* could thus be said,   **489**
"You will rejoice at what you see be-
cause you see it to rejoice."

project — Outside of the Kingdom the *law* that prevails   **106**
inside is adapted to "What you project,
you believe."

reality — Reality observes the *laws* of God, and not the   **589**
rules you set.

sin — The *laws* of sin demand a victim.   **498**

truth — The extension of truth, which is the *law* of the   **107**
Kingdom, rests only on the knowledge
of what truth is.

universe — The *laws* of the universe do not permit con-   **181**
tradiction.

voices — The shadow voices do not change the *laws* of   **513**
time nor of eternity.

yours — (God's) are the *laws* of freedom, but yours are   **174**
the *laws* of bondage.

LAWFUL

creation — Creation is perfectly *lawful,* and the chaotic   **174**
is without meaning because it is with-
out God.

LEARN

alone — Remember that you *learn* not for yourself   **287**
alone, no more than I did.

aright — You really want to *learn* aright, and nothing   **211**
can oppose the decision of God's Son.

gratitude — As you *learn,* your gratitude to your Self,   **313**
who teaches you what He is, will grow
and help you honor Him.

power — Your power to *learn* is strong enough to teach   **600**
you that your will is not your own,
your thoughts do not belong to you,
and even you are someone else.

projected — This (teaching) form implies that you will *learn* what you are from what you have projected on others, and therefore believe they are.   **106**

value — Indeed, many of the things you want to *learn* may be chosen because their value will not last.   **60**

value — The ability to *learn* has no value when change is no longer necessary.   **17**

value — You *learn* best when you believe what you are trying to *learn* is of value to you.   **60**

want — But perhaps you do not realize, even yet, that there is something you want to *learn,* and that you can learn it because it is your choice to do so.   **211**

waste — You but waste time unless you go beyond what you have learned to what is yet to *learn.*   **608**

yourself — (The Holy Spirit) becomes your Resource because of yourself you cannot *learn.*   **210**

LEARNED

experiences — Ask to be taught, and do not use your experiences to confirm what you have *learned.*   **277**

God — When you have *learned* to decide with God, all decisions become as easy and right as breathing.   **260**

love — Love is not *learned.* Its meaning lies within itself.   **369**

power — No one who understands what you have *learned,* how carefully you *learned* it, and the pains to which you went to practice and repeat the lessons endlessly, in every form you could conceive of them, could ever doubt the power of your learning skill.   **600**

present — Nothing you have ever *learned* can help you understand the present, or teach you how to undo the past.   **275**

recognize — You need only recognize that everything you *learned* you do not want.   **277**

recognized — Miracles demonstrate that learning has 213
    occurred under the right guidance, for
    learning is invisible and what has been
    learned can be recognized only by its
    results.

transfer — You cannot transfer what you have not 210
    learned, and the impairment of the
    ability to generalize is a crucial learning
    failure.

LEARNER

guiltless — The guiltless *learner* learns easily because his 255
    thoughts are free.

happy — The happy *learner* cannot feel guilty about
    learning. 255

LEARNING

ability — *Learning* is an ability you made and gave your- 601
    self.

body — *Learning* must lead beyond the body to the re- 142
    establishment of the power of the mind
    in it.

change — *Learning* is change. 615

change — Many stand guard over their ideas because 48
    they want to protect their thought sys-
    tems as they are, and *learning* means
    change.

condition — *Learning* applies only to the condition in 260
    which it happens of itself.

corrective — Corrective *learning* always begins with 22
    awakening of spirit, and the turning
    away from the belief in physical sight.

Creator — *Learning* is useless in the Presence of your 369
    Creator, Whose acknowledgement of
    you and yours of Him so far transcend
    all *learning* that everything you learned
    is meaningless, replaced forever by the
    knowledge of love and its one meaning.

depression — Whenever the reaction to *learning* is de- 141
    pression, it is because the true goal of
    the curriculum has been lost sight of.

dissatisfaction — Dissatisfaction with *learning* outcomes is a sign of *learning* failure, since it means that you did not get what you wanted. **128**

ego — *Learning* is ultimately perceived as frightening because it leads to the relinquishment, not the destruction, of the ego to the light of the Spirit. **48**

failure — Good teachers never terrorize their students. To terrorize is to attack, and this results in the rejection of what the teacher offers. The result is *learning* failure. **33**

fight — You fight against all *learning* and succeed, for that is what you want. **211**

God — Where *learning* ends there God begins, for *learning* ends before Him Who is complete where He begins, and where there is no end. **369**

handicaps — You have *learning* handicaps in a very literal sense. **210**

happiness — From this lowest point will *learning* lead to heights of happiness, in which you see the purpose of the lesson shining clear, and perfectly within your *learning* grasp. **608**

hurt — For every *learning* that would hurt you, God offers you correction and complete escape from all its consequences. **320**

joyful — *Learning* is joyful if it leads along your natural path, and facilitates the development of what you have. **130**

Kingdom — In the Kingdom there is no teaching or *learning*, because there is no belief. **106**

learn — *Learning* and wanting to learn are inseparable. **60**

manifest — *Learning* has been accomplished before its effects are manifest. **276**

meaningful — Only while there is a belief in differences is *learning* meaningful. **17**

memory — *Learning* is impossible without memory since it must be consistent to be remembered.   **107**

past — *Learning* is therefore in the past, but its influence determines the present by giving it whatever meaning it holds for you.   **276**

past — Your past *learning* must have taught you the wrong things, simply because it has not made you happy.   **128**

potential — Your *learning* potential, properly understood, is limitless because it will lead you to God.   **211**

power — The power of your *learning* will be proved to you by all the many different witnesses it finds.   **537**

power — True *learning* is constant, and so vital in its power for change that a Son of God can recognize his power in one instant and change the world in the next.   **112**

purpose — Are you willing to accept this (seeing yourself as limited to a body), when your whole purpose for *learning* should be to escape from limitations?   **143**

rewards — *Learning* through rewards is more effective than *learning* through pain, because pain is an ego illusion, and can never induce more than a temporary effect.   **61**

temporary — *Learning* itself, like the classrooms in which it occurs, is temporary.   **17**

transfer — All *learning* aims at transfer, which becomes complete within two situations that are seen as one, for only common elements are there.   **536**

transfer — Leave, then, the transfer of your *learning* to One Who really understands its laws, and Who will guarantee that they remain unvioleted and unlimited.   **537**

universe — The universe of *learning* will open before you in all its gracious simplicity.   **254**

world — On your *learning* depends the welfare of the world. 449

world — The *learning* of the world is built upon a concept of the self adjusted to the world's reality. 610

LEARNING DEVICE(S)

body — Only the mind can create because spirit has already been created, and the body is a *learning device* of the mind. 20

errors — (A *learning device*) has no power to introduce actual learning errors. 20

faulty — The worst a faulty use of a *learning device* can do is fail to facilitate learning. 20

goal — To confuse a *learning device* with a curriculum goal is a fundamental confusion that blocks the understanding of both. 142

teacher — A *learning device* is not a teacher. 145

LESSON(S)

ancient — An ancient *lesson* is not overcome by the opposing of the new and old. 603

believe — Never believe that any *lesson* you have learned apart from Him means anything. 276

dark — But to accomplish this (learning of his happiness), all your dark *lessons* must be brought willingly to truth, and joyously laid down by hands open to receive, not closed to take. 276

dark — Every dark *lesson* that you bring to Him Who teaches light He will accept from you, because you do not want it. 276

God's — If you are wholly free of fear of any kind, and if all those who meet or even think of you share in your perfect peace, then you can be sure that you have learned God's *lesson*. 276

guiltless — The outcome of the *lesson* that God's Son is guiltless is a world in which there is no fear, and everything is lit with hope and sparkles with a gentle friendliness. 601

guilty — The certain outcome of the *lesson* that God's   601
    Son is guilty is the world you see.

hardest — (That truth is true) is the hardest *lesson* you   253
    will ever learn, and in the end the only
    one.

joyous — Begin to learn the joyous *lessons* that come   254
    quickly on the firm foundation that
    truth is true.

teach — The *lessons* you would teach yourself He has   277
    corrected already.

trials — Trials are but *lessons* that you failed to learn   620
    presented once again, so where you
    made a faulty choice before you now
    can make a better one, and thus escape
    all the pain that what you chose before
    has brought to you.

two — The *lessons* to be learned are only two.   601

LIFE

accomplished — Everything is accomplished through   96
    life, and *life* is of the mind and in the
    mind.

creation — Nothing alive is fatherless, for *life* is creation.   179

death — *Life* makes not death, creating like itself.   462

death — Death yields to *life* simply because destruction   265
    is not true.

death — It cannot be the "sinner's" wish for death is just   494
    as strong as is God's Will for *life.*

denial — Denial of *life* perceives its opposite, as all forms   175
    of denial replace what is with what is
    not.

God — Death is the result of thought we call the ego, as   388
    surely as *life* is the result of the
    Thought of God.

God — For God is *Life,* and they abide in *Life.*   271

God — The death penalty is the ego's ultimate goal, for   216
    it fully believes that you are a criminal,
    as deserving of death as God knows
    you are deserving of *life.*

Heaven — There is no *life* outside of Heaven.   459

Holy Spirit — To the Holy Spirit the goal is *life,* which   280
        has no end.

hopelessness — Hopelessness and death must disappear   529
        before the ancient clarion call of *life.*

instant — Every instant offers *life* to (the Son of God)   518
        because his Father wills that he should
        live.

miracle — The miracle of *life* is ageless, born in time but   390
        nourished in eternity.

peace — *Life* is peace.   541

price — You pay no price for *life,* for that was given you,   209
        but you do pay a price for death, and a
        very heavy one.

world — *Life is given you to give the dying world.*   536

LIGHT

come — For, like your brothers, you do not realize the   254
        light has come and freed you from the
        sleep of darkness.

create — Perceiving the spark will heal, but knowing the   175
        light will create.

darkened — *Light* must come into the darkened world to   241
        make Christ's vision possible even
        here.

darkness — As the *light* comes nearer, you will rush to   353
        darkness, shrinking from the truth,
        sometimes retreating to the lesser;
        forms of fear, and sometimes to stark
        terror.

darkness — *Light* does not attack darkness, but it does   134
        shine it away.

darkness — Nor is it possible that what gives *light* be one   423
        with what depends on darkness to be
        seen.

darkness — The children of *light* cannot abide in dark-   185
        ness, for darkness is not in them.

darkness — Whenever *light* enters darkness, the dark-   28
        ness is abolished.

darkness — You have been willing to bring darkness to *light,* and this willingness has given strength to everyone who would remain in darkness.   354

darkness — Your *light* will join with theirs in power so compelling, that it will draw the others out of darkness as you look on them.   236

Heaven — Not one *light* in Heaven but goes with you.   354

holy — The holy *light* you saw outside yourself, in every miracle you offered to your brothers, will be returned to you.   242

in — Child of *light,* you know not that the *light* is in you.   235

kept — The *light* is kept from everything you see.   617

likeness — Clear in Your likeness does the *light* shine forth from everything that lives and moves in You.   622

mind — When mind has only *light,* it knows only *light.*   127

peace — Child of peace, the *light* has come to you.   448

recognize — The *light* you bring you do not recognize, and yet you will remember.   448

see — Each one you see in *light* brings your *light* closer to your awareness.   235

travels — He Who travels with you has the *light.*   605

universe — The *light* that joins you shines throughout the universe, and because it joins you, so it makes you one with your Creator.   450

unlimited — *Light* is unlimited and spreads across this world in quiet joy.   236

walls — *Light* cannot penetrate through walls you make to block it, and it is forever unwilling to destroy what you have made.   56

way — But deny (the dark companions) instead, for the *light* is here and the way is very near.   185

witnesses — Yet you will find *(light)* through its witnesses, for having given light to them they will return it.   235

world — Each of us is the *light* of the world, and by join-   **91**
ing our minds in this *light* we proclaim
the Kingdom of God together and as
one.

world — Let not the world's *light,* given unto you, be   **619**
hidden from the world.

world — There is a *light* that this world cannot give.   **235**

you — The *light* is in you.   **352**

LIMIT(S)

ego — *Limits* are demanded by the ego, and represent its   **300**
demands to make little and ineffectual.

everywhere — No one can be beyond the limitless, be-   **180**
cause what has no *limit* must be every-
where.

fear — For what you think is sin is limitation, and whom   **422**
you try to *limit* to the body, you hate
because you fear.

give — To give without *limit* is God's will for you, be-   **181**
cause only this can bring you the joy
that is His and that He wills to share
with you.

God — Think not the *limits* you impose on what you see   **506**
can *limit* God in any way.

world — You on earth can have no conception of limit-   **272**
lessness, for the world you seem to live
in is a world of *limits.*

LIMITATION

everything — No one who knows he has everything   **463**
could seek for *limitation,* nor could he
value the body's offerings.

sacrifice — Sacrifice is invariably a means for *limitation,*   **423**
and thus for hate.

LIMITLESS

beyond — No one can be beyond the *limitless,* because   **180**
what has no limits must be every-
where.

LIMITLESSNESS

earth — You on earth can have no conception of *limit-lessness*, for the world you seem to live in is a world of limits.   **272**

LITTLE

function — Your function is not *little*, and it is only by finding your function and fulfilling it that you can escape from littleness.   **285**

littleness — With the grandeur of God in you, you have chosen to be *little* and to lament your littleness.   **164**

satisfied — Believe that the *little* can content you and by limiting yourself you will not be satisfied.   **285**

LITTLENESS

arrogance — To accept your *littleness* is arrogance, because it means that you believe your evaluation of yourself is truer than God's.   **167**

content — Be not content with *littleness*.   **285**

content — It is essential that you accept the fact, and accept it gladly, that there is no form of *littleness* that can ever content you.   **285**

function — For your function is not little, and it is only by finding your function and fulfilling it that you can escape from *littleness*.   **285**

give — Neither give *littleness*, nor accept it.   **286**

glory — *Littleness* and glory are the choices open to your striving and your vigilance.   **285**

God — It is beyond all your *littleness* to give the gift of God, but not beyond you.   **286**

grandeur — *Littleness* and grandeur cannot coexist, nor is it possible for them to alternate.   **166**

grandiosity — *Littleness* and grandiosity can and must alternate, since both are untrue and are therefore on the same level.   **166**

interferers — Let not the little interferers pull you to *littleness*.   **451**

knowledge — Not to question your *littleness* therefore is   165
    to deny all knowledge, and keep the
    ego's whole thought system intact.

magnitude — *Littleness* is the offering you give yourself,   285
    you offer this in place of magnitude,
    and you accept it.

peace — Choose *littleness* and you will not have peace,   285
    for you will have judged yourself
    unworthy for it.

purpose — Your purpose is at variance with *littleness* of   451
    any kind.

striving — All striving must be directed against *littleness*,   285
    for it does require vigilance to protect
    your magnitude in this world.

temptation — Let not *littleness* lead God's Son into temp-   451
    tation.

truth — Truth and *littleness* are denials of each other be-   166
    cause grandeur is truth.

LOGIC

world — The *logic* of the world must therefore lead to   251
    nothing, for its goal is nothing.

world — There is nothing in the world to teach him that   252
    the *logic* of the world is totally insane
    and leads to nothing.

LONELINESS

God's — The *loneliness* of God's Son is the *loneliness* of his   298
    Father.

relationship — You are forever in a relationship so holy   299
    that it calls to everyone to escape from
    loneliness, and join you in your love.

relationship — You whose relationship shares the Holy   344
    Spirit's goal are set apart from *loneliness*
    because the truth has come.

Will — Who dwells in shadows is alone indeed, and *lone-*   514
    liness is not the Will of God.

LOOK

guide — As you *look* in, you choose the guide for seeing.   215

in — I said before that what you project or extend is up 215
to you, but you must do one or the
other, for that is a law of mind, and you
must *look* in before you *look* out.

LOSE
deserves — No one deserves to *lose*. 502

LOSS
fear — Future *loss* is not your fear. 519

God — What God has given cannot be a *loss*, and what is 557
not of Him has no effects.

impossible — *Loss* of any kind is impossible. 141

incomplete — If *loss* in any form is possible, then is God's 517
Son made incomplete and not himself.

misunderstanding — Yet all *loss* comes only from your 141
own misunderstanding.

thought — In any thought of *loss* there is no meaning. 597

LOVE(S)
accept — You can accept insanity because you made 226
it, but you cannot accept *love* because
you did not.

afraid — You do not realize that you are not afraid of 353
love, but only of what you have made of
it.

answers — *Love* always answers, being unable to deny a 237
call for help, or not to hear the cries of
pain that rise to it from every part of
this strange world you made but do
not want.

attack — If you seek *love* in order to attack it, you will 217
never find it.

attraction — What God did not give you has no power 219
over you, and the attraction of *love* for
love remains irresistible.

barriers — Your task is not to seek for *love* but to find the 315
barriers in yourself that you have built
against it.

belief — Hold back but one belief, one offering, and *love* is gone, because you asked a substitute to take its place.   464

bodies — *Love* knows no bodies, and reaches to everything created like itself.   365

boundless — Your *love* is as boundless as (God's) because it is His.   181

call — What you call with *love* will come to you.   237

certainty — *Love* rests in certainty.   446

change — For hate is an illusion, and what can change was never *love*.   314

changeless — (*Love*) is changeless but continually exchanged, being offered by the eternal to the eternal.   230

charity — Charity is really a weaker reflection of a much more powerful *love* encompassment that is far beyond any form of charity you can conceive of as yet.   23

confused — You cannot safely make this division (between *love* and the call for *love*) for you are much too confused either to recognize *love*, or to believe that everything else is nothing but a call for *love*.   274

content — Whenever any form of special relationship tempts you to seek for *love* in ritual, remember *love* is content, and not form of any kind.   319

create — Make way for *love*, which you did not create, but which you can extend.   568

creates — This is perception's form, adapted to this world, of God's more basic law; that *love* creates itself and nothing but itself.   487

creation — All fear is implicit in (miscreation), and all *love* in creation.   28

decide — Let *love* decide and never fear that you, in your unfairness, will deprive yourself of what God's justice has allotted you.   501

defense — If you would look upon *love*, which is the   **202**
world's reality, how could you do
better than to recognize, in every
defense against it, the underlying
appeal for it?

deny — If you deny *love* you will not know it because   **151**
your cooperation is the law of its being.

deny — It is impossible to deny what *love* is and still   **305**
recognize it.

die — Only the eternal can be loved, for *love* does not die.   **177**

draws — Everyone draws nigh unto what he *loves*, and   **231**
recoils from what he fears.

ego — Yet I assure you that without the ego, all would   **290**
be *love*.

enemy — Let him be what he is, and seek not to make of   **394**
love an enemy.

enter — You are more afraid of God than the ego, and   **226**
love cannot enter where it is not wel-
come.

everything — Fear is really nothing and *love* is every-   **28**
thing.

exceptions — *Love* is incapable of any exceptions.   **112**

exempt — Exempt no one from your *love*, or you will be   **227**
hiding a dark place in your mind where
the Holy Spirit is not welcome.

extended — *Love* must be extended.   **550**

extends — *Love* extends outward simply because it can-   **104**
not be contained.

extension — *Love* is extension.   **464**

fair — *Love* is fair and cannot chasten without cause.   **500**

Father — You cannot understand how much your   **261**
Father *loves* you, for there is no parallel
in your experience of the world to help
you understand it.

fear — As *love* must look past fear, so must fear see *love*   **382**
not.

fear — Fear and *love* are the only emotions of which you   **202**
are capable.

fear — Healing must be as complete as fear, for *love* cannot enter where there is one spot of fear to mar its welcome. **227**

fear — *Love* is treacherous to those who fear, since fear and hate can never be apart. **563**

fear — *Love*, where fear has entered, cannot be depended on because it is not perfect. **291**

fear — Say to yourself that you must somehow have chosen not to *love*, or the fear could not have arisen. **26**

fear — There is no fear in *love*. **398**

fear — Truth does not struggle against ignorance, and *love* does not attack fear. **267**

fear — Where fear has gone, there *love* must come, because there are but these alternatives. **558**

fear — You have chosen to fear *love* because of its perfect harmlessness, and because of this fear you have been willing to give up your own perfect helplessness and your own perfect Help. **173**

flows — Unbroken and uninterrupted *love* flows constantly between the Father and the Son, as both would have it be. And so it is. **269**

forever — *Love* offers everything forever. **464**

freedom — *Love* is freedom. **321**

function — Learn first of (your brothers) and you will be ready to hear God. That is because the function of *love* is one. **63**

function — For it is the function of *love* to unite all things unto itself, and to hold all things together by extending its wholeness. **219**

give — You cannot really give anything but *love* to anyone or anything, nor can you really receive anything but *love* from them. **215**

given — (The *love* between the Father and His Son) is the only *love* that is fully given and fully returned. **294**

gladly — *Love* leads so gladly! **237**

God — That is how God Himself created you; in under-   113
standing, in appreciation and in *love*.

God — Never forget the *Love* of God, Who has remem-   258
bered you.

God — You can *love* as God *loves*.   247

God's — Do not interpret against God's *Love*, for you   310
have many witnesses that speak of it
so clearly that only the blind and deaf
could fail to see and hear them.

guilt — *Love* and guilt cannot coexist, and to accept one   221
is to deny the other.

guilt — *Love* contains the end of guilt, as surely as fear   382
depends on it.

guilt — The attraction of guilt produces fear of *love*, for   382
love would never look on guilt at all.

happy — *Love* asks only that you be happy, and will give   311
you everything that makes for happi-
ness.

hate — The symbols of hate against the symbols of *love*   314
play out a conflict that does not exist.

hate — For it is the attempt to balance hate with *love* that   314
makes *love* meaningless to you.

hates — No one who hates but is afraid of *love*, and   563
therefore must he be afraid of God.

hatred — If you seek *love* outside yourself you can be   315
certain you perceive hatred within, and
are afraid of it.

Heaven — Everyone you welcome will bring *love* with   366
him from Heaven for you.

Heaven — In Heaven, where the meaning of *love* is   317
known, *love* is the same as union.

holiest — The holiest of all spots on earth is where an   522
ancient hatred has become a present
love.

illusion — As long as the illusion of hatred lasts, so long   315
will *love* be an illusion to you.

illusion — *Love* is not an illusion. It is a fact.   314

illusion — *Love* is wholly without illusion, and therefore wholly without fear.   **316**

illusion — The illusion of *love* can triumph over the illusion of hate, but always at the price of making both illusion.   **315**

illusion — The illusion of *love* will never satisfy, but its reality, which awaits you on the other side, will give you everything.   **314**

illusions — *Love* is in you and will lead you (beyond illusions.)   **228**

impartial — *(Love)* is completely impartial in its giving, encompassing only to preserve and keep complete what it would give.   **365**

imperfect — (The Apostles') own imperfect *love* made them vulnerable to projection, and out of their own fear they spoke of the "wrath of God" as His retaliatory weapon.   **87**

increase — *Love* would always give increase.   **300**

joy — There is no difference between *love* and joy.   **66**

justice — In justice, then, does *love* correct mistakes, but not in vengeance.   **500**

justice — *Love* and justice are not different.   **499**

justice — *Love* without justice is impossible.   **500**

justice — Without *love* is justice prejudiced and weak.   **500**

kill — *Love* does not kill to save.   **220**

kill — You would be willing to look even upon your savage wish to kill God's Son, if you did not believe that it saves you from *love*.   **225**

known — *Love* wishes to be known, completely understood and shared.   **407**

lack — In reality you are unaffected by all expressions of lack of *love*.   **15**

laws — The laws of *love* are not suspended because you sleep.   **236**

leads — *Love* always leads to *love*.   **235**

learned — *Love* is not learned.   **369**

like — *Love* must be forever like itself, changeless for-   **360**
    ever, and forever without alternative.

limit — *Love* does not limit, and what it creates is not   **181**
    limited.

limits — Limits on *love* will always seem to shut (God)   **364**
    out, and keep you apart from Him.

little — *Love* is not little and *love* dwells in you, for you   **287**
    are host to Him.

make — Fear and *love* make or create, depending on   **114**
    whether the ego or the Holy Spirit
    begets or inspires them, but they will;
    return to the mind of the thinker and
    they will affect his total perception.

meaning — The meaning of *love* lies in what you have   **305**
    cast outside yourself, and it has no
    meaning apart from you.

meaning — You do not know the meaning of *love*, and   **210**
    that is your handicap.

messengers — *Love*, too, is recognized by its messengers.   **215**

messengers — If you make *love* manifest, its messengers   **215**
    will come to you because you invited
    them.

messengers — *Love's* messengers are gently sent, and   **382**
    return with messages of *love* and
    gentleness.

mind — *Love* will enter immediately into any mind that   **55**
    truly wants it, but it must want it
    truly.

minds — You have gone past fear, for no two minds can   **354**
    join in the desire for *love* without *love's*
    joining them.

murder — What is not *love* is murder.   **461**

obstacles — From beyond each of the obstacles to *love*,   **392**
    Love Itself has called.

offer — Offer *(love)* and it will come to you because it is   **217**
    drawn to itself.

offering — And thus you will exempt yourself from (the Holy Spirit's) healing power, for by not offering total *love* you will not be healed completely.   **227**

overlook — If you overlook *love* you are overlooking yourself, and you must fear unreality because you have denied yourself.   **190**

part — No part of *love* calls on the whole in vain.   **366**

peace — He walks in peace who travels sinlessly along the way *love* shows him.   **451**

peace — *Love's* arms are open to receive you and give you peace forever.   **409**

"peace" — You do not see how limited and weak is your allegiance, and how frequently you have demanded that *love* go away and leave you quietly alone in "peace."   **564**

perfect — Perfect *love* casts out fear.   **12**

perfect — Perfect *love* is the Atonement.   **26**

perfect — The only remedy for lack of *love* is perfect *love*.   **26**

perfect — There is no fear in perfect *love*.   **204**

perfect — You cannot learn of perfect *love* with a split mind, because a split mind has made itself a poor learner.   **210**

power — *Love* is your power, which the ego must deny.   **115**

power — What is kept apart from *love* cannot share its healing power, because it has been separated off and kept in darkness.   **264**

recognize — You do not recognize that *love* has come because you have not let go of all the barriers you hold against your brother.   **366**

relationship — Be sure of this; *love* has entered your special relationship, and entered fully at your weak request.   **366**

relationships — (*Love*) does not seek for power, but for relationships.   **407**

remembrance — The remembrance of *love* therefore brings invulnerability with it.   **171**

297

return — Fear and *love* make or create, depending on whether the ego or the Holy Spirit begets or inspires them, but they will return to the mind of the thinker. **114**

right — *Love* does not conquer all things, but it does set all things right. **63**

savior — Your savior gives you only *love,* but what you would receive of Him is up to you. **403**

shares — Arrogance is the denial of *love,* because *love* shares and arrogance withholds. **178**

sin — What is not *love* is sin, and either one perceives the other as insane and meaningless. **495**

sinless — It is as certain you will fear what you attack as it is sure that you will *love* what you perceive as sinless. **451**

sinners — *Love* is the basis for a world perceived as wholly mad to sinners, who believe theirs is the way to sanity. **495**

Sonship — *(Love)* comes freely to all the Sonship, being what the Sonship is. **111**

special — *Love* is not special. **247**

strong — Only *love* is strong because it is undivided. **209**

suffer — *Love* cannot suffer because it cannot attack. **171**

suffering — *Love* would prove all suffering is but vain imagining, a foolish wish with no effects. **529**

symbol — Symbols stand for something else, and the symbol of *love* is without meaning if *love* is everything. **314**

thought — Every thought of *love* you offer (the Son of God) brings you nearer to your wakening to peace eternal and to endless joy. **570**

toward — You go toward *love* still hating it, and terribly afraid of its judgment upon you. **353**

transfers — *Love* transfers to *love* without any interference, for the two are one. **213**

treacherous — *Love* is seen as treacherous, because it   564
      seems to come and go uncertainly, and
      offer no stability to you.

triumphs — There are no triumphs of *love*.   314

trust — You cannot trust your own *love* when you attack   210
      it.

want — When you want only *love* you will see nothing   215
      else.

weakness — You associate *love* with weakness and   226
      hatred with strength, and your own
      real power seems to you as your real
      weakness.

welcome — *Love* waits on welcome, not on time, and the   238
      real world is but your welcome of what
      always was.

witnesses — Those who accept *love* of you become your   236
      willing witnesses to the *love* you gave
      them, and it is they who hold it out to
      you.

world — (In the world), where the illusion of *love* is   317
      accepted in *love's* place, *love* is perceived
      as separation and exclusion.

world — The world is safe from *love* to everyone who   494
      thinks sin possible.

world — Therefore, you have used the world to cover   226
      your *love*, and the deeper you go into
      the blackness of the ego's foundation,
      the closer you come to the *Love* that is
      hidden there. And it is this that
      frightens you.

you — You are only *love*, but when you deny this you   92
      make what you are something you
      must learn to remember.

yourself — *Love* yourself with the *love* of Christ, for so   187
      does your Father *love* you.

LOVED

concealed — What is concealed cannot be *loved*, and so it   264
      must be feared.

LOVING

attack — What is not *loving* must be an attack.　　　**461**

MADNESS

forgive — Forgive yourself your *madness*, and forget all　　**609**
　　　　senseless journeys and all goal-less
　　　　aims.

God — It must be so that either God is mad or is this　　**494**
　　　　world a place of *madness*.

Holy Spirit — What *madness* would conceal, the Holy　　**429**
　　　　Spirit holds out, for everyone to look
　　　　upon with gladness.

lovely — Be not deceived when *madness* takes a form you　　**459**
　　　　think is lovely. What is intent on your
　　　　destruction is not your friend.

protects — What protects *madness* is the belief that it is　　**458**
　　　　true.

reality — *Madness* holds out no menace to reality, and　　**453**
　　　　has no influence upon it.

reason — *Madness* and reason see the same things, but it　　**428**
　　　　is certain that they look upon them
　　　　differently.

reason — *Madness* is an attack on reason that drives it out　　**428**
　　　　of mind, and takes its place.

reason — The home of *madness* cannot be the home of　　**428**
　　　　reason.

wants — No one wants *madness*, nor does anyone cling to　　**458**
　　　　his *madness* if he sees that this is what it
　　　　is.

MAGIC

body — All material means that you accept as remedies　　**20**
　　　　for bodily ills are restatements of *magic*
　　　　principles.

ego — Myths and *magic* are closely associated, since　　**53**
　　　　myths are usually related to ego
　　　　origins, and *magic* to the powers the ego
　　　　ascribes to itself.

healer — *Magic* always sees something "special" in the　　**111**
　　　　healer, which he believes he can offer
　　　　as a gift to someone who does not have
　　　　it.

healing — This situation, too, can be used either for   **111**
　　　healing or for *magic*, but you must
　　　remember that *magic* always involves
　　　the belief that healing is harmful.

mind — *Magic* is the mindless or miscreative use of   **21**
　　　mind.

reconciling — All *magic* is the attempt at reconciling the   **173**
　　　irreconcilable.

weaken — *Magic* always tries to weaken.   **111**

MAGNITUDE

content — You will be content only in *magnitude* which is   **285**
　　　your home.

defiance — You are afraid (God's Love) would sweep   **226**
　　　you away from yourself and make you
　　　little, because you believe that *magnitude*
　　　lies in defiance, and that attack is
　　　grandeur.

individuals — When two individuals seek to become   **321**
　　　one, they are trying to decrease their
　　　magnitude.

instant — The instant in which *magnitude* dawns upon   **288**
　　　you is but as far away as your desire for
　　　it.

vigilance — All striving must be directed against little-   **285**
　　　ness, for it does require vigilance to
　　　protect your *magnitude* in this world.

MANIFEST

want — What you want in yourself you will make   **215**
　　　manifest, and you will accept it from the
　　　world because you put it there by
　　　wanting it.

MEANING

deny — To deny *meaning* is to fail to understand.   **183**

gives — Nothing gives *meaning* where no *meaning* is.   **516**

God — This (one) *meaning* comes from God and is God.   **107**

God — Your *meaning* cannot be out of accord with (God's), because your whole *meaning* and your only *meaning* comes from His and is like His. **112**

God — Your task is only to meet the conditions for *meaning,* since *meaning* itself is of God. **148**

God's — God's *meaning* is incomplete without you, and you are incomplete without your creations. **163**

God's — God's *meaning* waits in the Kingdom, because that is where He placed it. **108**

God's — How can you who are God's *meaning* perceive yourself as absent from it? **108**

God's — Yet your return to *meaning* is essential to (God's), because your *meaning* is part of His. **148**

judge — You do not have to judge, for you have learned one *meaning* has been given everything. **596**

looks — *Meaning* always looks within to find itself, and then looks out. **414**

world — All *meaning* that you give the world outside must thus reflect the sight you saw within, or better, if you saw at all or merely judged against. **414**

MEANINGLESS

Holy Spirit — (The Holy Spirit) will not attempt to communicate the *meaningless*. **266**

meaningful — You cannot make the *meaningless* meaningful. This can only be an insane attempt. **117**

undertakes — No one undertakes to do what he believes is *meaningless*. **395**

MEANS

alignment — The alignment of *means* and purpose is an undertaking impossible for you to understand. **357**

end — Perception is a part of what it is your purpose to behold, for *means* and end are never separate. **483**

God — You are the *means* for God; not separate nor with a life apart from His.   **483**

MEMORY(IES)

body — Life to the body, (*memory*) is purposeless within itself.   **548**

God — Give up gladly everything that would stand in the way of your remembering, for God is in your *memory*.   **170**

God — Because of your Father's love you can never forget Him, for no one can forget what God Himself placed in his *memory*.   **218**

heal — (*Memory*) can be used to heal and not to hurt, if you so wish it to be.   **547**

Holy Spirit — The Holy Spirit can indeed make use of *memory*, for God Himself is there.   **547**

Holy Spirit's — The Holy Spirit's use of *memory* is quite apart from time.   **548**

lives — He who lives in *memories* alone is unaware of where he is.   **512**

message — *Memory* holds the message it receives, and does what it is given it to do.   **548**

past — The Holy Spirit does not seek to use (*memory*) as a means to keep the past, but rather as a way to let the past go.   **548**

past — There is no link of *memory* to the past.   **547**

perception — *Memory*, like perception, is a skill made up by you to take the place of what God gave you in your creation.   **547**

MIND(S)

accept — What you accept into your *mind* does not really change it.   **312**

allegiance — Your *mind* is dividing its allegiance between two kingdoms, and you are totally committed to neither.   **116**

anxiety — Without anxiety the *mind* is wholly kind, and because it extends beneficence it is beneficent.   **92**

ascend — Let us ascend in peace together to the Father, 336
by giving Him ascendance in our *minds*.

Atonement — (Accepting the Atonement for yourself) 22
means you recognize the *mind* is the
only creative level, and that its errors
are healed by the Atonement.

attack — *Mind* cannot attack, but it can make fantasies 359
and direct the body to act them out.

attack — To fragment is to break into pieces, and the 121
mind cannot attack or be attacked.

attack — (The *mind*) cannot attack, but it maintains it 359
can, and uses what it does to hurt the
body to prove it can.

attack — The *mind* that accepts attack cannot love. 114

attack — The purpose of attack is in the *mind*, and its 472
effects are felt but where it is.

attacked — The *mind* cannot attack, but it can deceive 359
itself. And this is all it does when it
believes it has attacked the body.

blocked — A *mind* that has been blocked has allowed 142
itself to be vulnerable to attack,
because it has turned against itself.

body — Each body seems to house a separate *mind*, a dis- 365
connected thought, living alone and in
no way joined to the Thought by which
it was created.

body — If the *mind* can heal the body, but the body can- 97
not heal the *mind*, then the *mind* must be
stronger than the body.

body — Only by assigning to the *mind* properties of the 359
body, does separation seem to be
possible.

body — The *mind* that thinks it is a body is sick indeed! 482

capable — This is because the *mind* is capable of creating 77
reality or making illusions.

change — *Minds* can change as they desire. 472

change — This places you in a position of needing to learn a lesson that seems contradictory; — you must learn to change your *mind* about your *mind*. **113**

changing — That is because, by changing his *mind*, (the Son of God) has changed the most powerful device that was ever given him for change. **112**

closed — The closed *mind* believes the future and the present will be the same. **36**

communicate — A divided *mind* cannot communicate, because it speaks for different things in the same *mind*. **150**

communicate — *Minds* need not the body to communicate. **405**

communicate — That is why the *mind* cannot totally lose the ability to communicate, even though it may refuse to utilize it on behalf of being. **64**

concrete — Part of the *mind* becomes concrete, however, when it splits. **63**

condition — Your *mind* is the means by which you determine your own condition, because *mind* is the mechanism of decision. **134**

conflict — Your Self is still in peace, even though your *mind* is in conflict. **46**

conflicted — A conflicted *mind* cannot be faithful to one meaning, and will therefore change the meaning to preserve the form. **106**

consistency — Further, the *mind* of the learner projects its own conflict, and thus does not perceive consistency in the *minds* of others, making him suspicious of their motivation. **99**

control — For you do have control over your *mind*, since the *mind* is the mechanism of decision. **207**

create — When it is understood that the *mind*, the only   20
      level of creation, cannot create beyond
      itself, neither type of confusion need
      occur.

create — It is essential to remember that only the *mind*   21
      can create, and that correction belongs
      at the thought level.

creative — The *mind* is very powerful, and never loses its   27
      creative force.

darkened — A darkened *mind* cannot live in light, and it   227
      must seek a place of darkness where it
      can believe it is where it is not.

decision — Your *mind* is the means by which you deter-   134
      mine your own condition, because *mind*
      is the mechanism of decision.

defining — By defining the *mind* wrongly, you perceive   174
      it as functioning wrongly.

divided — Your divided *mind* is blocking the extension of   117
      the Kingdom, and its extension is your
      joy.

ego — If you enthrone the ego in your *mind*, your   77
      allowing it to enter makes it your
      reality.

ego — Your *mind* is filled with schemes to save the face   57
      of your ego, and you do not seek the
      face of Christ.

ego — Your *mind* cannot be unified in allegiance to the   108
      ego, because the *mind* does not belong
      to it.

encompasses — (The *mind*) encompasses you entirely;   360
      you within it and it within you.

exist — Everything else that you have placed within   262
      your *mind* cannot exist.

extends — Therefore, what extends from *mind* is still in   91
      it, and from what it extends it knows
      itself.

fear — Only your *mind* can produce fear.   26

fragment — You cannot perpetuate an illusion about another without perpetuating it about yourself. There is no way out of this, because it is impossible to fragment the *mind*. 121

function — The *mind* returns to its proper function only when it wills to know. 38

future — Your *mind* does make your future, and it will turn it back to full creation at any minute if it accepts the Atonement first. 79

gift — Every gift (the *mind*) offers depends on what it wants. 397

gives — In the state of being the *mind* gives everything always. 64

God — God has lit your *mind* Himself, and keeps your *mind* lit by His Light because His Light is what your *mind* is. 109

God — Miracles make *minds* one in God. 2

God — There are no strange images in the *Mind* of God, and what is not in His *Mind* cannot be in yours, because you are of one *mind* and that *mind* belongs to Him. 175

God — You dwell in the *Mind* of God with your brother, for God Himself did not will to be alone. 180

God's — God's *Mind* cannot be lessened. 181

God's — Your *mind* is one with God's. 57

God's — Your *mind* must be as pure as (God's), if you would know what belongs to you. 185

Godlike — Your Godlike *mind* can never be defiled. 91

guilt — *Minds* that are joined and recognize they are, can feel no guilt. 489

guilt — (The *mind*) can project its guilt, but it will not lose it through projection. 359

guilt — If you withhold agreement and accept the part 553
    you play in making sickness real, the
    other *mind* cannot project its guilt with-
    out your aid in letting it perceive itself
    as separate and apart from you.

guiltless — The guiltless *mind* cannot suffer. 78

harmful — Nor is the *mind* limited; so it must be that 472
    harmful purpose hurts the *mind* as one.

healed — Once your *mind* is healed it radiates health, and 103
    thereby teaches healing.

healed — Only the healed *mind* can experience revela- 66
    tion with lasting effect, because revela-
    tion is an experience of pure joy.

higher — The higher *mind* thinks according to the laws 67
    the spirit obeys, and therefore honors
    only the laws of God.

honor — (Innocent *minds*) can only honor other *minds*, 33
    because honor is the natural greeting
    of the truly loved to others who are
    like them.

illumination — Only the *mind* is capable of illumination. 22

illusions — The *mind* can, however, make up illusions, 115
    and if it does so it will believe in them,
    because that is how it made them.

innocent — Innocence is incapable of sacrificing any- 33
    thing, because the innocent *mind* has
    everything and strives only to protect
    its wholeness.

innocent — (Innocent *minds*) cannot project. 33

integration — The *mind* always strives for integration, 215
    and if it is split and wants to keep the
    split, it will still believe it has one goal
    by making it seem to be one.

invulnerable — The *mind* that serves spirit is invul- 9
    nerable.

joined — *Minds* are joined; bodies are not. 359

learn — For *mind* can learn, and there is all change made. 607

learner — Further, the *mind* of the learner projects its   99
own conflict, and thus does not per-
ceive consistency in the *minds* of others,
making him suspicious of their motivation.

level — I have repeatedly emphasized that one level of   73
the *mind* is not understandable to
another.

limits — Yet though the order you impose upon your   273
mind limits the ego, it also limits you.

me — The *Mind* that was in me is still irresistably drawn   75
to every *mind* created by God because
God's Wholeness is the wholeness of
His Son.

medium — If it elects to do so, the *mind* can become the   10
medium by which spirit creates along
the line of its own creation.

mine — Your *mind* and mine can unite in shining the ego   58
away, releasing the strength of God
into everything you think and do.

mine — Your *mind* will elected to join with mine, and   59
together we are invincible.

miracles — Miracles restore the *mind* to its fullness.   3

miscreate — The *mind* can miscreate only when it be-   34
lieves it is not free.

miscreations — None of these errors is meaningful,   21
because the miscreations of the *mind* do
not really exist.

misperceptions — You may let your *mind* misperceive,   73
but the Holy Spirit lets your *mind* rein-
terpret its own misperceptions.

one — Our *minds* are whole because they are one.   147

peace — Peace and guilt are both conditions of the *mind*,   386
to be attained.

perceive — You perceive from your *mind*, and project   90
your perceptions outward.

perception — Every response you make to everything   168
you perceive is up to you, because your
mind determines your perception of it.

physical — *Mind* cannot be made physical, but it can be made manifest through the physical if it uses the body to go beyond itself.   **142**

power — (Spiritual vision) re-establishes the power of the *mind* and makes it increasingly unable to tolerate delay, realizing that it only adds unnecessary pain.   **18**

power — (The *mind*) is the power by which you separate or join, and experience pain or joy accordingly.   **134**

power — The power of one *mind* can shine into another, because all the lamps of God were lit by one spark.   **175**

power — Yet it is also your *mind* that has the power to deny the ego's existence, and you will surely do so when you realize exactly what the journey is on which the ego sets you.   **208**

power — You cannot remove the power to change your *mind,* and see another purpose there.   **572**

project — Every *mind* must project or extend, because that is how it lives, and every *mind* is life.   **120**

protection — The *mind* asks: "Where can I go for protection?"   **60**

pure — A pure *mind* knows the truth and this is its strength.   **33**

questioning — The questioning *mind* perceives itself in time, and therefore looks for future answers.   **36**

quiet — The memory of God comes to the quiet *mind.*   **452**

reaches — *Mind* reaches to itself.   **360**

reality — The only part of your *mind* that has reality is the part that links you still with God.   **262**

reality — Whatever you accept into your *mind* has reality for you.   **77**

reality — Yet you could not have seen reality, for the reality of your *mind* is the loveliest of God's creations.   **216**

receive — Only the *mind* can value, and only the *mind*   397
    decides on what it would receive and
    give.

release — In your own *mind,* though denied by the ego,   56
    is the declaration of your release.

reproduces — *Mind* always reproduces as it was pro-   115
    duced.

right — No right *mind* can believe that its will is stronger   150
    than God's.

right — Your right *mind* sees only brothers, because it   108
    sees only in its own light.

salvation — Your Self does not need salvation, but your   186
    mind needs to learn what salvation is.

sane — The sane *mind* cannot conceive of illness because   78
    it cannot conceive of attacking anyone
    or anything.

self-fulness — The full appreciation of the *mind's* self-   123
    fulness makes selfishness impossible
    and extension inevitable.

separate — *Minds* cannot be separate.   426

separate — There are no separate parts in what exists   587
    within God's *Mind.*

separate — Your *minds* are not separate, and God has   171
    only one channel for healing because
    He has but one Son.

separated — The separated or divided *mind* must be   38
    confused.

separated — (A separated *mind*) has to be in conflict   38
    because it is out of accord with itself.

separation — The *mind* had no calling until the separa-   69
    tion, because before that it had only
    being.

shared — (The Holy Spirit) always tells you that only   97
    the *mind* is real, because only the *mind*
    can be shared.

sick — No *mind* is sick until another *mind* agrees that   553
    they are separate.

sick — His desire to be a sick and separated *mind* cannot remain without a witness or a cause.   557

sleeps — (The *mind*) never sleeps.   27

spirit — (The fact that spirit is incapable of darkness) makes (it) almost inaccessible to the *mind* and entirely inaccessible to the body.   38

spirit — This places (the *mind*) in the service of spirit, because it is from spirit that it derives its whole power to make and create.   38

split — A split *mind* cannot perceive its fullness, and needs the miracle of its wholeness to dawn upon it and heal it.   123

split — A split *mind* is endangered, and the recognition that it encompasses completely opposed thoughts within itself is intolerable.   206

split — Any split in the *mind* must involve rejection of part of it, and this is the belief in separation.   88

split — Therefore the *mind* projects the split, not the reality.   206

thought — (The *mind's* direction is always automatic, because the *mind* cannot but be dictated by the thought system to which it adheres.   54

thoughts — The insane thoughts (of God's Son), too, must be in His *mind,* but an eternal conflict of this magnitude he cannot tolerate.   206

war — (The memory of God) cannot come where there is conflict, for a *mind* at war against itself remembers not eternal gentleness.   452

whole — A whole *mind* is not idolatrous and does not know of conflicting laws.   172

wholeness — The wholeness of God, which is His peace,   88
cannot be appreciated except by a
whole *mind* that recognizes the wholeness of God's creation.

world — Therefore, seek not to change the world, but   415
choose to change your *mind* about the
world.

world — If only the loving thoughts of God's Son are   206
the world's reality, the real world must
be in His *mind.*

worlds — Your *mind* is capable of creating worlds, but it   177
can also deny what it creates because it
is free.

MIRACLE(S)

acceptance — You cannot perform a *miracle* for yourself,   163
because *miracles* are a way of giving
acceptance and receiving it.

act — The *miracle* is the act of a Son of God who has laid   175
aside all false gods, and calls on his
brothers to do likewise.

action — Revelation induces only experience. *Miracles,*   5
on the other hand, induce action.

appeal — Each (*miracle*) is a gentle winning over from the   381
appeal of guilt to the appeal of love.

appearances — The *miracle* is means to demonstrate that   598
all appearances can change because
they are appearances, and cannot have
the changelessness reality entails.

arise — *Miracles* arise from a miraculous state of mind,   4
or a state of *miracle*-readiness.

Atonement — *Miracles* are part of an interlocking chain   2
of forgiveness which, when completed,
is the Atonement.

Atonement — The ability (to work *miracles*) is the po-   6
tential, the achievement is its
expression, and the Atonement, which
is the natural profession of the
Children of God, is the purpose.

Atonement — The *miracle* turns the defense of the   17
Atonement to your real protection,
and as you become more and more
secure you assume your natural talent
of protecting others, knowing yourself
as both a brother and a Son.

beginnings — *Miracles* are both beginnings and endings,   1
and so they alter the temporal order.

blessed — *Miracles* offer you the testimony that you are   251
blessed.

blessing — A *miracle* is a universal blessing from God   3
through me to all my brothers.

blessing — That is why the *miracle* gives equal blessing   273
to all who share in it, and that is also
why everyone shares in it.

body — Each *miracle* He brings is witness that the body is   538
not real.

body — *Miracles* transcend the body.   2

brother — The *miracle* acknowledges everyone as your   4
brother and mine.

brother — The *miracle* enables you to see your brother   234
without his past, and so perceive him as
born again.

brother — The *miracle* is proof (your brother) is not   598
bound by loss or suffering in any form,
because it can so easily be changed.

brothers — Unless you think that all your brothers have   502
an equal right to *miracles* with you, you
will not claim your right to them because you were unjust to one with
equal rights.

Cause — The *miracle* reminds you of a Cause forever   549
present, perfectly untouched by time
and interference.

changeless — Because reality is changeless is a *miracle*   598
already there to heal all things that
change, and offer them to you to see in
happy form, devoid of fear.

Christ — The *miracle* is an expression of an inner awareness of Christ and the acceptance of
His Atonement.   4

closeness — *Miracles*, however, are genuinely interpersonal, and result in true closeness to
others.   4

communication — The Holy Spirit is the highest communication medium. *Miracles* do not
involve this type of communication,
because they are temporary communication devices.   4

communication — The whole aim of the *miracle* is to
raise the level of communication, not
to lower it by increasing fear.   20

communion — (The *miracle*) thus dispels illusions about
yourself, and puts you in communion
with yourself and God.   9

concern — The *miracle* alone is your concern at present.   553

contains — Every *miracle* you do contains them all, as
every aspect of reality you see blends
quietly into the one Reality of God.   241

control — (*Miracles*) should not be under conscious
control.   1

correction — However, as a correction, the *miracle* need
not await the right-mindedness of the
receiver.   21

creation — The *miracle* compares what you have made
with creation, accepting what is in
accord with it as true, and rejecting
what is out of accord as false.   4

creation — This is the *miracle* of creation; that it is one
forever.   241

device — (The *miracle*) is a device for perception-
correction, effective quite apart from
either the degree or the direction of the
error.   4

device — The *miracle* is a learning device that lessens
the need for time.   4

device — The *miracle* is the only device at your immediate disposal for controlling time.   **4**

devoted — Each day should be devoted to *miracles*.   **2**

differences — The *miracle* is the one thing you can do that transcends order, being based not on differences but on equality.   **272**

difficulty — There is no order of difficulty in *miracles*.   **1**

directed — *Miracles* are selective only in the sense that they are directed toward those who can use them for themselves.   **8**

does — The *miracle* does nothing. All it does is to undo.   **547**

done — You have done *miracles*, but it is quite apparent that you have not done them alone.   **309**

dreamer — (*Miracles*) are the dream's alternative, the choice to be the dreamer, rather than deny the active role in making up the dream.   **553**

dreams — Their equal lack of truth becomes the basis for the *miracle*, which means that you have understood that dreams are dreams; and that escape depends, not on the dream, but only on waking.   **568**

dreams — You have asked (the *miracle*) be withheld from power to heal all dreams.   **598**

earth — The *miracles* you do on earth are lifted up to Heaven and to (God.)   **242**

effects — *Miracles* are expressions of love, but they may not always have observable effects.   **3**

ego — *Miracles* seem unnatural to the ego because it does not understand how separate minds can influence each other.   **426**

error — The *miracle* dissolves error because the Holy Spirit identifies error as false or unreal.   **3**

errors — (*Miracles*) atone for your errors by freeing you from your nightmares.   **3**

eternity — *Miracles* have no place in eternity, because they are reparative.   **162**

extends — The *miracle* extends without your help, but   535
you are needed that it can begin.

faith — (The *miracle*) is an act of faith, because it is the   175
recognition that his brother can do it.

fear — *Miracles* are a way of earning release from fear.   3

fear — *Miracles* are associated with fear only because of   2
the belief that darkness can hide.

fear — *Miracles* represent freedom from fear.   2

fear — The *miracle* returns the cause of fear to you who   553
made it.

forgiveness — *Miracles* are natural signs of forgiveness.   2

forgiveness — Only forgiveness offers *miracles*.   503

forgives — The *miracle* forgives because it stands for   539
what is past forgiveness and is true.

given — There is no *miracle* that can be given you unless   598
you want it.

God — All *miracles* mean life, and God is the Giver of life.   1

God — Every *miracle* that you accomplish speaks to you   183
of the Fatherhood of God.

God — (God) offers you a *miracle* with every one you let   278
Him do through you.

God — *Miracles* praise God through you.   3

God — The power of God, and not of you, engenders   273
miracles.

God's — God's *miracles* are as total as His Thoughts   41
because they are His Thoughts.

God's — The *miracle* acknowledges (God's) changeless-   277
ness by seeing His Son as he always
was, and not as he would make himself.

God's — The only *miracle* that ever was is God's most   241
holy Son, created in the one Reality
that is his Father.

God's — To know God's *miracle* is to know Him.   41

gratitude — *Miracles* should inspire gratitude, not awe.   3

guilt — (*Miracles*) bestow an equal gift of full deliverance   529
from guilt upon your brother and
yourself.

guilt — The *miracle* would leave no proof of guilt to bring 555
you witness to what never was.

guiltlessness — The *miracle* acknowledges the guiltless- 263
ness that must have been denied to
produce the need of healing.

guiltlessness — The *miracle* brings the effects that only 277
guiltlessness can bring, and thus
establishes the fact that guiltlessness
must be.

heal — A *miracle* has come to heal God's Son, and close 621
the door upon his dreams of weakness,
opening the way to his salvation and
release.

heal — It must be true the *miracle* can heal all forms of 594
sickness, or it cannot heal.

heal — There is no sadness where a *miracle* has come to 535
heal.

healed — Thus is the body healed by *miracles* because 553
they show the mind made sickness, and
employed the body to be victim, or
effect, of what it made.

healing — *Miracles* are healing because they supply a 1
lack; they are performed by those who
temporarily have more for those who
temporarily have less.

healing — In every *miracle* all healing lies, for God gave 517
answer to them all as one.

healing — There is no *miracle* you cannot have when you 598
desire healing.

holiness — (*Miracles*) intercede for your holiness and 3
make your perceptions holy.

Holy Spirit — Each *miracle* (offered by the Holy Spirit) 278
corrects your use of time and makes it
His.

Holy Spirit — (The *miracle*) is a call to the Holy Spirit in 175
his mind, a call that is strengthened by
joining.

Holy Spirit — The Holy Spirit is the mechanism of 3
miracles.

Holy Spirit — The Holy Spirit is the motivation for *miracle*-mindedness; the decision to heal the separation by letting it go.   69

Holy Spirit's — *Miracles* are merely the sign of your willingness to follow the Holy Spirit's plan of salvation, recognizing that you do not understand what it is.   158

Identity — The *miracle* becomes the means of sharing (your Identity).   275

illusion — Every *miracle* is but the end of an illusion.   381

Judgment — (The length of the last Judgment), however, can be greatly shortened by *miracles,* the device for shortening but not abolishing time.   30

justice — A *miracle* is justice.   502

justice — Each *miracle* is an example of what justice can accomplish when it is offered to everyone alike.   503

justice — *Miracles* depend on justice.   502

lack — A major contribution of *miracles* is their strength in releasing you from a false sense of isolation, deprivation and lack.   4

lack — (*Miracles*) thus correct or atone for faulty perception of lack.   4

language — This means that a *miracle,* to attain its full efficacy, must be expressed in a language that the recipient can understand without fear.   20

laws — *Miracles* therefore reflect the laws of eternity, not of time.   2

learning — *Miracles* demonstrate that learning has occurred under the right guidance.   213

learning — The *miracle* is much like the body in that both are learning aids for facilitating a state in which they become unnecessary.   9

learning — The *miracle* substitutes for learning that might have taken thousands of years.   6

less — A *miracle* can offer nothing less to him than it has given unto you.   529

lesson — Every *miracle* is a lesson in truth, and by offering truth you are learning the difference between pain and joy.   126

lesson — Like every lesson that the Holy Spirit requests you learn, the *miracle* is clear.   552

lesson — The *miracle* is therefore a lesson in what joy is.   126

levels — By recognizing spirit, *miracles* adjust the levels of perception and show them in proper alignment.   3

limitless — *Miracles* are not in competition, and the number of them that you can do is limitless.   272

lost — A *miracle* is never lost.   4

lovable — *Miracles* honor you because you are lovable.   3

love — (A *miracle*) is a way of loving your neighbor as yourself.   2

love — *Miracles* are expressions of love, but they may not always have observable effects.   3

love — (*Miracles*) bring more love both to the giver and the receiver.   1

love — *Miracles* occur naturally as expressions of love.   1

love — Only a *miracle* could change your mind so that you understand love cannot be feared.   510

love — The *miracle* is therefore a sign of love among equals.   5

meaning — meaning of *miracles*.   1-4

means — The means on which you can depend for *miracles* has been provided for you.   277

mind — As an expression of what you truly are, the *miracle* places the mind in a state of grace.   8

mind — *Miracles* arise from a mind that is ready for them.   8

mind — *Miracles* restore the mind to its fullness.   3

mind — (The *miracle* was sent to teach) the mind was sick that thought the body could be sick.   553

minds — *Miracles* make minds one in God.   2

minds — The *miracle* does nothing just because the minds are joined, and cannot separate. 554

misperceptions — (The *miracle*) makes no distinctions among misperceptions. 15

name — The *miracle* but calls your ancient name, which you will recognize because the truth is in your memory. 518

names — The *miracle* makes no distinctions in the names by which sin's witnesses are called. 538

natural — I have asked you to perform *miracles* and have made it clear that *miracles* are natural, corrective, healing and universal. 15

natural — *Miracles* are as natural as fear and agony appeared to be before the choice for holiness was made. 620

natural — *Miracles* are natural. 1

natural — *Miracles* are natural to the One Who speaks for God. 310

nature — Concern yourself not with the extension of holiness, for the nature of *miracles* you do not understand. 309

nothing — The *miracle* does nothing but to show him that he has done nothing. 552

now — A *miracle* is now. 520

one — There is one *miracle*, as there is one reality. 241

past — The *miracle* but shows the past is gone, and what has truly gone has no effects. 547

past — Yet by doing so you are aligning past and future, and not allowing the *miracle*, which could intervene between them, to free you to be born again. 234

perceives — The *miracle* perceives everything as it is. 34

perception — (A *miracle*) places you under the Atonement principle, where perception is healed. 3

perception — Every *miracle* you offer to the Son of God is but the true perception of one aspect of the whole. 241

perception — *Miracles* rearrange perception and place all levels in true perspective.   **2**

perception — The *miracle* is a lesson in total perception.   **123**

perceptions — *Miracles* are examples of right thinking, aligning your perceptions with truth as God created it.   **3**

possible — Every *miracle* is possible the instant that the Son of God perceives his wishes and the Will of God are one.   **516**

possible — The *miracle* is possible when cause and consequence are brought together, not kept separate.   **517**

prayer — Prayer is the medium of *miracles.*   **1**

principles — principles of *miracles.*   **1-4**

purpose — *Miracles* are merely change of purpose from hurt to healing.   **472**

quietly — The *miracle* comes quietly into the mind that stops an instant and is still.   **549**

quietness — In quietness, see in the *miracle* a lesson in allowing Cause to have its Own effects, and doing nothing that would interfere.   **549**

reality — *Miracles* but show that you have interposed between reality and your awareness is unreal, and does not interfere at all.   **598**

reality — Offer Christ's gift to everyone and everywhere, for *miracles,* offered the Son of God through the Holy Spirit, attune you to reality.   **242**

reality — Since the *miracle* aims at restoring the awareness of reality, it would not be useful if it were bound by laws that govern the error it aims to correct.   **8**

receive — The *miracle* that you receive, you give.   **503**

reflect — And you will understand the *miracles* reflect the simple statement: "I have done this thing, and it is this I would undo."   **546**

relationship — In the *miracle* of your holy relationship, without this barrier, is every *miracle* contained. 381

release — *Miracles* are the instants of release you offer, and will receive. 282

response — The *miracle* offers exactly the same response to every call for help. 273

revelation — The impersonal nature of the *miracle* is an essential ingredient, because it enables me to direct its application, and under my guidance *miracles* lead to the highly personal experience of revelation. 7

reverse — Like all expressions of love, which are always miraculous in the true sense, (*miracles*) reverse the physical laws. 1

right — *Miracles* are everyone's right, but purification is necessary first. 1

service — A *miracle* is a service. 2

shift — However, the *miracle* entails a sudden shift from horizontal to vertical perception. 6

sickness — (*Miracles*) are the glad effects of taking back the consequence of sickness to its cause. 553

simultaneous — (*Miracles*) can be simultaneous and legion. 272

Sonship — *Miracles* are affirmations of Sonship, which is a state of completion and abundance. 10

speaks — A *miracle* speaks not but for itself, but what it represents. 539

spectacles — The use of *miracles* as spectacles to induce belief is a misunderstanding of their purpose. 1

spirit — *Miracles* reawaken the awareness that the spirit, not the body, is the altar of truth. 2

step — The *miracle* is the first step in giving back to cause the function of causation, not effect. 552

teaches — The *miracle* teaches you that you have chosen guiltlessness, freedom and joy. 256

teaching — *Miracles* are teaching devices for demon- 2
    strating it is as blessed to give as to
    receive.

thoughts — Both *miracles* and fear come from thoughts. 28

thoughts — *Miracles* are thoughts. 1

time — Miracles wait not on time. 535

transcends — The *miracle* is the one thing you can do that 272
    transcends order, being based not on
    differences but on equality.

translation — *Miracles* are merely the translation of 203
    denial into truth.

true — (A *miracle*) can make what always has been true 518
    be recognized by those who know it
    not; and by this little gift of truth but
    let to be itself, the Son of God allowed
    to be Himself, and all creation freed to
    upon the Name of God as one.

truth — (A *miracle*) merely lifts the veil and lets the truth 576
    shine unencumbered, being what it is.

truth — *Miracles* bear witness to truth. 2

truth — Reality belongs only to the spirit, and the *miracle* 9
    acknowledges only truth.

understand — It is not necessary that you understand 309
    miracles.

undone — Thus does the *miracle* undo all things the 529
    world attests can never be undone.

unite — *Miracles* unite you directly with your brother. 5

will — The *miracle* itself is a reflection of this union of 69
    will between Father and Son.

Will — *Miracles* are in accord with the Will of God, 125
    Whose Will you do not know because
    you are confused about what you will.

Will — The *Miracles* we do bear witness to the Will of the 136
    Father for His Son, and to our joy in
    uniting with His Will for us.

willingness — (*Miracles*) attest to your willingness to be 282
    released, and to offer time to the Holy
    Spirit for His use of it.

witness — As fear is witness unto death, so is the *miracle*   538
    witness unto life.

witness — Be you witness to the *miracle*, and not the   539
    laws of sin.

witness — The *miracle* itself is but the witness that you   273
    have the power of God in you.

witnesses — Yet while you still need healing, your   163
    miracles are the only witnesses to your
    reality you can recognize.

world — As *miracles* in this world join you to your   242
    brothers, so do your creations establish
    your fatherhood in Heaven.

world — Be not afraid, but let your world be lit by   555
    miracles.

world — There is no situation to which *miracles* do not   214
    apply, and by applying them to all
    situations you will gain the real world.

world — The world is full of *miracles*.   553

world — What (the Holy Spirit) enables you to do is   214
    clearly not of this world, for *miracles*
    violate every law of reality as this
    world judges it.

worthy — I have emphasized that the *miracle,* or the ex-   26
    pression of Atonement, is always a sign
    of respect from the worthy to the
    worthy.

"MIRACLES, A COURSE IN"

believed — ("A Course in Miracles") will be believed   440
    entirely or not at all.

changeless — If you could realize nothing is changeless   494
    but the Will of God, ("A Course in
    Miracles") would not be difficult for
    you.

clear — ("A Course in Miracles") is perfectly clear.   192

clear — If you do not see ("A Course in Miracles") clearly, it   192
    is because you are interpreting against
    it, and therefore do not believe it.

compromise — *("A Course in Miracles")* is easy just be-   **460**
cause it makes no compromise.

compromise — *("A Course in Miracles")* seems difficult to   **461**
those who still believe that compro-
mise is possible.

consistent — Being so simple and direct, ("A Course in   **409**
Miracles") has nothing in it that is not
consistent.

decision — The decision whether or not to listen to *("A*   **320**
Course in Miracles") and follow it is but
the choice between truth and illusion.

dismiss — You often dismiss *("A Course in Miracles")* more   **224**
readily than you dismiss the ego's
thought system.

fearful — If the purpose of this course is to help you   **149**
remember what you are, and if you
believe what you are is fearful, then it
must follow you will not learn *("A
Course in Miracles.")*

free — You have been told again and again that *("A*   **224**
Course in Miracles") will set you free, yet
you sometimes react as if it is trying to
imprison you.

goal — *("A Course in Miracles")* has explicitly stated that   **224**
its goal for you is happiness and peace.
Yet you are afraid of it.

God — Some of the later steps in *("A Course in Miracles,")*   **13**
however, involve a more direct ap-
proach to God Himself.

Guide — *"A Course in Miracles"* offers a very direct and a   **161**
very simple learning situation, and
provides the Guide Who tells you what
to do.

ideas — *("A Course in Miracles")* is not a course in the play   **196**
of ideas, but in their practical applica-
tion.

Identity — Earlier I said *("A Course in Miracles")* will teach   **275**
you how to remember what you are,
restoring to you your Identity.

know — ("A Course in Miracles") is a course in how to know yourself.   **312**

knowledge — ("A Course in Miracles") will lead to knowledge, but knowledge itself is still beyond the scope of our curriculum.   **369**

learn — To learn ("A Course in Miracles") requires willingness to question every value that you hold.   **464**

learning — ("A Course in Miracles") is not beyond immediate learning, unless you believe that what God wills takes time.   **288**

learning — ("A Course in Miracles") offers a very direct and a very simple learning situation, and provides the Guide Who tells you what to do.   **161**

learning — To some extent, then, you must believe that by not learning ("A Course in Miracles") you are protecting yourself.   **224**

love — ("A Course in Miracles") is a course on love, because it is about you.   **228**

means — You have surely begun to realize that "A Course in Miracles" is a very practical course, and one that means exactly what it says.   **147**

motivation — Knowledge is not the motivation for learning ("A Course in Miracles"). Peace is.   **464**

oppose — You would oppose ("A Course in Miracles") because it teaches you you are alike.   **466**

purpose — If the purpose of ("A Course in Miracles") is to help you remember what you are, and if you believe that what you are is fearful, then it must follow that you will not learn this course.   **149**

purpose — The only purpose of ("A Course in Miracles") is to teach what is the same and what is different, leaving room to make the only choice that can be made.   **509**

purpose — The whole purpose of *("A Course in Miracles")* is to teach you that the ego is unbelievable and will forever be unbelievable.   **122**

purpose — You must remember, however, that *("A Course in Miracles")* states, and repeatedly, that its purpose is the escape from fear.   **152**

study — Some of the later parts of *("A Course in Miracles")* rest too heavily on these earlier sections not to require careful study.   **13**

teach — *("A Course in Miracles")* attempts to teach no more than that the power of decision cannot lie in choosing different forms of what is still the same illusion and the same mistake.   **609**

teach — *("A Course in Miracles")* makes no attempt to teach what cannot easily be learned.   **480**

teaches — Perhaps you feel you do not need *("A Course in Miracles")* which, in the end, teaches that only reality is true.   **195**

training — *("A Course in Miracles")* is a course in mind training.   **13**

MIRACLE WORKER(S)

fear — Before *miracle workers* are ready to undertake their function in this world, it is essential that they fully understand the fear of release.   **21**

God's — Because the *miracle worker* has heard God's Voice, he strengthens it in a sick brother, by weakening his belief in sickness, which he does not share.   **175**

light — The *miracle worker* begins by perceiving light, and translates his perception into sureness by continually extending it and accepting its acknowledgement.   **161**

mind — It is essential, however, that the *miracle worker* be in his right mind, however briefly, or he will be unable to establish right-mindedness in someone else.   **21**

principles — (Special principles of *miracle workers*). 23-24

respect — The *miracle worker* must have genuine respect 27
for true cause and effect as a necessary
condition for the miracle to occur.

responsibility — The sole responsibility of the *miracle* 22
worker is to accept the Atonement for
himself.

task — The task of the *miracle worker* thus becomes to 203
deny the denial of truth.

thinking — All *miracle workers* need that kind of training 27
(miracle minded thinking).

MIRROR(S)

brother — (Your brother) is the *mirror* of yourself, 477
wherein you see the judgment you
have laid on both of you.

images — You need but leave the *mirror* clean and clear 271
of all images of hidden darkness you
have drawn upon it.

spotless — In this world you can become a spotless 271
mirror, in which the holiness of your
Creator shines forth from you to all
around you.

truth — You are a *mirror* of truth, in which God Himself 58
shines in perfect light.

MISCREATION

conflict — The fundamental conflict in this world, then, 28
is between creation and *miscreation*.

fear — All fear is implicit in *(miscreation)*, and all love in 28
(creation).

MISERY

escape — Reason will tell you that the only way to es- 439
cape from *misery* is to recognize it and
go the other way.

escape — You will either escape from *misery* entirely or 440
not at all.

made — All the *misery* you made has been your own. 441

MISPERCEPTION(S)

disappear — All that can literally disappear in the twinkling of an eye because it is merely a *misperception*. **14**

fear — *Misperceptions* produce fear and true perceptions foster love, but neither brings certainty because all perception varies. **35**

Holy Spirit — You may let your mind misperceive, but the Holy Spirit lets you mind reinterpret its own *misperceptions*. **73**

I — I cannot unite your will with God's for you, but I can erase all *misperception* from your mind if you will bring it under my guidance. **39**

knowledge — It is necessary only because *misperception* is a block to knowledge, while accurate perception is a steppingstone towards it. **54**

perceive — If you perceive truly you are cancelling out *misperceptions* in yourself and in others simultaneously. **35**

MISSION

fail — You will not fail in your *mission* because I did not fail in mine. **204**

Holy Spirit — As the Holy Spirit fulfills His *mission* He will teach you yours, for your *mission* is the same as His. **209**

MISTAKE(S)

corrected — What you see clearly as a *mistake* you want corrected. **377**

Holy Spirit — (The Holy Spirit) recognizes *mistakes*, and would correct them all as God entrusted Him to do. **377**

loss — For there is but one *mistake;* the whole idea that loss is possible, and could result in gain for anyone. **506**

overlook — It is not difficult to overlook *mistakes* that have been given no effects. **595**

MOTIVATION

change — Change in *motivation* is a change of mind, and this will inevitably produce fundamental change because the mind is fundamental.   **98**

interpretation — There is but one interpretation of *motivation* that makes any sense.   **201**

MOTIVE(S)

analyzing — Analyzing the *motives* of others is hazardous to you.   **200**

MURDER

function — It is not sinful to believe the function of the Son is *murder,* but it is insanity.   **462**

love — What is not love is *murder.*   **461**

will — This is your part; to realize that *murder* in any form is not your will.   **462**

wish — You are not asked to fight against your wish to *murder.*   **461**

MURDERER(S)

Father — Either the Father and Son are *murderers,* or neither is.   **462**

MYTH(S)

ambiguous — *Myths* are entirely perceptual, and so ambiguous in form and characteristically good-and-evil in nature that the most benevolent of them is not without fearful connotations.   **53**

ego — *Myths* and magic are closely associated, since *myths* are usually related to ego origins and magic to the powers the ego ascribes to itself.   **53**

God — The creations of God do not create *myths,* although creative effort can be turned to mythology.   **53**

NEED(S)

deprive — *Needs* arise only when you deprive yourself.   **11**

God's — God's Son can make no *needs* His Father will not   **277**
    meet, if he but turn to him ever so
    little.

unmet — No *needs* will long be left unmet if you leave   **308**
    them all to His Whose function is to
    meet them.

NIGHTMARE(S)

darkest — Learn that even the darkest *nightmare* that dis-   **250**
    turbs the mind of God's sleeping Son
    holds no power over him.

defeat — You still want what God wills, and no *night-*   **204**
    mare can defeat a Child of God in his
    purpose.

ego — The ego would preserve your *nightmares,* and   **229**
    prevent you from awakening and un-
    derstanding they are past.

NOW

gentleness — The stillness and peace of *now* enfold you   **325**
    in perfect gentleness.

given — Now it is given to you to heal and teach, to   **246**
    make what will be *now.*

"NOW"

encounters — For only *"now"* is here, and only *"now"*   **230**
    presents the opportunities for the holy
    encounters in which salvation can be
    found.

eternity — (The Holy Spirit's) is therefore on the only   **230**
    aspect of time that can extend to the
    infinite, for *"now"* is the closest approx-
    imation of eternity that this world
    offers.

NOTHING

content — I said before, "Be not content with *nothing,"*   **254**
    for you have believed that *nothing* could
    content you.

power — By giving power to *nothing* he throws away the   **256**
           joyous opportunity to learn that *nothing*
           has no power.

NOTHINGNESS

overlook — To overlook *nothingness* is merely to judge   **174**
           correctly, and because of your ability to
           evaluate it truly, to let it go.

reality — Only the anticipation will frighten you, for   **204**
           the reality of *nothingness* cannot be
           frightening.

OFFEND(S)

perceive — If what you perceive *offends* you, you are   **198**
           offended in yourself and are condemn-
           ing God's Son whom God condemneth
           not.

OFFENSE(S)

brother — If you perceive *offense* in a brother, pluck the   **198**
           offense from your mind, for you are
           offended by Christ and are deceived in
           Him.

Christ — Heal in Christ and be not offended by Him, for   **198**
           there is no *offense* in Him.

Holy Spirit — Let the Holy Spirit remove all *offenses* of   **198**
           God's Son against himself and perceive
           no one but through His guidance, for
           He would save you from all condemna-
           tion.

ONENESS

conflicts — Nothing conflicts with *oneness*.   **508**

giving — (God and His Son) are joined in giving you the   **269**
           gift of *oneness*, before which all separa-
           tion vanishes.

God — God's teacher is as like to His Creator as is His   **278**
           Son, and through His Teacher does
           God proclaim His *Oneness* and His
           Son's.

Holy Spirit — (The Holy Spirit) teaches the miracle of *oneness,* and before His lesson division disappears.   278

reality — You can lose sight of *oneness,* but cannot make sacrifice of its reality.   505

separate — All this takes note of time and place as if they were discrete, for while you think that part of you is separate the concept of a *oneness* joined as one is meaningless.   484

OPPOSITE(S)
together — *Opposites* must be brought together, not kept apart.   266

OVERLEARNED
task — However much you may have *overlearned* your chosen task, the lesson that reflects the Love of God is stronger still.   601

OVERLEARNING
truth — Now does your ancient *overlearning* stand implacable before the Voice of truth, and teach you that Its lessons are not true; too hard to learn, too difficult to see, and too opposed to what is really true.   601

PAIN
attack — Every *pain* you suffer do you see as proof that he is guilty of attack.   525

attack — Whenever you consent to suffer *pain,* to be deprived, unfairly treated or in need of anything, you but accuse your brother of attack upon God's Son.   525

body — *Pain* demonstrates the body must be real.   537

Christ — (Christ) would not leave one source of *pain* unhealed, nor any image left to veil the truth.   620

crucified — The crucified give *pain* because they are in *pain.*   395

free — There is no *pain* from which he is not free, if you would have him be what he is.   **599**

God — *Pain* is not of (God), for He knows no attack and His peace surrounds you silently.   **184**

God — (God) denied you only your request for *pain,* for suffering is not of His Creation.   **228**

joy — What is joyful to you is painful to the ego, and as long as you are in doubt about what you are, you will be confused about joy and *pain.*   **124**

learn — There is no need to learn through *pain.*   **416**

past — Unless you learn that past *pain* is an illusion, you are choosing a future of illusions and losing the many opportunities you could find for release in the present.   **229**

purpose — (The purpose of *pain*) is the same as pleasure, for both are means to make the body real.   **537**

"sacrifice" — *Pain* is the only "sacrifice" the Holy Spirit asks, and this He would remove.   **384**

separation — The cause of *pain* is separation, not the body, which is only its effect.   **554**

source — If it is true attack in any form will hurt you, and will do so just as much as in another form that you do recognize, then it must follow that you do not always recognize the source of *pain.*   **460**

unreal — Pleasure and *pain* are equally unreal, because their purpose cannot be achieved.   **538**

want — All your *pain* comes simply from a futile search for what you want, insisting where it must be found.   **573**

PAINFUL

recognize — You no more recognize what is *painful* than you know what is joyful, and are, in fact, very apt to confuse the two.   **124**

PARDON

fear — The fear of God is the sure result of seeing *pardon* as unmerited.   **594**

forgiveness — If you can see your brother merits *pardon*, you have learned forgiveness is your right as much as his.   **594**

justified — *Pardon* is always justified.

PAST

anger — Your *past* was made in anger, and if you use it to attack the present, you will not see the freedom that the present holds.   **234**

attack — They carry the spots of pain in your mind, directing you to attack in retaliation for a *past* that is no more.   **229**

binds — The *past* binds Him not, and therefore binds not you.   **278**

blame — Do not seek to lay the blame for deprivation on it, for the *past* is gone.   **324**

changed — The *past*, too, was changed and interposed between what always was and now.   **270**

darkness — Everyone seen without the *past* thus brings you nearer to the end of time by bringing healed and healing sight into the darkness, and enabling the world to see.   **241**

ego — The *past* becomes the justification for entering into a continuing unholy alliance with the ego against the present.   **332**

ego's — The *past* is the ego's chief learning device, for it is in the past that you learned to define your own needs and acquire methods for meeting them on your own terms.   **290**

escape — The shadowy figures from the *past* are precisely what you must escape.   **229**

failed — Its *past* has failed.   **485**

fear — Let not time worry you, for all the fear that you and your brother experience is really *past*.   **354**

free — He Who has freed you from the *past* would teach   278
you are free of it.

God's — The cloud that obscures God's Son to you is the   234
past, and if you would have it *past* and
gone, you must not see it now.

gone — Forgive the *past* and let it go, for it is gone.   513

in — The *past* is not in you.   245

live — You think you live in what is *past*.   511

mind — Give the *past* to Him Who can change your mind   332
about it for you.

peace — The peace of God passeth your understanding   238
only in the *past*.

present — *Past*, present and future are not continuous,   234
unless you force continuity on them.

present — The *past* can cast no shadow to darken the   233
present, unless you are afraid of light.

relationship — The *past* is gone; seek not to preserve it in   324
the special relationship that binds you
to it, and would teach you salvation is
past and so you must return to the
past to find salvation.

remember — The *past* that you remember never was,   270
and represents only the denial of what
always was.

risen — This is the way to Heaven and to the peace of   399
Easter, in which we join in glad aware-
ness that the Son of God is risen from
the *past*, and has awakened to the
present.

separate — Only the *past* can separate, and it is nowhere.   234

taught — Your *past* is what you have taught yourself.   276

value — The only value that the *past* can hold is that you   484
learn it gave you no rewards which you
would want to keep.

world — Only in the *past* — an ancient *past*, too short to   512
make a world in answer to creation, —
did this world appear to rise.

PATIENCE

attack — Every attack is a call for His *patience,* since His *patience* can translate attack into blessing.   **119**

infinite — Infinite *patience* calls on infinite love, and by producing results now it renders time unnecessary.   **81**

infinite — Now you must learn that only infinite *patience* produces immediate results.   **81**

PEACE

abide — Abide in *peace* where God would have you be.   **518**

absence — The absence of perfect *peace* means but one thing: You think you do not will for God's Son what his Father wills for him.   **276**

accept — You could accept *peace* now for everyone, and offer them perfect freedom from all illusions because you heard His Voice.   **172**

Atonement — *Peace* abides in every mind that quickly accepts the plan God set for its Atonement, relinquishing its own.   **257**

battleground — It has been hopeless to attempt to find the hope of *peace* upon a battleground.   **565**

brother's — It will be given you to see your brother's worth when all you want for him is *peace.*   **405**

Christ — (Christ) would bring *peace* to everyone, and how can He do this except through you?   **380**

come — It is through us that *peace* will come.   **294**

come — Make way for *peace,* and it will come.   **279**

conflict — Conflict and *peace* are opposites.   **455**

dream — You will first dream of *peace,* and then awaken to it.   **238**

dwell — You dwell in *peace* as limitless as its Creator, and everything is given those who would remember Him.   **454**

ego — *Peace* is the greatest enemy of the ego because, according to its interpretation of reality, war is the guarantee of its survival. 73

enemies — The secret enemies of *peace*, your least decision to choose attack instead of love, unrecognized and swift to challenge you to combat and to violence far more inclusive than you think, are there by your election. 465

excluding — When you give up *peace*, you are excluding yourself from it. 128

expand — The *peace* that already lies deeply within must expand, and flow across the obstacles you placed before it. 379

extended — *Peace* is extended from you only to the eternal, and it reaches out from the eternal in you. 384

extends — As *peace* extends from deep inside yourself to embrace all the Sonship and give it rest, it will encounter many obstacles. 379

extends — *Peace*, looking on itself, extends itself. 454

favor — You were at *peace* until you asked for special favor. 227

find — You cannot find *peace* outside you. 15

find — You will not find *peace* until you have removed the nails from the hands of God's Son, and taken the last thorn from His forehead. 193

forgiveness — Forgiveness is your *peace*, for herein lies the end of separation and the dream of danger and destruction, sin and death; of madness and of murder, grief and loss. 572

forgiveness — You who want *peace* can find it only by complete forgiveness. 11

give — If you want to have *(peace)* of me, you must give it. 134

339

"given" — You have "given" your *peace* to the gods you made, but they are not there to take it from you, and you cannot give it to them.   **174**

goal — The goal of *peace* cannot be accepted apart from its conditions, and you had faith in it for no one accepts what he does not believe is real.   **364**

God — God has established (the conditions for *peace*).   **355**

God — Guilt is the condition of sacrifice, as *peace* is the condition for the awareness of your relationship with God.   **305**

God — (Nothing) will prevail against the *peace* God wills for you.   **249**

God — Only at the altar of God will you find *peace*.   **173**

God — *Peace* comes from God through me to you.   **172**

God — *Peace* could no more depart from you than from God.   **380**

God — *Peace* is yours because God created you.   **175**

God — When you are not at *peace* it can only be because you do not believe you are in (God).   **133**

God's — *Peace* will be yours because it is God's Will.   **464**

guilt — *Peace* and guilt are antithetical, and the Father can be remembered only in *peace*.   **221**

healing — *Peace* be to you to whom is healing offered.   **537**

illusion — For fantasy solutions bring but the illusion of experience, and the illusion of *peace* is not the condition in which truth can enter.   **342**

infinity — The still infinity of endless *peace* surrounds you gently in its soft embrace, so strong and quiet, tranquil in the might of its Creator, nothing can intrude upon the sacred Son of God within.   **570**

Kingdom — *Peace* is the condition of the Kingdom.   **102**

knowledge — *Peace* is the prerequisite for knowledge.   **128**

limitlessness — Your *peace* lies in its limitlessness.   **186**

love — *Peace* is the state where love abides and seeks to share itself.   **455**

love — *Peace* will never come from the illusion of love, but only from its reality.   **315**

means — Be the means whereby your brother finds the *peace* in which your wishes are fulfilled.   **518**

messengers — *Peace* will send its messengers from you to all the world, and barriers will fall away before their coming as easily as those that you interpose will be surmounted.   **380**

mission — When you have accepted your mission to extend *peace* you will find *peace*, for by making it manifest you will see it.   **216**

nothing - In *peace* (you) needed nothing and asked for nothing.   **227**

obstacle — The first obstacle that *peace* must flow across is your desire to get rid of it.   **380**

obstacle — The second obstacle that *peace* must flow across, and closely related to the first, is the belief the body is valuable for what it offers.   **384**

obstacle — The third obstacle (that *peace* must flow across is) the attraction of death.   **388**

obstacle — The fourth obstacle (that *peace* must surmount is) the fear of God.   **391**

offer — Those who offer *peace* to everyone have found a home in Heaven the world cannot destroy.   **490**

perfect — Think not you understand anything until you pass the test of perfect *peace*, for *peace* and understanding go together and never can be found alone.   **278**

realization — When *peace* comes at last to those who wrestle with temptation and fight against the giving into sin; when the light comes at last into the mind given to contemplation; or when the goal is finally achieved by anyone, it always comes with just one happy realization; "I need do nothing."   **363**

rest — You can rest in *peace* only because you are awake.   **147**

spirit — *Peace* is a natural heritage of spirit.   **44**

stronger — *Peace* is stronger than war because it heals.   **70**

substitute — There is no substitute for *peace*.   **464**

teach — Since (your) mind is whole, you are teaching   **102**
    peace because you believe in it.

teach — The only way to have *peace* is to teach *peace*.   **92**

teacher — The teacher of *peace* will never abandon you.   **279**

truce — Mistake not truce for *peace*, nor compromise for   **461**
    the escape from conflict.

truth — If *peace* is the condition of truth and sanity, and   **341**
    cannot be without them, where *peace* is
    they must be.

truth — If you experience *peace*, it is because truth has   **341**
    come to you and you will see the
    outcome truly, for deception cannot
    prevail against you.

truth — When a situation has been devoted wholly to   **371**
    truth, *peace* is inevitable.

understanding — Think not you understand anything   **278**
    until you pass the test of perfect *peace*,
    for *peace* and understanding go together
    and can never be found alone.

understanding — For understanding is in you, and from   **279**
    it *peace* must come.

war — The means of war are not the means of *peace*, and   **452**
    what the warlike would remember is
    not love.

world — This world has much to offer to your *peace*, and   **488**
    many chances to extend your own
    forgiveness.

world — Do you not think the world needs *peace* as much   **134**
    as you do?

yours — *Peace* will be yours because His *peace* still flows to   **250**
    you from Him Whose Will is *peace*.

PENALTY

God's — No *penalty* is ever asked of God's Son except by   **256**
    himself and of himself.

PERCEIVE(S)

anew — To *perceive* anew is merely to *perceive* again, implying that before, or in the interval between, you were not perceiving at all.   **194**

Atonement — Since perception rests on lack, those who *perceive* have not totally accepted the Atonement and given themselves over to truth.   **41**

body — The ability to *perceive* made the body possible, because you must *perceive* something and with something.   **38**

brother — This means that you *perceive* a brother only as you see him now.   **233**

convinces — Everyone convinces you of what you want to *perceive,* and of the reality of the Kingdom you have chosen for your vigilance.   **192**

good — For if you *perceive* both good and evil, you are accepting both the false and the true and making no distinction between them.   **195**

healing — Perception is based on a separated state, so that anyone who *perceives* at all needs healing.   **41**

Holy Spirit — Nothing (the Holy Spirit) *perceives* can induce fear.   **22**

interpretation — Yet you cannot be aware without interpretation, for what you *perceive* is your interpretation.   **192**

love — When you love someone, you *perceive* him as he is, and this makes it possible for you to know him.   **36**

meaning — You do not know the meaning of anything you *perceive.*   **196**

thinketh — As a man thinketh, so does he *perceive.*   **415**

truly — To *perceive* truly is to be aware of all reality through the awareness of your own.   **233**

witness — Everything you *perceive* is a witness to the thought system you want to be true.   **192**

PERCEPTION(S)

accurate — It is necessary only because misperception is a block to knowledge, while accurate *perception* is a stepping-stone towards it.   **54**

believe — Yet you believe that you do understand your (*perceptions*).   **203**

believe — Look, then, beyond error and do not let your *perception* rest upon it, for you will believe what your *perception* holds.   **157**

body — Even in its most spiritualized form *perception* involves the body.   **36**

body — The interpretive function of *perception*, a distorted form of creation, then permits you to interpret the body as yourself in an attempt to escape from the conflict you have induced.   **38**

brother — Correct *perception* of your brother is necessary, because minds have chosen to see themselves as separate.   **41**

change — Since *perceptions* change, their dependence on time is obvious. How you perceive at any given time determines what you do, and actions must occur in time.   **36**

choice — *Perception* is a choice and not a fact.   **425**

choice — *Perception* is the choice of what you want yourself to be; the world you want to live in, and the state in which you think your mind will be content and satisfied.   **483**

choice — And it is given you to make another choice, and use *perception* for a different purpose.   **481**

chooses — (*Perception*) chooses where you think your safety lies, at your decision.   **483**

choosing — *Perception* rests on choosing; knowledge does not.   **487**

complete — *Perception*, at its loftiest, is never complete.   **241**

conflict — The alternating investment in the two levels of *perception* is usually experienced as conflict, which can become very acute.   **18**

conflict — There is no conflict anywhere in (perfect)   91
perception, because it means that all
perception is guided by the Holy Spirit,
Whose Mind is fixed on God.

distorted — Your distorted *perceptions* produce a dense   12
cover over miracle impulses, making it
hard for them to reach your own
awareness.

distorts — There are many instances of how what you   145
want distorts *perception*.

error — Redeemed *perception* is easily translated into   219
knowledge, for only *perception* is capable
of error and *perception* has never been.

evaluation — Evaluation is a central part of *perception*,   41
because judgments are necessary in
order to select.

experience — *Perceptions* are built up on the basis of   192
experience, and experience leads to
beliefs.

faith — Faith and belief, upheld by reason, cannot fail to   427
lead to changed *perception*.

faithful — And always is (*perception*) faithful to your   483
purposes from which it never
separates, nor gives the slightest
witness unto anything the purpose in
your mind upholdeth not.

fear — As an attribute of the belief in space and time,   35
(*perception*) is subject either to fear or
love.

guidance — Two ways of looking at the world are in   215
your mind, and your *perception* will
reflect the guidance you have chosen.

healed — Your *perception* was healed in the holy instant   378
Heaven gave you.

higher — I have spoken before of the higher or "true"   68
perception, which is so near to truth that
God Himself can flow across the little
gap.

holy — Yet no *perception*, however holy, will last forever.   241

Holy Spirit — The Holy Spirit is the Christ Mind which   68
    is aware of the knowledge that lies
    beyond *perception.*

Holy Spirit — Even the *perception* of the Holy Spirit, as   241
    perfect as *perception* can be, is without
    meaning in Heaven.

impossible — *Perception,* on the other hand, is impossible   41
    without belief in "more" and "less."

incorrect — Perceived improperly, it induces a *perception*   109
    of conflict with something else, as all
    incorrect *perception* does.

instruction — Instruction in *perception* is your great need,   196
    for you understand nothing.

interpretation — You can see in many ways because   35
    perception involves interpretation, and
    this means that it is not whole or
    consistent.

judgments — What happens to *perceptions* if there are no   41
    judgments and nothing but perfect
    equality? *Perception* becomes impossible.

knowledge — *Perception* is not knowledge, but it can be   68
    transferred to knowledge, or cross
    over into it.

knowledge — True *perception* is the basis for knowledge,   35
    but knowing is the affirmation of truth
    and beyond all *perceptions.*

law — *Perception's* basic law could thus be said, "You will   489
    rejoice at what you see because you see
    it to rejoice."

laws — Yet *perception* cannot escape the basic laws of   90
    mind.

limits — You have no conception of the limits you have   301
    placed on your *perception*, and no idea of
    all the loveliness that you could see.

love — Misperceptions produce fear and true *perceptions*   35
    foster love, but neither brings
    certainty because all *perception* varies.

made — You made *perception* that you might choose among your brothers, and seek for sin with them.   **422**

manifest — *Perception* tells you you are manifest in what you see.   **483**

meaning — *Perception* cannot be in constant flux, and make allowance for stability of meaning anywhere.   **596**

meaning — *Perception* derives meaning from relationships.   **73**

meaningless — The meaninglessness of *perception* based on the unbelievable is apparent, but may not be recognized as being beyond belief, because it is made by belief.   **122**

meaningless — *Perception* will be meaningless when it has been perfected, for everything that has been used for learning will have no function.   **329**

medium — *Perception* is the medium by which ignorance is brought to knowledge.   **267**

mind — *Perception* involves some misuse of mind, because it brings the mind into areas of uncertairty.   **38**

miracle — (The miracle) acts as a catalyst, breaking up erroneous *perception* and reorganizing it properly.   **3**

miracles — By recognizing spirit, miracles adjust the levels of *perception* and show them in proper alignment.   **3**

miracles — (Miracles) intercede for your holiness and make your *perceptions* holy.   **3**

obey — *Perception* cannot obey two masters, each asking for messages of different things in different languages.   **382**

perfect — Perfect *perception*, then, has many elements in common with knowledge, making transfer to it impossible.   **241**

process — *Perception* is a continual process of accepting and rejecting, organizing and reorganizing, shifting and changing. — 41

projection — Projection makes *perception* and you cannot see beyond it. — 231

proper — Properly perceived, it can be used as a way out of conflict, as all proper *perception* can. — 109

redeemed — Redeemed *perception* is easily translated into knowledge, for only *perception* is capable of error and *perception* has never been. — 219

result — *Perception* is a result and not a cause. — 415

right — Right *perception* is necessary before God can communicate with His altars, which He established in His Sons. — 36

right — The strength of right *perception* is so great that it brings the mind into accord with His, because it serves His Voice, which is in all of you. — 110

right — The whole value of right *perception* lies in the inevitable realization that all *perception* is unnecessary. — 54

sane — Sane *perception* induces sane choosing. — 39

seem — *Perceptions* are determined by their purpose, in that they seem to be what they are for. — 570

selective — Selective *perception* chooses its witnesses carefully, and its witnesses are consistent. — 191

selects — *Perception* selects, and makes the world you see. — 425

separation — *Perception* did not exist until the separation introduced degrees, aspects and intervals. — 37

sick — Only *perception* can be sick, because only *perception* alone can be distorted. — 146

Sonship — And *perception* will last until the Sonship knows itself as whole. — 118

specialness — (*Perception*) is not bound to specialness but by your choice. — 481

specific — *Perception* is always specific. — 51

straightened — This is because *perception* must be straightened out before you can know anything.   35

teach — *Perception* seems to teach you what you see.   480

temporary — *Perception* is temporary.   35

time — Since *perceptions* change, their dependence on time is obvious.   36

true — For *perceptions* cannot be partly true.   195

unreal — Although *perception* of any kind is unreal, you made it and the Holy Spirit can therefore use it well.   90

whole — You can see in many ways because *perception* involves interpretation, and this means that it is not whole or consistent.   36

wish — (*Perception*) is the outward picture of a wish; an image that you wanted to be true.   480

wrong — Wrong *perception* is the wish that things be as they are not.   146

PERFECT

God — God, who knows that His creations are *perfect*, does not affront them.   95

God — If God created you *perfect*, you are perfect.   173

PERFECTION

denied — For *perfection* is, and cannot be denied.   204

know — You cannot know your own *perfection* until you have honored all those who were created like you.   119

sickness — Sickness and *perfection* are irreconcilable.   173

world — Yet in this world, your *perfection* is unwitnessed.   242

PERSECUTED

cannot — The message the crucifixion was intended to teach was that it is not necessary to perceive any form of assault in persecution, because you cannot be *persecuted*.   85

free — You are free to perceive yourself as *persecuted* if you choose.   85

PERSECUTION

teaching — If you react as if you are persecuted, you are teaching *persecution*.   85

PLAN

accept — How could this readiness (to accept His *plan* for salvation in the place of yours) be reached save through the sight of all your misery, and the awareness that your *plan* has failed, and will forever fail to bring you peace and joy of any kind?   469

PLEASURE

God's — All real *pleasure* comes from doing God's will.   12

pain — *Pleasure* and pain are equally unreal, because their purpose cannot be achieved.   538

POOR

abundance — The *poor* do not understand that they dwell in abundance and that salvation is come.   206

attack — Remember that those who attack are *poor*. Their poverty asks for gifts, not for further impoverishment.   205

ego — To identify with the ego is to attack yourself and make yourself *poor*.   206

invested — The *poor* are those who have invested wrongly, and they are *poor* indeed!   205

POVERTY

acting — You who could help (those who attack) are acting destructively if you accept their *poverty* as yours.   205

ego — *Poverty* is of the ego and never of God.   206

lack — For *poverty* is lack, and there is but one lack, since there is but one need.   205

lesson — Consider how perfectly your lesson would be learned if you were unwilling to share their *poverty*.   205

POWER

accepting — By accepting this *power* as yours you have learned to remember what you are.   **104**

all — By teaching the *power* of the Kingdom of God Himself (the Holy Spirit) teaches you that all *power* is yours.   **107**

belonging — (*Power*) was created to be shared, and therefore cannot be meaningfully perceived as belonging to anyone at the expense of another.   **108**

claim — You claim this *power* when you become vigilant only for God and His Kingdom.   **104**

creative — Only you can limit your creative *power*, but God wills to release it.   **122**

efforts — Join your efforts to the *power* that cannot fail and must result in peace.   **263**

forgiveness — Give welcome to the *Power* beyond forgiveness, and beyond the world of symbols and of limitations.   **533**

give — It is not up to you to give *power* at all.   **402**

give — Yet you give *power* as the laws of this world interpret giving; as you give you lose.   **402**

glory — *Power* and glory belong to God alone.   **133**

God — All *power* is of God.   **188**

God — *Power* is of God, given by Him and reawakened by the Holy Spirit, who knows that as you give you gain.   **402**

God — Therefore, look only to the *power* that God gave to save you, remembering that it is yours because it is His, and join with your brothers in His peace.   **186**

God — The *power* of God is limitless.   **273**

God — The *power* that God has given to His Son is his, and nothing else can His Son see or choose to look upon without imposing on himself and penalty of guilt, in place of all the happy teaching the Holy Spirit would gladly offer him.   **256**

God — What is not of (God) has no *power* to do anything.   **188**

God — Yet all that stands between you and the *power* of   275
God in you is but your learning of the
false, and of your attempts to undo the
true.

God — You have not usurped the *power* of God, but you   43
have lost it.

God — You will not see yourself beyond the *power* of   263
God if you teach only this (teaching.)

God's — The whole *power* of God's Son lies in all of us,   139
but not in any of us alone.

healing — For healing comes of *power*, and attack of   432
helplessness.

keep — You who have tried to keep *power* for yourself   275
have "lost" it.

Kingdom — You have *power* to add to the Kingdom,   104
though not to add to the Creator of the
Kingdom.

limitation — What you experience when you deny your   186
Father is still for your protection, for
the *power* of your will cannot be
lessened without the intervention of
God against it, and any limitation on
your *power* is not the Will of God.

mind — Banish not *power* from your mind, but let all that   269
would hide your glory be brought to
the judgment of the Holy Spirit, and
there be undone.

obscure — Everything you have taught yourself has   275
made your *power* more and more
obscure to you.

obscured — In the darkness you have obscured the glory   269
God gave you, and the *power* He
bestowed upon His guiltless Son.

oppose — *Power* cannot oppose.   531

peace — You do not know the peace of *power* that   533
opposes nothing.

power — For *power* is not a seeming strength, and truth   275
is beyond semblance of any kind.

semblance — You have made a semblance of power and a show of strength so pitiful that it must fail you. **275**

Son — For you have the *power* to save the Son of God because his Father willed that it be so. **518**

unweakened — Unweakened *power* with no opposite is what creation is. **532**

weaken — Weak strength is meaningless and *power* used to weaken is employed to limit. **531**

POWERLESS

army — The army of the *powerless* is weak indeed. **431**

army — The army of the *powerless* must be disbanded in the presence of strength. **431**

misery — Do you not see that all your misery comes from the strange belief that you are *powerless* **430**

(PSYCHO) THERAPIST

heal — A *therapist* does not heal; he lets healing be. **161**

healer — The *psychotherapist* as unhealed healer. **159-161**

Holy Spirit — The Holy Spirit is the only *therapist*. **161**

light — A *therapist* cannot bring light of himself, for light is not of him. **161**

PRAYER(S)

answered — The Bible emphasizes that all *prayer* is answered, and this is indeed true. **152**

asking — *Prayer* is a way of asking for something. **40**

brothers — The answer to all *prayer* lies in my brothers (to whom God's Voice speaks). **154**

failure — Everyone who has tried to use *prayer* to ask for something has experienced what appears to be failure. **152**

forgiveness — But the only meaningful *prayer* is for forgiveness, because those who have been forgiven have everything. **40**

forgiveness — The *prayer* for forgiveness is nothing more than a request that you may be able to recognize what you already have. **40**

inclusion — *Prayer* is the restatement of inclusion, directed by the Holy Spirit under the law of God.   **153**

know — If you would know your *prayers* are answered, never doubt a Son of God.   **153**

miracles – (*Prayer*) is the medium of miracles.   **40**

PRESENT

birth — And Heaven will not change, for birth into the holy *present* is salvation from change.   **282**

ego's — But what is obvious is that the *present* is useless to you while you pursue the ego's goal as its ally.   **324**

forever — And the *present* extends forever.   **281**

forgiveness — For the *present* is forgiveness.   **332**

healing — All healing lies within (the *present*) because its continuity is real.   **234**

past — Past, *present* and future are not continuous, unless you force continuity upon them.   **234**

Son — This is the way to Heaven and to the peace of Easter, in which we join in glad awareness that the Son of God is risen from the past, and has awakened to the *present*.   **399**

Sonship — (The *present*) extends to all aspects of the Sonship at the same time, and thus enables them to reach each other.   **234**

time — The *present* is before time was and will be when time is no more.   **234**

true — Look lovingly upon the *present* for it holds the only things that are forever true.   **234**

PRICE

getting — The *price* for getting is to lose sight of value, making it inevitable that you will not value what you receive.   **154**

PRIDE

miracles — *Pride* will not produce miracles, and will therefore deprive you of the true witnesses to your reality. **167**

returned — It is easy to distinguish grandeur from grandiosity, because love is returned and *pride* is not. **167**

PRISON

body — (The body) holds in *prison* but the willing mind that would abide in it. **606**

escape — For everyone is seeking to escape from the *prison* he has made, and the way to find release is not denied him. **221**

hate — The home of vengeance is not yours; the place you set aside to house your hate is not a *prison*, but an illusion of yourself. **360**

separate — You see yourself locked in a separate *prison*, removed and unreachable, incapable of reaching out as being reached. **360**

PRISONER

body — (The body) sickens at the bidding of the mind that would become its *prisoner*. **606**

body — Yet is the body *prisoner* and not the mind. **606**

God — If you be *prisoner*, then God Himself could not be free. **585**

PROBLEM(S)

absurd — The choice will not be difficult, because the *problem* is absurd when clearly seen. **540**

error — Every *problem* is an error. **506**

faith — Had you not lacked faith that it could be solved, the *problem* would be gone. **342**

faith — The *problem* was the lack of faith, and it is this you demonstrate when you remove it from its source and place it elsewhere. **342**

faith — There is no *problem* in any situation on that faith will not solve. **342**

healing — Each time you keep a *problem* for yourself to 507
solve or judge that it is one that has no
resolution, you have made it great, and
past the hope of healing.

Holy Spirit — The Holy Spirit will answer every specific 196
problem, as long as you believe that
problems are specific.

Holy Spirit — To give a *problem* to the Holy Spirit to 502
solve for you means that you want it
solved.

Holy Spirit — You have never given any *problem* to the 311
Holy Spirit He has not solved for you,
nor will you ever do so.

Holy Spirit — You have no *problems* (the Holy Spirit) 277
cannot solve by offering you a miracle.

Holy Spirit's — The Holy Spirit's *problem* solving is the 502
way in which the *problem* ends.

identification — Perceived *problems* in identification at 116
any level are not *problems* of fact.

impossible — There is no shift in any aspect of the 342
problem but will make solution
impossible.

just — If God is just, then can there can be no *problems* 507
that justice cannot solve.

justice — (The *problem*) has been solved because it has 502
been met with justice.

loses — And when the situation is worked out so that no 506
one loses, is the *problem* gone, because it
was an error in perception that has
now been corrected.

nature — The very nature (of a *problem*) is that it is not. 536

perceived — If *problems* are perceived, it is because the 343
thoughts are judged to be in conflict.

remove — To remove the *problem* elsewhere is to keep it, 342
for you remove yourself from it and
make it unsolvable.

shift — For if you shift part of the *problem* elsewhere, the meaning of the problem must be lost, and the solution to the *problem* is inherent is its meaning.   343

sins — The little *problems* that you keep and hide become your secret sins, because you did not choose to let them be removed for you.   503

solved — And it will also be apparent that your many different *problems* will be solved as any one of them has been escaped.   537

solved — Is it not possible that all your *problems* have been solved, but you have removed yourself from the solution?   343

suffer — (All *problems*) are the same to (the Holy Spirit) because each one, regardless of the form it seems to take, is a demand that someone suffer loss and make a sacrifice that you might gain.   506

understands — And no one understands the nature of his *problem*.   536

world — The world was made that *problems* could not be escaped.   608

PROJECT

afraid — (Those who *project*) are afraid that their projections will return and hurt them.   121

disown — What you *project* you disown, and therefore do not believe it is yours.   89

judged — Since you have also judged against what you *project*, you continue to attack it because you continue to keep it separated.   89

real — What you *project* or extend is real for you.   106

vigilant — That is why those who *project* are vigilant for their own safety.   121

you — I said before that what you *project* or extend is up to you, but you must do one or the other, for that is a law of mind, and you must look in before you look out.   215

PROJECTED

antagonistic — You have *projected* outward what is antagonistic to what is inward, and therefore you would have to perceive it this way.　　206

PROJECTING

want — When you think you are *projecting* what you do not want, it is still because you do want it.　　215

PROJECTION

alternative — We have learned, however, that there is an alternative to *projection*.　　89

anger — *Projection* means anger, anger fosters assault, and assault promotes fear.　　85

anger — We have said that without *projection* there can be no anger, but it is also true that without extension there can be no love.　　120

attack — *Projection* and attack are inevitably related because *projection* is always a means of justifying attack.　　89

belief — (*Projection*) reinforces your belief in your own split mind, and its only purpose is to keep the separation going.　　89

device — (*Projection*) is solely a device of the ego to make you feel different from your brothers and separated from them.　　89

hurt — Yet *projection* will always hurt you.　　89

love — (The Apostles') imperfect love made them vulnerable to *projection*, and out of their own fear they spoke of the "wrath of God" as His retaliatory weapon.　　87

make — You make by *projection*, but God creates by extension.　　179

motivation — *Projection* is a confusion in motivation, and given this confusion, trust becomes impossible.　　125

perception — *Projection* makes perception.　　415

purpose — (*Projection*) reinforces your belief in your own   89
split mind, and its only purpose is to
keep the separation going.

purpose — The ultimate purpose of *projection* is always to   223
get rid of guilt.

separation — We have said before that the separation   88
was and is dissociation, and that once it
occurs *projection* becomes the main
defense, or the device that keeps it
going.

wishes — *Projection* always sees your wishes in others.   119

PROMISE

faithlessness — Yet all (sickness) means is that you tried   562
to keep a *promise* to be true to faithless-
ness.

gap — The *promise* that there is no gap between Himself   561
and what He is cannot be false.

God's — God's *promise* is a *promise* to Himself, and there is   561
no one who could be untrue to what He
wills as part of what He is.

PUNISHMENT

deserving — Yet *punishment* is but another form of guilt's   376
protection, for what is deserving
punishment must have really been done.

projection — Any concept of *punishment* involves the   88
projection of blame, and reinforces the
idea that blame is justified.

right-mindedness — *Punishment* is a concept totally   30
opposed to right-mindedness, and the
aim of the Last Judgment might be
called a process of right evaluation.

sin — *Punishment* is always the great preserver of sin,   376
treating it with respect and honoring
its enormity.

world — For this world is the symbol of *punishment*, and   220
all the laws that seem to govern it are
the laws of death.

Friend — Yet it is given you to see this *purpose* in your holy Friend, and recognize it as your own. 395

fulfill — You need take thought for nothing, careless of everything except the only *purpose* that you would fulfill. 404

goal — Think not that you can set a goal unlike God's *purpose* for you and establish it as changeless and eternal. 572

God — For your *purpose* was given you by God, and you must accomplish it because it is His Will. 204

God — God has one *Purpose* which He shares with you. 268

God — The *purpose* God ascribed to anything is its only function. 333

God's — Believe you can interfere with (God's) *purpose*, and you need salvation. 143

Holy Spirit's — The Holy Spirit's *purpose* rests in peace within you. 380

Holy Spirit's — Those who have accepted the Holy Spirit's *purpose* as their own share also His vision. 398

Holy Spirit's — You do not even realize you have accepted the Holy Spirit's *purpose* as your own, and you would merely bring unholy means to its accomplishment. 357

littleness — Your *purpose* is at variance with littleness of any kind. 451

means — And when you hesitate it is because the *purpose* frightens you, and not the means. 410

means — A *purpose* is attained by means and if you want a *purpose* you must be willing to want the means as well. 410

means — The alignment of means and *purpose* is an undertaking impossible for you to understand. 357

mind — *Purpose* is of the mind. 472

PURIFICATION

God — *Purification* is of God alone, and therefore for you. **356**

PURITY

confined — *Purity* is not confined. **550**

creation — Creation is the natural expression of perfect *purity*. **262**

peace – Peace is the acknowledgement of perfect *purity*, from which no one is excluded. **263**

PURPOSE(S)

accomplish — For your *purpose* was given you by God, and you must accomplish it because it is His Will. **204**

afraid — No one who has a single *purpose*, unified and sure, can be afraid. **405**

awake — Awake and remember your *purpose*, for it is your will to do so. **204**

body — The body has no *purpose* and must be solitary. **463**

brother — You (and your brother) are joined in *purpose*, but remain still separate and divided on the means. **340**

brother — You have no *purpose* apart from your brother, nor apart from the one you asked the Holy Spirit to share with you. **380**

brother's — And you will perceive (your brother's) *purpose* is the same as yours. **605**

changed — Your *purpose* has not changed and will not change, for you accepted what can never change. **346**

constant — Only a constant *purpose* can endow events with stable meaning. **596**

desires — No one allows a *purpose* to be replaced while he desires it, for nothing is so cherished and protected as a goal the mind accepts. **421**

faith — Your faith will call the others to serve your *purpose*, as the same *purpose* calls forth the faith in you. **344**

newborn — Your newborn *purpose* is nursed by angels,   **390**
cherished by the Holy Spirit and pro-
tected by God Himself.

possible — Only two *purposes* are possible. And one is sin,   **413**
the other holiness.

salvation — (The salvation of the Son of God) is your   **346**
only *purpose*.

shares — What shares a common *purpose* is the same.   **537**

single — In single *purpose* is the end of all ideas of   **596**
sacrifice, which must assume a dif-
ferent *purpose* for the one who gains and
him who loses.

survives — Nothing survives its *purpose*.   **572**

unification — The unification of *purpose*, then, is the   **148**
Holy Spirit's only way of healing.

unified — Joy is unified *purpose*, and unified *purpose* is only   **143**
God's.

unifies — Only a *purpose* unifies, and those who share a   **463**
purpose have a mind as one.

QUESTION(S)

answers — Just as the body's witnesses are but the   **534**
senses from within itself, so are the
answers to the *questions* of the world
contained within the *questions* that are
asked.

hate — A *question* asked in hate cannot be answered, be-   **533**
cause it is an answer in itself.

honest — An honest *question* is a learning tool that asks   **534**
for something that you do not know.

honest — Only within the holy instant can an honest   **534**
question honestly be asked.

pseudo- — A pseudo*question* has no answer.   **534**

world — All *questions* asked within this world are but a   **533**
way of looking, not a question asked.

world — The *questions* of the world but ask of whom is   **534**
sacrifice demanded, asking not if sacri-
fice is meaningful at all.

QUESTIONING

propaganda — Thus is all *questioning* within the world a   534
    form of propaganda for itself.

selective — You have been as selective in your *questioning*   228
    as in your perception.

QUIET

turmoil — Learn to be *quiet* in the midst of turmoil, for   204
    quietness is the end of strife and this
    is the journey to peace.

QUIETNESS

answered — In *quietness* are all things answered, and is   533
    every problem quietly resolved.

RADIANCE

sorrow — *Radiance* is not associated with sorrow.   66

READINESS

accomplishment — *Readiness* is only the prerequisite for   29
    accomplishment. The two should not
    be confused.

confidence — *Readiness* is only the beginning of confi-   29
    dence.

mind — The state (of *readiness*) does not imply more than   29
    a potential for a change of mind.

REAL

mind — For nothing *real* has ever left the mind of its   312
    creator.

REALITY(IES)

accepted — The only sane solution is not to try to   49
    change *reality,* which is indeed a fearful
    attempt, but to accept it as it is.

appreciated — *Reality* cannot be partly appreciated.   118

aspect — And every miracle you do contains them all, as   241
    every aspect of *reality* you see blends
    quietly into the one *Reality* of God.

aspects — Aspects of *reality* can be seen in everything   241
    and everywhere.

attack — You believe that attack is your *reality*, and that   228
    your destruction is the final proof that
    you were right.

change — It is, then, only your wish to change *reality* that   327
    is fearful, because by your wish you
    think that you have accomplished what
    you wish.

change — *(Reality)* cannot change with time or mood or   271
    chance.

change — (There is but one Teacher who) does not   201
    change His Mind about *reality* because
    reality does not change.

changeless — *Reality* is changeless.   597

conflict — There is but one response to *reality*, for *reality*   201
    evokes no conflict at all.

cooperation — *Reality* needs no cooperation from you to   425
    be itself.

decide — Yet it is no more up to you to decide what is   218
    visible and what is invisible, than it is
    up to you to decide what *reality* is.

deciding — By deciding against your *reality* you have   170
    made yourself vigilant against God and
    the Kingdom.

definition — The definition of *reality* is God's, not yours.   218

denial — Your denial of *reality* may arrest it in time, but   180
    not in eternity.

denial — Your denial of *reality* precludes the acceptance   170
    of God's gift, because you have ac-
    cepted something else in its place.

different — Different *realities* are meaningless, for *reality*   271
    must be one.

disaster — Today, let us resolve together to accept the   311
    joyful tidings that disaster is not real
    and that *reality* is not disaster.

distort — And if you do distort *reality* you will experience   152
    anxiety, depression and ultimately
    panic, because you are trying to make
    yourself unreal.

everything — *Reality* is everything, and you have every-   152
thing because you are real.

faith — How can faith in *reality* be yours while you are   310
bent on making it unreal?

Father — It is not the *reality* of your brothers or your   198
Father or yourself that frightens you.

fearful — You cannot make the unreal because the ab-   152
sence of *reality* is fearful, and fear can-
not be created.

form — *Reality* is ultimately known without a form, un-   532
pictured and unseen.

form — *(Reality)* must transcend all form to be itself.   597

goal — Willing against *reality*, though impossible, can be   151
made into a very persistent goal even
though you do not want it.

God's — And you who share God's Being with Him   219
could never be content without *reality*.

harmless — The *reality* of everything is totally harmless,   146
because total harmlessness is the con-
dition of its *reality*.

Heaven — In Heaven *reality* is shared and not reflected.   272

hurled — Fear not that you will be abruptly lifted up and   322
hurled into *reality*.

illusions — *Reality* cannot "threaten" anything except   149
illusions, since *reality* can only uphold
truth.

join — You cannot join anything except *reality*.   269

know — To know *reality* must involve the willingness to   174
judge unreality for what it is.

laws — *Reality* observes the laws of God, and not the   589
rules you set.

love — You cannot love parts of *reality* and understand   290
what love means.

madness — Madness may be your choice, but not your   258
reality.

mind — *Reality* can dawn only on an unclouded mind.   174

nothing — *Reality* opposes nothing.   445

nothing — There is nothing you can hold against *reality*.   **325**

obstructions — *Reality* cannot break through obstructions you interpose, but it will envelop you completely, when you let them go.   **174**

order — There is no order in *reality*, because everything there is true.   **328**

orders — Different orders of *reality* merely appear to exist, just as different orders of miracles do.   **141**

orders — Orders of *reality* is a perspective without understanding; a frame of reference for *reality* to which it cannot really be compared at all.   **327**

part — You are part of *reality*, which stands unchanged beyond the reach of your ego but within easy reach of the spirit.   **49**

question — The Answer merely undoes the question by establishing the fact that to question *reality* is to question meaninglessly.   **109**

safe — *Reality* is safe and sure, and wholly kind to everyone and everything.   **311**

safety — *Reality* is the only safety.   **150**

seek — You do not have to seek *reality*.   **146**

share — You share *reality* with (God), because *reality* is not divided.   **173**

spirit — *Reality* belongs only to spirit, and the miracle acknowledges only truth.   **9**

task — Your task is not to make *reality*.   **261**

Teacher — There is but one Teacher of *reality*.   **201**

Thought — An idol or the Thought God holds of you is your *reality*.   **588**

truth — *Reality* cannot "threaten" anything except illusions, since *reality* can only uphold truth.   **149**

usurpation — *Reality* is "lost" through usurpation, which produces tyranny.   **13**

witnesses — (Others) will become the created witnesses   162
    to your *reality*, as you were created
    witnesses to God's.

yours — *Reality* is yours because you are *reality*.   108

REASON

awareness — *Reason* lies in the other self you have cut off   426
    from your awareness.

awareness — And nothing you have allowed to stay in   426
    your awareness is capable of *reason*.

brother — Yet *reason* tells you that you cannot see your   428
    brother or yourself as sinful and still
    perceive the other innocent.

correction — *Reason* can see the difference between sin   442
    and mistakes, because it wants correc-
    tion.

ego — The ego never uses *(reason)*, because it does not   427
    realize that it exists.

ego — The introduction of *reason* into the ego's thought   442
    system is the beginning of its undoing,
    for *reason* and the ego are contradictory.

ego — Your *reason's* alien nature to the ego is proof you   426
    will not find the answer there.

ego's — For *reason* is beyond the ego's range of means.   427

error — *Reason* will tell you that the form of error is not   442
    what makes it a mistake.

Heaven — *Reason* assures you Heaven is what you want,   429
    and all you want.

insane — The partially insane have access to *(reason)*, and   427
    only they have need of it.

insanity — The part of your mind where *reason* lies was   427
    dedicated, by your will in union with
    your Father's, to the undoing of in-
    sanity.

love — *Reason*, like love, would reassure you and seeks   429
    not to frighten you.

madness — But *reason* has no part at all in madness, nor   427
    can it be adjusted to fit its end.

madness — For *reason,* kind as is the purpose for which it   429
is the means, leads steadily away from
madness toward the goal of truth.

madness — Madness and *reason* see the same things, but   428
it is certain that they look upon them
differently.

madness — *Reason* does not attack but takes the place of   428
madness quietly, replacing madness if
it be the choice of the insane to listen
to it.

madness — The home of madness cannot be the home   428
of *reason.*

means — *Reason* is a means that serves the Holy Spirit's   427
purpose in its own right.

open — But *reason* can serve to open doors you closed   427
against it.

salvation — *Reason* is not salvation in itself, but it makes   442
way for peace and brings you to a state
of mind in which salvation can be given
you.

save — Thus does the ego damn, and *reason* save.   442

see — What *reason* points to you can see, because the wit-   427
nesses on its behalf are clear.

sin — *Reason* cannot see sin but can see errors, and leads   428
to their correction.

sin — *Reason* will also tell you that when you think you   428
sin, you call for help.

vision — You can see *reason.* This is not a play on words,   442
for here is the beginning of a vision
that has meaning.

world — *Reason* would tell you that the world you see   435
through eyes that are not yours must
make no sense to you.

REBORN

Son — Each instant is the Son of God *reborn* until he   518
chooses not to die again.

RECEIVE(S)

accept — But to *receive* is to accept, not to get.   **154**

choose — Everyone gives as he receives, but he must   **395**
          choose what it will be that he *receives.*

desire — For if what you desire you *receive,* and happi-   **434**
          ness is constant, then you need ask for
          it but once to have it always.

give — To give is no more blessed than to *receive.*   **430**

give — You will *receive* because it is His will to give.   **325**

RECEIVED

give — Give as you have *received.*   **346**

give — Yet it is done already, and unless you give all   **194**
          that you have *received* you will not know
          that your Redeemer liveth.

RECEIVING

giving — The cost of giving is *receiving.*   **256**

RECOGNITION

vision — For *recognition* comes of vision and suspended   **419**
          judgment.

RECOGNIZE

"know" — To *recognize* means to "know again," implying   **35**
          that you knew before.

REDEEMED

joy — But the *redeemed* give joy because they have been   **395**
          healed of pain.

REDEEMER

brother — For sin would keep you separate, but your   **378**
          Redeemer would have you look upon
          your brother as yourself.

call — To you who have acknowledged the call of your   **345**
          Redeemer, the strain of not responding
          to His call seems to be greater than
          before.

REDEMPTION

afraid — In the extreme, you are afraid of *redemption* and   225
you believe it will kill you.

crucifixion — For the undoing of the crucifixion of   193
God's Son is the work of *redemption*, in
which everyone has a part of equal
value.

crucifixion — You would rather be a slave of the cruci-   226
fixion than a Son of God in *redemption*.

everyone — Everyone in the world must play his part in   214
its *redemption*, in order to recognize that
the world has been redeemed.

give — Fear not to give *redemption* over to your Re-   298
deemer's love.

give — Let us give *redemption* to each other and share in it,   394
that we may rise as one in resurrection,
not separate in death.

given — *Redemption* has been given you to give each   394
other, and thus receive it.

mine — Bring only this awareness (of salvation) to the   194
Sonship and you will have a part in the
redemption as valuable as mine.

mission — The mission of *redemption* will be fulfilled as   250
surely as the creation will remain un-
changed throughout eternity.

part — You have assumed your part in (the *redemption* of   345
the Son of God) and are fully respon-
sible to him.

sharing — *Redemption* is recognized only by sharing it.   194

terror — Your real terror is of *redemption*.   225

voice — Each voice has a part in the song of *redemption*,   235
the hymn of gladness and thanksgiving
for the light to the Creator of light.

REFLECTION(S)

eternity — The *reflections* you accept into the mirror of   272
your mind in time but bring eternity
nearer or farther.

God — The *reflection* of God needs no interpretation.   271

light — *Reflections* are seen in light.   271

truth — For the *reflection* of truth draws everyone to truth, and as they enter into it they leave all *reflections* behind.   **272**

RELATIONSHIP(S)

beautiful — The beautiful *relationship* you have with all your brothers is part of you because it is a part of God Himself.   **561**

brother — In your *relationship* with your brother, where He has taken charge of everything at your request, (the Holy Spirit) has set the course inward to the truth you share.   **349**

Christ — For at the center (of your holy *relationship*) Christ has been reborn, to light His home with vision that overlooks the world.   **441**

Christ — I am within your holy *relationship*, yet you would imprison me behind the obstacles you raise to freedom, and bar my way to you.   **385**

close — To join in close *relationship* with Him is to accept *relationships* as real, and through their reality to give over all illusions for the reality of your *relationship* with God.   **326**

each — Use no *relationship* to hold you to the past, but with each one each day be born again.   **245**

ego — But everything seems to come between the fragmented *relationships* the ego sponsors to destroy.   **347**

ego — Now the ego counsels thus; substitute for this another *relationship* to which your former goal was quite appropriate.   **338**

ego's — The ego's use of *relationships* is so fragmented that it frequently goes even farther; one part of one aspect suits its purpose, while it prefers different parts of another aspect.   **291**

faith — Enter each situation with the faith you give your brother, or you are faithless to your own *relationship.*   **344**

goals — For your *relationship* has been made clean of special goals.   **466**

God — In any *relationship* in which you are wholly willing to accept completion, and only this, there is God completed, and His Son; with Him.   **316**

guilt — All *relationships* that guilt has touched are used but to avoid the person and the guilt.   **245**

guilt — It is impossible to use one *relationship* at the expense of another and not suffer guilt.   **292**

healing — Your *relationship* is now a temple of healing; a place where all the weary ones can come and rest.   **378**

Heaven — Heaven is restored to all the Sonship through your *relationship,* for in it lies the Sonship, whole and beautiful, safe in your love.   **349**

holiness — A *relationship,* undertaken by two individuals for their unholy purposes, suddenly has holiness for its goal.   **338**

holiness — For you have asked that nothing stand between the holiness of your *relationship* and your awareness of its holiness.   **434**

holiness — The holiness of your *relationship* forgives you and your brother, undoing the effects of what you both believed and saw.   **435**

holiness — The holiness of your *relationship* is established in Heaven.   **353**

holy — A holy *relationship* is one in which you join with what is part of you in truth.   **424**

holy — A holy *relationship,* however newly born, must value holiness above all else.   **443**

holy — And as the unholy *relationship* is a continuing hymn of hate in praise of its maker, so is the holy *relationship* a happy song of praise to the Redeemer of *relationships*. 337

holy — Before a holy *relationship* there is no sin. 448

holy — Beyond the bodies that you interposed between you, and shining in the golden right that reaches it from the bright endless circle that extends forever, is your holy *relationship*, beloved of God Himself. 441

holy — For what is born into a holy *relationship* can never end. 436

holy — From your holy *relationship* truth proclaims the truth, and love looks on itself. 385

holy — (In a holy *relationship*) each one has looked within and seen no lack. 435

holy — In all its aspects, as it begins, develops and becomes accomplished, (the holy *relationship*) represents the reversal of the unholy *relationship*. 337

holy — In this world, God's Son comes closest to himself in a holy *relationship*. 404

holy — In your holy *relationship* is your Father's Son. 385

holy — No *relationship* is holy unless its holiness goes with it everywhere. 343

holy — Peace to your holy *relationship* which has the power to hold the unity of the Son of God together. 405

holy — So in each holy *relationship* is the ability to communicate instead of separate reborn. 437

holy — Such is the function of a holy *relationship*; to receive together and give as you received. 445

holy — The holy *relationship* has the power to heal all pain, regardless of its form. 448

holy — The holy *relationship* is a means of saving time. 363

holy — The holy *relationship* is a constant reminder of the experience in which the *relationship* became what it is. 337

holy — (The holy *relationship*) is the old unholy *relationship*   **337**
transformed and seen anew.

holy — The holy *relationship* is the expression of the holy   **337**
instant in living in this world.

holy — The holy *relationship* reflects the true *relationship*   **408**
the Son of God has with his Father in
reality.

holy — There is no obstacle that you can place before   **385**
our union, for in your holy *relationship*
I am there already.

holy — Think not your choice will leave you comfort-   **339**
less, for God Himself has blessed your
holy *relationship*.

holy — This holy *relationship*, lovely in its innocence,
mighty in strength, and blazing with a   **448**
light far brighter than the sun that
lights the sky you see, is chosen of your
Father as a means for His Own plan.

holy — This *relationship* has been reborn as holy.   **339**

holy — (To bless each other) is the purpose of the holy   **401**
relationship.

holy — Through your holy *relationship*, reborn and   **357**
blessed in every holy instant you do not
arrange, thousands will rise to Heaven
with you.

holy — What God has given to your holy *relationship* is   **441**
there.

holy — Yet a holy *relationship*, so recently reborn itself   **437**
from an unholy *relationship*, and yet
more ancient than the old illusion it has
replaced, is like a baby now in its rebirth.

holy — Yet reason sees a holy *relationship* as what it is; a   **444**
common state of mind, where both
give errors gladly to correction, that
both may happily be healed as one.

holy — You did not set (the goal of holiness) because holiness cannot be seen except through faith, and your *relationship* was not holy because your faith in your brother was so limited and little.   343

Holy Spirit — Any *relationship* you would substitute for another has not been offered to the Holy Spirit for His use.   291

Holy Spirit — In your *relationship* the Holy Spirit has gently laid the real world; the world of happy dreams, from which awakening is so easy and so natural.   352

Holy Spirit — Under (the teaching of the Holy Spirit), every *relationship* becomes a lesson in love.   291

Holy Spirit — When the Holy Spirit changed the purpose of your *relationship* by exchanging yours for his, the goal He placed there was extended to every situation you enter, or will ever enter.   344

Holy Spirit — You undertook, together, to invite the Holy Spirit into your *relationship*.   339

Holy Spirit's — You can place any *relationship* under (the Holy Spirit's) care and be sure that it will not result in pain.   291

light — In your *relationship* is this world's light.   353

love — The special love *relationship* is the ego's most boasted gift, and one which has the most appeal to those unwilling to relinquish guilt.   317

love — The special love *relationship* is the ego's chief weapon for keeping you from Heaven.   317

love — The special love *relationship* is but a shabby substitute for what makes you whole in truth, not in illusion.   315

Love — The lovely light of your *relationship* is like the Love of God.   462

lovely — How lovely and how holy is your *relationship*, with the truth shining upon it!   349

one — But forget not that your *relationship* is one, and so   358
    it must be that whatever threatens the
    peace of one is an equal threat to the
    other.

order — There is no order in *relationships*.   408

part — The idea of part-whole *relationship* has meaning   144
    only at the level of perception, where
    change is possible.

peace — And no illusion can disturb the peace of a *rela-*   448
    tionship that has become the means of
    peace.

purpose — Every situation in which you find yourself is   343
    but a means to meet the purpose set
    for your *relationship*.

purpose — Only a radical shift in purpose could induce a   338
    complete change of mind about what
    the whole *relationship* is for.

real — And you forgot that real *relationships* are holy, and   245
    cannot be used by you at all.

real — No real *relationship* can rest on guilt, or even hold   245
    one spot of it to mar its purity.

real — You cannot enter into any real *relationships* with   247
    God's Sons unless you love them all
    and equally.

real — You have a real *relationship* and it has meaning.   409

sanity — And your *relationship* has sanity as its purpose.   338

situation — There is no situation that does not involve   344
    your whole *relationship,* in every aspect
    and complete in every part.

special — (A special *relationship*) is a kind of union from   318
    which union is excluded.

special — A special *relationship* is a strange and unnatural   318
    ego device for joining hell and Heaven,
    and making them indistinguishable.

special — A special *relationship* is a device for limiting   321
    your self to a body, and for limiting
    your perception of others to theirs.

special — All special *relationships* have sin as their goal.   421

special — (All special *relationships*) are bargains with reality, toward which the seeming union is adjusted.   **421**

special — Be sure of this; love has entered your special *relationship,* and entered fully at your weak request.   **366**

special — Because of guilt, all special *relationships* have elements of fear in them.   **291**

special — Every special *relationship* you have made has, as its fundamental purpose, the aim of occupying your mind so completely that you will not hear the call of truth.   **333**

special — Every special *relationship* you have made is a substitute for God's Will, and glorifies yours instead of His because of the illusion that they are different.   **333**

special — Everyone on earth has formed special *relationships,* and although this is not so in Heaven, the Holy Spirit knows how to bring a touch of Heaven to them here.   **291**

special — For the special *relationship* is an attempt to re-enact the past and change it.   **323**

special — For the special *relationship* is the renunciation of the Love of God, and the attempt to secure for the self the specialness that He denied.   **317**

special — For your special *relationship* has not been disrupted. It has been saved.   **339**

special — Hear Him gladly, and learn of Him that you have no need of special *relationships* at all. You but seek in them what you; have thrown away.   **298**

special — I have said repeatedly that the Holy Spirit would not deprive you of your special *relationships,* but would transform them.   **333**

special — In a sense, the special *relationship* was the ego's answer to the creation of the Holy Spirit.   **334**

special — In His function as interpreter of what you made, the Holy Spirit uses special *relationships,* which you have chosen to support the ego, as learning experiences that point to truth. — 291

special — In looking at the special *relationship,* it is necessary first to realize that it involves a great amount of pain. — 317

special — In seeking the special *relationship* you look not for glory in yourself. — 324

special — (In the special *relationship*) each partner tries to sacrifice the self he does not want for one he thinks he would prefer. — 318

special — (In the special *relationship*) where both partners see this special self in each other, the ego sees "a union made in heaven." — 318

special — It is in the special *relationship,* born of the hidden wish for special love from God, that the ego's hatred triumphs. — 324

special — It is impossible to let go of the past without relinquishing the special *relationship.* — 323

special — It is in the special love from God, that the ego's hatred triumphs. — 317

special — No special *relationship* is experienced in the present. — 324

special — Nothing you seek to strengthen in the special *relationship* is really part of you. — 322

special — See in the special *relationship* nothing more than a meaningless attempt to raise other Gods before Him, and by worshipping them to obscure their tininess and His greatness. — 320

special — The central theme in the litany to sacrifice (of the special *relationship*) is that God must die so you can live. — 319

special — The conviction of littleness lies in every special *relationship,* for only the deprived could value specialness. — 319

special — The gift (of the special *relationship*) is given you   335
for your damnation, and if you take it
you will believe that you are damned.

special — The real purpose of the special *relationship*, in   319
strict accordance with the ego's goals,
is to destroy reality and substitute
illusion.

special — The search for a special *relationship* is the sign   321
you equate yourself with the ego and
not God.

special — The special *relationship* is totally meaningless   321
without a body.

special — The special *relationship* is a ritual of form, aimed   319
at raising the form to take the place of
God at the expense of content.

special — The special *relationship* will remain, not as a   351
source of pain and guilt, but as a source
of joy and freedom.

special — The special *relationship* takes vengeance on the   323
past.

special — To believe that special *relationships,* with special   290
love, can offer salvation is the belief
that separation is salvation.

special — Yet the closer you look at the special *relation-*   321
ship, the more apparent it becomes that
it must foster guilt and therefore must
imprison.

special — Yet the one thing the ego never allows to   324
reach awareness is that the special
relationship is the acting out of
vengeance on yourself.

special — Yet the special *relationship* the ego seeks does   321
not include even one whole individual.

special — You could not long find even the illusion of   322
love in any special *relationship* here.

special — You seek to answer this question in your   303
special *relationships* in which you seem to
be both destroyer and destroyed in
part, but able to be neither completely.

special — You have but little difficulty now in realizing that the thought system the special *relationship* protects is but a system of delusions.   334

special — You will find many opportunities to blame your brother for the "failure" of your (special) *relationship*, for it will seem at times to have no purpose.   339

special — Your special *relationship* will be a means for undoing guilt in everyone blessed through your holy relationship.   351

special — Whenever your thoughts wander to a special *relationship* which still attracts you, enter with (the Holy Spirit) into a holy instant, and there let Him release you.   323

special — While (the special *relationship*) remains you will not let go (of other aspects of the ego's thought system.)   334

truth — Praise be to your *relationship* with (God) and to no other. The truth lies there and nowhere else.   326

truth — When you accepted truth as the goal for your *relationship*, you became a giver of peace as surely as your Father gave peace to you.   346

unholy — An unholy *relationship* is no *relationship*.   408

unholy — Every step taken in the making, the maintaining and the breaking off of the unholy *relationship* is a move toward further fragmentation.   331

unholy — For an unholy *relationship* is based on differences, where each one thinks the other has what he has not.   435

unholy — For once the unholy *relationship* has accepted the goal of holiness, it can never again be what it was.   337

unholy - In an unholy *relationship*, each one is valued because he seems to justify the other's sin.   443

unholy — In the unholy *relationship*, it is not the body of the other with which union is attempted, but the bodies of those who aren't there.   **331**

unholy — Set firmly in the unholy *relationship*, there is no choice except to change the unholy *relationship* to fit the goal.   **338**

unholy — That bodies are central to all unholy *relationships* is evident.   **331**

unholy — The attraction of the unholy *relationship* begins to fade and to be questioned almost at once.   **331**

unholy — Time is indeed unkind to the unholy *relationship*.   **331**

union — For when you have accepted it with gladness, you will realize that your *relationship* is a reflection of the union of the Creator and His Son.   **450**

world — *Relationships* in this world are the result of how the world is seen.   **382**

RELEASE

certain — Your *release* is certain.   **346**

function — *Release* yourself to Him Whose function is *release*.   **356**

given — *Release* is given the instant you desire it.   **362**

released — As you *release* so will you be released.   **321**

reserve — What you reserve for yourself, you take away from Him Who would *release* you.   **327**

Son — The Son of God looks unto you for his *release*.   **398**

RELIGION

reconciled — All *religion* is the recognition that the irreconcilable cannot be reconciled.   **173**

REMEMBER

eternal — When you *remember* you will know that what you *remember* is eternal, and therefore is now.   **169**

everything — You will *remember* everything the instant   169
    you desire it wholly, for if to desire
    wholly is to create, you will have willed
    away the separation, returning your
    mind simultaneously to your Creator
    and your creations.

God — To perceive the healing of your brother as the   203
    healing of yourself is thus the way to
    remember God.

Holy Spirit — Offer the Holy Spirit only your willing-   170
    ness to *remember*, for He retains the
    knowledge of God and of yourself for
    you, waiting for your acceptance.

made — If you *remember* what you have made, you are   261
    remembering nothing.

make — You do not make what you *remember;* you   170
    merely accept again what is already
    there, but was rejected.

mind — To *remember* is merely to restore to your mind   170
    what is already there.

what — What you *remember* never was.   549

REMEMBERED

God — But your remembering is His, for God cannot be   203
    remembered alone.

REMEMBERING

give — Give up gladly everything that would stand in   170
    the way of your *remembering*, for God is
    in your memory.

God — What your *remembering* would witness to is but   549
    the fear of God.

REMEMBRANCE

God — Call forth in everyone only the *remembrance* of   287
    God, and of the Heaven that is in Him.

reality — *Remembrance* of reality is in Him, and therefore   261
    in you.

RESURRECTION

allegiance — *Resurrection* must compel your allegiance   193
 gladly, because it is the symbol of joy.

Atonement — The crucifixion did not establish the   32
 Atonement; the *resurrection* did.

believe — Believe in the *resurrection* because it has been   193
 accomplished, and it has been
 accomplished in you.

Christ — Nor can the *resurrection* be complete till your   396
 forgiveness rests on Christ, along with
 mine.

Christ — The *resurrection* is the complete triumph of   192
 Christ over the ego, not by attack but
 by transcendence.

crucifixion — Each day, each hour and minute, even   255
 every second, you are constantly
 deciding between the crucifixion and
 the *resurrection*, between the ego and the
 Holy Spirit.

death — And now you are part of *resurrection*, not of   512
 death.

God — This is as true now as it ever will be, for the   193
 resurrection is the Will of God, which
 knows no time and no exception.

knowledge — I have also made it clear that the *resur-*   39
 rection was a means for the return to
 knowledge, which was accomplished
 by the union of my will with the
 Father's.

power — (The *resurrection's*) whole compelling power lies   193
 in the fact that it represents what you
 want to be.

prepare — So will we prepare together the way unto the   395
 resurrection of God's Son, and let him rise
 again to glad remembrance of his
 Father, Who knows no sin, no death,
 but only life eternal.

redemption — Here is the holy place of *resurrection*, to   394
 which we will come again; to which we
 will return until redemption is
 accomplished and received.

truth — The *resurrection* demonstrates nothing can   33
    destroy truth.

your — Your *resurrection* is your awakening.   86

REVELATION

doubt — *Revelation* induces complete but temporary   4
    suspension of doubt and fear.

experience — *Revelation* induces only experience.   5

God — (*Revelation*) proceeds from God to you.   6

God — *Revelation* unites you directly with God.   4

God — (*Revelation*) reflects the original form of com-   4
    munication between God and His
    creations, involving the extremely
    personal sense of creation sometimes
    sought in physical relationships.

joy — Only the healed mind can experience *revelation*   67
    with lasting effect, because *revelation* is
    an experience of pure joy.

love — *Revelation* is literally unspeakable because it is   5
    an experience of unspeakable love.

miracle — Only *revelation* transcends (the miracle),   4
    having nothing to do with time at all.

personal — *Revelation* is intensely personal, and cannot   5
    be meaningfully translated.

time — I said before that *revelation* transcends time.   23

RIGHT-MINDED(NESS)

miracles — I have already said that miracles are expres-   21
    sions of miracle-mindedness, and
    miracle-mindedness means *right-
    mindedness*.

One-mindedness — Salvation is nothing more than   53
    "*right-mindedness*," which is not the One-
    mindedness of the Holy Spirit, but
    which must be achieved before One-
    mindedness is restored.

perception — The term *right-mindedness* is properly used   38
    as the correction for wrong-
    mindedness, and applies to the state of
    mind that induces accurate perception.

perfection — If nothing but the truth exists, *right-minded*   **34**
seeing cannot see anything but perfection.

ROAD(S)

confusion — All *roads* that lead away from what you are   **609**
will lead you to confusion and despair.

Him — There is no *road* that leads away from Him.   **609**

purpose — And every *road* that leads the other way will   **609**
not advance the purpose to be found.

SACRIFICE

altars — Kneel not before the altars to *sacrifice*, and seek   **240**
not what you will surely lose.

asked — Are you not glad that Heaven cannot be sacri-   **385**
ficed, and *sacrifice* cannot be asked of you?

attack — And it is this that you must look upon; *sacrifice*   **302**
is attack, not love.

body — For *sacrifice* must be exacted of a body, and by   **423**
another body.

body — The body is itself a *sacrifice*, a giving up of power   **504**
in the name of saving just a little for yourself.

demand — You think that everyone outside yourself   **303**
demands your *sacrifice*, but you do not
see that only you demand *sacrifice*, and
only of yourself.

ego — No partial *sacrifice* will appease this savage guest   **303**
(the ego), for it is an invader who but
seems to offer kindness, but always to
make the *sacrifice* complete.

faith — Your faith in *sacrifice* has given it great power in   **423**
your sight, except you do not realize
you cannot see because of it.

fear — (*Sacrifice*) arises solely from fear, and frightened   **33**
people can be vicious.

freedom — It is no *sacrifice* that (your brother) be saved,   **491**
for by his freedom will you again your
own.

glory — But it is *sacrifice* to accept anything less than glory.   286

God — For God has said there is no *sacrifice* that can be asked; there is no *sacrifice* that can be made.   607

God — The memory of God must be denied if any *sacrifice* is asked of anyone.   504

guilt — For *sacrifice* brings guilt as surely as love brings peace.   305

guilt — Guilt cannot last when the idea of *sacrifice* has been removed.   302

guilt — Guilt is the condition of *sacrifice*, as peace is the condition for the awareness of your relationship with God.   305

Holy Spirit — Brother, the Holy Spirit knows that *sacrifice* brings nothing.   422

Holy Spirit — The Holy Spirit never asks for *sacrifice*, but the ego always does.   125

Holy Spirit — Your little part is but to give the Holy Spirit the whole idea of *sacrifice*.   386

I — I am as incapable of receiving *sacrifice* as God is, and every *sacrifice* you ask of yourself you ask of me.   302

idea — In the "dynamics" of attack is *sacrifice* a key idea.   504

idea — *Sacrifice* is an idea totally unknown to God.   33

limitation — Learn now that *sacrifice* of any kind is nothing but a limitation imposed on giving.   302

love — You who believe that *sacrifice* is love must learn that *sacrifice* is separation from love.   304

love — And without *sacrifice* there love must be.   304

love — Your confusion of *sacrifice* and love is so profound that you cannot conceive of love without *sacrifice*.   302

nothing — You can see no other alternatives, for you cannot accept the fact that *sacrifice* gets nothing.   302

pain — Pain will be brought to us and disappear in our presence, and without pain there can be no *sacrifice*. 304

pay — For if there is *sacrifice*, someone must pay and someone must get. 302

recognize — Fear not to recognize the whole idea of *sacrifice* as solely of your making. 304

relationships — All *sacrifice* entails the loss of your ability to see relationships among events. 597

tiny — A tiny *sacrifice* is just the same in its effects as is the whole idea of *sacrifice*. 517

total — *Sacrifice* is total. 525

truth — Yet to the dedication to the truth as God established it no *sacrifice* is asked, no strain called forth. 478

SACRIFICING

merciful — *Sacrificing* in any way is a violation of my injunction that you should be merciful even as your Father in Heaven is merciful. 33

SAFE

benign — The perfectly *safe* are wholly benign. 92

bless — (The perfectly *safe*) bless, because they know they are blessed. 92

Father — God's Son is as *safe* as his Father, for the Son knows his Father's protection and cannot fear. 217

SAFETY

attack — *Safety* is the complete relinquishment of attack. 92

Holy Spirit — The only *safety* lies in extending the Holy Spirit, because as you see His gentleness in others your own mind perceives itself as totally harmless. 92

SALVATION

Atonement — For it is the complete equality of the Atonement in which *salvation* lies. 290

belief — Yet it is certain the belief that *salvation* is impossible cannot uphold a quiet, calm assurance it has come.   **461**

borderland — *Salvation* is a borderland where place and time and choice have meaning still, and yet it can be seen that they are temporary, out of place, and every choice has been already made.   **508**

bringers — You who are now the bringers of *salvation* have the function of bringing light to darkness.   **354**

brother — *Salvation* is of your brother.   **153**

brother — Yet in (the hands of your brother) is your *salvation*.   **393**

complete — (*Salvation*) is complete for everyone.   **460**

compromise — *Salvation* is no compromise of any kind.   **460**

condemn — Condemn *salvation* not for it has come to you.   **339**

death — *Salvation* challenges not even death.   **471**

death — *Salvation* seeks to prove there is no death, and only life exists.   **575**

dreams — For *salvation* is the end of dreams, and with the closing of the dream will have no meaning.   **330**

easy — *Salvation* is easy just because it asks nothing you cannot give right now.   **356**

ego — Since you cannot not teach, your *salvation* lies in teaching the exact opposite of everything the ego believes.   **92**

ego — Be glad you have escaped the mockery of *salvation* the ego offered you, and look not back with longing on the travesty it made of your relationships.   **322**

faith — *Salvation* rests on faith there cannot be some forms of guilt that you cannot forgive.   **595**

forgive — (*Salvation*) asks you but that you forgive all things that no one ever did; to overlook what is not there, and not to look upon the unreal as reality.   **590**

God — And knowing (we will be not lost but found), nothing in the plan God has established for *salvation* will be left undone.   **395**

God — But ask yourself if it is possible that God would have a plan for your salvation that does not work.   **404**

God — If you are wholly willing to leave *salvation* to the plan of God and unwilling to attempt to grasp for peace yourself, *salvation* will be given to you.   **287**

God — *Salvation* is as sure as God.   **250**

God — *Salvation* is of Him to Whom God gave it for you.   **258**

God — *Salvation* is simple, being of God, and therefore very easy to understand.   **304**

God's — God's plan for your *salvation* could not have been established without your will and your consent.   **426**

God's — God's Son could never be content with less than full *salvation* and escape from guilt.   **517**

God's — *Salvation* is (God's) Will because you share it.   **497**

guilt — You want *salvation*, not the pain of guilt.   **385**

hands — And in your hands does all *salvation* lie, to be both offered and received as one.   **518**

Heaven — *Salvation* stops just short of Heaven, for only perception needs *salvation*.   **509**

Holy Spirit — The Holy Spirit can use all that you give to Him for your *salvation*.   **497**

Holy Spirit — (The Holy Spirit) uses everyone who calls on Him as means for the *salvation* of everyone.   **352**

Holy Spirit's — *Salvation* is the Holy Spirit's goal.   **411**

illusions — *Salvation* lies in the simple fact that illusions are not fearful because they are not true.   **320**

illusions — And even in illusions (*salvation*) but asks forgiveness be the substitute for fear.   **590**

immediate — *Salvation* is immediate.   **519**

joined — That you are joined is your *salvation;* the gift of Heaven, not the gift of fear.   **429**

justice — There is a kind of justice in *salvation* of which the world knows nothing.   **497**

learn — You will learn *salvation* because you will learn how to save.   **250**

middle — There is no middle ground in any aspect of *salvation.*   **561**

mind — *Salvation* is for the mind, and it is attained through peace.   **206**

nothing — *Salvation* gives up nothing.   **460**

perception — *Salvation* stops just short of Heaven, for only perception needs *salvation.*   **509**

plan — You have not been asked to work out the plan of *salvation* yourself because, as I told you before, the remedy could not be of your making.   **82**

purpose — (*Salvation*) is your purpose.   **380**

purpose — *Salvation* (of the Son of God) is your only purpose.   **346**

real — *Salvation* merely asks that you respond appropriately to what is not real by not perceiving what has not occurred.   **593**

reality — (*Salvation*) asks for nothing in reality.   **590**

rebirth — *Salvation* is the rebirth of the idea that no one can lose for anyone to gain.   **496**

"right" — *Salvation* is nothing more than "right-mindedness," which is not the One-mindedness of the Holy Spirit, but which must be achieved before One-mindedness is restored.   **53**

saved — But remember *salvation* is not needed by the saved.   **497**

secret — The secret of *salvation* is but this: That you are doing this unto yourself.   **545**

secret — This is the obvious; (*salvation* is) a secret kept from no one but yourself.   **546**

serve — All that you made can serve *salvation* easily and well.   **493**

Sonship — Never forget that the Sonship is your *salvation*, for the Sonship is your Self.   **186**

space — *Salvation* would wipe out the space you see between you still, and let you instantly become as one.   **519**

spirit — However, *salvation* does not apply to spirit, which is not in danger and does not need to be salvaged.   **53**

spirit — *Salvation* does not ask that you behold the spirit and perceive the body not.   **614**

time — Now is the time of *salvation*, for now is the release of time.   **235**

true — All (*salvation*) says is what was never true is not true now, and never will be.   **600**

true — *Salvation*, perfect and complete, asks but a little wish that what is true be true; a little willingness to overlook what is not there; a little sight that speaks for Heaven as a preference to this world that death and desolation seem to rule.   **516**

undoing — *Salvation* is undoing.   **614**

unfair — *Salvation* cannot seek to help God's Son be more unfair than he has sought to be.   **502**

venture — *Salvation* is a collaborative venture.   **63**

vision — The means (of *salvation*) is vision.   **411**

ways — You are very new in the ways of *salvation*, and think you have lost your way.   **339**

withheld — *Salvation* cannot be withheld from you.   **380**

world - *Salvation* is no more than a reminder this world is not your home.   **493**

world — (*Salvation*) will give you the real world, trembling with readiness to be given you.   **330**

SANE

insanity — Only the *sane* can look on stark insanity and raving madness with pity and compassion, but not with fear.   **393**

SANITY

brothers — *Sanity* is wholeness, and the *sanity* of your brothers is yours. 82

Holy Spirit — The Holy Spirit will restore your *sanity* because insanity is not the Will of God. 249

inward — Inward is *sanity;* insanity is outside you. 348

separation — You who prefer separation to *sanity* cannot obtain it in your right mind. 227

wholeness — *Sanity* is wholeness, and the *sanity* of your brothers is yours. 82

SAVIOR(S)

brother's — You are your brother's *savior.* 429

condemn — Condemn your *savior* not because he thinks he is a body. 567

dead — Your *savior* is not dead, nor does he dwell in what was built as a temple unto death. 567

enemy — It is impossible to look upon your *savior* as your enemy and recognize him. 441

enemy — There is a shock that comes to those who learn their *savior* is their enemy no more. 564

forgiven — Forgiven by you, your *savior* offers you salvation. 491

grace — And to each one has He allowed the grace to be a *savior* to the holy ones especially entrusted to his care. 617

healing — Your *savior* waits for healing, and the world waits with him. 561

illusions — Those who would let illusions be lifted from their minds are this world's *saviors,* walking the world with their Redeemer, and carrying His message of hope and freedom and release from suffering to everyone who needs a miracle to save him. 445

judge — A *savior* cannot be a judge, nor mercy condemnation. 440

learn — But he must learn he is a *savior* first, before he can remember what he is. 567

released — You will see your value through your brother's eyes, and each one is released as he beholds his *savior* in place of the attacker who he thought was there.   448

world — The *saviors* of the world, who see like Him, are merely those who choose (Christ's) strength instead of their own weakness, seen apart from Him.   620

SCARCITY

illusion — Do not share (your brother's) illusions of *scarcity*, or you will perceive yourself as lacking.   119

love — In the world of *scarcity*, love has no meaning and peace is impossible.   293

SECRET(S)

dark — Save no dark *secrets* that (the Holy Spirit) cannot use, but offer Him the tiny gifts He can extend forever.   449

God - God has no *secrets*.   436

"guilty" — Your "guilty *secret*" is nothing, and if you will but bring it to the Light, the Light will dispel it.   225

nothing — Nothing lives in *secret*, and what you would hide from the Holy Spirit is nothing.   275

you — Yet you believe that you have *secrets*.   436

SEE

alone — It is the recognition that nothing you *see* means anything alone.   268

alone — You cannot *see* alone.   268

aware — For you can be aware of what you cannot *see*, and it can become compellingly real to you as Its Presence becomes manifest through you.   214

decide — As you decide, so will you *see*.   216

desire — What you desire, you will *see*.   419

either — You either *see* or not.   410

expect — You *see* what you expect, and you expect what you invite.   **214**

Holy Spirit — Sharing perception with (the Holy Spirit) Whom God has given you teaches you how to recognize what you *see*.   **268**

look — For you will believe in what you manifest, and as you look out so will you *see* in.   **214**

made — Yet what you *see* is only what you made, with the blessing of your forgiveness on it.   **329**

not — You do not *see*.   **415**

reality — You who would judge reality cannot *see* it, for whenever judgment enters reality has slipped away.   **237**

seek — Remember always that you *see* what you seek, for what you seek you will find.   **215**

support — For one thing is sure; the way you *see*, and long have seen, gives no support to base your future hopes, and no suggestions of success at all.   **484**

vision — Only your vision can convey to you what you can *see*.   **437**

will — Those who would see will *see*.   **354**

wish — The Wish to *see* calls down the grace of God upon your eyes, and brings the gift of light that makes sight possible.   **492**

yourself — You but behold yourself in what you *see*.   **599**

SEEING

darkness — Do not seek vision through your eyes, for you made your way of *seeing* that you might see in darkness, and in this you are deceived.   **232**

Holy Spirit — *Seeing* with (the Holy Spirit) will show you that all meaning, including yours, comes not from double vision, but from the gentle fusing of everything into one meaning, one emotion, and one purpose.   **268**

outward — *Seeing* is always outward.   **252**

perceiver — All *seeing* starts with the perceiver, who judges what is true and what is false.   **237**

sinless — For what the *seeing* look upon is sinless.   **411**

wish — For *seeing* can but represent a wish, because it has no power to create.   **618**

wish — *Seeing* adapts to wish, for sight is always secondary to desire.   **410**

SEEK

find — Remember always that you see what you *seek*, for what you *seek* you will find.   **215**

yourself — *Seek* not outside yourself.   **573**

SEEKING

finding — Yet *seeking* and finding are the same, and if you seek for two goals you will find them, but you will recognize neither.   **215**

SEEN

Holy Spirit — What can be *seen* is what the Holy Spirit sees.   **218**

judge — How foolish it is to attempt to judge what could be *seen* instead.   **415**

SELF

denial — Denial of *Self* results in illusions, while correction of the error brings release from it.   **12**

God's — Your *self* and God's *Self* are in opposition.   **48**

SELF-FULLNESS

boundless — Your *self-fullness* is as boundless as God's.   **123**

extension — The full appreciation of the mind's *self-fullness* makes selfishness impossible and extension inevitable.   **123**

joy — You do not know your joy because you do not know your own *self-fullness*.   **123**

Spirit — Selfishness is of the ego, but *self-fullness* is of Spirit because that is how God created it.   **122**

SEPARATION

communication — The *separation* was not a loss of perfection, but a failure of communication. 95

corrected — For *separation* must be corrected where it was made. 331

denial — What is one cannot be perceived as separate, and the denial of the *separation* is the reinstatement of knowledge. 213

descent — Yet in the returning the little light must be acknowledged first, for the *separation* was a descent from magnitude to littleness. 175

exclusion — Exclusion and *separation* are synonymous, as are *separation* and dissociation. 88

fear — All who believe in *separation* have a basic fear of retaliation and abandonment. 98

God — Sickness and *separation* are not of God, but the Kingdom is. 106

guilt — For *separation* is the source of guilt, and to appeal to it for salvation is to believe you are alone. 290

healed — For this wish (to kill God's Son) caused the *separation*, and you have protected it because you do not want the *separation* healed. 226

know — *Separation* is only the decision not to know yourself. 320

mind — The *separation* is merely another term for a split mind. 73

projection — We have said before that the *separation* was and is dissociation, and that once it occurs projection becomes its main defense, or the device that keeps it going. 88

reality — The *separation* is merely a faulty formulation of reality, with no effect at all. 241

rejection — The *separation* is the notion of rejection. 88

thought — The *separation* is a system of thought real enough in time, though not in eternity. 45

union — For the love of God, no longer not seek for   321
    union in *separation*, nor for freedom in
    bondage!

union — For the *separation* is only the denial of union, and   202
    correctly interpreted, attests to your
    eternal knowledge that union is true.

union — *Separation* is overcome by union.   134

will — The *separation* is nothing more than the belief   150
    that (your will) is different (from
    God's).

SHARE

Christ — Nor can you use what (Christ has) given   398
    unless you *share it*.

Son — Sharing the perfect Love of the Father the Son   187
    must *share* what belongs to Him, for
    otherwise he will not know the Father
    or the Son.

SHARED

world — Nothing in this world can give this peace, for   249
    nothing in this world is wholly *shared*.

SHARING

substituting — In the mad world outside you nothing   349
    can be shared but only substituted, and
    sharing and substituting have nothing
    in common in reality.

task — You have set yourself the task of *sharing* what   252
    cannot be shared.

SICK

accusers — The *sick* remain accusers.   528

body's — (The body's) nothingness is a guarantee it can   566
    not be *sick*.

Christ — If you are *sick* you are withdrawing from   147
    (Christ.)

gods — If you believe you can be *sick* you have placed   173
    other gods before Him.

gods — Unless you are *sick* you cannot keep the gods you 　176
made, for only in sickness could you
possibly want them.

heal — The *sick* must heal themselves, for the truth is in 　203
them.

love — If to love oneself is to heal oneself, those who are 　203
sick do not love themselves.

love — The *sick*, who ask for love, are grateful for it, and 　235
in their joy they shine with holy
thanks.

merciless — The *sick* are merciless to everyone, and in 　526
contagion do they seek to kill.

not — You are not *sick* and you cannot die. 　177

reason — The *sick* have reason for each one of their 　526
unnatural desires and strange needs.

union — No one is *sick* if someone else accepts his union 　557
with him.

value — When you do not value yourself you become 　172
sick, but my value of you can heal you,
because the value of God's Son is one.

SICKNESS

anger — *Sickness* is anger taken out upon the body, so 　560
that it will suffer pain.

answer — *Sickness* is merely another example of your 　145
insistence on asking guidance of a
teacher who does not know the
answer.

attempt — For *sickness* is a meaningless attempt to give 　551
effects to causelessness, and make it be
a cause.

body — *Sickness* is a demand that the body be a thing that 　566
it is not.

body — *Sickness* is meaningful only if the two basic 　145
premises on which the ego's
interpretation of the body rests are
true; that the body is for attack, and
that you are a body.

cause — Always in *sickness* does the Son of God attempt to make himself his cause, and not allow himself, to be his Father's Son.   **551**

choice — The choice of *sickness* seems to be of form, yet it is one, as is its opposite.   **562**

confusion — *Sickness* or "not-right-mindedness" is the result of level confusion, because it always entails the belief that what is amiss on one level can aversely affect another.   **19**

death — *Sickness* and death seem to enter the mind of God's Son against his will.   **176**

desired — And *sickness* is desired to prevent a shift in balance in the sacrifice.   **530**

fear — All forms of *sickness*, even unto death, are physical expressions of the fear of awakening.   **146**

futility — The strongest witness to futility, that bolsters all the rest and helps them paint the picture in which sin is justified, is *sickness* in whatever form it takes.   **526**

god — If you accept (the god of *sickness*) you will bow down and worship him because he was made as God's replacement.   **173**

god — If you attack (the god of *sickness*) you will make him real to you.   **173**

god — (The god of *sickness*) is the symbol of deciding against God.   **173**

god — The rituals of the god of *sickness* are strange and very demanding.   **175**

god — You can give up the god of *sickness* for your brothers; in fact, you would have to do so if you gave him up for yourself.   **173**

god — You made the god of *sickness*, and by making him you made yourself able to hear him.   **173**

God — God is not at war with the god of *sickness* you made, but you are.   **173**

God — *Sickness* and separation are not of God, but the Kingdom is.   **106**

heal — Your vigilance against this *sickness* is the way to heal it. 10ɔ

hurt — *Sickness* is a way of demonstrating that you can be hurt. 145

illusion — The acceptance of peace is the denial of illusion, and *sickness* is an illusion. 172

love — Perceive in *sickness* but another call for love, and offer your brother what he believes he cannot offer himself. 203

mind — All forms of *sickness* are signs that the mind is split, and does not accept a unified purpose. 148

perceive — You will be made whole as you make whole, for to perceive in *sickness* the appeal for health is to recognize in hatred the call for love. 203

perfection — *Sickness* and perfection are irreconcilable. 173

remedy — Whatever the *sickness*, there is but one remedy. 203

separating — And thus is *sickness* separating off the self from good and keeping evil in. 558

separation — All *sickness* comes from separation. 514

separation — The seeds of *sickness* come from the belief that there is joy in separation, and its giving up would be a sacrifice. 557

side — Do not side with *sickness* in the presence of a Son of God even if he believes in it, for your acceptance of God in him acknowledges the Love of God he has forgotten. 171

vengeance — *Sickness* is but a "little" death; a form of vengeance not yet total. 526

witness — It is hard to perceive *sickness* as a false witness, because you do not realize that it is entirely out of keeping with what you want. 144

world — In the real world there is no *sickness*, for there is no separation and no division. 197

SIGHT

understand — And what your *sight* would show you, you will understand because it is the truth.   437

understand — You do not understand how what you see arose to meet your *sight*.   614

your — Your *sight* was given you, along with everything that you can understand.   437

SIN(S)

abide — For here are you made *sin,* and *sin* cannot abide the joyous and the free, for they are enemies which *sin* must kill.   607

arise — Look upon your Redeemer, and behold what He would show you in your brother, and let not *sin* arise again to blind your eyes.   378

attack — *Sin* is belief attack can be projected outside the mind where the belief arose.   517

attack — *Sin* is the proclamation that attack is real and guilt is justified.   375

attack — Attack and *sin* are bound as one illusion, each the cause and aim and justifier of the other.   490

attack — You do not see that every *sin* and every condemnation that you perceive and justify is an attack upon your Father.   449

belief — The belief in *sin* is a adjustment.   399

belief — The belief in *sin* is necessarily based on the firm idea that minds, not bodies, can attack.   374

belief — *Sin* is the fixed belief perception cannot change.   488

beliefs — *Sins* are beliefs that you impose between your brother and yourself.   516

bodies — *Sins* are in bodies. They are not perceived in minds.   606

body — If you are *sin* you are a body, for the mind acts not.   606

brother — And not one *sin* you see in (your brother) but keeps you both in hell.   476

brother — You can never hate your brother for his *sins* but only for your own.   606

brother's — For what you are has now become (your brother's) *sin*. **611**

brothers — Only the lonely and alone, who see their brothers different from themselves, have need for *sin*. **435**

condemnation — For *sin* and condemnation are the same, and the belief in one is faith in the other, calling for punishment instead of love. **243**

creation — For *sin* has changed creation from an Idea of God to an ideal the ego wants; a world it rules, made up of bodies, mindless and capable of complete corruption and decay. **375**

death — For *sin* is a request for death. **494**

death — For the wages of *sin* is death, and how can the immortal die? **375**

death — Yet each one knows the cost of *sin* is death. **494**

denial — And therefore those who look on *sin* are seeing the denial of the real world. **433**

die — In death is *sin* preserved, and those who think that they are *sin* must die for what they think they are. **607**

ego — Any attempt to reinterpret *sin* as error is always indefensible to the ego. **375**

end — The end of *sin,* which nestles quietly in the safety of your relationship, protected by your union with your brother, and ready to grow into a mighty force for God is very near. **390**

enemy — There can be no faith in *sin* without an enemy. **431**

error — It is essential that error be not confused with *sin*, and it is this distinction that makes salvation possible. **374**

error — *Sin* is but error in a special form the ego venerates. **442**

error — *Sin* is not an error, for *sin* entails an arrogance which the idea of error lacks. **375**

error — *Sin* is not error, for it goes beyond correction to impossibility. **515**

errors — In (the undoing of *sins*) lies the proof that they are merely errors. **529**

evil — *Sin* is an idea of evil that cannot be corrected, and yet will be forever desirable. **376**

faith — It is impossible to have faith in *sin*, for *sin* is faithlessness. **376**

faith — Your faith that *sin* is there but witnesses to your desire that it be there to see. **423**

fear — Belief in *sin* arouses fear, and like its cause, is looking forward, looking back, but overlooking what is here and now. **520**

fear — Let not your fear of *sin* protect it from correction, for the attraction of guilt is only fear. **437**

forgive — But to forgive *sin* is to change its state from error into truth. **489**

forgive — Yet no one can forgive a *sin* that he believes is real. **528**

forgiveness — *Sins* are beyond forgiveness just because they would entail effects that cannot be undone and overlooked entirely. **529**

healed — You will be healed of *sin* and all its ravages the instant that you give it no power over your brother. **378**

healing — If you choose *sin* instead of healing, you would condemn the Son of God to what can never be corrected. **429**

Heaven — For *sin* will not prevail against a union Heaven has smiled upon. **378**

Heaven — *Sin* has no place in Heaven, where its results are alien and can no more enter than can their source. **403**

Heaven — See *sin* in (your brother) instead, and Heaven is lost to you. **403**

Holy Spirit — The Holy Spirit cannot punish *sin*. **377**

Holy Spirit — The Holy Spirit can teach you to look on time differently and see beyond it, but not while you believe in *sin*. — 377

Holy Spirit — Those who believe in *sin* must think the Holy Spirit asks for sacrifice, for this is how they think their purpose is accomplished. — 422

Holy Spirit's — But on His vision *sin* cannot encroach, for *sin* has been corrected by (the Holy Spirit's) sight. — 488

illusion — *Sin* is the grand illusion underlying all the ego's grandiosity. — 375

lack — The ego does not perceive *sin* as a lack of love, but as a positive act of assault. — 78

looked — What if you looked within and saw no *sin*. — 424

love — But *sin* is equally insane within the sight of love, whose gentle eyes would look beyond the madness and rest peacefully on truth. — 495

love — Darkness is lack of light as *sin* is lack of love. — 9

love — What is not love is *sin*, and either one perceives the other as insane and meaningless. — 495

mistake — What could *sin* be but a mistake you would keep hidden; a call for help that you would keep unheard and thus unanswered? — 377

no — There is no *sin*. — 516

paradox — To witness *sin* and yet forgive it is a paradox that reason cannot see. — 528

peace — For *sin* is carved into a block out of your peace, and laid between you and its return. — 446

peace — *Sin* is a block, set across like a heavy gate, locked and without a key, across the road to peace. — 442

perceived — *Sin* is perceived as mightier than God, before which God Himself must bow, and offer His creation to its conqueror. — 378

perception — *Sin* is a strictly individual perception, seen   435
in the other yet believed by each to be
within himself.

perception — But *sin* is the belief that your perception is   377
unchangeable, and that the mind must
accept as true what it is told through it.

place — The holy place on which you stand is but the   510
place where *sin* has left.

possible — But *sin*, were it possible, would be irrever-   374
sible.

punished — No one is punished for *sins*, and the Sons of   88
God are not sinners.

purposes — (*Sins*) are not seen as purposes, but actions.   606

real — If *sin* is real, both God and you are not.   377

real — If *sin* is real, God must be at war with Himself.   377

real — If *sin* is real, it must forever be beyond the hope of   378
healing.

real — *Sin* is not real because the Father and Son are not   495
insane.

reality — While you believe your reality or your   377
brother's is bounded by a body, you will
believe in *sin*.

see — You will not see *sin* long.   378

separate — *Sin* would maintain you must be separate.   428

Son — But (the Son of God) cannot *sin*.   375

Son — The Son of God could never *sin*, but he can wish   489
for what would hurt him.

Son of God — Forgive me all the *sins* you think the Son   385
of God committed.

spot — The tiny spot of *sin* that stands between you still   510
is holding back the happy opening of
Heaven's gate.

suffer — Suffer, and you decided *sin* was your goal.   418

symbol — And you are each the symbol of your *sins* to   611
one another, silently, and yet with
ceaseless urgency, condemning still
your brother for the hated thing you
are.

405

weakness — The sinless cannot fear, for *sin* of any kind   **451**
      is weakness.

world — *Sin* is the only thing in all the world that cannot   **494**
      change.

SINFUL
Holy Spirit — The Holy Spirit will never teach you that   **423**
      you are *sinful.*

SINLESS
fear — The *sinless* cannot fear, for sin of any kind is   **451**
      weakness.

love — It is as certain you will fear what you attack as it   **451**
      is sure that you will love what you
      perceive as *sinless.*

perceive — The *sinless* must perceive that they are one,   **510**
      for nothing stands between to push the
      other off.

receive — The *sinless* gave as they received.   **403**

SINLESSNESS
attack — The state of *sinlessness* is merely this: The   **490**
      whole desire to attack is gone, and so
      there is no reason to perceive the Son
      of God as other than he is.

fear — And as you ask, forget not that (your brother's)   **411**
      sinlessness is your escape from fear.

opposite — Do you not see the opposite of frailty and   **451**
      weakness is *sinlessness.*

see — One is given you to see in him his perfect *sin-*   **507**
      lessness.

SINNED
Atonement — The Atonement is the final lesson (God's   **221**
      Son) need learn, for it teaches him that,
      never having *sinned,* he has no need of
      salvation.

past — You have *"sinned"* in the past, but there is no past.   **221**

Son — In the strange world that you have made the Son   **221**
      of God has *sinned.*

SLEEP

alone — In *sleep* you are alone, and your awareness is narrowed to yourself.   **236**

Christ — Even in *sleep* Christ has protected you, ensuring the real world for you when you awake.   **236**

death — *Sleep* is no more a form of death than death is a form of unconsciousness.   **147**

die — What (God) created can *sleep*, but cannot die.   **182**

"drugged" — You can be indeed "drugged" by *sleep*, if you have misused it on behalf of sickness.   **147**

wake — *Sleep* (of God's Son) will not withstand the call to wake.   **250**

withdrawing — *Sleep* is withdrawing; waking is joining.   **146**

SLEEPING

awake — You cannot dream some dreams and wake from some, for you are either *sleeping* or awake.   **569**

cost — Yet you must learn the cost of *sleeping*, and refuse to pay it.   **212**

SOLITUDE

savior — To each who walks this earth in seeming *solitude* is a savior given, whose special function here is to release him, and so to free himself.   **403**

SONSHIP

accomplish — Being a perfect accomplishment, the *Sonship* can only accomplish perfectly, extending the joy in which it was created, and identifying itself with both its Creator and its creations, knowing they are one.   **117**

appreciated - You can appreciate the *Sonship* only as one.   **114**

Christ — We are the joint will of the *Sonship*, whose wholeness is for all.   **137**

creations — Yet when the *Sonship* comes together and accepts its oneness it will be known by its creations, who will witness to its reality as the Son does to the Father.   **162**

deny — It is impossible to deny a part of the *Sonship* as it is to love it in part.　117

fragmented — Although you can love the *Sonship* only as one, you can perceive it as fragmented.　114

gifts — Do not withhold your gifts to the *Sonship*, or you withhold yourself from God!　122

God — Think but an instant on this: God gave the *Sonship* to you, to ensure your perfect creation.　299

healing — And in your healing is the *Sonship* healed because your wills are joined.　448

illusions — All illusions about the *Sonship* are dispelled together as they were made together.　118

increase — (God) created the *Sonship* and you increase it.　104

indebted — The term "holy" can be used here because, as you learn how much you are indebted to the whole *Sonship*, which includes me, you come as close to knowledge as perception can.　61

meaning — This is because you have no meaning apart from the *Sonship*, and the rightful place of the Sonship is God.　73

miracles — Miracles are affirmations of the *Sonship*, which is a state of completion and abundance.　10

oneness — Now you must be vigilant to hold the one-ness (of the *Sonship*) in your mind because, if you let doubt enter, you will lose awareness of its wholeness and will be unable to teach it.　102

oneness — The *Sonship* in its oneness transcends the sum of its parts.　29

place — You cannot understand yourself alone. This is because you have no meaning apart from your rightful place in the Sonship, and the rightful place of the *Sonship* is God.　73

power — The power of the whole *Sonship* and of its Creator is therefore spirit's own fullness, rendering its creations equally whole an equal in perfection. — 122

restoration — Complete restoration of the *Sonship* is the only goal of the miracle-minded. — 13

salvation — Never forget that the *Sonship* is your salvation, for the *Sonship* is yourself. — 186

sick — The *Sonship* cannot be perceived as partly sick, because to perceive it that way is not to perceive it at all. — 174

united — The ego cannot prevail against the Kingdom because the *Sonship* is united. — 74

will — The joint will of the *Sonship* is the only creator that can create like the Father, because only the complete can think completely, and the thinking of God lacks nothing. — 76

will — The undivided will of the *Sonship* is the perfect creator, being wholly in the likeness of God, Whose Will it is. — 136

SOUL

perceive — You cannot perceive your *soul* but you will not know it while you perceive something else as more valuable. — 212

sell — You cannot sell your *soul*, but you can sell your awareness of it. — 212

SPACE

meaningless — Ultimately, *space* is as meaningless as time. — 11

SPECIAL

asleep — The *special* ones are all asleep, surrounded by a world of loveliness they do not see. — 471

enemies — Only the *special* could have enemies, for they are different and not the same. — 465

illusions — Those who are *special* must defend illusions against the truth. — 466

messages — The *special* messages the *special* hear convince them they are different and apart: each in his *special* sins and "safe" from love, which does not see his specialness at all. 467

perspective — What perspective can the *special* have that does not change with every seeming blow, each slight, or fancied judgment on itself? 466

weak — The *special* ones feel week and frail because of differences, for what would make them special is their enemy. 465

you — You are not *special*. 467

SPECIALNESS

attack — For what is *specialness* but an attack upon the Will of God? 466

attacked — It is your *specialness* that is attacked by everything that walks and breathes, or creeps or crawls, or even lives at all. 470

belief — All that is ever cherished as a hidden belief, to be defended though unrecognized, is faith in *specialness*. 465

body — The hope of *specialness* makes it seem possible God made the body as the prison that keeps His Son from Him. 469

brother — A sinless brother is (the) enemy of (*specialness*), while sin, if it were possible, would be its friend. 472

brother — Let (your brother) forgive you all your *specialness*, and make you whole in mind and one with him. 468

comparisons — *Specialness* always makes comparisons. 466

creations — Yet *specialness* stands in place of your creations, who are son to you, that you might share the Fatherhood of God, not snatch it from Him. 478

death — The death of *specialness* is not your death, but your awakening into life eternal. 469

decisions — *Specialness* is the great dictator of wrong decisions.   **465**

defended — *Specialness* must be defended.   **465**

dream — Let not the dream of *specialness* remain between you (and your brother).   **468**

dream — There is no dream of *specialness*, however hidden or disguised the form, however lovely it may seem to be, however much it delicately offers the hope of peace and the escape from pain, in which you suffer not your condemnation.   **473**

enemies — Your brother's *specialness* and yours are enemies, and bound in hate to kill each other and deny they are the same.   **468**

eyes — Let not your eyes be blinded by the veil of *specialness* that hides the face of Christ from him, and you as well.   **476**

fear — The fear of God and of each other comes from each unrecognized belief in *specialness*.   **466**

forgiveness — Forgiveness is the end of *specialness*.   **470**

function — *Specialness* is the function that you gave yourself.   **477**

given — What you have given *specialness* has left you bankrupt and your treasure house barren and empty, with an open door inviting everything that would disturb your peace to enter and destroy.   **472**

God — And never doubt but that your *specialness* will disappear before the Will of God.   **477**

God — You can defend your *specialness*, but never will you hear the Voice for God beside it.   **467**

illusion — For what your brother must become to keep your *specialness* is an illusion.   **465**

love — *Specialness* is the seal of treachery upon the gift of love.   **469**

one — The unity that *specialness* denies will save them all, for what is one can have no *specialness*.   **518**

pain — But the pursuit of *specialness* must bring you pain.   **467**

peace — Pursuit of *specialness* is always at the cost of peace.   **467**

savior — Here is your savior from your *specialness*.   **468**

share — *Specialness* can never share, for it depends on goals that you alone can reach.   **465**

sin — *Specialness* is the idea of sin made real.   **467**

sin — Whatever form of *specialness* you cherish, you have made sin.   **470**

slaves — The slaves of *specialness* will yet be free.   **471**

triumph — For *specialness* is triumph, and its victory is (your brother's) defeat and shame.   **465**

trust — *Specialness* is a lack of trust in anyone except yourself.   **472**

truth — But *specialness* is not the truth in you.   **470**

truth — How bitterly does everyone tied to this world defend the *specialness* he wants to be the truth!   **478**

truth — Only *specialness* could make the truth of God and you as one seem anything but Heaven, with the hope of peace at last in sight.   **469**

truth — Seek not to make your *specialness* the truth, for if it were you would be lost indeed.   **479**

value — To value *specialness* is to esteem an alien will to which illusions of yourself are dearer than the truth.   **467**

worth — How can you know your worth while *specialness* claims you instead?   **479**

SPIRIT

attack — (*Spirit*) does not attack.   **53**

body — The exaltation of the body is given up in favor of the *spirit*, which you love as you could never love the body.   **392**

choose — But choose the *spirit*, and all Heaven bends to touch your eyes and bless your holy sight, that you may see the world of flesh no more except to heal and comfort and bless.   **614**

clash — Egos can clash in any situation, but *spirit* cannot clash at all. 49

communication — (*Spirit*) is in complete and direct communication with every aspect of creation, because it is in complete and direct communication with its Creator. 63

Creator — Your ego and your *spirit* will never be co-creators, but your *spirit* and your Creator will always be. 54

darkness — *Spirit*, which knows, could not be reconciled with this loss of power, because it is incapable of darkness. 38

ego — Nothing can reach *spirit* from the ego, and nothing can reach the ego from *spirit*. 48

Father — Having everything, *spirit* holds everything by giving it, and thus creates as the Father created. 67

fatigued — To be fatigued is to be dis-spirited but to be inspired is to be in the *spirit*. 47

flesh — You see the flesh or recognize the *spirit*. 614

free — Your mind can be possessed by illusions, but *spirit* is eternally free. 9

function — The extension of God's Being is *spirit's* only function. 123

getting — To *spirit* getting is meaningless and giving is all. 67

God - *Spirit* knows God completely. 41

having — Remember that *spirit* knows no difference between having and being. 67

humility — *Spirit* is beyond humility, because it recognizes its radiance and gladly sheds its light everywhere. 50

immortal — *Spirit* is immortal, and immortality is a constant state. 54

journeys — The ego may desire them, but *spirit* cannot embark on (useless journeys) because it is forever unwilling to depart from its Foundation. 47

levels — *Spirit* has no levels, and all conflict arises from the concept of levels.   **37**

mind — At the altar of God, the holy perception of God's Son becomes so enlightened that light streams into it, and the *spirit* of God's Son shines in the mind of the Father and becomes one with it.   **213**

perceive — (Your self and God's Self) are fundamentally irreconcilable, because *spirit* cannot perceive and the ego cannot know.   **48**

permanence — Against this sense of temporary existence *spirit* offers knowledge of permanence and unshakable being.   **55**

save — Of your ego you can do nothing to save yourself or others, but of your *spirit* you can do everything for the salvation of both.   **50**

share — *Spirit* yearns to share its being as its Creator did.   **122**

taught — *Spirit* need not be taught, but the ego must be.   **48**

threat — Thereafter, *spirit* is perceived as a threat, because light abolishes darkness merely by showing you it is not there.   **38**

true — In contrast, *spirit* reacts in the same way to everything it knows is true, and does not respond at all to anything else.   **63**

unalterable — *Spirit* is therefore unalterable because it is already perfect, but the mind can elect what it chooses to serve.   **10**

will — For *spirit* is will, and will is the "price" of the Kingdom.   **209**

will — (*Spirit*) does not wish to contain God, but wills to extend His Being.   **122**

will — Created by sharing, (*Spirit's*) will is to create.   **122**

SPIRITUAL VISION (SIGHT)

Atonement — *Spiritual vision* literally cannot see error, and merely looks for Atonement.   **18**

mind — Because of the strength of its vision, (*Spiritual vision*) brings the mind into its service.   **18**

perception — (*Spiritual sight*) is, however, a means of right perception, which brings it into the proper domain of the miracle.   **36**

symbolic — *Spiritual sight* is symbolic, and therefore not a device for knowing.   **36**

truth — Perfectly aware of the right defense (*Spiritual vision*) passes over all others, looking past error to truth.   **18**

STRONG

attack — The *strong* do not attack because they see no need to do so.   **209**

enemy — No one is *strong* who has an enemy, and no one can attack unless he thinks he has.   **451**

treacherous — Those who are *strong* are never treacherous, because they have no need to dream of power and to act out their dream.   **431**

SUBSTITUTE(S)

accept — To *substitute* is to accept instead.   **347**

brother — In you there is no separation, and no *substitute* can keep you from your brother.   **349**

call — (The) call (of *substitutes*) is but an echo of the original error that shattered Heaven.   **349**

choose — To *substitute* is to choose between, renouncing one aspect of the Sonship in favor of the other.   **347**

God — Whom God has called should hear no *substitutes*.   **349**

Holy Spirit — The Holy Spirit never uses *substitutes*.   **347**

reality — Your reality was God's creation, and has no *substitute*.   **349**

SUBSTITUTING

sharing — In the mad world outside you nothing can be shared but only substituted, and sharing and *substituting* have nothing in common in reality.   **349**

SUBSTITUTION(S)

different — *Substitution* is clearly a process in which (people) are perceived as different.   **347**

ego — To fragment is to exclude, and *substitution* is the strongest defense the ego has for separation.   **347**

fear — Fear involves *substitution* by definition, for it is love's replacement.   **347**

God — You who believe that God is fear made but one *substitution*.   **347**

little — Your little senseless *substitutions*, touched with insanity and swirling lightly off on a mad course like feathers dancing insanely in the wind, have no substance.   **348**

love — The one emotion in which *substitution* is impossible is love.   **347**

SUFFERING

cause — Here is the cause of *suffering*, the space between your little dreams and your reality.   **542**

cause — And this is what you choose if you deny the cause of *suffering* is in your mind.   **541**

Holy Spirit — (The Holy Spirit) does not understand *suffering*, and would have you teach it is not understandable.   **307**

kill — In your *suffering* of any kind you see your own concealed desire to kill.   **613**

name — It matters not the name by which you called your *suffering*.   **538**

source — And he cannot escape (his *suffering*) because its source is seen outside himself.   **539**

world — *Suffering* is an emphasis upon all that the world has done to injure you.   **539**

SYMBOL(S)

ideas — *Symbols* which but represent ideas that cannot be must stand for empty space and nothingness.   **531**

no — For (creation) there are no *symbols*.   **532**

Self — Seek not your Self in *symbols.*   **613**

totality — As nothingness cannot be pictured, so there   **532**
is no *symbol* for totality.

TEACH

lesson — Every lesson you *teach* you are learning.   **92**

lesson — That is why you must *teach* only one lesson.   **92**

TEACHER(S)

conflicted — A conflicted *teacher* is a poor *teacher.*   **121**

ego — (The ego-oriented *teacher*) is concerned with the   **49**
effect of his ego on other egos, and
therefore interprets their interaction
as a means of ego preservation.

"ego" — If you perceive a *teacher* as merely "a larger ego"   **49**
you will be afraid, because to enlarge a
ego would be to increase anxiety about
separation.

equal — Believe with me, and we will become equal as   **86**
teachers.

everyone — Everyone is a *teacher,* and teaches all the   **84**
time.

excellent - Under proper learning conditions, which you   **211**
can neither provide nor understand,
you will become an excellent learner
and an excellent *teacher.*

God — God gave His *Teacher* to replace the one you   **511**
made, not to conflict with it.

good — A good *teacher* clarifies his own ideas and   **47**
strengthens them by teaching them.

good — A good *teacher* must believe in the ideas he   **47**
teaches, but he must meet another
condition; he must believe in the
students to whom he offers the ideas.

good — All good *teachers* realize that only fundamental   **98**
change will last, but they do not begin
at that level.

good — Every good *teacher* hopes to give his students so   **48**
much of his own learning that they will
one day no longer need him.

good — Good *teachers* never terrorize their students. 33

innocence — *Teachers* of innocence, each in his own way, have joined together, taking their part in the unified curriculum of the Atonement. 263

motivation — Increasing motivation for change in the learner is all that a *teacher* need do to guarantee change. 98

own — Resign now as your own *teacher*. 211

patient — *Teachers* must be patient, and repeat their lessons until they are learned. 49

pupil — *Teacher* and pupil are alike in the learning process. 47

two — There are two *teachers* only, who point in different ways. 511

wise — (A wise *teacher*) does not emphasize what you must avoid to escape from harm, but what you need to learn to have joy. 96

wise — A wise *teacher* teaches through approach, not avoidance. 96

TEACHING

always — Yet you are always *teaching*. 108

change — *Teaching* aims at change, but God created only the changeless. 95

comfort — You may have taught well, and yet you may not have learned how to accept the comfort of your *teaching*. 311

example — *Teaching* is done in many ways, above all by example. 75

healing — *Teaching* should be healing, because it is the sharing of ideas and the recognition that to share ideas is to strengthen them. 75

joy — For the joy of *teaching* is in the learner, who offers it to the *teacher* in gratitude, and shares it with him. 313

joy — Though you seem to suffer for it, the joy of *teaching* will yet be yours. 313

judge — For it is certain that you judge yourself according to your *teaching*. 311

Kingdom — In the Kingdom there is no *teaching* or learning, because there is no belief. 106

TEMPTATION

alternatives — Consider what *temptation* is, and see the real alternatives you choose between. 619

choose — Be never fearful of *temptation*, then, but see it as it is; another chance to choose again, and let Christ's strength prevail in every circumstance and every place you raised an image of yourself before. 620

lesson — *Temptation* has one lesson it would teach, in all its forms, wherever it occurs. 619

sickness — What you behold as sickness and pain, as weakness and as suffering and loss, is but *temptation* to perceive yourself defenseless and in hell. 621

THOUGHT SYSTEM(S)

allegiance — Your capacity for allegiance to a *thought system* may be misplaced, but it is still a form of faith and can be redirected. 84

centers — This is because everyone identifies himself with his thought system, and every *thought system* centers on what you believe you are. 98

ego — Perceive any part of the ego's *thought system* as wholly insane, wholly delusional, and wholly undesirable, and you have correctly evaluated all of it. 120

fear — I do not want you to allow any fear to enter into the *thought system* toward which I am guiding you. 88

God — Any *thought system* that confuses God and the body must be insane. 60

identifies — This is because everyone identifies with his *though system,* and every *thought system* centers on what you believe you are. 98

identify — If you identify with your *thought system*, and you cannot escape this, and if you accept two *thought systems* which are in complete disagreement, peace of mind is impossible.   **99**

life — (Teaching) is a responsibility you inevitably assume the moment you accept any premise at all, and no one can organize his life without some *thought system*.   **84**

opposing — The way out of conflict between two opposing *thought systems* is clearly to choose one and relinquish the other.   **99**

teach — Once you have developed a *thought system* of any kind, you live by it and teach it.   **84**

weak — It is a mistake to believe that a *thought system* based on lies is weak.   **44**

THOUGHT(S)

basis — It will seem difficult for you to learn that you have no basis at all for ordering your *thoughts*.   **273**

beliefs — The *thoughts* (God's Son) shares with God are beyond his belief, but those he made are his beliefs.   **252**

borderland — There is a borderland of *thought* that stands between this world and Heaven.   **508**

communication — Yet *thought* is communication, for which the body can be used.   **141**

consequences — Yet consider what has happened, for *thoughts* do have consequences to the thinker.   **206**

disordered — Every disordered *thought* is attended by guilt at its inception, and maintained by guilt in its continuance.   **78**

endure — For *thoughts* endure as long as does the mind that *thought* of them.   **587**

exclude — You will never be able to exclude yourself from your *thoughts*.   **118**

extends — Consider how this self perception must extend, and do not overlook the fact that every *thought* extends because that is its purpose, being what it really is.   530

fearful — The ego is quite literally a fearful *thought*.   77

flesh — *Thought* cannot be made flesh except by belief, since *thought* is not physical.   141

form — There are no idle *thoughts*. All thinking produces form at some level.   27

given — *Thoughts* increase by being given away.   67

God — Beyond all idols is the *Thought* God holds of you.   588

God — God Himself orders your thought because your *thought* was created by Him.   78

God — In perfect sureness of its changelessness and of its rest in its eternal home, the *Thought* God holds of you has never left the Mind of its Creator, Whom it knows as its Creator knows that it is there.   588

God — The *Thoughts* of God are with you.   76

God — Only the *Thoughts* of God are true.   333

God — The *Thoughts* of God are far beyond all change, and shine forever.   587

God — The *Thought* of God surrounds your little kingdom, waiting at the barrier you built to come inside and shine upon the barren ground.   365

God — The *Thought* God holds of you is perfectly unchanged by your forgetting.   587

God — The *Thought* God holds of you is like a star, unchangeable in an eternal sky.   587

God — You can share only the *thoughts* that are of God and that He keeps for you.   75

guard — It is much more helpful to remind you that you do not guard your *thoughts* carefully enough.   27

harbor — You believe you can harbor *thoughts* you would not share, and that salvation lies in keeping *thoughts* to yourself alone.   289

healing — Every healing *thought* that you accept, either
from your brother or in your own
mind, teaches you that you are God's
Son.   **183**

hidden — Every *thought* you would keep hidden shuts
communication off because you would
have it so.   **289**

hurtful — In every hurtful *thought* you hold, wherever
you perceive it, lies the denial of God's
Fatherhood and of your Sonship.   **183**

impossible — Only your *thoughts* have been impossible.   **441**

irrational — Irrational *thought* is disordered *thought*.   **78**

kill — The *thoughts* that seem to kill are those that teach
the thinker that he can be killed.   **433**

loving — Every loving *thought* is true.   **200**

loving — Every loving *thought* that the Son of God ever
had is eternal.   **195**

loving — If all but loving *thoughts* has been forgotten,
what remains is eternal.   **331**

loving — Every loving *thought* held in any part of the
Sonship belongs to every part.   **75**

loving — The loving *thoughts* (the) mind (of the Son of
God) perceives are the world's only
reality.   **195**

mind — The *thoughts* you think are in your mind, as you
are in the Mind Which *thought* of you.   **587**

mind — *Thoughts* begin in the mind of the thinker, from
which they reach outward.   **90**

power — The *thoughts* the mind of God's Son projects or
extends have all the power that He
gives to them.   **252**

power — No *thought* but has the power to release or kill.   **433**

powerful — Yet (the *thought* of God's Sons) is so powerful that they can imprison the mind of
God's Son if they so choose.   **139**

reality — You have allowed the *Thought* of your reality
to enter your mind, and because you
invited it, it will abide with you.   **322**

separate — No *thought* of God's Son can be separate or isolated in its effects.   257

share — It is impossible to share opposing *thoughts*.   75

true — No one *thought* you hold is wholly true.   196

TIME

belief — And all of *time* is but the mad belief that what is over is still here and now.   513

belong — You do not belong in *time*.   79

brother — *Time* has been saved for you because you and your brother are together.   363

change — *Time* is inconceivable without change, yet holiness does not change.   282

change — Only the timeless must remain unchanged, but everything in *time* can change with *time*.   439

choice — *Time* itself is your choice.   178

constructively — The purpose of *time* is to enable you to learn how to use *time* constructively.   2

disposal — You must learn that *time* is solely at your disposal, and that nothing in the world can take this responsibility from you.   168

ego — Delay is of the ego, because *time* is its concept.   72

ego's — There is no escape from fear in the ego's use of *time*.   281

elected — You have elected to be in *time* rather than in eternity, and therefore believe you are in *time*.   79

end — *Time* can set no end to its fulfillment nor its changelessness.   572

eternity — The other picture is lightly framed, for *time* cannot contain eternity.   336

eternity — *Time* and eternity cannot both be real, because they contradict each other.   178

forgiveness — Forgiveness does not aim at keeping *time*, but at its ending, when it has no use.   572

friend — *Time* is your friend, if you leave it to the Holy Spirit to use.   283

given — He to Whom *time* is given offers thanks for every quiet instant given Him.   **549**

God — What holds remembrance of God cannot be bound by *time*.   **283**

God's — Only in *time* does interference in God's completion seem to be possible.   **316**

guilt — Guilt feelings are the preservers of *time*.   **79**

healing — Accept only the function of healing in *time*, because that is what *time* is for.   **156**

Holy Spirit's — Begin to practice the Holy Spirit's use of *time* as a teaching aid to happiness and peace.   **282**

illusion — When (the Son of God) finds (release) is only a matter of *time*, and *time* is but an illusion.   **222**

immortality — And immortality is the opposite of *time*, for *time* passes away, while immortality is constant.   **222**

instant — Practice giving this blessed instant of freedom to all who are enslaved by *time*, and thus make *time* their friend for them.   **282**

interpret — And *time* will be as you interpret it, for of itself it is nothing.   **230**

interpret — You, too, will interpret the function of *time* as you interpret yours.   **230**

intrude — Do not let *time* intrude upon your sight of (God's Son).   **451**

join — So do the parts of God's Son gradually join in *time*, and with each joining is the end of *time* brought nearer.   **404**

lasted — *Time* lasted but an instant in your mind, with no effect upon eternity.   **511**

lost — Nothing is ever lost but *time*, which in the end is meaningless.   **511**

lost — Only in *time* can anything be lost, and never lost forever.   **404**

made — For *time* you made, and *time* you can command.   **440**

making — The making of *time* to take the place of timelessness lay in the decision to be not as you are. 270

meaning — Waiting is only possible in *time*, but *time* has no meaning. 180

mind — *Time* and eternity are both in your mind, and will conflict until you perceive *time* solely as a means to regain eternity. 168

much — Yet while in *time*, there is still much to do. 493

need — When you have learned that (giving and receiving) are the same, the need for *time* is over. 163

neutral — *Time* is as neutral as the body is, except in terms of what you see it for. 519

nothing — Yet *time* is but another phase of what does nothing. 548

now — The only aspect of *time* that is eternal is now. 73

place — There is a place in you which *time* has left, and echoes of eternity are heard. 570

purpose — The purpose of *time* is solely to "give you *time*," to achieve (your own last) judgment. 30

release — *Time* can release as well as imprison. 234

separate — *Time* cannot separate you from God if you use it on behalf of the eternal. 186

takes — *Time* neither takes away nor can restore. 548

takes — It has taken *time* to misguide you so completely, but it takes no *time* at all to be what you are. 282

waken — Waken from *time*, and answer fearlessly the call of Him Who gave eternity to you in creation. 316

war — Eternity and peace are as closely related as are *time* and war. 73

waste — *Time* can waste as well as be wasted. 10

TIMELESS

minds — No trace of anything in time can long remain in minds that serve the *timeless*. 448

TIRED

capable — You are not really capable of being *tired*, but you are very capable of wearying yourself.   **42**

TREASURE(S)

death — If death is your *treasure*, you will sell everything else to purchase it.   **209**

defends — Everyone defends his *treasure*, and will do so automatically.   **16**

dreams — Count, then, the silver miracles and golden dreams of happiness as all the *treasures* you would keep within the storehouse of the world.   **554**

function — Your function is to add to God's *treasure* by creating yours.   **138**

God's — God wants only His Son because His Son is His only *treasure*.   **138**

investment — If you have no investment in anything in this world, you can teach the poor where their *treasure* is.   **205**

unworthy — Yet you cannot make yourself unworthy because you are the *treasure* of God, and what He values is valuable.   **138**

TRUE

contrast — The contrast between what is *true* and what is not is perfectly apparent.   **253**

explained — This is *true*, but it is hard to explain in words because words are symbols, and nothing that is *true* need be explained.   **105**

Father — For death is not your Father's Will nor yours, and whatever is *true* is the Will of the Father.   **209**

Father — Yet everything *true* is like (the Father).   **195**

visible — When you made visible what is not *true*, what is *true* became invisible to you.   **217**

TRULY

see — Yet you can see (another) *truly* because it is possible for you to see yourself *truly*.   **156**

TRUST

brother — And as you give your *trust* to what is good in (your brother), you give it to the good in you.   **616**

Christ — Is it too much to ask a little *trust* for him who carries Christ to you, that you may be forgiven all your sins, and left without a single one you cherish still?   **521**

intentions — *Trust* not your good intentions.   **355**

learn — But whenever they *trust* themselves, they will not learn.   **278**

problem — And you cannot believe that *trust* would settle every problem now.   **519**

willingness — But *trust* implicitly your willingness, whatever else may enter.   **355**

TRUSTWORTHY

Holy Spirit — The Holy Spirit is perfectly *trustworthy*, as you are.   **125**

TRUTH

"cost" — This is the only "cost" of *truth:* You will no longer see what never was, nor hear what makes no sound.   **468**

ability — The ability to accept the *truth* in this world is the perceptual counterpart of creating in the Kingdom.   **170**

abundant — *Truth* is always abundant.   **9**

alien — Nothing is so alien to you as the simple *truth*, and nothing are you less inclined to listen to.   **253**

asked — All that is asked of you is to make room for *truth.*   **419**

attack — By believing you have successfully attacked *truth*, you are believing that attack has power.   **190**

battle — There is an ancient battle being waged against the *truth*, but *truth* does not respond.   **603**

be — Let *truth* be what it is.   **345**

before — With *truth* before you, you will not look back.   **254**

belief — The Holy Spirit will teach you to perceive be-   **121**
yond your belief, because *truth* is
beyond belief and His perception is
true.

believe — But *truth* is real in its own right, and to believe   **200**
in *truth* you do not have to do anything.

belongs — *(Truth)* belongs to you because, as an exten-   **74**
sion of God, you created it with Him.

brother — You and your brother stand together in the   **340**
holy presence of *truth* itself.

choose — But remember that to choose *(truth)* is to let   **332**
(illusion) go.

conceals — What conceals the *truth* is not where you   **541**
should look to find the *truth*.

concepts — Where concepts of the self have been laid by   **613**
is *truth* revealed exactly as it is.

connected — But illusions are always connected, as is   **372**
truth.

constant — But *truth* is constant, and implies a state   **432**
where vacillations are impossible.

convince — No evidence will convince you of the *truth* of   **310**
what you do not want.

dawn — Together we can meet its conditions, but *truth*   **139**
will dawn upon you of itself.

decide — Decide for *truth* and everything is yours.   **586**

decide — Let *truth* decide if you be different or the same,   **450**
and teach you which is true.

decisions — The *truth* makes no decisions, for there is   **508**
nothing to decide between.

dedicated — Yet we also said that peace without faith   **371**
will never be attained, for what is
dedicated to *truth* as its only goal is
brought to *truth* by faith.

defend — Ask, then, for what is yours, and do not   **196**
defend yourself against *truth*.

defense — And *truth* needs no defense to make it true.   **516**

deny — You cannot deny part of *truth*.   **127**

described — *(Truth)* cannot be described and it cannot be explained. **139**

destroy — *Truth* is beyond your ability to destroy, but entirely within your ability to accept. **74**

enter — Let *(truth)* enter, and it will call forth and secure for you the faith you need for peace. **345**

environment — Out of your natural environment you may well ask, "What is *truth*" since *truth* is the environment by which and for which you were created. **127**

error — *Truth* overcomes all error, and those who live in error and emptiness can never find lasting solace. **35**

experienced — *Truth* can only be experienced. **139**

extends — For *truth* extends inward, where the idea of loss is meaningless and only increase is conceivable. **348**

falter — You have come far along the way of *truth;* too far to falter now. **468**

Father — Your Father can no more forget the *truth* in you than you can fail to remember it. **316**

fear — Fear not to look upon the lovely *truth* in you. **246**

fear — The association of *truth* and fear, which would be highly artificial at most, is particularly inappropriate in the minds of those who do not know what *truth* is. **149**

fear — Under each cornerstone of fear on which you have erected your insane system of belief, the *truth* lies hidden. **267**

fills — For *(truth)* fills every place and every time, and makes them wholly indivisible. **559**

follows — *Truth* follows faith and peace, completing the process of making lovely that they begin. **374**

forever — Yet *truth* will stay forever. **374**

forgotten — Yet *truth* can never be forgotten by itself, and you have not forgotten what you are. **453**

fragment — To fragment *truth* is to destroy it by rendering it meaningless.   **327**

frail — *Truth* is not frail.   **470**

free — You have not made *truth*, but *truth* can still set you free.   **74**

function — The function of *truth* is to collect information that is true.   **145**

give — What you give to *truth* to use for you is safe from fantasy.   **327**

given — But it is given you to know the *truth*, and not to seek for it outside yourself.   **573**

goal — In the goal of *truth* which you accepted must all illusions end.   **381**

God — If you understand that this is always an attack on *truth*, and *truth* is God, you will realize why it is always fearful.   **170**

God's — *Truth* is God's Will.   **124**

holy — The holy do not interfere with *truth*.   **400**

Holy Spirit — Like you, the Holy Spirit did not make the *truth*.   **253**

Holy Spirit — (The Holy Spirit) brings the light of *truth* into the darkness, and lets it shine on you.   **253**

idea — Reserve not one idea aside from *truth*, or you establish orders of reality that must imprison you.   **328**

ignorance — *Truth* does not struggle against ignorance, and love does not attack fear.   **267**

illusion — Every illusion is an assault on *truth*, and every one does violence to the idea of love because it seems to be of equal *truth*.   **461**

illusion — Is it not welcome news to hear not one of the illusions that you made replaced the *truth*.   **441**

illusion — One illusion cherished and defended against the *truth* makes all *truth* meaningless, and all illusions real.   **439**

illusion — Recognize this, for it is true, and *truth* must   315
be recognized if it is to be distinguished
from illusion: the special love relationship is an attempt to bring love into
fear, and make it real in fear.

illusion — The opposite of illusions is not disillusion-   438
ment but *truth*.

illusion — *Truth* and illusion have no connection.   372

illusion — *Truth* has no meaning in illusion.   328

illusion — What you can decide between is fixed, be-   255
cause there are no alternatives except
truth and illusion.

illusions — And you will see the means you once em-   344
ployed to lead you to illusions trans-
formed to means for *truth*.

illusions — But to give illusions to *truth* enables *truth* to   328
teach that the illusions are unreal, and
thus enable you to escape from them.

illusions — Illusions cannot triumph over *truth*, nor can   453
they threaten it in any way.

illusions — *Truth* is without illusions and therefore   103
within the Kingdom.

indivisible — But *truth* is indivisible, and far beyond   453
(illusions') little reach.

invisible — For what you have made invisible is the only   218
truth, and what you have not heard is
the only Answer.

is — *Truth* is.   267

Kingdom — The extension of *truth*, which is the law of   107
the Kingdom, rests only on the
knowledge of what *truth* is.

Kingdom — The world is not left by death but by *truth*,   46
and *truth* can be known by all those for
whom the Kingdom was created, and
for whom it waits.

Kingdom — *Truth* is without illusions and therefore   103
within the Kingdom.

laws — The laws of *truth* forever will be true, and cannot   515
    be reversed; yet can be seen as upside
    down.

listening — Listening to *truth* is the only way you can   153
    hear it now, and finally know it.

littleness — *Truth* and littleness are denials of each other   166
    because grandeur is *truth*.

lofty — The *truth* about you is so lofty that nothing un-   165
    worthy of God is worthy of you.

lost — *(Truth)* can neither be lost nor sought nor found.   267

meet — *Truth* has rushed to meet you since you called   353
    upon it.

mind — *Truth* is whole, and cannot be known by part of a   174
    mind.

near — For you have come too near to *truth* to renounce   310
    it now, and you will yield to its com-
    pelling attraction.

nothing — Not even faith is asked of you, for *truth* asks   345
    nothing.

obscure — *Truth* is not obscure nor hidden, but its   167
    obviousness to you lies in the joy you
    bring to its witnesses, who show it to
    you.

offered — Yet *truth* is offered first to be received, even as   259
    God gave it first to His Son.

offering — Every miracle is thus a lesson in *truth*, and by   126
    offering *truth* you are learning the
    difference between pain and joy.

one — What is one is joined in *truth*.   468

peace — We have said before that when a situation has   371
    been dedicated wholly to *truth*, peace is
    inevitable.

perceived — Whatever is perceived as means for *truth*   479
    shares in its holiness, and rests in light
    as safely as itself.

points — Nothing points beyond the *truth*, for what can   532
    stand for more than everything?

presence — In the presence of *truth*, there are no un-   151
    believers and no sacrifices.

present — Let no dark cloud out of the past obscure (your brother) from you, for *truth* lies only in the present. 234

recognize — Nothing is so easy to recognize as *truth*. 127

recognized — *Truth* can only be recognized and need only be recognized. 109

reconciliation — It is this reconciliation with *truth*, and and only *truth*, in which the peace of Heaven lies. 250

restored — *Truth* is restored to you through your desire, as it was lost to you through your desire for something else. 412

safe — Yet you cannot be safe from *truth*, but only in *truth*. 150

save — The *truth* will save you. 348

search — The search for *truth* is but the honest searching out of everything that interferes with *truth*. 267

simple — Nothing is so alien to you as the simple *truth*, and nothing are you less inclined to listen to. 253

simple — The *truth* is simple; it is one, without an opposite. 508

star — The *truth* in you remains as radiant as a star, as pure as light, as innocent as love itself. 615

substitute — There is no substitute for *truth*. 270

teach — When you teach anyone that *truth* is true, you learn it with him. 254

time — *Truth* is so far beyond time that all of it happens at once. 283

total — If *truth* is total, the untrue cannot exist. 116

union — In union, everything that is not real must disappear, for *truth* is union. 266

vacillate — *Truth* does not vacillate; it is always true. 166

want — Dreams will be impossible because you will want only *truth*, and being at last your will, it will be yours. 169

way — The way to *truth* is open. 317

will — *Truth* comes of its own will unto its own. **249**

withhold — No one can withhold *truth* except from him- **196**
self.

within — When you feel (anxiety, depression, panic), do **152**
not try to look beyond yourself for
truth, for *truth* can only be within you.

THIS NEED NOT BE

anxious — When you are anxious, realize that anxiety **57**
comes from the capriciousness of the
ego and know *this need not be.*

guilty — While you feel guilty your ego is in command, **57**
because only the ego can experience
guilt. *This need not be.*

joyous — When your mood tells you that you have **57**
chosen wrongly, and this is so when-
ever you are not joyous, then know
this need not be.

sad — When you are sad, know *this need not be.* **57**

vigilant — Yet you are not sufficiently vigilant against **58**
the demands of the ego to disengage
yourself. *This need not be.*

UNDERSTAND

accept — Accept with gladness what you do not *under-* **339**
stand, and let it be explained to you as
you perceive its purpose work in it to
make it holy.

messages — You have received no messages at all you **436**
understand.

nothing — Instruction in perception is your great need, **196**
for you *understand* nothing.

nothing — Yet we have emphasized that you need *under-* **356**
stand nothing.

wish — All that was necessary was merely the wish to **353**
understand.

UNDERSTANDING

appreciation — As I have already said, *understanding*   **115**
    brings appreciation, because what you
    understand you can identify with, and
    by making it part of you, you have
    accepted it with love.

appreciation — *Understanding* is appreciation.   **113**

asked — You are not asked to make or do what lies be-   **419**
    yond your *understanding.*

consistency — *Understanding* means consistency, because   **112**
    God means consistency.

form — For sight of form means *understanding* has been   **443**
    obscured.

God — That is how God Himself created you; in *under-*   **113**
    standing, in appreciation and in love.

inheritance — Recognize (you understand nothing) but   **196**
    do not accept it, for *understanding* is your
    inheritance.

know — Only those who recognize they cannot know   **278**
    unless the effects of *understanding* are
    with them, can really learn at all.

light — *Understanding* is light, but you yourself do not   **73**
    know this.

necessary — You do not understand what you accepted,   **353**
    but remember that your *understanding* is
    not necessary.

peace — Think not you understand anything until you   **278**
    pass the test of perfect peace, for peace
    and *understanding* go together and never
    can be found alone.

powerful — You are still convinced that your *understand-*   **356**
    ing is a powerful contribution to the
    truth, and makes it what it is.

Self — The *understanding* that you need comes not of you,   **500**
    but from a larger Self, so great and
    holy that He could not doubt His
    innocence.

UNDERSTOOD

forgiven — And it is recognized that all things must be first forgiven, and then *understood*. 591

UNDOING

indirect — *Undoing* is indirect, as doing is. 252

mind — The *undoing* is necessary only in your mind, so that you will not project, instead of extend. 101

prepare — Prepare you now for the *undoing* of what never was. 357

process — The first step in the reversal or *undoing* process is the *undoing* of the getting concept. 99

task — *Undoing* is not your task, but it is up to you to welcome it or not. 419

true — Yet true *undoing* must be kind. 532

unreality — *Undoing* is for unreality. 271

UNDONE

fear — And every fear or pain or trial you have has been *undone*. 277

reality — (Reality) cannot be *undone*. 271

UNFAIR

Holy Spirit — To (the Holy Spirit), what is *unfair* must be corrected because it is *unfair*. 501

projection — Projection of the cause of sacrifice is at the root of everything you perceive to be *unfair*. 523

UNFAIRLY

error — And every error is a perception in which one, at least, is seen *unfairly*. 501

treated — You cannot be *unfairly* treated. 523

UNFAIRNESS

attack — *Unfairness* and attack are one mistake, so firmly joined that where one is perceived the other must be seen. 523

Holy Spirit — It is impossible the Holy Spirit could see *unfairness* as a resolution. 501

treated — And if you are unfairly treated, (your brother) must suffer the *unfairness* that you see. 525

world — And each *unfairness* that the world appears to lay upon you, you have laid on it by rendering it purposeless, without the function that the Holy Spirit sees. 524

UNFORGIVEN

voice — The *unforgiven* is a voice that calls from out a past forevermore gone by. 512

UNHEALED

pardon — The *unhealed* cannot pardon. 528

UNION

caused — Nothing can be caused without some form of *union*, be it a dream of judgment or the Voice for God. 584

separate — Each would deny his power, for the separate *union* excludes the universe. 321

separation — For the love of God, no longer seek for *union* in separation, nor for freedom in bondage! 321

together — Opposites must be brought together, not kept apart. For their separation is only in your mind, and they are reconciled by *union*, as you are. 266

truth — In *union*, everything that is not real must disappear, for truth is *union*. 266

UNIVERSE

God — There are no beginnings and no endings in God, Whose *universe is* Himself. 180

God — Unless the *universe* were joined in you it would be apart from God, and to be without Him is to be without meaning. 305

lost — Nothing is lost to you in all the *universe*.   **476**

love — The *universe* of love does not stop because you do   **181**
not see it, nor have your closed eyes
lost the ability to see.

right — You have the right to all the *universe;* to perfect   **500**
peace, complete deliverance from all
effects of sin, and to the life eternal,
joyous and complete in every way, as
God appointed for His holy Son.

we — There is no end to God and His Son, for we are the   **181**
universe.

UNJUST

be — No one can be *unjust* to you, unless you have   **502**
decided first to be *unjust.*

UNKNOWING

defined — (The *unknowing*) have defined themselves as   **267**
they were not created.

God — To God, *unknowing* is impossible.   **267**

UNLOVING

happy — If you choose to see yourself as *unloving* you will   **164**
not be happy.

UNREAL

despair — You looked upon the *unreal* and found despair.   **218**

VALUE

appreciation — The hidden is kept apart, but *value*   **265**
always lies in joint appreciation.

attack — Nothing can attack (your *value*) nor prevail   **167**
over it.

brother's — It is impossible to overestimate your   **405**
brother's *value.*

brother's — You will see your *value* through your   **448**
brother's eyes, and each one is released
as he beholds his savior in place of the
attacker who he thought was there.

ego — And *value* no plan of the ego before the plan of 288
God.

establish — You did not establish your *value* and it needs 167
no defense.

God — God could not offer His Son what has no *value*, 218
nor could His Son receive it.

God — *Value* is where God placed it and the *value* of what 248
God esteems cannot be judged, for it
has been established.

is — (Your *value*) merely is. 167

nothing — For if you *value* one thing made of nothing, 253
you have believed that nothing can be
precious, and that you can learn how to
make the untrue true.

self- — As self — *value* comes from self-extension, so 212
does the perception of self — *value* from
the extension of loving thoughts outward.

special — Think not you lack a special *value* here. 493

wholly — For nothing that you *value* here you *value* 248
wholly, and so you do not *value* it at all.

world — To justify one *value* that the world upholds is to 495
deny your Father's sanity and yours.

world — You see the world you *value*. 321

VENGEANCE

bodies — And finally, why all relationships become 331
attempts at union through the body,
for only bodies can be seen as means
for *vengeance*.

fairness — Fairness and *vengeance* are impossible, for 498
each one contradicts the other and
denies that it is real.

love — But *vengeance* without love has gained in strength 499
by being separate and apart from love.

merit — You can be perfect witness to the power of love 500
and justice if you understand it is
impossible the Son of God could merit
vengeance.

problem — Problem solving cannot be *vengeance*, which at best can bring another problem added to the first, in which the murder is not obvious.   **502**

safe — And you are safe from *vengeance* in all forms.   **500**

VIGILANCE

beliefs — (*Vigilance*) is necessary against beliefs that are not true, and would never have been called upon by the Holy Spirit if you had not believed the untrue.   **116**

effort — *Vigilance* does require effort, but only until you learn that effort itself is unnecessary.   **103**

essential — This is why *vigilance* is essential.   **102**

God — And it is this *vigilance* (against God) that makes you afraid to remember Him.   **170**

me — *Vigilance* was required of me as much as of you, and those who choose to teach the same thing must be in agreement about what they believe.   **103**

power — Your *vigilance* does not establish (power) as yours, but it does enable you to use it always and in all ways.   **107**

sign — Your *vigilance* is the sign that you want (the Holy Spirit) to guide you.   **103**

VIGILANT

choose — As long as you must be *vigilant* against anything, however, you are not recognizing this mutual exclusiveness, and still believe that you can choose either (chaos or consistency).   **101**

ego — I have already told you that you can be as *vigilant* against the ego as for it.   **101**

God's — This (doubt) is why you must be *vigilant* on God's behalf.   **102**

VISION(S)

body — To see the body is the sign that you lack *vision*, and have denied the means the Holy Spirit offers you to serve His purpose.   **411**

brain — The brain cannot interpret what your *vision* sees. **436**

Christ — Beyond your darkest dreams (Christ) sees God's guiltless Son within you, shining in perfect radiance that is undimmed by your dreams, and this you will see as you look with Him, for His *Vision* is His gift of love to you, given Him of the Father for you. **233**

Christ — Beyond this darkness, and yet still within you, is the *vision* of Christ, Who looks on all in light. **232**

Christ's — In the sanity of (Christ's) vision they looked upon themselves with love, seeing themselves as the Holy Spirit sees them. **233**

correct — A Voice will answer every question you ask, and a *vision* will correct the perception of everything you see. **218**

damn — And *vision* cannot damn, but only bless. **440**

denied — When *vision* is denied, confusion of cause and effect becomes inevitable. **419**

dreams — *Vision* is the means by which the Holy Spirit translates your nightmares into happy dreams; your wild hallucinations that show you all the fearful outcomes of imagined sin into the calm and reassuring sights with which He would replace them. **414**

extends — *Vision* extends beyond itself, as does the purpose that it serves, and all the means for its accomplishment. **427**

faith — Faith and belief become attached to *vision*, as all the means that once served sin are redirected now toward holiness. **422**

fear — And let the fear of God no longer hold the *vision* you were meant to see from you. **476**

fear — Your "*vision*" comes from fear, as His from love. **232**

glimpses — *Vision* will come to you at first in glimpses, but they will be enough to show you what is given you who see your brother sinless. 411

God's — God's Son can be seen because his *vision* is shared. 218

healed — Everything looked upon with *vision* is healed and holy. 415

Holy Spirit's — Those who accept the Holy Spirit's purpose as their own share also His *vision*. 398

illusions — You have *vision* now to look past all illusions. 398

judgment — *Vision* would not be necessary had judgment not been made. 412

last — That is why *visions*, however holy, do not last. 36

learned — Judgment you taught yourself; *vision* is learned from Him who would undo your teaching. 411

light — For the light of perfect *vision* is freely given as it is freely received, and can be accepted only without limit. 235

light — *Vision* depends on light. 232

obstacles — You cannot lay aside the obstacles to real *vision* without looking upon them, for to lay aside means to judge against. 204

order — For *vision*, like relationships, has no order. 410

redeemed — All is redeemed when looked upon with *vision*. 413

savior's — (The savior's *vision*) sees no past in anyone at all. 618

savior's — (The world) needs the light, for it is dark indeed, and men despair because the savior's *vision* is withheld and what they see is death. 619

see — See through the *vision* that is given you, for through Christ's vision He beholds Himself. 233

seek — Do not seek *vision* through your eyes, for you   **232**
made your way of seeing that you
might see in darkness, and in this you
are deceived.

sense — *Vision* is sense, quite literally.   **442**

shows — Judgment will always give you false direction,   **415**
but *vision* shows you where to go.

sight — But let the darkness go and all you made you   **232**
will no longer see, for sight of it
depends upon denying *vision*.

true — True *vision* is the natural perception of spiritual   **36**
sight, but it is still a correction rather
than a fact.

world — One *vision*, clearly seen, that does not fit the   **615**
the picture as it was perceived before
will change the world for eyes that
learn to see, because the concept of the
self has changed.

VOICE

brother — The *voice* you hear in (your brother) is but   **604**
your own.

question — A *Voice* will answer every question you ask,   **218**
and a vision will correct the perception
of everything you see.

WAKE

decision — The decision to *wake* is the reflection of the   **147**
will to love, since all healing involves
replacing fear with love.

sleep — How you *wake* is a sign of how you have used   **147**
sleep.

WAKENED

yourself — Yet you can let yourself be *wakened*.   **568**

WAKING

rest — Rest does not come from sleeping but from   **71**
waking.

WANT

really — Having forgotten your will, you do not know   **183**
what you really *want*.

WAR

between — Yet if he could but realize the *war* is between   **248**
real and unreal powers, he could look
upon himself and see his freedom.

demanded — In *war* (God's Son) demanded everything   **227**
and found nothing.

escape — You are but trying to escape a bitter *war* from   **248**
which you have escaped.

fear — *War* is the condition in which fear is born, and   **454**
grows and seeks to dominate.

freedom — Yet as you made not freedom, so you made   **248**
not a *war* that could endanger freedom.

God - Do you not realize a *war* against yourself would   **452**
be a *war* on God?

God — This is no *war*; only the mad belief the Will of   **452**
God can be attacked and overthrown.

gone — The *war*, the guilt, the past are gone as one into   **248**
the unreality from which they came.

impossible — *War* is impossible unless belief in victory is   **452**
cherished.

means — The means of *war* are not the means of peace,   **452**
and what the warlike would remember
is not love.

yourself — Brother, the *war* against yourself is almost   **453**
over.

yourself — The *war* against yourself is but the battle of   **453**
two illusions, struggling to make them
different from each other, in the belief
the one that conquers will be true.

yourself — The *war* against yourself was undertaken to   **453**
teach the Son of God that he is not
himself, and not his Father's Son.

WAY

dark — But the dark journey is not the *way* of God's Son.   **185**

dark — The dark companions, the dark *way* are all illusions.   185

God — You will never lose your *way* for God leads you.   185

pain — Yours is the *way* of pain, of which God knows nothing.   185

WEAK

attack — Before attack can enter your mind, you must have perceived yourself as *weak*.   209

Holy Spirit's — As long as you avoid (the Holy Spirit's) guidance in any way, you want to be *weak*.   125

lose — Someone must always lose if you perceive yourself as *weak*.   293

Will — Belief in enemies is therefore the belief in weakness, and what is *weak* is not the Will of God.   451

WEAKENING

attack — You use attack to ("equalize" the situation you made) because you believe that attack was successful in *weakening* you.   209

WEAKNESS

Christ — For you have brought your *weakness* unto (Christ), and He has given you His strength instead.   620

frightening — Yet *weakness* is frightening.   125

love — The meaning of love is lost in any relationship that looks to *weakness*, and hopes to find love there.   308

power — Simple by never using *weakness*, to direct your actions, you have given it no power.   620

triumph — The triumph of *weakness* is not what you would offer to a brother.   308

WEARY

hurt — When you are *weary*, remember you have hurt yourself.   184

WHOLE

God — Whom God remembers must be *whole*.   **316**

made — We are made *whole* in our desire to make *whole*.   **354**

made — You will be made *whole* as you make *whole*, for to perceive in sickness the appeal for health is to recognize in hatred the call for love.   **203**

perception — In perception the *whole* is built of parts that can separate and reassemble in different constellations.   **144**

recognition — The recognition of the part as *whole*, and of the *whole* in every part is perfectly natural, for it is the way God thinks, and what is natural to Him is natural to you.   **309**

WHOLENESS

acceptance — The appreciation of *wholeness* comes only through acceptance, for to analyze means to break down or to separate out.   **190**

extension — The power of *wholeness* is extension.   **143**

form — *Wholeness* has no form because it is unlimited.   **586**

healing — By healing you learn of *wholeness*, and by learning of *wholeness* you learn to remember God.   **110**

heals — *Wholeness* heals because it is of the mind.   **146**

learn — Wholeness is indivisible, but you cannot learn of your *wholeness* until you see it everywhere.   **162**

message — And this willingness opens your ears to the Voice of the Holy Spirit, Whose message is *wholeness*.   **183**

understand — For you cannot understand *Wholeness* unless you are whole, and no part of the Son can be excluded if he would know the *Wholeness* of his Father.   **186**

WILL

"price" — For spirit is *will*, and *will* is the "price" of the Kingdom.   **209**

afraid — Yet as long as you are afraid of your *will*, (what you don't want) is precisely what you are asking for.   **150**

asked — You are but asked to let your *will* be done, and seek no longer for the things you do not want.   **590**

behold — Behold your *will*, accepting it as His, with all His Love as yours.   **268**

born — Not one created thing but gives you thanks, for it is by your *will* that it was born.   **585**

boundless — Your *will* is boundless; it is not your *will* that it be bound.   **585**

deny — By denying (you are God's Son), you deny your own *will*, and therefore do not know what it is.   **181**

destroy — No one can *will* to destroy himself.   **171**

difference — There is no difference between your *will* and God's.   **150**

done — And you are worthy that your *will* be done!   **615**

ego's — Your *will* is not the ego's, and that is why the ego is against you.   **149**

fear — Now hear God speak to you, through Him Who is His Voice and yours as well, reminding you that it is not your *will* to hate and be a prisoner to fear, a slave to death, a little creature with a little life.   **585**

free — In a holy state the *will* is free, so that its creative power is unlimited and choice is meaningless.   **70**

free — The ego cannot teach you anything as long as your *will* is free, because you will not listen to it.   **130**

free — This unnatural lesson cannot be learned, and the attempt to learn it is a violation of your own freedom, making you afraid of your *will* because it is free.   **130**

given — Yet *will* was given them because it is holy, and will bring to them all that they need, coming as naturally as peace that knows no limits.   **257**

God — It is not a world of *will* because it is governed by the desire to be unlike God, and this desire is not *will*.   **207**

God — God asks you do your *will*.   **585**

God's — If you are God's *Will* and do not accept His *Will*, you are denying joy.   **125**

Heaven — And Heaven itself but represents your *will*, where everything created is for you.   **585**

Holy Spirit — (The Holy Spirit) tells you but your *will;* He speaks for you.   **585**

imprisoned — What you made has imprisoned your *will*, and gave you a sick mind that must be healed.   **103**

imprisoned — You have imprisoned your *will* beyond your own awareness, where it remains, but cannot help you.   **149**

know — Yet what you *will* you do not know.   **181**

life — Your *will* is His life, which He has given to you.   **182**

limitless — (God) would but keep your *will* forever and forever limitless.   **585**

nature — Your *will* is in your nature, and therefore cannot go against it.   **130**

obliterate — Your *will* is still in you because God placed it in your mind, and although you can keep it asleep you cannot obliterate it.   **69**

power — God gave your *will* its power, which I can only acknowledge in honor of His.   **135**

power — What you experience when you deny your Father is still for your protection, for the power of your *will* cannot be lessened without the intervention of God against it, and any limitation on your power is not the *Will* of God.   **186**

powerful — Your *will* is as powerful as (God's) because it is His.   **124**

salvation — Your *will* is your salvation because it is the same as God's.   **150**

strong — No force except your own *will* is strong enough or worthy enough to guide you.   **55**

universal — But your *will* is universal, being limitless.   **586**

universal — There is no living thing that does not share the universal *will* that it be whole, and that you do not leave its call unheard.   **602**

unlimited — In the holy state the *will* is free, so that its creative power is unlimited and choice is meaningless.   **70**

value — There is nothing their *will* fails to provide that offers them anything of value.   **257**

world — For it is by your *will* the world is given freedom.   **586**

world — To give this sad world over and exchange your errors for the peace of God is but your *will*.   **237**

WILLING

salvation — If you did not have a split mind, you would recognize that *willing* is salvation because it is communication.   **150**

WILLINGNESS

perfect — Your *willingness* need not be perfect, because His is.   **184**

signified — The attraction of light must draw you willingly, and *willingness* is signified by giving.   **236**

strength — You do not need the strength of *willingness* to come from you, but only from His Will.   **355**

WISH

ego — Any *wish* that stems from the ego is a *wish* for nothing, and to ask for it is not a request.   **151**

given — And what you *wish* is given you to see.   **529**

power — The power of a *wish* upholds illusions as strongly as does love extend itself.   **473**

true — What you *wish* is true for you.   **473**

WITNESS(ES)

Christ — The (*witnesses*) are silent because Christ speaks to them, and it is His words they speak.   **191**

God — *Witnesses* for God stand in His Light and behold what He created.   **191**

God - God waits your *witness* to His Son and to Himself.   **242**

God's — God's *Witness* sees no *witnesses* against the body.   **538**

God's — So (God's Son) has never ceased to be his Father's *witness* and his own.   **236**

Holy Spirit — For (the Holy Spirit) will send you His *witnesses* if you will but look upon them.   **215**

investment — No one with a personal investment is a reliable *witness*, for truth to him has become what he wants it to be.   **201**

one — For just one *witness* is enough, if he sees truly.   **500**

perfect — You can be perfect *witness* to the power of love and justice, if you understand it is impossible the Son of God could merit vengeance.   **500**

power — The power of *witness* comes from your belief.   **529**

power — The power of *witness* is beyond belief because it brings conviction in its wake.   **252**

silence — (The) silence (of *witnesses*) is the sign that they have beheld God's Son, and in the Presence of Christ they need demonstrate nothing, for Christ speaks to them of Himself and of His Father.   **191**

sin's — Sin's *witnesses* hear but the call of death.   **538**

true — You do not make a *witness* true because you called him by truth's name.   **538**

WORLD(S)

"sacrifice" — The *world* you see is based on "sacrifice" of oneness.   504

abandon — It seems to you the *world* will utterly abandon you if you but raise your eyes.   392

afraid — You are afraid of the *world* as you see it, but the real world is still yours for the asking.   197

another — Therefore, there must be another *world* that you do not see.   194

attempt — The *world* is an attempt to prove your innocence, while cherishing attack.   517

blind — The *world* can add nothing to the power of God and His holy Sons, but it can blind the Sons to the Father if they behold it.   138

both — You cannot see both *worlds*, for each of them involves a different kind of seeing, and depends on what you cherish.   236

causeless — This *world* is causeless, as is every dream that anyone has dreamed within the *world*.   551

change — Therefore, seek not to change the *world*, but choose to change your mind about the *world*.   415

choice — Because (the *world*) is a place where choice among illusions seems to be the only choice.   607

choice — The learning that the *world* can offer but one choice, no matter what its form may be, is the beginning of acceptance that there is a real alternative instead.   608

choose — And if you choose to see a *world* without an enemy, in which you are not helpless, the means to see it will be given you.   432

Christ — (Christ is) come as a light into a *world* that does deny itself everything.   133

control — You still cannot will against (your Father), and that is why you have no control over the *world* you made.   207

451

crucifixion — This *world* is a picture of the crucifixion of God's Son.   **220**

deceives — The *world* deceives, but it cannot replace God's justice with a version of its own.   **501**

decide — You can decide to see (the *world*) right.   **215**

denied — The *world* you see must be denied, for sight of it is costing you a different kind of vision.   **236**

depicts — The *world* you see depicts exactly what you thought you did.   **544**

difference — Nor is there any difference between yourself and (the *world*) in your perception.   **400**

distracted — No one in this distracted *world* but has seen some glimpses of the other *world* about him.   **237**

dream — The *world* is but a dream that you can be alone, and think without affecting those apart from you.   **562**

dying — A dying *world* asks only that you rest an instant from attack on yourself, that it be healed.   **536**

ego — Everything you perceive as the outside *world* is merely your attempt to maintain your ego identification, for everyone believes that identification is salvation.   **206**

end — The end of the *world* is not its destruction, but its translation into Heaven.   **196**

exist — The *world* you see does not exist, because the place where you perceive it is not real.   **559**

forgive — But you will not forgive the *world* until you have forgiven Him Who gave your will to you.   **585**

forgive — When you forgive the *world* your guilt, you will be free of it.   **546**

forgiven — From the forgiven *world* the Son of God is lifted easily into his home.   **329**

forgiveness — How lovely is the *world* whose purpose is forgiveness of God's Son!   573

forgiveness — In (God's) perception of the *world*, nothing is seen but justifies forgiveness and the right of perfect sinlessness.   488

forgotten — There is a place in you where this whole *world* has been forgotten; where no memory of sin and of illusion linger still.   570

freedom — This *world* awaits the freedom you will give when you have recognized that you are free.   585

gain — For in this *world* it seems that one must gain because another lost.   496

gap — What is the *world* except a little gap perceived to tear eternity apart, and break it into days and months and years?   554

God — You cannot behold the *world* and know God.   138

God's — And in (God's) sight there is another *world*.   616

ground — You stand no longer on the ground that lies between the *worlds*.   513

guilt — (The) only purpose (of this *world*) is to prove guilt real.   526

guilty — To see a guilty *world* is but the sign your learning has been guided by the *world*, and you behold it as you see yourself.   613

healing — Thus is your healing everything the *world* requires, that it may be healed.   536

holy — The *world* the holy see is beautiful because they see their innocence in it.   401

holy — The *world* the holy see is one with them, just as the *world* the ego looks upon is like itself.   401

Holy Spirit — The Holy Spirit has the power to change   495
the whole foundation of the *world* you
see to something else; a basis not
insane, on which a sane perception can
be based, another *world* perceived.

Holy Spirit's — And as (the Holy Spirit's) purpose is   404
fulfilled, a new *world* rises in which sin
can enter not, and where the Son of
God can enter without fear, and where
he rests a while, to forget imprisonment and to remember freedom.

hope — To open up a road of hope, you need but to   574
decide you do not know the purpose of
the *world*.

insane — It is through these strange and shadowy   231
figures that the insane relate to their
insane *world*.

judgment — The *world* you see is but a judgment on   400
yourself.

judgment — Your judgment has been lifted from the   584
world by your decision for a happy day.

justice — To the *world*, justice and vengeance are the   497
same, for sinners see justice as their
only punishment, perhaps sustained by
someone else, but not escaped.

kill — The *world* will bind your feet and tie your hands   573
and kill your body only if you think that
it was made to crucify God's Son.

laws — The *world* goes against your nature, being out of   126
accord with God's laws.

learning — There will be some confusion every time   613
there is a shift (in perception), but be
you thankful that the learning of the
world is loosening its grasp upon your
mind.

loneliness — If I am with you in the loneliness of the   133
world, the loneliness is gone.

love — The *world* must therefore despise and reject me, because the *world* is the belief that love is impossible.   134

magic — The magic of the *world* can seem to hide the pain of sin from sinners, and deceive with glitter and with guile.   494

make — You make the *world* and then adjust to it, and it to you.   400

Maker — The Maker of the *world* of gentleness has perfect power to offset the *world* of violence and hate that seems to stand between you and His gentleness.   488

maker — You maker of a *world* that is not so, take rest and comfort in another *world* where peace abides.   489

meaning — Nothing that the *world* believes has any meaning in (God's) Mind at all.   494

meaning — The *world* you made is therefore totally chaotic, governed by arbitrary and senseless "laws," and without meaning of any kind.   207

meaningless — This *world* is meaningless because it rests on sin.   495

means — The means are given you by which to see the *world* that will replace the one you made.   615

merciless — Yet it was you who made (the *world*) merciless, and now if mercilessness seems to look back at you, it can be corrected.   400

merciless — The *world* is merciless, and were it outside you, you should indeed be fearful.   400

mind — Yet the *world* is only in the mind of its maker, along with his real salvation.   207

motivation — It is not will for life but wish for death that is the motivation for this *world*.   526

needful — It is needful that you recognize you made the *world* you see, as that you recognize that you did not create yourself.   420

new — For the whole new *world* rests in the hands of   404
    every two who enter here to rest.

odds — You have become at odds with the *world* as you   206
    perceive it, because you think it is
    antagonistic to you.

orders — The *world* perceives orders of difficulty in   126
    everything.

outside — He (who identifies with the ego) does not   206
    realize that he makes this *world*, for
    there is no *world* outside of him.

over — This *world* was over long ago.   547

pain — (God's Son) must deny the *world* of pain the   238
    instant he perceives the arms of love
    around him.

past — Each one peoples his *world* with figures from his   231
    individual past, and it is because of this
    that private *worlds* do differ.

perceive — The *world* as you perceive it cannot have   194
    been created by the Father, for the
    world is not as you see it.

private — It is given you to learn how to deny insanity,   232
    and come forth from your private *world*
    in peace.

purpose — The real purpose of this *world* is to use it to   11
    correct your unbelief.

real — If only the loving thoughts of God's Son are the   206
    world's reality, the real *world* must be in
    his mind.

real — In the real *world* there is no sickness, for there is   197
    no separation and no division.

real — Love waits on welcome, not on time, and the real   238
    world is but your welcome of what
    always was.

real — Make the *world* real unto yourself, for the real   212
    world is the gift of the Holy Spirit, and
    so it belongs to you.

purpose — The *world* has no purpose as it blends into the   213
    Purpose of God.

real — (The) reality (of the real *world*) will make everything else invisible, for beholding (the
real *world*) is total perception. **219**

real — The real *world* can actually be perceived. **195**

real — The real *world* is achieved when you perceive the
basis of forgiveness is quite real and
fully justified. **594**

real — The real *world* is all that the Holy Spirit has
saved for you out of what you have
made, and to perceive only this is
salvation, because it is the recognition
that reality is only what is true. **195**

real — The real *world* is a state in which the mind has
learned how easily idols do go when
they are still perceived but wanted not. **591**

real — The real *world* is attained simply by the complete
forgiveness of the old, the *world* you see
without forgiveness. **329**

real — The real *world* is the state of mind in which the
only purpose of the *world* is seen to be
forgiveness. **590**

real — The real *world* is the way that leads you to
remembrance of the one thing that is
wholly true and wholly yours. **238**

real — This *world* of light, this circle of brightness is
the real *world*, where guilt meets with
forgiveness. **368**

real — Yet the real *world* has the power to touch you
even here, because you love it. **237**

real — You are afraid of the *world* as you see it, but the
real *world* is yours for the asking. **197**

real — When you perceive the real *world*, you will
recognize you did not believe it. **195**

real — We need remember only that whoever attains
the real *world*, beyond which learning
cannot go, will go beyond it, but in a
different way. **369**

reality — What you made of (this *world*) is not its reality,
for its reality is only what you give it. **215**

reinterpretation — The reinterpretation of the *world* is the transfer of all perception to knowledge.   **196**

resolution — (The *world*) sees resolution as a state in which it is decided who shall win and who shall lose; how much the one shall take, and how much can the loser still defend.   **502**

resurrection — The resurrection of the *world* awaits your healing and your happiness, that you may demonstrate the healing of the *world*.   **539**

road — Seek not another signpost in the *world* that seems to point to still another road.   **608**

road — You did not come to learn to find a road the *world* does not contain.   **609**

see — The *world* you see is what you gave it, nothing more than that.   **415**

see — And what you see the *world* will witness, and will witness to.   **536**

see — (The *world* you see) is the witness to your state of mind, the outside picture of an inward condition.   **415**

split — Yet as long as you perceive the *world* as split, you are not healed.   **215**

striving — Anything in this *world* that you believe is good and valuable and worth striving for can hurt you, and will do so.   **513**

strong — You must perceive that what is strong enough to make a *world* can let it go, and can accept correction if it is willing to see that it was wrong.   **418**

suffering — But there is need that you be healed, because the suffering and sorrow of the *world* have made it deaf to its salvation and deliverance.   **539**

think — (The *world*) is a picture of what you think you are.   **400**

unreal — The unreal *world* is a thing of despair, for it can never be. 219

value — The only thing of value in (the *world*) is whatever part of it you look upon with love. 212

want — You do not really want the *world* you see, for it has disappointed you since time began. 237

want — You do not want the *world*. 212

will — For it is by your will the *world* is given freedom. 586

witness — The *world* you see is but the idle witness that you were right. 418

witness — It is not (eyes and ears) that hear and see, but you, who put together every jagged piece, each senseless scrap and shred of evidence, and make a witness to the *world* you want. 559

wrong — You have been wrong about the *world* because you have misjudged yourself. 237

your — (Your *world*) is a *world* of scarcity in which you find yourself because you are lacking. 238

WORSHIPPERS

idols — The idols are nothing, but their *worshippers* are the Sons of God in sickness. 171

WORTH

established — Again, — nothing you do or think or wish or make is necessary to establish your *worth*. 49

God — Your *worth* is established by God. 49

YOURSELF

advice — Therefore ask not of *yourself* what you need, for you do not know, and your advice to *yourself* will hurt you. 239

give — And like (your Father) you can give *yourself* completely, wholly without loss and only with gain. 293

made — You made neither *yourself* nor your function. 138

not — You are not of *yourself*. 141

nothing — Of *yourself* you can do nothing, because of   **135**
    yourself you are nothing.

replace — You cannot replace the Kingdom, and you   **167**
    cannot replace *yourself*.

suffering — If you will accept *yourself* as God created   **177**
    you, you will be incapable of suffering.

tasks — You are not asked to do mighty tasks *yourself*.   **268**

value — It is not my merit that I contribute to you but   **172**
    my love, for you do not value *yourself*.

wait — You wait but for *yourself*.   **237**

world — To believe that you can perceive the real world   **195**
    is to believe that you can know *yourself*.

NOTES